Rainer Funk, Neil McLaughlin (Eds.)
Towards a Human Science

The series BIBLIOTHEK DER PSYCHOANALYSE (Library of Psychoanalysis) wishes to create a forum of discussion which stimulates the basic, human and cultural aspects of psychoanalysis as a science and as a clinical theory and practice. The different currents within psychoanalysis will be given space, and the critical dialogue with the neighbouring academic fields will be intensified. So far, the following thematic focuses have developed:

The rediscovery of psychoanalytic classics which have long been out of print – such as the works of Otto Fenichel, Karl Abraham, W. R. D. Fairbairn, Otto Rank and others – will strengthen the common roots of the psychoanalytic movement, which is threatening to split. Another component of the psychoanalytic identity is the treatment of both the person and the works of Sigmund Freud, and of the discussions and conflicts of the psychoanalytic movement's early days.

In the course of the process during which psychoanalysis established itself as a medical-psychological therapy, it neglected its multidisciplinarity regarding the humanities, cultural analysis and politics. By resuming the dialogue with the neighbouring academic fields, the culture-critical and socio-critical heritage of psychoanalysis will be revitalised and advanced.

Psychoanalysis now competes with neighbouring psychotherapeutic methods and with biological psychiatry more than it used to. Being the most sophisticated among the psychotherapeutic methods, psychoanalysis should face an empirical-scientific verification of its procedures and its therapeutical success, but it should also develop its own criteria and concepts to control results. This context also includes the revival of the discussion about the particular scientific-theoretical status of psychoanalysis.

One hundred years after its creation by Sigmund Freud, psychoanalysis faces new challenges which it can only meet by focussing on its critical potential.

BIBLIOTHEK DER PSYCHOANALYSE

EDITED BY HANS-JÜRGEN WIRTH

Rainer Funk, Neil McLaughlin (Eds.)

Towards a Human Science

The Relevance of Erich Fromm for Today

With contributions by Kevin Anderson, Burkhard Bierhoff,
Joan Braune, Sandra Buechler, Mauricio Cortina,
Takeshi Deguchi, Jan Dietrich, Rainer Funk,
Sonia Gojman de Millán, Jürgen Hardeck,
Luis Jimenez, Helmut Johach, Adrian Kind,
Michael Maccoby, Neil McLaughlin, Dietmar Mieth,
Salvador Millán, Anna Müller-Hermann,
Nikolai Omelchenko, Rainer Otte, Tatiana Panfilova
and Manfred Zimmer

Psychosozial-Verlag

Thanks to the Karl Schlecht Stiftung for their support.

KSG Karl Schlecht Stiftung

Bibliographic information
of the Deutsche Nationalbibliothek (The German Library)
The Deutsche Nationalbibliothek lists this publication
in the Deutsche Nationalbibliografie; detailed bibliographic data
are available in the internet at http://dnb.d-nb.de.

Original edition
© 2015 Psychosozial-Verlag
Walltorstr. 10, 35390 Gießen, Germany
Phone: +49 - 6 41 - 96 99 78 - 18; Telefax: +49 - 6 41 - 96 99 78 - 19
info@psychosozial-verlag.de
www.psychosozial-verlag.de
Cover: Erich Fromm, photo by Thea Goldmann (© Rainer Funk)
Cover design & layout based on drafts by Hanspeter Ludwig, Wetzlar
www.imaginary-world.de
ISBN 978-3-8379-2535-7

Content

Introduction

Rainer Funk and Neil McLaughlin

No theoretical system can be successful "unless we recognize that, and why, every system as it is developed and presented by its author *is necessarily* erroneous". When Erich Fromm wrote these lines at the end of his life in his *Greatness and Limitations of Freud's Thought* (1979a, p. 1) he had in mind the creative ideas of Sigmund Freud. Fromm was a great admirer of psychoanalytic insights, but he had the courage and insight in the 1930s to challenge Freud's view that most of the psychic strivings and irrationality are the outcome of drives inherent in the biological constitution of man (Roazen 1996). Fromm replaced Freud's libido theory by a theory based on the psychic need to be related – to other individuals, to reality, to social groups he belongs to and to oneself, and thus created his own unique and influential social criticism and theory of social character in such works of critical social science as *Escape from Freedom* (1941a), *Man for Himself* (1947a), *The Sane Society* (1955a), *The Heart of Man* (1964a) *The Anatomy of Human Destructiveness* (1973a) and *To Have Or to Be?* (1976a). The goal of this edited book is to document the global reception, continuing influence and contemporary relevance of Erich Fromm's theories while discussing some of his limitations in the spirit of Fromm's own understanding of how theoretical systems work.

All thinkers have their personal limitations, of course, something Fromm documented in his writings about Sigmund Freud to the distress of the founder of psychoanalysis' most uncritical followers; we aim to go deeper than this obvious point because Fromm's insistence on the need to constantly revise and refine theoretical systems, was based on a more profound philosophical, historical and sociological account of the nature of knowledge production than one based on critiquing individual thinkers. One important dynamic at play in the creation of theoretical systems is that when a creative and innovative author has something new to say that has not been thought or said before, he or she has no choice but to express this new thought in the spirit of the time in which they lived. Moreover, because different societies have different kinds of 'common sense,' different categories of thinking, and different systems of logic therefore every society has its own 'social filter' that makes it difficult to see, understand or experience some truths that will be obvious to later generations.

In *Greatness and Limitations of Freud's Thought* (1979a) Fromm also states that for the one who revises the idea of another thinker the same holds true:

> The process of revision of an author, which distinguishes the essential and new from the contingent, time-conditioned elements, is in itself also the product of a certain historical period that influences the interpretation. In this creative interpretation, again creative and valid elements are mixed with time-bound and accidental ones. The revision is not simply true as the original was not simply false. (Fromm 1979a, p. 4)

Thirty five years after these lines were written we may ask which of Fromm's creative ideas are groundbreaking and in which way these ideas were expressed in a time-conditioned frame of reference? That is to say, we aim to build on Fromm insights all the time looking for new evidence and looking critically at the concepts that highlight what Fromm sensed and perceived but expressed in concepts that in our days are limited or even obsolete.

These themes of the relevance of Fromm's creative ideas for today, the review of Fromm's reception and this kind of critical reappraisal of his work were topics of discussion for the first International Erich Fromm Research Conference that took place end of June 2014 at the International Psychoanalytic University in Berlin. Most papers presented in this volume have their origins in presentations given at this conference participated in by some fifty specialists from all over the world. A major focus of the conference consisted in providing a differentiated survey of the various and widespread fields and cultural contexts in which Fromm's ideas are being discussed. This is important not simply because of the global influence of his work, but also because it is essential to understand the varied ways he was interpreted and used according to the different pressing social issues and existing social filters of the various cultural contexts his work was read in. This volume will thus document the continuing influence of Fromm in Germany and throughout Europe and Latin America, and a revival of interest in his work in North America and Japan and new space for his ideas in Russia and, most surprisingly in China. The interest in Fromm's ideas is remarkable in China, a nation leading along with European scholars what can only be called a world revival of interest in his work that is happening in the social scientists particularly sociology, psychology and psychoanalysis, and the study of philosophy, theology and religious studies. But this volume does not simply document Fromm's continuing use and relevance, it centrally engages with his theoretical system directly and critically, suggesting ways that new research, theories and insights in neurosciences, evolutionary psychology, sociology, philosophy, religious studies and radical humanist public intellectual work can help us move beyond some of the limitations of his work so that we can better reformulate his insights in order to address the current crisis of inequality, violence, cultural crisis and environmental destruction and climate change in the 21st century.

What did Fromm mean by Science?

Before talking about Fromm's core concepts and his global and interdisciplinary reception, we must step back for a moment to clarify what Fromm meant by "science." Fromm's view on the time-limited nature of all theoretical systems was rooted in a broader philosophy of science, and for this reason this volume begins with the republication of a 1957 essay called "The Humanistic Science of Man" originally sketched under the title "Institute for the Science of Man".

According to Erich Fromm, science means

> an attitude of objectivity. It is a human attitude (...) to have the courage (...) to examine whether the data that we gathered confirmed our idea or disproved it, and whether one had the courage to change a theory if the data showed that they had not proved it (Fromm 1991e, p. 64).

11

This attitude of objectivity was particularly important in the modern society of the 1950s where Fromm observed that

> the average person has become the consumer of science and expects that the scientist knows it all (...) people are convinced that scientists are like priests, who have complete certainty about the world. (...) There is somebody at least who has certainty and conviction, and one feels a sense of security oneself (Fromm 1991e, p. 65).

Some twenty years later Horst-Eberhard Richter called this phenomenon "Gotteskomplex" (Richter 1979), and the public attitudes it describes still are widespread. In contemporary society, however, the unquestioned status of science has been eroded by the influence of various relativist philosophies of knowledge and the attacks on scientific reasoning lead by religious fanatics of various faiths and the influence of conservative and left-wing populism empowered by the failure of established elites to solve the growing social and economic problems facing the world at the beginning of the 21st century. Fromm's open attitude toward existing theories and insistence on following the data where it leads is thus even more important today than it was in the 1950s, as reason itself is under siege in large parts of the world just as it was in Europe of the 1930s.

Yet science, for Fromm, is not "positivism" or "scientism" where the method of the natural science are aped by social thinkers in a simplistic way that distorts the insights of what must be a human science. Fromm made this criticism as early as 1957 when he pointed out that

> the social sciences of today (with a number of notable exceptions), impressed by the success and prestige of the natural sciences, try to apply the methods of the natural sciences to the furthering of mankind. Not only do they not ask themselves whether the method which is valid for the study of things is also valid for the study of man, but they even fail to question whether this concept of the scientific method is not naive and outdated. They believe that only a method that counts and weighs can be called *scientific*, forgetting that the most advanced natural sciences today, such as theoretical physics, operate with bold hypotheses based on imaginative inferences. (...) There is a difference between 'the objective' approach, in which 'the object' is nothing but an object, and an approach in which the observer at the same time relates empathically to the persons he observes. (Fromm 1991e, pp. 102–3.)

Fromm has an enormous influence on the social sciences starting in the 1930s through the early 1960s, but he was never central to the disciplines of sociology, political science anthropology, not to mention economics and psychology, largely because of the dominance of the outmoded model of science Fromm critiques in his work. While Fromm developed his model of science to a very large extent by critiquing the positivist strains within Freud's system, psychoanalysis has generally been more open to moving beyond a simplistic positivist model than most social science with the possible exception of cultural anthropology. It is no accident that the conference was sponsored by the International Psychoanalytic University of Berlin; the model Fromm outlined for a psychoanalytic social science is consistent with the dominant approach in that association.

President Teising opened the conference in Berlin stressing how influential Fromm was as both a role model and intellectual inspiration for him individually along with a couple of generations of analysts now, and central to this influence was the power of his scientific thinking for the development of a human science engaged in healing and social reform outside the ivory academic tower. And this influence was centrally due to the power of Fromm's critique of libido theory, a major residue of outdated 19th century positivism in Freud's thought and a limitation Fromm transcended precisely by seeing psychoanalytic theory as created in a particular time and place as well as insisting that it be tested against empirical data.

According to Fromm, Freud's thought was limited by his adherence to a 19th century mechanistic theory that led him to look for a biological root for neurosis, something Fromm challenged directly. As President Teising quotes Fromm succinctly, Fromm believes that

> the basic inner forces which determine man's life (...) are not his instinctual needs (although they are important too) but those which stem from the very nature and condition of human existence and its inherent contradictions (Fromm 1991e, p. 54).

And furthermore, for Fromm

> these fundamental needs include the necessity for relatedness, rootedness, transcendence (creativity and destruction), sense of identity and frame of

13

> orientation and devotion. (...) Man is a "freak of nature"; lacking the ins-
> tinctive equipment which regulates the life of all animals, but gifted instead
> with reason, imagination, and self-awareness, life becomes for him a problem
> which must be solved (Fromm 1991e, p. 54).

Teising emphasizes that in the paper of 1955 that leads off this book, "Fromm defines his own position in the field of psychoanalysis. Fromm stresses his connection to Freud, recognizing that the most important of Freud's findings have been widely accepted, at the same time not refraining from accentuating his differences with Freud." In particular, Teising points out that for Fromm, "the polarity of Freud's late drive theory never found the same applications to clinical data" as did some of his earlier theories and thus he, operating with the same kind of scientific objectively we will bring to our examination of Fromm's ideas here, rejected Freud's view that destructiveness was "an expression of the death-drive." Fromm's critique of Freudian orthodoxy, as well as his critical engagement with Marxism and various forms of Jewish messianism defined his powerful set of ideas that shaped so much of 20th century intellectual in Europe, and North and South America, but we have now entered a new stage of the reception of Fromm that we hope this volume represents. In order to contribute to this new discussion, this introduction will 1) briefly review some global trends in the reception of Fromm; 2) outline some trends in his reception among the professions and selected academic disciplines, and 3) suggest some ways forward for the development of Fromm's theory of social character. Each of these three goals is reflected in various contributions in this book, and we will highlight the some important work not included in this volume as well as discuss how the various essays in the book contribute to this larger goal of looking at the greatness, influence and limitations of Fromm's work with an eye towards the development of a human science.

A Global Public Intellectual and Scholar: The Maturation of Contemporary Fromm Scholarship

Fromm was arguably one of the first truly global public intellectuals, after emerging on the world intellectual scene with his hugely influential and powerful analysis of Nazism in *Escape from Freedom* (1941a). Fromm had been influential among the critical theorists we now know of as the Frankfurt School in Germany in the late 1920s and early 1930s but it was in his exile and adventure in America that he gained world-wide fame and a global audience with his own unique synthesis of Freudian, Marxist, sociological and Jewish radical intellectual traditions. The theoretical synthesis was developed in scholarly publications in the 1920s and 1930s, but with *Man for Himself* (1947a), *The Sane Society* (1955a) and *The Art of Loving* (1956a), Fromm was widely read by mass publics around the world, particularly in the English speaking world (the United States, Britain and Canada, in particular) most of Western and Central and Eastern Europe and throughout Latin America, where he lived from 1950 to his retirement years back in Europe. There has been a distortion in the reception of Fromm's work, however, because in North America, in particular, his intellectual reputation was damaged severely during the Cold War period and the 1960s by attacks on his work by orthodox Freudians, dogmatic Marxists and neo-conservatives intellectuals. It has even been argued that by the 1970s and 1980s, Fromm had become a "forgotten intellectual" among elite intellectuals and scholars in the English-speaking world.

Fromm was never really forgotten, however, in large parts of Europe, and indeed the reception of his work has been steadily growing in Germany since the late 1970s when he spent his last years in Switzerland and appeared extensively in German media. Rainer Funk's Dissertation (*Mut zum Menschen*, published 1978 and translated to English as *The Courage to Be Human*, New York 1982) was the first publication that pulled together a discussion of Fromm's live and his various influences, shaping the reception of Fromm after his death. There were numerous other dissertations published in German language in the eighties (mostly importantly Wehr, Klein, Bierhoff, Hardeck, Bader). European conferences on Fromm took place as early as 1981 in Yugoslavia in Dubrovnik and more or less from 1986 on every year in Italy and the Fromm Society's national and international conferences from 1985 on in various German and European cities. This book thus has a strong representation of this continuing influence of Fromm in Europe and Germany, with two essays by Rainer Funk, and one by Jürgen Hardeck.

The same relative continuity in the reception of Fromm's work can be seen in Latin America, led by the participatory action research agenda and psychoanalytic theorizing of Sonia Gojman de Millán and Salvador Millán from Mexico. While the German reception of Fromm has seen an emphasis also on Fromm's contributions as a philosopher, education researcher and student of religion, the Latin American scholarship particularly has emphasized Fromm's engaged research on social character, represented here by the Milláns' summary of their three decades of research with poor communities in Mexico. It makes sense, of course, that Fromm scholarship in Latin America would emphasize the engaged elements of his work, given his years spent in Mexico City where he founded the Mexican psychoanalytic Institute, dialogued with a generation of Latin American intellectuals temporary exiled from dictatorships in Brazil, Argentina and elsewhere. The Milláns held the first conference on Fromm, in Mexico in 1981, and have been refining and developing the method Fromm outlined first in *Social Character in a Mexican Village* (1970b) for three decades now. In the social sciences since the 1970s, there has been an enormous growth of participatory action research, particularly in North American sociology and social work, although little of it has taken into account the tradition of social character research represented by Maccoby in the United States and the Milláns in Mexico.

Even in North America where a number of myths about Fromm became almost conventional wisdom (he allegedly was a Freudian revisionist hostile to Freud, a simplistic popularize who was never a theoretically important member of the Frankfurt School, and his political views were dangerous and naïve), there has been a revival of Fromm's ideas beginning in the early years of the 1980s and 1990s. With the English translation of Rainer Funk *The Courage to be Human* (1982) and later Daniel Burston's *The Legacy of Erich Fromm* (1991) we had two full-length studies on Fromm's ideas and influence that began to revive interest in his work in North America after a couple of decades of attacks on his ideas. Michael Maccoby's research group based in Washington had continued the development of Fromm's social character theory after his death, based on Maccoby's own co-authorship and training with Fromm that produced *Social Character in a Mexican Village* (1970b) and his own interest in organizational leadership. This was an uphill battle in North America, because of the concerted efforts of Fromm's many enemies among orthodox Freudians, dogmatic Marxists, neo-conservative Cold warriors and the academic establishments in sociology, philosophy, anthropology, political science and religious studies and theology had left Fromm relatively isolated among the intellectual elite in the English speaking world. Fromm's central role in the creation of Frankfurt School critical theory had previously been erased from historical memory. And his influence within humanist psychology, early feminist thinking and the social scientific study of religion had been largely forgotten.

The North America Fromm revival continues with historian Lawrence Friedman's biography *Love's Prophet: The Lives of Erich Fromm* (2013). Written over a ten year period by a major American biographer and intellectual historian, and published by the prestigious Columbia University Press, *Love's Prophet* has been widely and largely positively reviewed and has been instrumental in reminding the intellectual public, in North America, at least, of Fromm's seminal contributions to psychoanalytic theory, social criticism and public intellectual life. Combined with the efforts of intellectual historian Thomas Wheatland *The Frankfurt School in Exile* (2009) and the critical theorists Stephen Eric Bronner (1994), Douglas Kellner (1992) and Kevin Anderson (1998), and political scientist Jack Jacobs (2014), Fromm's role in bringing Freud and Marx together in a critical theory research agenda in Frankfurt and at Columbia in the late 1920s and early 1930s that laid the foundation for the theory of the authoritarian personality research tradition is now indisputable. This volume has essays by many of the major contributors to the revival of Fromm's reputation in North America, including Maccoby, the psychoanalyst Mauricio Cortina, the prominent America Marxist sociologist Kevin Andersen and the philosopher Joan Braune. A similar revival of Fromm's influence in Japan is happening, as he was highly influential in the 1950s but lost status in the social sciences in later years, only to find new audiences in the early 21st century as discussed by Takeshi Deguchi in this volume.

There is enormous room for growth in the reception of Erich Fromm in the Global South and countries that lived under communist dictatorships during the height of Fromm's influence in the West. Probably the biggest surprise in this book is the data presented that shows a massive interest in Fromm's work in China over the past couple of decades. There have been more dissertations written in China on Erich Fromm over the past 10 years than in the rest of the world in the same period, and the scholarship there tends to emphasize themes of belletristic literature, social theory, concepts of man, alienation, religion while psychoanalytic theory or psychological research is not the focus of interest. The Marxist Fromm was once also influential in Japan and interest is returning to these ideas given the economic conditions in the country today (cf. Takechi Deguchi's contribution). Fromm is being discussed more frequently in Russia in recent years, with translations of his work and new debates about his relevance, as reflected in the contributions of two Russian philosophers here (Tatiana Panfilova and Nikolai Omelchenko). And while we do not have contributors in the book from Arab or Muslim majority countries or Africa, the visibility of Fromm's writings during the Arab spring suggests that Fromm's focus on freedom and skepticism towards consumerist modernity and critique of the inequalities of capitalism will find a new audience in coming decades.

We are thus entering a stage of the reception of Erich Fromm where the reach of his work is now truly global. Fromm, of course, was never a parochial thinker, having grown up in Germany, spent years in cosmopolitan New York, and lived in Mexico for 23 years. And Fromm's theories were concerned with a universal human science; his work always dealt with global politics from a comparative perspective. Yet his influence was strongest in North America, Japan, and Latin America in the middle years of the 20th century and especially in Germany in the 1970s and among intellectuals of socialist and humanist circles in Europe in the sixties and seventies (Poland, Hungary, and the former Yugoslavia and Czechoslovakia). Fromm's ideas often spread during times of social crisis and change, and the fall of the Iron Curtain and the period of the Arab Spring created a tremendous interest in Fromm in Eastern and Central Europe and now in the Middle East. One of the contributions of this volume is to frame the reception of Fromm's work in comparative and global terms, suggesting the need for new research on the influence and applicability of Fromm's theory of social character in China, Russia and in Arab and/or Muslim majority states.

Fromm's growing influence among the professions and academic disciplines

A major dynamic that is fueling this new global reception of Fromm is that there is now new room for Fromm's ideas within various applied professions and academic disciplines and applied professions that did not exist previously when Fromm was under attack by his many critics. Fromm, of course, was influential with American psychoanalysis in the 1940s and 1950s, but there was a number decades where orthodox Freudian hostility to Fromm's revision of Freud pushed his ideas to the margins of the profession. Jay Greenberg's and Stephen Mitchell's influential 1983 book *Object relations in psychoanalytic theory* was the beginning of a new trend in writings on the history of psychoanalysis in North America that restored Fromm's place in the development of cutting edge theory in the field, a trend that has increased as relational and object relations have gained influence. The magnificent historical research and psychoanalytic theorizing of the late Stephen Mitchell has re-introduced Fromm's role in 20th century psychoanalysis as an important precursor to the influential contemporary relational, object relations and self psychology schools of thought.

Recent decades have seen a global trend towards integrating Fromm's contribution to the psychoanalytic profession. Romano Biancoli pioneered the application of Fromm's social character theory to psychotherapy and psychoanalytic treatment and founded a Frommian training institute in Bologna in the late 1980s. Marco Bacciagaluppi of Milan applied Fromm's relational psychoanalytic approach to psychotherapeutic treatment and published his papers in both English (in the influential journal *Contemporary Psychoanalysis*) and Italian. And Fromm's influence remains strong and has been developed further in Mexico by Jorge Silva and Salvador Millán and Sonia Gojman de Millán of the *Seminario Sociopsicoanalítico*. Rainer Funk's edited collection *The Clinical Erich Fromm: Personal Accounts and Papers on Therapeutic Technique* (2009) published also in German and Spanish has pulled together a discussion of Fromm's global influence on analytic technique in a volume that will likely help frame the debate over the next decade.

Much of the scholarship on Fromm has tended to emphasize the ways his psychoanalytic thinking helped influence therapists, social workers, clergy and educators, and recent years have also seen a revival and expansion of interest in Fromm's work in the helping professions and applied professions. We have seen calls for bringing Fromm's work back into social work practices (Rasmussen and Salhani 2008) and an explosion of literature on critical pedagogy based on the work of Paulo Freire, some of which takes account of Fromm's contributions to radical educational thinking (Matias and Allen 2013). We have also seen a new focus on the kind of participatory action research tradition pioneered by Fromm in *Social Character in a Mexican Village* (1970b, pp. 203–25).

In addition, while so much of the response to Fromm's work among theologians and religious scholars in 1940s, 1950s and 1960s was critical, we are seeing as revival of work among Christian, Jewish and humanist scholars concerned with questions of spirituality and Fromm's radical humanism. Some of the most important works that deal with Fromm's religious thought are Angelo M. Caligiuri (1966), Brian Richard Betz (1974), Jörg Jeremias (1983), Jürgen Hardeck 1992, Svante Lundgren (1998). This trend is represented in this volume by Jan Dietrich's contribution on "Erich Fromm in Hebrew Bible research" and in Dietmar Mieth's discussion of Fromm's position in the reception of Master Eckhart.

One of the important developments in recent years in Fromm scholarship in English has been the publication of three major books of political philosophy and social theory addressing Fromm's contributions in sophisticated ways. Lawrence Wilde *Erich Fromm and the quest for solidarity* (2004) and, more recently, Kieran Durkin's *The radical humanism of Erich Fromm.* (2014) and Joan Braune's *Erich Fromm's revolutionary hope: Prophetic Messianism as a Critical Theory of the future* (2014) have put Fromm's philosophical thinking back on the agenda for scholars. While the influence of Fromm's ideas on applied fields like psychoanalysis, social work and education is vitally important, in the end, it is Fromm's theoretical contribution that must be emphasized and refined. So we will conclude by talking about what we see as the central contribution of Fromm's ideas represented by his concept of man as a relational and social being and by his theory of social character, and suggest some directions for its development in light of new developments in the human sciences since Fromm's death.

Conclusion: Building on the greatness and limitations of Fromm's thought

By returning to where we started with our discussion of what we mean by a human science, it must be said that despite the excitement created by both the continuing and new interest in the work of Erich Fromm, the full potential of his ideas will not be felt unless we address head on the time-bound aspects of Fromm's work as he himself did with Sigmund Freud, Karl Marx, Johann Jacob Bachofen and all the major thinkers he engaged with to produce his theory of social character. The debate and discussion about Fromm's work has shifted in recent decades away form a concern with whether he is really a Freudian or a Marxist, and what he disagrees with in these systems of thought, to a new level of debate about Fromm's own theory on its own terms. From our perspective, the core of Fromm's ideas worth building on for the 21st century is his scientifically sound concept of man as a social being and his theory of social character.

Fromm's own theoretical system was built, of course, on the foundation of Freud's theory of character and Marx's historical materialism but with an innovative revision of both. What is special about both Fromm's psychoanalytic approach and his sociological-historical analysis is that he understands the person as having always been related to others not only in the sense of interactive sociality but as a social relatedness that precedes all concrete perceptions of relatedness because it is rooted in a larger social structure. This larger social structure has its psychic representation in the social character. The social character has the same function that Steven Mitchell assigns to the "relational matrix" (Mitchell 1988, pp. 41ff.) as the connection between the intrapsychic and the interpersonal therefore the various relational and interpersonal versions of psychoanalysis that emerged since Fromm's early theoretical writings have created new space for social character theory. It is more possible today to connect Freudian insights on character to sociological perspectives on history and social structure than it was in the 1930s and 1940s when orthodox Freudian theories dominated the field. And Fromm's theory of social character does a far better job of connecting the intrapsychic to the social than anything that has yet been developed within either psychoanalysis or sociology. For Fromm, the interpersonal is subordinated to the social. It is involved in two intrapsychic structural dimensions: the social character and the individual character. For the intersubjective construction of reality, this means (expressed in Mitchell's terms) that not only the personal, but also the social "microcosms of the relational field" (Mitchell 2003, p. 57) play a part in organizing the self and the outside world.

According to Fromm

The members of the society and/or the various classes or status groups within it have to behave in such a way as to be able to function in the sense required by society. It is the function of the social character to shape the energies of the members of society in such a way that their behavior is not left to conscious decisions whether or not to follow the social pattern but that *people want to act as they have to act* and at the same time find gratification in acting according to the requirements of the culture. In other words, the social character has the function of molding human energy for the purpose of the functioning of a given society. (Fromm 1949c, p. 5.)

Fromm always tries to see the person, even in his intersubjectivity and relatedness, as a social being. He thus overcomes, theoretically and clinically, a social amnesia that social scientists, in particular, accuse psychoanalytic theory and practice of showing. Sociologists have begun again to examine their own traditions critically with regards to their ignoring of the power of feeling and emotions and are making finding their way to the more sociological oriented currents within psychoanalysis such as object relations, relational and self-psychology (Chancer and Andrews 2014).

We argue, however, that the false dichotomy of individual psychology and social structure is not really transcended by relational psychoanalysis or the intersubjective paradigms. Comparing Fromm's approach with the intersubjective approach, as Stolorow and Atwood developed it, Fromm's perspective surpasses the dimension of intersubjectivity in order to allow us to do justice to the social imprint of society's norms on individual people. A person's sociability is defined in the intersubjective paradigm only from the interactive social position, and not from that which the person has to develop in terms of irrational pathogenic drives to adjust to the demands of a certain society. The intersubjective paradigm thus lacks the potential for social critique that allowed Freud to recognize the meaning of repressed sexual urges in the development of psychic illnesses and brought Fromm to unmask authoritarianism as pathogenic, given its inherent quest for both power and subordination. At issue is a social-psychological approach that highlights what society needs to function and how this is manifested in the person as a powerful striving. And crucially for Fromm's theory of social character, we can use it to help understand when society's needs and the passions this creates also make human beings sick.

We would argue that there are three major social crises in the contemporary world situation that cannot be fully understood theoretically without the insights of a rediscovered and revised version of social character theory: the threat of human extinction due to climate change, the outbreak of violence we are seeing around the world in the early years of the 21st century and the accelerating inequality we see globally and internally within most nations.

Looking beyond the specific scientific debates about the causes of climate change, and the policy differences addressing solutions, the reality is there is no realistic way to limit carbon emissions and thus halt global warming without dealing with excessive consumerism. There is no competing social psychological theory that is more focused and useful on this question than Fromm's concept of social character. This social psychoanalytic approach lets us recognize, for example, that the socially required and promoted striving for security, predictability, and quantifiability stifles a person's ability to trust and to love. These powerful internalized consumerist passions prevent critical distance from the consumerism that is omnipresent today, where what goes into a person and what he can acquire and become are the only things that count, rather than what he can bring out of himself by his own abilities. Such consumerism occurs today especially with respect to the experience of feelings and passions. The production of emotions, affects, and passions are in full force and bring the individual to relinquish his innermost perception of feelings and affective powers in order to experience the proffered emotions. The pathogenic effects of this can be seen in insurance companies' statistics of depression and in the inner emptiness and lifelessness that overcome people more and more if they do not let themselves be animated, entertained, stimulated, and enlivened (cf. Funk 2011). Without addressing these issues, the vast majority of people will resist the kinds of societal changes that would be required to prevent catastrophic climate change, leaving us a choice between the destruction of human life on the planet or some kind of anti-democratic imposed solution, enforced by elites.

Similar dynamics are at play, as we watch the emergence of mass movements around the world promoting various hatreds and scapegoating, something that inevitably leads to violence. Elite interests often lay behind state violence, something Fromm highlighted in *Escape from Freedom* (1941a) and *May Man Prevail?* (1961a). But it is not possible to fully understand

the re-emergence of neo-Nazism and fascism throughout Europe, the surprising popularity of Putin in Russia, the violence of radical Islam and the
irrationality of the American tea party without some account of the social
characters that create a passion for violence, revenge and irrationality in
particular historical contexts. As Sagall (2013) has worked out by referring
to Fromm's concept of necrophilia sociological and economic theories that
operate purely at the structural and rational levels are inadequate, as are
social psychological perspectives that connect individual psyches to societal
dynamics without a theoretical perspective on human passions that avoids
the biological determinism we find in orthodox Freudian theory.

And finally, recent debates about inequality globally and inside Europe,
the United States and Latin America, for example, are unproductively polarized between structural perspectives that highlight economic factors and
moral and social psychological perspectives that put an emphasis on the
individual's role in re-producing the unhealthy patterns of behavior that
led to drug abuse and alcoholism, passivity and violence and criminality.
Only Fromm's theory of social character allow us to connect the emotions
and passions that are imprinted in human psyches by society to the larger
historical and structural patterns that must be understood as central to any
discussion of poverty, inequality and human hopelessness. From our perspective, one of the important tasks for building a human science in the
21st century will be taking this theory of social character, and developing it
further while identifying the aspects of Fromm's original formulations that
were limited by Fromm's own historical conditioning and the theoretical
limitations that flow from this.

Fromm's theory of social character for the 21st century

We are fortunate to have an essay by Michael Maccoby in this book, and
as Fromm's co-author in the most extensive development of the theory in
Social Character in a Mexican Village (1970b) he is well positioned to frame
the history of social character research for us as a living tradition that he
has developed over several decades of research with corporate leaders and
public sector managers. It is unfortunate that this social character research
tradition has not been taken up and developed within contemporary soci-

ology, although recent scholarship has been suggesting that Fromm's ideas could usefully be combined with the work of French sociologist Pierre Bourdieu whose theory of habitus has affinity with theory of social character (Cheliotis 2011). Bourdieu's theory is more sociologically and methodological advanced than the work Fromm did before Bourdieu emerged as a major scholar in the 1970s while at the same time, lacking Fromm's psychoanalytic depth. Kieran Durkin (2014) has also called for more work synthesizing Fromm and Bourdieu, and we think this is a vitally important direction for future research. And we have seen a new opening to psychoanalysis within sociology in recent years, something that bodes well for the further reception of Fromm in that discipline (Chancer and Andrews, 2014; Cheliotis 2011; David-West 2014).

It would be a mistake, however, to think that Fromm's theory can simply be applied to culture sociological questions without addressing current research in the natural sciences, as Fromm did himself in *The Anatomy of Human Destructiveness* (1973a). Mauricio Cortina's essay in this volume raises important theoretical issues about how Fromm's social character theory must take into account developments in neuro-sciences, attachment theory and our understanding of socio-biology and evolutionary psychology since the publication of *The Anatomy of Human Destructiveness* (1973a). Fromm actually stands out from most radical social critics because he was deeply committed to an engagement with all the social and biological sciences. Cortina's provocative essay suggests that Fromm overemphasized the human break with the psychological mechanisms we can see operating in various mammals and our own evolutionary ancestors, calling for a revision of social character theory. There is much debate on this question among the contributors to this book, some of whom would put more emphasis on Fromm's original argument for an existential break with instincts and biology rooted in the human condition. Leaving aside the specifics, we are sympathetic to this call for cooperation between the social sciences, Fromm scholars and cutting edge biological researchers while also insisting that social character theory also remain linked to social philosophy and its roots in radical humanism. This debate is likely to be one of the mostly lively and productive as social character theory is developed in the 21st century.

It is hard to deny, moreover, that many biological scientists in the 20th century shared Fromm's relative inattention to questions of full equality for gay and lesbians, a issue put on the agenda for us here in Luis Jimenez's contribution that challenges Fromm's views on homosexuality while suggesting ways that his theories could be used and revised productively in light of modern awareness of the sexual diversity and rights. Similar points could be made regarding Fromm's views about gender and women, and we note that many radical feminism today are returning to Fromm's work for inspiration based on his earlier influence on Mary Daly while questioning some of his views about the essential differences between men and woman in light of current scholarship (Daly 1978; Kellner 1992). There will be differences among Fromm's scholars as to what is useful and what is problematic in his views about gender, but debating this issue is interesting precisely because Fromm was a pioneer in critically addressing gender question from his early writing on, particularly with his reception of Bachofen and Briffault and his papers on sex and character in the forties (see Fromm 1994a: *Love, Sexuality, and Matriarchy: About Gender*). More work must be done, in addition, to refine Fromm's insights in light of recent scholarship on race and racism (Traoré, Mergler and McLaughlin forthcoming; Matias and Allen 2013).

Fromm's vision of science, to be sure, was rooted in a vision of human potential and a commitment to social change, but we will not attempt to resolve this important debate that this edited book hopes to contribute it. Indeed, it ultimately will not be the many esteemed and established Fromm scholars in this volume who will determine the best way to build on and revise Fromm's thought for the 21st century, since this a task for a new generation of intellectuals and scholars. For this reason, we end the book not with a definitive statement on Fromm's theories but some questions raised by two graduate student participants from the Fromm Research Conference.

It remains only for us to thank the Karl Schlecht Foundation and Karl Schlecht, in particular, for making the First Fromm Research Conference and this book possible. And to encourage our readers to think about the prospects of a human science in the 21st century along with Fromm and this collection of scholarship in the open ended tradition of a human science he helped establish.

References

Anderson, K. (1998). The Young Erich Fromm's Contribution to Criminology. Justice Quarterly, 15(4), pp. 667–96.

Bambery, M., and Abell, S. (2006). Relocating the Nexus of Psychopathology and Treatment: Thoughts on the Contribution of Erich Fromm to Contemporary Psychotherapy. Journal of Contemporary Psychotherapy, 36(4), pp. 175–82.

Betz, B.R. (1974). An Analysis of the Prophetic Character of the Dialectical Rhetoric of Erich Fromm, Northwestern University Dissertation 1974.

Braune, J. (2014). Erich Fromm's Revolutionary Hope. Prophetic Messianism as a Critical Theory of the Future, Rotterdam et al.: Sense Publishers.

Bronner, S.E. (1994). Of Critical Theory and Its Theorists, Oxford and Cambridge: Blackwell.

Burston, D. (1991). The Legacy of Erich Fromm. Cambridge and London: Harvard University Press.

Caligiuri, A.M. (1966). The Concept of Freedom in the Writings of Erich Fromm. An Exposition and Evaluation, Universitas Gregoriana Roma Dissertation 1966.

Chancer, L., and Andrews, J. (Eds.). (2014). The Unhappy Divorce of Sociology and Psychoanalysis: Diverse Perspectives on the Psychosocial. New York: Palgrave Macmillan.

Cheliotis, L.K. (2011). For a Freudo-Marxist Critique of Social Domination: Rediscovering Erich Fromm through the Mirror of Pierre Bourdieu. Journal of Classical Sociology, 11(4), pp. 438–61.

Cortina, M., and Maccoby, M. (Eds.). (1996). A Prophetic Analyst: Erich Fromm's Contributions to Psychoanalysis. Nothvale and London: Jason Aronson Incorporated.

Daly, M. (1978). Gyn/Ecology: The Metaphysics of Radical Feminism. Boston: Beacon Press.

David-West, A. (2014). Erich Fromm and North Korea: Social Psychology and the Political Regime. Critical Sociology, 40(4), pp. 575–600.

Durkin, K. (2014). The Radical Humanism of Erich Fromm. New York: Palgrave Macmillan.

Friedman, L. (2013). The Lives of Erich Fromm: Love's Prophet. New York: Columbia University Press.

Fromm, E. (1941a). Escape from Freedom. New York: Farrar and Rinehart.

Fromm, E. (1947a). Man for Himself. An Inquiry into the Psychology of Ethics. New York: Rinehart and Co.

Fromm, E. (1949c). Psychoanalytic Characterology and Its Application to the Understanding of Culture. In: S. Stansfeld Sargent and Marian W. Smith (Eds.), Culture and Personality. New York: Viking Press, pp. 1–12.

Fromm, E. (1955a). The Sane Society. New York: Rinehart and Winston, Inc.

Fromm, E. (1956a). The Art of Loving. An Inquiry into the Nature of Love. New York: Harper and Row.

Fromm, E. (1961a). May Man Prevail? An Inquiry into the Facts and Fictions of Foreign Policy. New York: Doubleday.

Fromm, E. (1964a). The Heart of Man. Its Genius for Good and Evil. New York: Harper and Row.

Fromm, E. (1973a). The Anatomy of Human Destructiveness. New York: Holt, Rinehart and Winston.

Fromm, E. (1976a). To Have Or to Be? New York: Harper and Row.

Fromm, E. (1979a). Greatness and Limitations of Freud's Thought. New York: Harper and Row, 1980.

Fromm, E. (1991e). Modern Man's Pathology of Normalcy [originated 1953]. In: E. Fromm, The Pathology of Normalcy. Contributions to a Science of Man. New York: American Mental Health Foundation, 2010, pp. 15–80.

Fromm, E. (1994a). Love, Sexuality, and Matriarchy: About Gender. New York: Fromm International Publishing Corporation, 1997.

Fromm, E., and Maccoby, M. (1970b). Social Character in a Mexican Village. A Sociopsychoanalytic Study. Englewood Cliffs: Prentice Hall.

Funk, R. (1978/1982). Mut zum Menschen. Stuttgart: Deutsche Verlags-Anstalt, 1978; English: Erich Fromm: The Courage to Be Human. New York: Continuum, 1982.

Funk, R. (Ed.) (2009). The Clinical Erich Fromm. Personal Accounts and Papers on Therapeutic Technique. Amsterdam and New York: Rodopi Publisher. German edition: Erich Fromm als Therapeut. Frühere Schüler erinnern sich an seine Praxis der Psychoanalyse. Gießen: Psychosozial-Verlag, 2009. Spanish edition: Recordando a Erich Fromm. Testimonios de sus alumnos sobre el hombre y el terapeuta. Barcelona et al.: Paidós, 2011.

Funk, R. (2011). Der entgrenzte Mensch. Warum ein Leben ohne Grenzen nicht frei, sondern abhängig macht [The unbounded self. Why a life without limitations and attachment leads to dependence]. Gütersloh: Gütersloher Verlagshaus.

Greenberg, J., and Mitchell, S. (1983). Object relations in psychoanalytic theory. Cambridge: Harvard University Press.

Hardeck, J. (1992). Vernunft und Liebe. Religion im Werk von Erich Fromm. Frankfurt am Main and Berlin: Ullstein.

Jacobs, J. (2014). The Frankfurt School: Jewish Lives and Anti-Semitism. Cambridge: Cambridge University Press.

Jeremias, J. (1983). Die Theorie der Projektion im religionskritischen Denken Sigmund Freuds und Erich Fromms, Dissertation Universität Oldenburg 1983.

Kellner, D. (1992). Erich Fromm, Feminism, and the Frankfurt School. In: M. Kessler and R. Funk (Eds.), Erich Fromm und die Frankfurter Schule. Tuebingen: Francke Verlag, pp. 111–30.

Lundgren, S. (1998). Fight Against Idols. Erich Fromm on Religion, Judaism and the Bible, Frankfurt and New York: Peter Lang.

Maccoby, M. (1995). The Two Voices of Erich Fromm: Prophet and Analyst. Society, 32(5), pp. 72–82.

Matias, C.E., and Allen, R.L. (2013). Loving Whiteness to Death: Sadomasochism, Emotionality, and the Possibility of Humanizing Love. Berkeley Review of Education, 4(2). Retrieved from: https://escholarship.org/uc/item/9sd900g8#page-1 (April 3, 2015).

Mitchell, S.A. (1988). Relational Concepts in Psychoanalysis: An Integration. Cambridge: Harvard University Press.

Mitchell, S.A. (2003). Relationality: From Attachment to Intersubjectivity. New York: Analytic Press.

Rasmussen, B., and Salhani, D. (2008). Resurrecting Erich Fromm. Smith College Studies in Social Work, 78(2–3), pp. 201–25.

Richter, H.E. (1979). Der Gotteskomplex. Die Geburt und die Krise des Glaubens an die Allmacht des Menschen. Reinbek bei Hamburg: Rowohlt.

Roazen, P. (1996). Erich Fromm's Courage. In: M. Cortina, and M. Maccoby (Eds.). A Prophetic Analyst: Erich Fromm's Contributions to Psychoanalysis. Nothvale and London: Jason Aronson Incorporated, 1996, pp. 427–53.

Sagall, S. (2013). Final Solutions. Human Nature, Capitalism and Genocide. London: Pluto Press.

Traoré, I., Mergler, I., and McLaughlin, N. Erich Fromm, 1900–1980. In: The Blackwell Encyclopedia of Race, Ethnicity and Nationalism (Forthcoming).

Wheatland, T. (2009). The Frankfurt School in Exile. Minneapolis: University of Minnesota Press.

Wilde, L. (2004). Erich Fromm and the Quest for Solidarity. New York: Palgrave Macmillan.

Zingale, N.C., and Piccorelli, J.T. (2012). Chains of Freedom: A View from Erich Fromm on Individuality Within Organizations. Administrative Theory & Praxis, 34(2), pp. 211–36.

The Humanistic Science of Man

Erich Fromm

Erich Fromm was convinced that our future depends decisively on whether one can motivate the most capable people to dedicate themselves to a science of man, which makes humans the center of interest once again. Only with concerted efforts can the psychic pathologies of modern society be overcome. His understanding of a humanistic science of man is nowhere expressed more clearly or more concretely than in a small programmatic piece of writing entitled "Institute for the Science of Man," which he sketched in 1957[1]. At the suggestion of publicist Ruth Nanda Anshen, Fromm pursued the idea of founding an Institute committed to a humanistic scientific ideal. The fact that the Institute was never created does not decrease the merit of his vision of a humanistic science of man.

Preliminary Considerations

Our present epoch is characterized by the discrepancy that exists between our scientific and technical knowledge on the one hand, and the little knowledge we as yet have about humankind on the other.

This is not just a theoretical discrepancy, but a most important practical

---

1 The draft was first published in the 1990 *Yearbook of the International Erich Fromm Society: Science of Man - Wissenschaft vom Menschen*. Münster (LIT-Verlag), pp. 12-17. Republished in: E. Fromm (2010). *The Pathology of Normalcy. Contributions to a Science of Man*, edited and with a Foreword by Rainer Funk, Riverdale (American Mental Health Foundation), pp. 101-108.

one as well: if man cannot know more about himself, and use this knowledge for the better organization of his life, he will be destroyed by the very products of his scientific knowledge. But isn't this need for man to gain a better knowledge of himself not already being met by the thousands of investigators in the fields of psychology, social psychology, psychoanalysis, human relations, and so forth? The answer to this question is vital with regard to the foundation of a new Institute for the Science of Man. If one feels that the aims of a science of man are being adequately covered by the existing social sciences, then indeed one should be strengthening the existing framework and not be founding new institutes.

Those participating in the discussions about the new Institute very clearly hold that the existing social sciences do not provide what is needed. These are some of the reasons for this conviction:

(1) The social sciences of today (with a number of notable exceptions), impressed by the success and prestige of the natural sciences, try to apply the methods of the natural sciences to the furthering of mankind. Not only do they not ask themselves whether the method is valid for the study of things is also valid for the study of man, but they even fail to question whether this concept of the scientific method is not naive and outdated. They believe that only a method that counts and weighs can be called *scientific,* forgetting that the most advanced natural sciences today, such as theoretical physics, operate with bold hypotheses based on imaginative inferences. Even intuition, according to Einstein, should not be despised. The result of this imitation of a badly understood scientific method is that the methodology of "facts and figures" determines the problems one studies. Researchers choose insignificant problems because the answers can be put into figures and mathematical formulas, instead of choosing significant problems and developing new methods suitable to the study of these problems.

The result is that there are thousands of research projects, most of which do not touch on the fundamental questions of mankind. The thinking applied in these projects is not rigorous but rather of a naive, practical-technical nature, and it is no wonder that the advanced natural sciences rather than the social sciences attract the best brains.

(2) Closely related to the problem of a misunderstood scientific method is the relativism with which the social sciences are imbued. Whereas

we still pay lip service to the great humanistic tradition, most social scientists have adopted an attitude of complete relativism, an attitude in which values are considered a matter of taste but of no objective validity. Because it is a difficult task to probe the objective validity of values, social science has chosen the easier path of throwing them out altogether. In doing so, it has neglected the fact that our whole world is endangered by the increasing loss of a sense of values, which has led to an increasing incapacity to use constructively the fruits of our thoughts and efforts in the natural sciences.

(3) Another aspect of this relativism is the loss of a concept of man as a definite entity underlying the various manifestations of man as they appear in various cultures. One studies man as if he were a blank sheet of paper on which every culture writes its own text, rather than as a being that is not only biologically but also psychologically a definable entity. If we do not regain this concept of man as an underlying reality, how can we expect to make fruitful use of the growing geographical and social unity of man, which is the historical trend of the future?

General Aims

In the light of these preliminary considerations, we arrive at the formulation of the general aim of the Institute, which is to pursue the scientific study of man in the spirit of humanism. More specifically, this has the following implications. Firstly, the study of man must be based on certain humane concerns, primarily those which have been the concern of the whole humanistic religious and philosophical tradition: the idea of the dignity of man and of his potentialities for love and reason, which can be actualized under favorable circumstances. Secondly, the study of man must be based on those concerns which result from our own historical situation: the breakdown of our traditional value system, the uncontrolled and unstructured growth of purely intellectual and technical activities, and the resulting need to find a new, rational foundation for the establishment of the values of the humanistic tradition. These concerns assume that in spite of all differences man is one species, not only biologically and physiologically but also mentally and psychologically.

These general aims can be accomplished only if methods proper to the study of man are examined and developed. The problem is not that of choosing between a scientific and a non-scientific study of man, but of determining what constitutes the proper rational method for the understanding of man and what does not.

A humanistic science of man must continue the work of the great students of man of the past, such as Aristotle and Spinoza. It will be enriched by the new data that biology, physiology, and sociology are giving us, and by our own experiences as contemporaries in this age of transition who are concerned with the future of man.

In this latter respect one more remark appears to be necessary. It is often said by social scientists that one condition of scientific enquiry is the absence of any self-interested or preconceived aims. That this is a naive assumption is clearly shown by the development of the natural sciences: they are to a large extent furthered and not hindered by practical aims and necessities. It is the task of the scientist to keep the data objective, not to study without aims—which are what give meaning and impulse to his work. Just as every age has its specific economic and technical problems, so it also has its specific human problems, and the study of mankind today must be prompted and guided by the problems engendered in this period of world history.

Specific Aims

The study of the methods proper for the science of man. It has to be established what differences in approach exist between the study of things and the study of living beings, especially man. For instance, there is a difference between "the objective" approach, in which "the object" is nothing but an object, and an approach in which the observer at the same time relates empathically to the persons he observes.

Study of the concept of man and of human nature. Although humanistic philosophy assumes the unity of all mankind, there is a great need for rational and demonstrable proof that there is indeed such a thing as man and human nature beyond the purely anatomical and physiological realm. The concept of human nature must be established by integrating what we know of man in the past with what we know of man in various highly developed and relatively primitive cultures today. The task is to go beyond a descriptive anthropology, and to study the basic human forces behind the manifold verities in which it is expressed. The thoroughgoing dynamic study of all manifestations of human nature will lead to the inference of a tentative picture of human nature and what the laws governing it are. A humanistic science of man must begin with the concept of human nature, while at the same time aiming to discover what this human nature is. Needless to say, a number of studies should be made of different societies (preindustrial, primitive) in which hypotheses on human nature should be tested.

Study of values. It must be shown that certain values are not simply matters of taste, but are rooted in the very existence of man. It has to be demonstrated which of these such-basic values are, and how they are rooted in the very nature of man. Values in all cultures must be studied in order to find any underlying unity; and a study of the moral evolution of mankind must also be attempted. Furthermore, it is necessary to investigate what effect the violation of basic ethical norms has on the individual and on the culture. According to the relativists, any norm is valid once it is established by the culture whether it is murder or love. Humanism claims that certain norms are inherent in man's existential situation, and that their violation results in certain consequences, which are inimical to life.

Study of destructiveness. Related to the above is the study of destructiveness in all its forms: destruction of others, self-destruction, sadism, and masochism. We know almost nothing about the causes of destructiveness, and yet there is an enormous field of empirical data that would permit us to establish at least hypotheses concerning the individual and social causes of destructiveness.

Study of creativeness. There is an equally broad field of observation for the study of creative impulses in children, adolescents, and adults, as well as of the factors that further impede these impulses. The study of creativeness, as of destructiveness, must transcend the American scene and, if possible, use material from as many diverse cultures as can be obtained.

Study of authority. The modern age of freedom and individualism has fought against authority and established as its ideal the complete absence of authority. This absence of overt authority, however, has helped to increase the power of anonymous authority, which, in turn, has led to a dangerous degree of conformity. It is necessary to study the problem of authority afresh and to differentiate empirically between irrational and rational forms of authority; also to study the phenomenon of conformism in all its manifestations.

Study of the psychological premises of democratic organization. The idea of the responsible and well-informed citizen who participates in the important decisions of the community is the central concept of democracy. But due to the quantitative increase in population and to the influence of methods of mass-suggestion, the substance of democracy is weakening. Studies are necessary to show what goes on in the mind of the voter (beyond polling his opinion), how suggestible he is, what the fact that he can do little to influence political action does to the alertness of political thinking. Experiments in group discussion and decision-making must be furthered, and their results studied.

Study of the educational process. The fact is that we enjoy more higher education than any people ever had anywhere in the world, but that our system of higher education does relatively little to stimulate critical thought and to influence character formation. As a number of studies have shown, the students are little affected by their teachers' personalities and, at best, get not much more than purely intellectual knowledge. New studies are needed to examine the learning situation and the student-teacher relationship. How can education can go beyond purely verbal intellectual processes into the realm of meaningful experience?

Study of history as the evolution of man. Conventional history was studied in a provincial way. The roots of our culture in Palestine, Greece, and Rome, and then European and American history, were at the center of attention. We need a true world history in which the evolution of mankind is shown in its right proportions. It must be shown how the same basic ideas have arisen in various branches of the human family, how some have merged and others remained separate, although the differences have been greatly overstated in comparison to the similarities. In a true History of Man, the evolution of humanity, his character and his ideas could be shown as well as his growth into an ever more integrated unity. Due emphasis would be given to the true proportions of various cultures and ages. Such a history should enable man to have an objective picture of the whole human race, its growth, integration, and unity. In recent years a number of universal histories more or less answering to this type have been written, but they do not meet the real need, which is that for a scholarly work of many volumes, written by a number of outstanding specialists united by a humanistic spirit.

General Remarks

(1) The Institute, in order to have any value, must have a distinctive image. This image cannot be adequately expressed in words (not so much because we have no words, but because they are misused in double-talk) but must rather be expressed by people who in their work and personalities express this image.

(2) The Institute should not follow the practice of the big foundations, which has been in practice to encourage many people to think about a scientific problem in terms of what they can "sell" to a foundation, to think first about the funding and only later about what one wants to discover. The Institute should make money available only to the extent that a project really needs it. As a matter of principle, budgets should be kept within a reasonable minimum and should be entirely functional. In this way, the Institute would try to encourage the return to an old-fashioned way of working in which thinking and studying, and not the obtaining of funds and their administration, are at the center of research.

(3) The Institute should support two kinds of activities (as well as building up a library devoted to the science of man):

> The work of outstanding scholars: here the goal should not be a specific problem, but rather to support a productive personality who should be enabled to pursue research into the science of man free from other restricting obligations.

> Specific research problems to be tackled by gifted people. The discovery of such persons could be one of the tasks of the Institute. Here, grants should be given for specific projects. The governing body of the Institute should develop its own research policy, not only choosing gifted people but also problems on the basis of an integrated study of the whole field. The governing body of the Institute would be, to an extent, a scientific planning body for the study of man.

(4) The Institute should support people and projects outside as well as inside of the United States. Under no circumstances should grants be given to universities or other such bodies. Only persons and specific projects suggested and accepted by the Institute should receive grants.

(5) It is suggested that the Institute has an active governing body of five-to-seven members that meet for at least a whole week twice a year, in order to discuss not only grants but the general plans for work, and to devote some time during the year to the preparation of this work in their own field. Such a body should be composed of representatives of various branches in the field of the science of man, but members should primarily be chosen on the basis of common principles, productivity, and individual imagination. The bureaucratic spirit should be kept to a minimum.

Building on Erich Fromm's Scientific Contributions

Michael Maccoby

Abstract: Erich Fromm's scientific contributions were based on his theory of social character and the methods he developed to test it. Social character describes the deep-rooted emotional attitudes shared by people raised in the same culture. Family, schooling, work, and play shape the social character so that people want to do what they need to do to prosper economically and socially in a particular culture. Fromm's first study of German employees and workers before the rise of Hitler showed that despite subscribing to a democratic ideology the majority would support whoever gained power. The second study of Mexican peasant villagers provided statistically significant results demonstrating that social character explained both productivity and psychopathology. These findings were reinforced by subsequent studies. The nucleus of social character is the psychoanalytic character types discovered by Freud and modified by Fromm. This theory makes use of knowledge from economics, sociology, anthropology, and history. Maccoby has continued to show the relevance of the concept of social character in understanding leadership and motivation at work.

We meet today in the context of extremist violence throughout the world, the unchecked spread of weapons of mass destruction, insufficient response to challenges posed by climate change and the lack of the visionary and ethical leadership we need to survive on this planet. The list goes on. We urgently need to understand the causes of these problems to generate solutions. But our current theories are inadequate. The most influential theories in contemporary scholarship can teach us a lot about micro processes of perception and emotions framed in the context of cognitive and neurosciences, but they have little to say about either the power of emotions from a depth psychological perspective, or from the point of view of economic, political, cultural structures and dynamics. The social sciences do address these larger structures and institutions that shape our world, but do so in ways that marginalize serious analysis of emotions and, what Erich Fromm termed, social character.

We need to understand and address both the causes of social pathology, and the factors that affect further human growth. On the one hand, we need to understand the roots of violence, the escapes from freedom, and the commercialization of culture. On the other hand, we need to promote models that will be conducive to human collaboration, or to use Fromm's terms, promote models that will value being over having lifestyles and develop a saner society. Erich Fromm's work is perhaps the best point of departure to try to understand these complex issues.

In this chapter, I will first discuss Fromm's impressive scientific output, then research that his work inspired, and finally elaborate on the work that still needs to be done for Fromm's contribution to continue improving our understanding of both human and socio-economic development.

In July, 1960, having just received a doctorate from Harvard and a research and training fellowship from the National Institute of Mental Health, I drove, together with my wife, Sandylee, from Cambridge, Massachusetts, to Cuernavaca, Mexico. The purpose of this journey was to study psychoanalysis with Erich Fromm and join him in a study of Mexican villagers. For eight years, I worked with Fromm as a student and a colleague. For another ten years I met and corresponded with him. Fromm helped me to better understand myself, to develop a philosophy of life that has guided my work and relationships, and to acquire theoretical knowledge that I have employed in my own research, writing and teaching.

Fromm wanted the Mexican study to achieve four goals. They were:

➤ To test and establish scientific evidence for his theory of social character.

➤ To understand what causes the social pathologies of alcoholism and violence in Mexican villages and what, in contrast, leads to sustainable social and economic development.

➤ To understand what is needed to facilitate individual development in peasant society.

➤ To give something back to Mexico which welcomed him and supported his work.

I believe the study published in our book, *Social Character in a Mexican Village* (Fromm/Maccoby 1970b) achieved Fromm's purposes.

Before describing Fromm's specific scientific contributions, I would like to talk about the widely discussed problem of defining science, particularly in relation to social science. Starting with Aristotle who described science as seeking the causes of phenomena, different definitions of science have been proposed. The Oxford English dictionary defines science as "theoretical perception of a truth as contrasted with moral conviction." This definition reflects the truth that "facts" without theory cannot be tested.

The Science Council of the UK proposes a definition demonstrating the way most scientists think about science. "Science is the pursuit and application of knowledge and understanding of the natural and social world following a systematic methodology based on evidence." The Scientific Council provides the following list of scientific methodologies:

➤ Objective observation: measurement and data (possibly although not necessarily using mathematics as a tool)

➤ Evidence

➤ Experiment and/or observation as benchmarks for testing hypotheses

➤ Induction: reasoning to establish general rules or conclusions drawn from facts or examples

➤ Repetition

➤ Critical analysis

➤ Verification and testing: critical exposure to scrutiny, peer review and assessment

Fromm's scientific contributions include theories that have been *tested* with evidence and measureable data and some that are *testable* but have not yet been tested. I will describe both kinds of Fromm's theories.

Tested – the Theory of Social Character

The theory of social character employed in Mexico and the principal method of studying it grew out of an earlier research project designed and undertaken in Germany. From 1929–31, Fromm and his collaborators studied the political attitudes of German factory workers and office workers. In a letter to Fromm in 1974, I asked him why he undertook this study. He wrote back (11ᵗʰ April, 1974):

> our main motive was that we wanted to know how many of the workers and employees would in fact resist the Nazis, in spite of the fact that it seemed obvious that they would to many people, who were impressed by the strength of the Social Democratic and Communist organizations... (...) I thought that the only way to find that out was to study their character, that is to say the relationship between the anti-Nazi 'opinion' and their character structure.

Using a questionnaire that elicited responses that were interpreted psychologically, Fromm contrasted conscious political opinions with unconscious attitudes to authority. The study (Fromm 1980a) showed that men holding similar leftist views had different emotional attitudes to authority. Some were "humanistic revolutionaries", some were "authoritarian rebels", and some lacked strong convictions. Fromm reasoned that only the humanistic revolutionaries would resist the National Socialists; the authoritarians would join the Nazis, and the others would fall in line with whatever regime was in power.

Fromm concluded from this study that if the Nazis came to power, the left lacked the unity and conviction to resist them. He also theorized that people holding the same political views had different social characters because their personalities were shaped in different cultural contexts.

Building on his study, Fromm began to develop the theory of social character as a way of integrating theories of Karl Marx and Sigmund Freud. In 1962, he wrote:

> Marx postulated the interdependence between the economic basis of society and the political and legal institutions, its philosophy, art, religion, etc. The former, according to Marxist theory, determined the latter, the 'ideological

superstructure.' But Marx and Engels did not show, as Engels admitted quite explicitly, *how* the economic basis is translated into the ideological superstructure. I believe that by using the tools of psychoanalysis, this gap in Marxian theory can be filled, and that economic basis structure and the superstructure are connected. One of these connections lies in what I have called the *social character* (Fromm 1962a, p. 71).

A key element of social character is Freud's dynamic and systemic concept of character. Fromm modified Freud's descriptions of three character types and added a new type (Freud 1931a). These are:

➤ *Erotic type.* The main interest is loving and more particularly, being loved. This type is dominated by the fear of losing love and therefore people with this character can become dependent on others from whom they seek love.

➤ *Obsessive type.* This type has a strong superego and is dominated by the fear of conscience rather than the fear of losing love. People with this character are inwardly rather than outwardly dependent. Freud saw this type as self-reliant and "the conservative pillar of civilization."

➤ *Narcissistic type.* The chief interest is directed to self-maintenance. The superego is weak. These individuals are independent and not easily intimidated.

In describing the normal narcissist, Freud wrote

> People of this type impress others as "personalities" and are particularly fitted to serve as support for others, to assume the role of leadership, to add new stimulus to cultural development or attack the existing order (Freud 1931a).

In contrast to Freud who theorized that these types were formed by the structuring of libidinal ties in childhood, Fromm theorized that the character types were ways of relating to the world to satisfy material needs and to relate to others, to survive materially and emotionally. He wrote that these character syndromes were shaped by socialization mediated by family, schooling, work and play. He also stated that each type can be more productive – active, self-directed, responsible, loving – or unproductive – passive, dependent and driven by internal drives.

Fromm's ideal of a fully productive person combined love and creative work. He termed Freud's erotic type *receptive* with the positive quality of caring for others. Furthermore, he labelled the obsessive type *hoarding* with positive qualities of patience, practicality, and tenacity and negative qualities of stubbornness and stinginess. Finally, he branded the narcissistic type *exploitative* adding to Freud's positive qualities the negatives of arrogance, seduction, and exploitation (Fromm 1947a, pp. 114–5).

Fromm pointed out that the behavior of people differed according to their social character. When Freud observed personalities in the early twentieth century, productive obsessives were the dominant model for character development. This was because their personality type fits the social character formed in the era of craft and bureaucratic-industrial production. An obsessive farmer or a craftsman, however, was likely to be more independent and hoarding than an obsessive bureaucrat. The farmer had to hoard to protect himself from damaging changes in the weather or in markets. The farmer, however, controlled his time, and when he worked and when he rested. The bureaucrats, on the other hand, were ruled by bosses and clocks but they tried to maximize autonomy within this role (cf. Crozier 1964).

As the mode of production and its cultural frame shifted from manufacturing to service, Fromm observed that a new personality type was emerging to adapt to the new, more service-economy oriented market. Fromm termed this chameleon-like type the *marketing personality*. It has become the dominant personality type of a new social character that I, in turn, have called the interactive social character (Maccoby 2007).

The productive marketing type combines independence with interactivity. Flexible to the point of being protean, marketing types adapt easily to changing situations. Their negative traits include lack of a center, insincerity and disloyalty. Like narcissists, marketing types lack a strong superego, because they don't identify strongly with parental figures. But unlike the narcissist who responds to the commands of an internalized ego ideal, the moral code of the marketing character is continually programmed and reprogrammed by groups considered essential for their success. They are controlled by anxiety of rejection by the group as contrasted with the narcissist's efforts to avoid the feelings of shame, even humiliation for not living up to an ideal image.

Fromm considered these character types as the nuclei of the social character, combined with the attitudes to authority. In the Mexican study, we defined social character as follows:

> The concept of social character does not refer to the complete or highly individualized, in fact, unique character structure as it exists in an individual, but to a "character matrix," a syndrome of character traits which has developed as an adaptation to the economic, social, and cultural conditions common to that group (Fromm/Maccoby 1970b, p. 16).

The Scientific Contributions of the Mexican Study

The most important contributions of *Social Character in a Mexican Village* to scientific knowledge concern the relationship between social character and behavior and the interaction between economic, social, cultural, historical, and psychological factors in explaining social pathologies.

At the start of the study, Fromm raised the following question: What happened to the peasant farmers (*campesinos*) after the Mexican revolution in the 1920s? Despite the fact that they were given land, many peasants failed to take advantage of their opportunities. Alcoholism increased, and there was a high incidence of violence. Why did this happen?

The study showed the importance of social character in explaining this failure of development. Those villagers brought up before the revolution in the culture of the semi-feudal hacienda lacked the self-confidence and the self-directed, hard-working character of successful peasants throughout the world. Their submissive, receptive, unproductive character that was adapted to life in the hacienda, made them vulnerable to alcoholism and exploitation after the revolution. Furthermore, the children of these villagers were apt to become like them.

In contrast, the villagers who came from free villages demonstrated adaptive, productive, hoarding traits. They farmed their land effectively, and they attempted to maintain conservative, patriarchal values and traditions. Those few villagers with a modern outlook and an entrepreneurial character, the productive exploitative types, proved best able to take advantage of the new opportunities, and they also took advantage of the unproductive villagers. They opened small businesses, and they rented land from those

45

unproductive receptive types, many of who were alcoholics. These entrepreneurs took the lead in transforming the culture, getting rid of costly fiestas, while building roads and schools.

The study demonstrated that although the revolution left the villagers in a state of equality, a class system emerged because of differences in social character. One of the most significant findings of the study is the relationship between character and the actual farming behavior of the *campesinos*. Those who were psychologically more productively hoarding, as interpreted from the questionnaires, were also economically more productive. This finding was statistically significant. These productive peasants planted the major part of their land in cash crops, such as rice and vegetables that demanded much care and hard work. Some of the receptive unproductive landholders rented out their land. The others farmed it with sugar cane, producing a much lower profit but greater security. Cane required fewer days of work and less care. The difficult and dirty job of harvesting the cane was done by migrant workers who occupied the lowest class in Mexican rural society and were hired by the sugar refinery, the so-called "cooperative" that took on the paternalistic role of the old hacienda. Some landholders who tried to escape the control of the cooperative found their crops ploughed under. Some of the most astute villagers planted a small percentage of their land in sugar cane, just enough to satisfy the cooperative, gain their benefits (scholarships for their children, health care, low cost loans) and avoid trouble, while optimizing their income.

Another major finding of the study had to do with relationships between the sexes. In the most successful village marriages, husband and wife shared a productive-hoarding social character and were hardworking, conservative, churchgoing, and supportive of each other. However, in those dysfunctional families where husbands and wives fought with each other, the husband and wife expressed different values. The men had unproductive receptive traits and were dependent on their mothers, but they covered it up by acting tough and independent or in other words *macho*. The women were long-suffering and self-denying, but with stubborn hoarding traits, tougher and more independent than the men. Fed up with male posturing and the underlying weakness of their husbands, these wives became hard and unloving, sometimes ridiculing the men who responded violently to the humiliation.

The study of alcoholism described the combination of social character, relationship between the sexes, economic factors, historical factors, and cultural context, which taken together explained the prevalence of alcoholism in the village. The typical alcoholic male was a receptive unproductive landholder with a social character, formed in the hacienda, who planted cane, spending his money and free time on drinking. The fact that he was in a culture where alcohol was relatively cheap and beer and liquor flowed freely at fiestas, increased the social support and impetus to drink. The alcoholism accounted for most of the village violence. Fights often broke out because of drunken insults about a person's masculinity or his mother.

Building on Fromm's Contributions

A number of studies using Fromm's theory of social character have expanded understanding of personality and motivation. Soon after its' publication, the concepts and findings of *Social Character in a Mexican Village* were applied to a study of village women, sponsored by the American Association for the Advancement of Science. I was a member of an advisory group that included the anthropologist Margaret Mead (Reining et al. 1977).

The study of village women explored why women in Kenya, Mexico, and the Philippines either have many children or limit the number of children they have. In two Mexican villages studied by Sonia Gojman, a Mexican psychoanalyst, social character, combined with economic factors, explained the findings concerning fertility. One village, called Santa Maria, was much like the village of *Social Character in a Mexican Village*, perhaps with an even more psychopathological environment. These villagers were descended from hacienda peons, with the receptive unproductive social character. Within families, men tried to dominate their wives by force and both parents treated their children as exploitable property. The men saw sons as future laborers who could either help them farm or could migrate to the United States and send money home. The women saw their children as potential allies against their husbands and as insurance to care for them in old age. Furthermore, because there was so much alcoholism and violence, women wanted many children to replace a son who might be murdered.

The institutions of Santa Maria also reflected this social character. The receptive villagers were constantly looking to the government to give them money and solve their problems. Village leadership was arbitrary, corrupt, and authoritarian.

The other village, called Tierra Alta, was no richer than Santa Maria and was poorer in land, but it had never been a hacienda. The villagers had a long tradition of independent landholding. The women supplemented their income by raising animals and through the cottage industry of sewing. Their economic independence allowed them to challenge the traditional patriarchy. But their economic activity could not be separated from character and values. In Santa Maria, the war between the sexes smoldered underground. The women appeared to accept male domination, but were in fact resentful, and both men and women undermined each other. In Tierra Alta, the struggle between men and women for control of the family was open and acknowledged, but it was tempered by values of human respect. Bringing women into the new economy strengthened their ability to limit their families, and the village's capacity to adapt to change. This process was supported by local leadership, both religious and secular, which was responsive and democratic.

While the social character of Tierra Alta supported economic and individual development, that of Santa Maria did not. The women of Tierra Alta said that they wanted to practice birth control in order to be free to enjoy life more or to have enough resources to provide for their children. In contrast, the mothers of Santa Maria, because they lived in a violent distrustful society, were interested neither in birth control, nor in planning for the education of their children. The researchers found that fertility rates were significantly lower in Tierra Alta even before the introduction of modern contraception. These findings have held up in other studies and supported programs to strengthen the economic independence of women.

Dr Gojman, together with Dr. Salvador Millán, have continued to employ the methods of social character to study issues of human development in rural and urban Mexico, and they have trained a number of students who have participated in this research.

Building on Fromm –
Studies of Leadership and Social Character

When I returned with my family to the United States in 1968, I joined Fromm in opposing the Vietnam War and supporting Senator Eugene McCarthy's anti-war campaign for president. Fromm and I constructed a survey to compare life-loving (biophilic) attitudes vs. anti-life attitudes with political choices such as support for the war. We found statistical evidence that a person's deep-rooted emotional attitudes could be more important than social class or identification with a political party in predicting political positions on issues of war and peace (cf. Maccoby 1972).

After the election I began a series of studies of leadership, and I organized projects to improve the quality of working life in the US, the UK, and Sweden. All of these projects made use of the concepts learned while working with Fromm.

The research questions I asked were:

➤ What are the values and social character of the leaders in the forefront of developing the new information technology that is changing the mode of production in the most advanced countries? Do these leaders care about the impact of what they produce on people and the environment?

➤ What is the social character of followers and what motivates them at work?

➤ How can work be changed to further human development?

I can only briefly summarize the findings of forty years of study about leaders and followers, and I will not have the time to describe the studies and projects to improve the quality of working life (see Maccoby 1981; Heckscher et al. 2003).

Types of Leaders

I found three types of change leaders (Maccoby 1976). One type has an extremely competitive marketing personality. This type leads change to beat the competition. They will shape decisions for the benefit of people and the

49

environment only if forced to by the government regulations, pressure from unions, or from customers.

The second type refers to productive narcissists who are motivated to change the way people live and work, as Freud wrote, "to add new stimulus to cultural development or attack the existing order." Some want to improve life and care about the environment. Others care only for their wealth and power. These leaders have succeeded only when they have been able to partner with colleagues who complement their abilities, especially their tendency to ignore the views of others. An example is Steve Jobs who was fired from Apple when he first became CEO, because of his arrogance and egocentrism. When he returned, he learned to partner with Tim Cook in operations and Jony Ives in design and the result was a historic success.

In contrast, narcissistic leaders even those with humanistic ideas, such as P.G. Gyllenhammar of Volvo and Jan Carlzon of SAS, failed because they did not listen to subordinates (cf. Maccoby 2003; 2007a; 2015).

The third type is a more productive mixed type. Their purpose is to improve life and they have been able to develop an organization as a collaborative community. My colleagues and I have described some of these leaders and their achievements in our recent book, *Transforming Health Care Leadership, A Systems Guide to Improve Patient Care, Decrease Costs, and Improve Population Health* (Maccoby et al. 2013).

Types of Followers

Fromm was prescient, observing that the shift from an industrial to a service mode of production was changing the social character. The cultural changes that shape the social character have accelerated since Fromm first wrote about the marketing character in 1947 (Fromm 1947a). Not only has most work in advanced societies become service (eighty-four percent in the U.S., seventy-four percent in Germany), but also the structure of the typical family and the experience of childhood development has changed.

In 1947, in the typical family in Western Europe and the US, the father went to work in an office or factory, and the mother stayed at home to care for the children and the house. Children were raised to identify with parents and their roles. The school prepared them for bureaucratic careers, passing tests and pleasing the teacher to move up a grade.

The ideal boss at work was like a good father, a fair and caring autocrat. The few women who moved up the pyramid grew up with strong father attachments that they transferred to the boss (Henning/Jardom 1977). To succeed in the bureaucratic industrial world, people needed to develop a social character with productive obsessive traits, oriented to pleasing authority.

The negative side of the *bureaucratic social character* is overcontrol, micromanagement, and as Fromm noted, authoritarian, sadomasochistic relationships at work. The negative bureaucrat has been described by novelists such as Gogol, Dickens, Melville and Kafka as well as by many sociologists.

The Interactive Social Character

In the 1980s, as both workplace and family began to change, so did the social character. The new knowledge-service mode of production required an *interactive social character* that was naturally collaborative and open to constant change. Besides the knowledge-service mode of production the following factors have also been instrumental in shaping the interactive social character:

1. Fewer two-parent homes with just the father working outside the home and more dual career and single-mother led households.
2. Children sent at an early age to day care centers, where they develop interactive skills and learn to depend emotionally on peers so they are less emotionally dependent on parents.
3. Early use of information/communication technology, interaction with people around the globe.
4. Schools increasingly emphasize teamwork, as well as individual achievement. Leaders of knowledge work like Bill Gates are at the forefront of changing schoolwork to prepare children for knowledge work.
5. Easy access to information on the Internet to challenge authority.
6. Less trust of companies and less lifetime employment in one company. Employees expect to be free agents, seeking the best deal and frequently moving from job to job.

7. Increased focus on continual learning to keep up with relevant new knowledge.

At best, the interactive social character is both independent and collaborative. Interactives expect continual change. But they are not loyal to companies, and do not expect companies to be loyal to them. They are adept at forming relationships, but also at dissolving them. They have learned to adapt their personalities, their self-presentation, to different situations and audiences. Their morality is based on what the group considers *appropriate* vs. an internalized conscience.

Brought up in single parent families, or families where both parents work, they are used to shared leadership. They are raised with democratic values, and they have no problem questioning or contradicting authority. They become expert at negotiating with parents, playing on parental guilt at not being at home for them. They see parents less as disciplinarians than as service providers who are concerned, above all, that they do well at school and activities that will prepare them for admission to college and for successful careers.

At an early age, interactives become adept at using social and information technologies. At work, they are prepared to use these tools to innovate and solve problems. In contrast to the best bureaucrats who evaluate their products in terms of excellence, interactives view value in terms of customer acceptance.

Given the continual development of new knowledge, interactives may come to work knowing more about their jobs than their bosses. They want transparent and fully credible leaders who treat them as collaborators, not as followers. The more productive ones are engaged only by leaders who articulate and practice a philosophy, including a meaningful purpose and values.

The negative sides of the interactive social character are the lack of loyalty and the lack of personality integration, the negative qualities of the marketing character. Interactives typically are connected to many people and are related to few, if any. They are so used to adapting to different situations, of wearing different masks, that they are in danger of losing their center, the person behind the mask.

Since 2008, my colleagues and I have given a questionnaire with statements that express bureaucratic vs. interactive attitudes to hundreds of participants in leadership workshops. Over time, an increasing number of participants have identified with interactive attitudes. Tim Scudder has run correlation tests that demonstrate the construct and differential validity of the questionnaire results.

Testing Fromm's Character Typology

Dr. Scudder heads Personal Strengths Publishing, a company built from Elias Porter's development of the Strengths Deployment Inventory (SDI), a method allowing people to gain self-understanding based on Fromm's character types (Scudder/Lacroi 2013). The usefulness of both Freud's and Fromm's types had been limited by the negative terms they used. People did not want to be identified by terms such as erotic-receptive, obsessive-hoarding, and narcissistic-exploitative, terms that seemed judgmental. Porter called the types *motivational value systems* and made them more acceptable by emphasizing their positive qualities and renaming them with colors. He also constructed a test that indicates how motivations change in conflict. Over two million employees from over one thousand companies, universities and government agencies in six continents have participated in SDI workshops that have helped them understand their own motivation and helped them improve relationships by understanding others. Statistical tests of construct and differential validity have supported the scientific validity of the Freud-Fromm theory of character types (Scudder 2013).

Fromm's Theories that Remain to be Tested

Fromm did not recommend that people develop the social character of their culture. The social character is a formula for adaptation and success within a culture. It is not a recipe for happiness. To the contrary, it may cripple a person's capacity for growth.

Fromm wrote about "the pathology of normalcy." However, he recognized that it takes effort and awareness to transcend the social character. He once said to me: "The question isn't why someone is insane. It is why anyone is sane, given the irrationality and the absurdity of life."

Most people stay sane by conforming. Their social character keeps them sane, but at the expense of full human development and the pursuit of happiness.

Fromm sought to understand both the nature of human development and its perversion to psychopathology. His theories integrated Aristotle's emphasis on productiveness, Spinoza's understanding of internal freedom, and Judeo-Christian lessons on love and wisdom.

In *The Heart of Man* (Fromm 1964a) Fromm presents a model of human development and psychopathology that he elaborates in that book and others. He proposes that the best solution to human existence is love, expressed in love of the stranger, and biophilia (love of life), combined with individuation, implying a humanistic conscience, a heart that listens.

This theory is not only testable; there is evidence supporting it in the conclusions of George E. Valliant in his book *Triumphs of Experience* (Valliant 2012). He writes: "There are two pillars of happiness revealed by the seventy-five-year-old Grant Study (of Harvard graduates). One is love. The other is finding a way of coping with life that does not push love away" (Valliant 2012, p. 50).

In contrast, Fromm viewed psychopathology either as a loss of freedom in conformity, sado-masochism, addiction, and dependency, or a perversion of transcendence in destructiveness, the extreme being necrophilia, an attraction to what is dead, the impulse to destroy all that is spontaneous, free and alive.

Fromm did not ignore genetic and biological causes of psychopathology. But these factors do not explain the alienation and destructiveness of people in tribes and nations. Fromm theorized that a society either pulls people in the direction of growth and development or in the direction of tribalism and toward decay and pathology.

Unlike Freud, who posited a destructive death instinct, Fromm viewed love and collaboration as primary human strivings. He viewed destructiveness as a perversion, the extreme being necrophilia (Fromm 1973a). Mauricio Cortina has presented evidence from anthropology and attachment theory in support of Fromm's view (Cortina 2013). Cortina cites evidence that our ape relatives demonstrated these social instincts that have been developed during the course of human evolution.

Fromm believed that societies and organizations could shape the social character in either a positive or negative direction. His book, *The Sane Society* (Fromm 1955a) proposed positive models. In *Social Character in a Mexican Village*, we describe *Nuestros Pequeños Hermanos* (NPH), a home for orphaned and abandoned children, founded in 1954 by Father William Wasson. Fr. Wasson's purpose was not only to provide a home for the children, but also to develop them as productive and caring citizens. To achieve this, he established a family based on love of the stranger (*agape*) with values of security, including education to prepare the children for the future; work so that each child would actively contribute to the community; sharing, caring for others; and responsibility, acting from a humanistic conscience, not just following rules.

Since we wrote about NPH, it has grown from its beginnings in Mexico to homes and schools in nine countries, with a pediatric hospital in Haiti that treated 96,000 patients in 2014. Five of the nine homes are led by people who grew up at NPH, and the executive director is a former *pequeño*. The other four are led by former volunteers from Europe and the U.S. NPH and their graduates demonstrate that a community based on humanistic values can develop the kind of social character that Fromm described in terms of human growth.

To conclude, ongoing theorizing and research continues to increase our understanding of the nature of human instincts. The distinguished biologist E. O. Wilson theorizes that through natural selection, humans have two genetically determined behavioral drives that sometimes clash – one individualistic and selfish, the other collaborative and altruistic (Wilson 2012). The logic of Wilson's argument is that our altruistic genes are fired up by threats to our identity group. He writes that humans are compulsive group-seekers; we are tribal animals that satisfy this need variously in extended families, organized religion, political groups, ethnic groups, and sports clubs. When people are threatened, their group identities are instinctively strengthened. They collaborate to survive, for sustenance or against an enemy.

Wilson's theories can expand our understanding of social character and its genetic roots. They do not contradict Fromm's theories of social and individual factors that lead to human development. Rather, they emphasize the importance of leadership that develops the kind of collaborative community that shapes a positive social character, one in which people collaborate to create rather than to destroy.

By building on Fromm's theory of social character, social scientists could expand our understanding of how different cultures develop their social characters and what it would take to shape a more humanly developed social character. But testing Fromm's theories requires a change in the dominant paradigms of the social science that favor reductionistic tests of cause and effect. Fromm's theories are systemic. They connect psychodynamic factors with society, culture, history, ideology, economy, and politics.

Erich Fromm gave us new truths that integrated his clinical observations and research with the theories of other humanistic thinkers and scientists. Yet, Fromm's paradigm has not been widely accepted, even though it could increase understanding of human and economic development. The Frommian paradigm requires interdisciplinary work, but the institutions of the social sciences, academic departments and scholarly journals, do not support this integration. I studied for my doctorate at Harvard's Department of Social Relations that combined psychology, sociology, and cultural anthropology. A few years after I received my doctorate, the department was disbanded into separate disciplinary departments. I taught Fromm's approach at the Washington School of Psychiatry, where Fromm was one of the founders together with Harry Stack Sullivan. Neither Fromm's work nor Sullivan's emphasis on integrating psychiatry with the social sciences exists today in a significant way. And the prevailing paradigm of the social sciences that claims to be value-free or that defines progress purely in material terms does not enable us to understand and address the problems that threaten humanity. For that we need Fromm's rational and critical approach that evaluates events in terms of biophilic ethics and productive human development. For those of us who have appreciated Erich Fromm's value based scientific contributions, the challenge is to engage a new generation to understand and build on them. This conference is a good place to begin.

References

Cortina, M. (2013). The Greatness and Limitations of Erich Fromm's Humanism. Paper presented at the Washington School of Psychiatry, November 16.
Crozier, M. (1964). The Bureacratic Phenomonon. Chicago (University of Chicago Press).
Freud, S. (1931a). Libidinal Types. Psychoanalytic Quarterly, 1 (36), pp. 3–6.
Fromm, E. (1947a). Man for Himself. New York (Rinehart and Company), pp. 114–5.

Fromm, E. (1955a). The Sane Society. New York (Rinehart and Company).

Fromm, E. (1962a). Beyond the Chains of Illusion, My Encounter with Marx and Freud. New York (Simon & Schuster).

Fromm, E. (1964a). The Heart of Man. New York (Harper & Row).

Fromm, E. (1973a). The Anatomy of Human Destructiveness. New York (Holt, Rinehart and Winston).

Fromm, E. (1980a). The Working Class in Weimar Germany, A Psychological and Sociological Study, Warwickshire (Berg Publishers) 1984. Originally published as Arbeiter und Angestellte am Vorabend des Dritten Reiches, ed. W. Bonss, Stuttgart (Deutsche Verlags-Anstalt).

Fromm, E., and Maccoby, M. (1970b). Social Character in a Mexican Village. Englewood Cliffs (Prentice-Hall) 1970. Reprinted with an introduction by Michael Maccoby, New Brunswick (Transaction Publishers), 1996.

Heckscher, Ch. et al. (2003). Agents of Change Crossing the Post-Industrial Divide. Oxford (Oxford University Press).

Henning, M./Jardim, A. (1977). The Managerial Woman. New York (Anchor Press/Doubleday).

Maccoby, M. (1972). Emotional Attitudes and Political Choices. Politics and Society, Winter, pp. 209–39.

Maccoby, M. (1976). The Gamesman, New York (Simon & Schuster). German translation: Gewinner um jeden Preis: Der neue Führungstyp in den Großunternehmen der Zukunftstechnologie. Rowohlt (Hamburg),1977.

Maccoby, M. (1981). The Leader. New York (Simon & Schuster).

Maccoby, M. (2003). The Productive Narcissist, The Promise and Peril of Visionary Leadership. New York (Broadway Books).

Maccoby, M. (2007). The Leaders We Need: And What Makes Us Follow. Boston (Harvard Business School Press).

Maccoby, M. (2007a). Narcissistic Leaders, Who Succeeds and Who Fails. Boston (Harvard Business School Press).

Maccoby, M. et al. (2013). Transforming Health Care Leadership, A Systems Guide to Improve Patient Care, Decrease Costs, and Improve Population Health. San Francisco (Jossey Bass).

Maccoby, M. (2015). Strategic Intelligence, Conceptual Tools for Leading Change. Oxford (Oxford University Press).

Reining, P. et. al. (1977). Village Women, Their Changing Lives and Fertility, Studies in Kenya, Mexico and the Philippines. Washington (American Association for the Advancement of Science).

Scudder T./Lacroi, D. (2013). Working with SDI, How to Build More Effective Relationships with the Strength Deployment Inventory. Carlsbad (Personal Strength Publishing).

Scudder, T. J. (2013). Personality Types in Relationship to Awareness Theory: The Validation of Freud's Libidinal Types and Explication of Porter's Motivational Typology. Dissertation in partial fulfillment of the requirements for the degree of Doctor of Philosophy, Fielding Graduate University.

Valliant, G. E. (2012). Triumphs of Experience. Cambridge (Harvard University Press).

Wilson, E. O. (2012). The Social Conquest of Earth. New York (Liveright).

The Reception of Erich Fromm's Writings and Ideas

Rainer Funk

The reception of Fromm's ideas and scientific contributions started during his lifetime and has continued to today, in various disciplines and professions and throughout the world. Some of this influence is well known and fully credited, while other times Fromm's contributions have been neglected. Helmut Johach, for instance, gives a striking example of the former case in his description of the influence which Fromm had on what is often called "Humanistic Psychology". My remarks in the following chapter will discuss only a few salient aspects of Fromm's reception, which I shall look at from the perspective of an editor of his (German) *Collected Works* and as Fromm's literary executor.

Concerning my own role, a first step toward promoting the reception of Fromm's ideas and writings was taken by Erich Fromm himself when he agreed to the publication of his *Collected Works* in German and asked me to edit the *Erich Fromm-Gesamtausgabe*. After five years of preparation, the publication of a collection of ten volumes begun in February 1980 while Fromm was still alive, with volumes one and four, and was completed in the fall of 1981. Volume ten of this omnibus edition contains a detailed index of some 360,000 entries, including, for instance, whether and where Fromm mentions Alfred Adler or discusses problems of authoritarianism or the aims of unions. Unfortunately, I have never succeeded in publishing Fromm's collected works in other languages because publishers were reluctant to invest money in an edited publication with an index volume.

As this work proceeded, Fromm re-wrote his last will and designated me as his "literary executor" and as the heir to his library and his scientific estate. After Fromm's death, I established the *Erich Fromm Archive* in Tuebingen and made major parts of Fromm's estate accessible for persons and scholars interested in Fromm.

Since that time, the Tuebingen Erich Fromm Archive has become not only a center for scholars from all over the world – many of whom were present and participated in the conference this volume is based on – but also, and in particular, it has become a venue for young German scientists

who wish to make use of Fromm's collected works and have gotten in touch with me as editor of the *Gesamtausgabe* and owner of the Fromm Archive. Meetings have been organized at the Fromm Archive, and in the fall of 1985 an International Erich Fromm Society was founded by this group of – mostly young – Fromm scholars.

The Fromm Society has always regarded itself as an international umbrella organization for other institutions and initiatives that are devoted to Fromm's ideas and their reception:

➤ After Fromm's death in 1980, a first international Fromm conference was organized by the philosophers of the Yugoslavian "praxis"-group in December 1981 in Dubrovnik.

➤ Simultaneously with the establishment of the International Erich Fromm Society, in Italy a group around *Pier Lorenzo Eletti* dedicated itself to Fromm's ideas and began organizing conferences in Florence.

➤ A first joint seminar with this group took place 1987 in Tuebingen. From then on, regular meetings and conferences have taken place, especially with the group around *Romano Biancoli* of Ravenna. He founded the Bolognese Fromm Training Institute in Bologna and, with the assistance of *Marco Bacciagaluppi* of Milan and *Jorge Silva* of Mexico, has offered training seminars for treating patients according to Fromm's psychoanalytic theory. There have been joint meetings in Bologna, Locarno, Florence, Grosseto, Verbania, Verona, Konstanz, Ascona, Magliaso and Ravenna. The photograph below was taken during a seminar in Verbania (Lago Maggiore) and shows Romano Biancoli and Marco Bacciagaluppi on the right (in squatting position), with Jorge and Inés Silva of Mexico behind them, and Ruth Lesser from New York in the middle; on the left side are Petra Tauscher (Berlin), Helmut Johach (Nuremberg) and Maarit Arppo from Finland.

➤ Another center of Fromm research emerged in Mexico, where the Seminario Socio-Psicoanalítico around Salvador Millán and *Sonia Gojman de Millán* began conducting training seminars in socio-psychoanalysis and has carried out many empirical studies on the application of Fromm's social character theory and method.

➤ *Michael Maccoby* also contributed greatly to Fromm's reception with the *Project on Technology, Work, and Character* which he directed for many years in Washington DC. As he reports in his chapter here, he and his colleagues have applied Fromm's theory and methods regarding social character, and this has led to many studies and publications. He organized joint meetings together with Mexican researchers and sponsored an international Fromm Conference in Washington in 1994. The photo shows the members of a meeting in 2000 (on the occasion of Fromm's centenary) in Washington, DC.

➤ Two other persons are also to be mentioned here, both Mexicans, who – quite independently of each other – spent many weeks every year abroad teaching other psychoanalysts about Fromm's theories and his way of treating patients. I am speaking of *Aniceto Aramoni* and *Jorge Silva*, both of whom, I am sad to say, passed away within the last two years. They had a tremendous influence on psychoanalytic groups in Spain, Italy, Greece, Germany, Norway, Sweden and South America.

While many conferences and study groups happen to take place in Germany, the Fromm Society has invariably tried to maintain contact with other local initiatives all over the world, particularly after the Iron Curtain dropped. Hence, conferences were arranged in Hungary, the Czech Republic, in Poland and in Slovakia. In 2013 the Fromm Society organized conferences in Latvia and Lithuania.

Starting about ten years ago, a growing interest in Fromm's work has been observed in the Arabic-speaking world on the one hand and in China on the other; in 2005 a conference took place in Rabat, and another one in 2007 in Fes, Morocco. However, an overwhelming interest in Fromm is to be found in China. Manfred Zimmer, a member of the Fromm Society who lives in Malaysia, did a thorough internet research about Fromm's reception in China and identified some 700 dissertations, master theses, and detailed books and articles on Fromm's ideas. (A poster which he prepared for this conference and is included in this volume gives an idea of this Fromm reception in China.)[1]

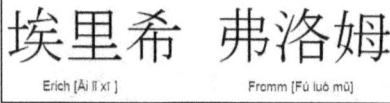

埃里希　弗洛姆

Erich [Āi lī xī]　　　　Fromm [Fú luò mǔ]

Most of the contributions presented at conferences have been published in yearbooks, journals or in other collections. The Mexican scholars have published a series of *Anuarios*, *Memorias* and *Cuaternos*; the Fromm Society published its *Yearbooks* from 1991 through 1996 and since1997 has continued to publish an annual *Fromm Forum* in both English and a German edition, given gratis to 700 members worldwide. Digital techniques, electronic media and the internet make all these papers more easily available to Fromm scholars and to people all over the world who value Fromm's work.

There are two websites which everyone interested in Fromm should be familiar with: the website of the Fromm Society (www.frommsociety.org

---

1 An English report on the reception of Fromm in China is available at: http://fromm-online.org/wp-content/uploads/Zimmer_M_2014.pdf (27.02.2015)

or www.fromm-gesellschaft.eu), and the official website of Erich Fromm (www.erich-fromm.com or www.erich-fromm.de).

The website of the Fromm Society presents not only announcements but also a huge collection of papers from the *Yearbook* series and the *Fromm Forum* for download. In addition, and also free to download, the website contains many important publications about Fromm. Here you will find the *Festschrift* on the occasion of Fromm's seventieth birthday, entitled *In the Name of Life* and edited by Landis and Tauber, or the publication of the Society's field research about the social character of East- and West-German primary school teachers in 1990, which was published in 1995 under the title *Die Charaktermauer* ("The Character Wall"). – The website of the Fromm Society is available in German, Italian, Russian, Spanish, French, Arabic, Bulgarian, Latvian, and English.

The official Fromm website (www.erich-fromm.com) is a treasure trove of subjects related to Fromm's life, writings and ideas. Just to give you some idea of what you can find on the Fromm website, here are some examples of what you can discover by using the menu buttons:

Life

> Important Dates

> Autobiographical Highlights

> Fromm's Credo

> Biographies on Erich Fromm

> Photo

> Audio Clips

> Video Clips

> Fromm Exhibition

Writings

> English and German Booktitles

> Original Writings 1918-1969

> Original Writings since 1970

> Translations, Copy Estimations

> Reception of Erich Fromm

> Audio and Video Indexes

> Copyright

> Erich Fromm Glossary

The website's menu button >*Life of Erich Fromm*< opens up a table of >*Important Dates*< in various languages as well as a list of >*Biographies on Erich Fromm*<. His most important findings and his concept of man are the content of Fromm's humanistic >*Fromm's Credo*< – also available in various translations. For all who wish to use a photograph of Fromm for their own purposes a colored photo is offered for free download. The same holds true for some audio and video clips in German and English.

The menu button >*Writings of Erich Fromm*< leads to a list of all original writings by Fromm; in addition, an English-German synopsis of the titles of Fromm's books is featured. The setup of the menu button >*Reception of Erich Fromm*< is still in progress, but offers an interesting overview showing which Fromm titles have been translated into which languages; an estimate is also given of how many copies of each Frommian book title have sold so far. Last but not least, this menu button gives access to two lists of some 700 academic publications (dissertations etc.) published in China in the last years and to abstracts of these titles.

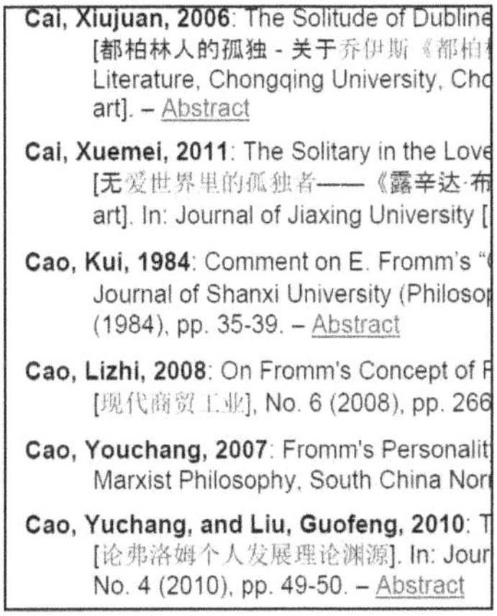
Cai, Xiujuan, 2006: The Solitude of Dubline
[都柏林人的孤独 - 关于乔伊斯《都柏
Literature, Chongqing University, Cho
art]. – Abstract

Cai, Xuemei, 2011: The Solitary in the Love
[无爱世界里的孤独者——《露辛达·布
art]. In: Journal of Jiaxing University [

Cao, Kui, 1984: Comment on E. Fromm's "
Journal of Shanxi University (Philoso
(1984), pp. 35-39. – Abstract

Cao, Lizhi, 2008: On Fromm's Concept of F
[现代商贸工业], No. 6 (2008), pp. 266

Cao, Youchang, 2007: Fromm's Personalit
Marxist Philosophy, South China Nor

Cao, Yuchang, and Liu, Guofeng, 2010: T
[论弗洛姆个人发展理论渊源]. In: Jour
No. 4 (2010), pp. 49-50. – Abstract

Particular attention should also be given to the >*Erich Fromm Glossary*< button: some 150 of the most important terms and concepts developed by Fromm are defined there in Fromm's own words. The quotations (in English and German) are verified and can be copied into the reader's own paper.

For Fromm scholars, the richest treasure is to be found in the >*Document Server*<: Just click on the "Document Server" link on the homepage or fill in the search mask with any term related to Erich Fromm. It is then forwarded to the advanced search engine OPUS that is offered by the Zuse Institute in Berlin, which includes some 25,000 titles from the Erich Fromm Archive and Institute of Tuebingen and c. 8,000 full text files (PDFs).

The following inventories are included in the "Document Server":

(1) All published *Writings by Erich Fromm* in all known translations and editions (now around 4,000), some 700 *Excerpts* by Fromm, and drafts, typescripts and proofs referring to publications by Fromm.
(2) All known *Writings about Erich Fromm* (c. 6,500).
(3) Fromm's *Reference library*, which he handed down to me (c. 3,500 books, journals and collective volumes, with some 15,000 single titles in total).
(4) The *Publications of the International Erich Fromm Society* (c. 750 single titles).

All collections of the Erich Fromm Archive are now located physically at the Erich Fromm Institute in downtown Tuebingen at Hintere Grabenstrasse 26. The opening hours for the public are published on the Fromm website and on the Fromm Society's website. The inventories and a growing number of full texts are also housed virtually in Berlin and are accessible via the Fromm website >http://erich-fromm.com< or directly via >http://opus4.kobv.de/opus4-Fromm/home<.

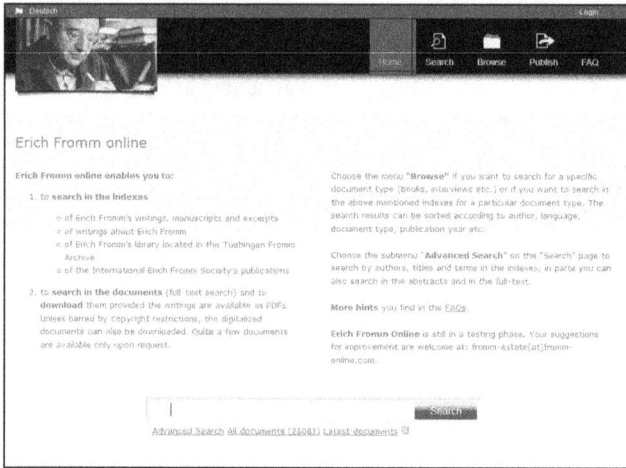

The >*Erich Fromm Document Server's*< search engine offers two ways to find dates and full texts concerning Fromm (a detailed description for optimal use of the search engine is given under the FAQ's at the homepage of the document server): simply write an author's name or some terms from a title in the search mask, and the result will be a listing of all data records in which the name or terminus you asked for is mentioned in the title or in the full text. Usually the search machine presents a very large list which can then be filtered according to language, author, document type, year of publication and which displays whether the full text is available or not.

The >*Browse*< button, makes an even more precise search possible, it allows to search in detail within the inventories, for instance in the inventory of >*Writings about Erich Fromm*<. Here, you can choose among >*articles*<, >*books*<, >*interviews*<, >*prefaces*<, >*reviews*<, and so on. If you are searching for >*books*< about Fromm, a scroll of some 300 titles is shown, all of which are concerned with Fromm's thought. From there you can filter your search (on the left side) according to language, author, document type, year of pub-

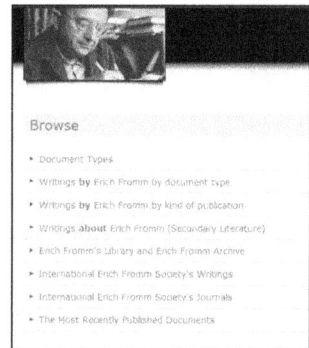

lication and whether or not a full text is available. Let's say that you have selected the Italian titles: you can then sort the books alphabetically by author and title as well as chronologically according to the year of publication.

Clicking on a title opens a list of all data referring to that title.

If a PDF file name is displayed (in the right corner at the top end), then the full text can be read and downloaded. If, on the other hand, >*File not available?*< appears, then the full text has to be ordered via inter-library loan. In that case, you must fill out a request form (displayed with the link "document request"), including the identification number (= name of the PDF) and your e-mail-address, in order to get the full text at the earliest opportunity sent as an e-mail attachment.

With the friendly support of the Karl Schlecht Foundation, we are now in the process of scanning the literature about Fromm and intend to make it available.

Up to this point, my overview of Fromm reception has focused on the local Fromm groups and on the activities of the Fromm Society. But over and above these institutional activities, there have been many Fromm scholars and students of Fromm who have contributed to this reception by their scientific work, research and publications. Happily, this group is represented at this conference by some of its most prominent figures.

As examples I want to mention Kevin Anderson and his publication on Fromm and criminology and Joan Braune, who contributed to a cumulative publication of American scientists about *Reclaiming the Sane Society*, which was recently published (Sense Publisher, 2014). Helmut Johach, Jan Dietrich and I have been editing the *Fromm Forum* for many years – and Rainer Otte had an enormous impact on Fromm's reception in Germany by producing two films on Fromm. Also, Lawrence Friedman's biography of Fromm stimulated interest in Fromm anew, especially in the United States, and Juergen Hardeck's intellectual biography is still influential in the German-speaking world. Finally, we expect that Thiago da Costa, a Brazilian based in California, will finish his documentary film on Fromm's life and work very soon.

The Fromm Prize, sponsored by a Fromm Society member living in Switzerland, turned out to be a most effective way to keep Fromm's legacy alive in the German-speaking countries. The idea of the present Fromm Prize is to give the award to a person who is well known to the public and who adopts or realizes Frommian ideas. Of international importance was the presentation of the prize to Noam Chomsky in 2010, but also in 2014 we were happy that the lecture of Dirk Schuemer, the award recipient, on Fromm's *To Have or to Be?* was published in one of the world's most renowned newspapers, the *Frankfurter Allgemeine Zeitung*, and evoked an enormous discussion through letters to the editor and on the internet.

As Fromm's literary executor, my own contribution to promoting the reception of his ideas has been and still is first and foremost to make Fromm's writings available all over the world. I have attempted to do so with the *Gesamtausgabe* and, following Fromm's death, with eight smaller volumes of posthumous published writings that have now been translated into many languages. These posthumous published writings were included in volumes eleven and twelve of the Fromm Collected Works in German, which came out on the occasion of Fromm's centenary, with some 7,700 pages and 20,000 copies sold.

Today, more and more readers prefer to read books and articles by using electronic media. Hence I have started an e-book publication of the English originals of Fromm's books with OPEN ROAD MEDIA.

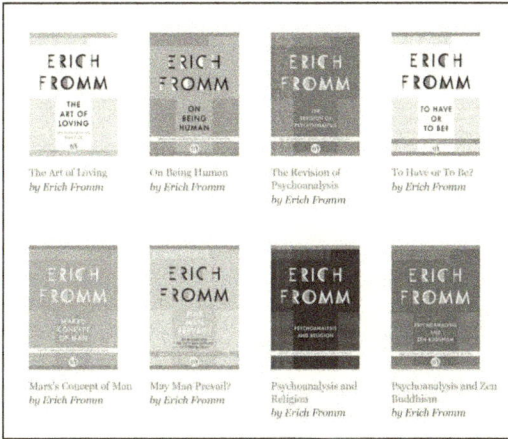

19 Fromm books are already available on the e-book market, and the next five titles should be available in 2015. Our aim is to achieve e-book publication of all English-language Fromm titles. Such a "Fromm library" will also include articles, forewords, interviews and reviews. What can be easily realized with the original English writings of Fromm will in the future be realized also with Fromm's writings in Spanish, Italian and other languages. Concerning a German e-book collection I am preparing a quite ambitious project with the e-book publisher OPEN PUBLISHING in Munich: Everything written by Erich Fromm in German or translated into German (c. 270 titles) will be published as e-books. Moreover, OPEN PUBLISHING will offer an e-book version of the German Collected Works that will permit a search for specific terms and quotations. This e-book, the *Gesamtausgabe*, will include updated editorial remarks of the print edition and will offer links to facilitate jumps from one Fromm title to another (and back). Since the end of 2014 the first German Fromm e-book titles are on the market.

Fact and Fiction
about Erich Fromm's Life and Work

Jürgen Hardeck

Abstract: Many authors have written about Erich Fromm since
Rainer Funk published a German Collected Works of Erich Fromm
in 1980/1981. Regrettably, however, there have also been many (intentional?) misunderstandings and misinterpretations as well as
conscious distortions by former colleagues of the Institute for Social
Research as well as by many practitioners of the school of orthodox
psychoanalysis; these have often been adopted uncritically by their
disciples and various authors and have continued to exert their influence until to the present day. In my paper I shall discuss some of the
main mistakes, that I found, made in biographies on Erich Fromm
and in publications about Fromm's role at the Institute for Social Research and histories of his contributions to psychoanalysis.

Many authors have written about Erich Fromm since Rainer Funk published the Collected Works of Erich Fromm in 1980/1981. Regrettably,
however, there have also been many misunderstandings and misinterpretations as well as conscious distortions by former colleagues of the Institute
for Social Research as well as many practitioners of the school of orthodox
psychoanalysis; these have often been adopted uncritically by their disciples
and various authors and have continued to exert their influence until the
present day. The central question for me has always been: What is provable
and what is not? Everything else is moot. In my contributions to Fromm
research, I have compared Fromm's statements with those of his critics and
have presented different points of view in order to arrive at the most realis-

tic overall picture possible in the light of different perspectives, to make the differences clear, and to give the reasons for these different points of view. I have published my results in numerous books and have also presented them at various events sponsored by the International Erich Fromm Society.

By training, Fromm was a sociologist and psychoanalyst. Inasmuch as his interdisciplinary approach is difficult to categorize, he is often described as a "social philosopher". It would be more correct, however, to call him a "social psychologist", since the focus of his publications was clearly on a psychoanalytically molded social psychology. In addition, he worked with others both as a therapist and as a trainer in psychoanalysis for nearly fifty years, and in doing so made a considerable contribution to the psychoanalytic theories of Sigmund Freud. Last but not least – and this is something which we can judge better in historical hindsight than during his lifetime – he was one of the most influential as well as one of the clearest-eyed social critics of the twentieth century. Nevertheless, the appraisals of his significance remain astonishingly disparate.[1] In spite of many publications, it therefore remains necessary even today to strip away the many misunderstandings of Fromm in order to come to a realistic impression of his life. I wish and must limit myself in my chapter here to just a few issues which are misunderstood – or misrepresented – with particular frequency.

Life and Work

After finishing my dissertation in 1989 on *"Religion in the Works of Erich Fromm"*, I found it necessary to write the following: "We still do not have enough detailed knowledge for a clear picture of Erich Fromm the human being" (Hardeck 1990, p. 207; cf. Hardeck 1992, p. 243). This has changed

---

1 One indication of this is what was written on his one hundredth birthday, in the year 2000, in German feuilletons about him. Whereas Richard Herzinger, for example, wrote in the *Tagesspiegel* on 23 March 2000 that he was in every sense of the word to be taken seriously, if not as a major social scientist who had left his stamp on the history of one of the most important intellectual movements of the last century," Michael Rutschky in the German publication *taz* found in Fromm only "intellectual lack of substance" and "puffed-up, book-long sermons about good will" (*taz* 18 March, 2000). Lorenz Jaeger in the *FAZ* (26 February 2000) even found a "neurosis in the name of God".

a great deal in the meantime. Today we have an abundance of information, most of which is now to be found in the collections of the Fromm Archive except for a few of Fromm's letters. For that reason, it is now possible to see Fromm's life more realistically. What is more, Rainer Funk's publications invariably give us utterly reliable biographical details. But good treatments of Fromm's life and works were available, for example, from Daniel Burston (1991) and Helmut Wehr (1990) even before Funk presented his Illustrated Biography in the year 2000, along with many important details to which he gained access only after his biographical introduction in Volume I of the Collected Works and his illustrated *Erich Fromm* monograph of 1983 (Funk 1983), Alfred Lévy's *Erich Fromm* (2002), written from the perspective of an Adlerian, contains not only many correct interpretations, but unfortunately also some misinterpretations. For example, Lévy writes that Fromm had hoped for a renaissance of the matriarchy (Levy 2002, p. 95–6), instead of a dialectic synthesis of patriarchy and matriarchy; in addition, he accused Fromm of saying nothing about some of the people who had formative influences on his life, such as Wilhelm Reich; Fromm not only knew Reich personally, but was also familiar with his Freudo-Marxian school of psychoanalysis and wrote about him in various books. And Reich himself writes in his memoirs that he quickly gave up the desire to convert Fromm to his – Reich's – way of thinking (Reich 1976, p. 137). Nevertheless, Fromm adopted ideas from Reich for his own therapeutic work just as gratefully as he did from many other psychoanalysts. For a person as open as Fromm, this practice was a matter of course.

In addition, Lévy is one of the authors who have failed to understand Fromm's concept of religion and who wish to explain Fromm's religious bent as the result of an inferiority complex, like that typical of religious persons (Levy 2002, p. 217). This understanding is reductionistic in the bad sense of the word. Fromm himself, in my view, provides many clear-cut indications about the nature of this "underlying sense of religion". In addition to his account of his relationship with his parents and his socialization in a completely Jewish environment, these include a "disquiet about the existential dichotomies of life", his longing to experience a world which he perceived as dysfunctional as being once again whole and pristine – and a deep-seated longing to overcome his own loneliness (Fromm 1966a, p. 58).

In 2013 the American historian Lawrence J. Friedman set down what is known about Fromm's life in an impressive, 400-page biography – including many quotations from Fromm's private letters (from the Fromm Archive) and an abundance of information gathered from interviews with persons who knew Fromm well (Friedman 2013). There is no doubt that Friedman's biography is excellent, a milestone in Fromm research. No other book presents more details from Fromm's life. On the other hand, however, and regrettably, the book also contains new errors and superfluous speculations. One major flaw in the book flows from Friedman's lack of German language skills, and the need for him to rely on a German speaking collaborator. As a result, he is lacking important information which he could have found, for example in the publications of Wolfgang Bonss (1984), Rolf Wiggershaus (1994), Helmut Wehr (1990), Burkhard Bierhoff (1991), Rainer Funk (above all 1983 and 2000), and myself (1993 and 2005). Thankfully, some of his most glaring factual errors have been carefully corrected by the translator team of Maren Klostermann, Maja Uebele-Pfaff and Christoph Trunk with the advisory assistance of Rainer Funk. For this reason, the German translation (Friedman 2013a) deviates – and rightly so – in some places from the American original, without, of course, changing Friedman's book in any essential way. Fromm is, by the way, just as much a prophet of reason and enlightenment as he is one of love. In the second place, Friedman shows a strong affinity for gossip and speculations about Fromm's private life, even without documentary evidence to support this.

Friedman succeeds well in summarizing Fromm's most important works in compact form. On the other hand, the same works lose a good deal of their original substance in the process. If we put aside the political climate of the United States in the 1950s and 1960s, it becomes clear that Friedman scrupulously avoids almost all discussion of the topics treated by Fromm, and also spends little time on the respective secondary literature and the reception history of Fromm's ideas. This does not mean, however, that it was Friedman's aim to circumvent these issues. His primary focus was on Fromm as a person. On the other hand, the picture which he paints of Fromm is not quite the same as that of Rainer Funk, who, after all, knows Fromm better than anyone else, or the one which I myself have gained during the course of my many years of studying Fromm. Friedman believes that he can identify numerous areas of discontinuity in Fromm. Funk and I, on the other hand, believe that we have solid reasons for per-

ceiving a continuity which permeates Fromm's life and work to an aston-
ishing degree.

Perhaps Friedman merely wishes in fact to say that Fromm was himself
affected by the many salient sojourns of his life, and by the fact that he
thought and wrote in three languages and explored so many different areas
of thought. Nevertheless, it is often difficult to avoid the impression (above
all at the end of his "Prologue") that Friedman is attempting to present
Fromm in the final analysis as a pathological case, a sort of multiple personality – and should this is in fact be his assertion, then I find it impossible
to understand why. In addition, Friedman is neither a psychologist nor a
psychoanalyst, but rather a historian. For that reason, it seems to me that he
should be more cautious in his ventures into the area of "psychologizing".

Fromm's Role at the Institute for Social Research

Certain critics of Fromm wish to untether a "critical", "scientific" Fromm,
the author of publications during his years at the Institute for Social Research in the 1930s (often also the Fromm of the *Escape from Freedom*, i.e.
the writer of the early 1940s) from a later, uncritical, allegedly "unscientific"
moral prophet, while at the same time acknowledging the importance of his
methods and results in "Psychoanalytic Social Psychology", his theory of
the "social character", and his view of the family as the "agency of society".
They appear not to know, or even to suppress the fact that it was Fromm
and not Adorno who developed and described the concept of the "authoritarian character" and presented the very first empirical, socio-psychological
study in Germany about the attitudes of workers and salaried employees.

Numerous critics who have attempted to distinguish between the "scientific" and the later Fromm have failed to recognize the fact that while his
terminology changed, his personal convictions did not, nor did his skill in
illusion-less analysis. When, for example, Gerhard P. Knapp writes in his
Erich Fromm that "his works from these years display a keen edge of argumentation, a realism and not least a precision of literary style which Fromm
had in no way possessed in earlier years and never attained again thereafter
(...) [because he] was challenged by the surroundings of the Institute to give
his best" (Knapp 1982, p. 27) he attributes too much importance – with all

due respect for Fromm's achievements there – to a Freudo-Marxian jargon which was in part still not fully developed and which Fromm apparently felt it necessary to use in his writings in order to achieve recognition.

In his book *The Frankfurt School*, Rolf Wiggershaus (1994) became the first author to truly and accurately describe the role of Erich Fromm at the Institute for Social Research. Martin Jay (1976) had taken a first step in this direction in his *Dialectic Imagination. The History of the Frankfurt School and of the Institute for Social Research 1923–1950*, but clearly shared certain pre-assumptions of the Frankfurt School regarding Fromm and was not in possession of all the facts. Wiggershaus was followed – with further revealing and detailed knowledge about "intentional taciturnity" (Burkhard Bierhoff) and re-evaluations of Fromm's important role for the school of Critical Theory – by Burkhard Bierhoff (1991) and Helmut Johach (1991), Daniel Burston (1991), Rainer Funk (2000), and myself (Hardeck 2005), inasmuch as I now had access to Horkheimer's complete correspondence with Fromm, Adorno and Karl Landauer (M. Horkheimer 1995; 1996). The same is true of Lawrence Friedman (2013), who gives a good picture of the developments leading up to Fromm's departure from the Institute and in doing so goes into an intensive study of the correspondence.

Horkheimer and Adorno even went so far as to falsify the Institute's history in order to cast a veil of silence over Fromm's role there. In the "Preface" to their publication of lectures from the series "Freud Today" at the universities of Frankfurt and Heidelberg in 1956, Horkheimer and Adorno wrote the following: "Since its founding in the years before 1933, the Institute has included psychoanalysis in its work, and this in its strict Freudian form" (quoted from Horkheimer 1996, Vol. 19, pp. 17–20). This is correct. But then the text goes on: "From the very beginning, a psychoanalytic department was an integral part of the Institute and was headed by Karl Landauer, the student of Freud who died in Bergen-Belsen." This is untrue. The department was headed from 1930 to 1939 by Erich Fromm.

The next sentence proceeds: "The Journal for Social Research contained in its first issue a programmatic essay about the tasks of analytic Social psychology" (Horkheimer 1932, reprint 1980). To quote the preface of the reprint: "The – often very long – papers are not devoted foremost to empirical research in sociology – as the title might seem to indicate – but rather to social philosophy above all, and to sociology, political theory, political economics, the sociology of art and literature, and to philosophical and social anthropology" (p. 3.). However, Theodor W. Adorno's five articles in total in the Institute journal up to 1940 deal exclusively with the sociology of music: *Zur gesellschaftlichen Lage der Musik* (1932), *Über Jazz* (1936), *Über den Fetischcharakter in der Musik und die Regression des Hörens* (1938), *Fragmente über Wagner* (1939) and, with George Simpson, *On Popular Music* (1940/41). This is correct. It was written by Erich Fromm – a fact which, however, was not mentioned.

Not admitting the relevance of Fromm's work is continued when the many years of "empirical studies at the Institute" are elaborated upon (Horkheimer 1932, reprint 1980, p. 18), but without connecting them with *Studies on Authority and Family*[2] – a volume which is named there and appeared in 1936 in Paris (Horkheimer 1936). Nor is there any mention of Erich Fromm's and Hilde Weiss's preliminary results from 1929 on – that is, even before Fromm joined the Institute for Social Research! – which are contained in that volume. These included the concept for a socio-psychological study which was then developed independently and carried out on an empirical basis by Fromm as a member of the Institute concerning the attitudes of workers and salaried employees (Fromm 1980a).

As Wolfgang Bonss correctly states, for some eight to nine years – that is, "as long as Fromm's role as an expert remained unquestioned in the Institute, work was carried on there for the most part more or less openly on the basis of concepts which he had developed" (Bonss 1979, p. 29). In his trailblazing description of the history of the Institute, Martin Jay was the first

---

2 *Studien über Autorität und Familie* is a joint work of the Institute for Social Research which was published as a collection of papers in 1936 in Paris by Felix Alcán. It contains the following dedication: "The Institute dedicates its first report on joint research to FELIX WEIL, our loyal friend". The theoretical sections form the *first section*: "General Remarks" (Max Horkheimer); "Socio-Psychological Section" (Erich Fromm); "History of Ideas" (Herbert Marcuse). Erich Fromm introduces in the *second section* the results of empirical data acquisition (among workers and salaried employees, on sexual mores, etc.). The *third section* contains individual studies and literature reviews by, among others, Karl A. Wittfogel (Wirtschaftsgeschichtliche Grundlagen der Entwicklung der Familienautorität), Paul Honigsheim (Materialien zur Beziehung zwischen Familie und Asozialität von Jugendlichen), Marie Jahoda (Autorität und Erziehung in der Familie, Schule und Jugendbewegung Österreichs) and Hans Mayer (Autorität und Familie in der Theorie des Anarchismus). The sociologist and historian Alfred Meusel also contributed an article.

to find that Fromm emerged "soon as the most important figure" (Jay 1976, p. 115) there and that direction of the socio-psychological department of the Institute was officially transferred to him for the rest of his life. Curiously, *The Authoritarian Personality*, a study from the year 1950 (Adorno et al. 1950), was ascribed foremost to Theodor W. Adorno because of his theoretical contribution to the results of the study workgroup; that it was indebted in large part to preparatory work was indeed mentioned here – but again without admitting that it was Erich Fromm, who carried out that work.

And finally, the name "Fromm" is not heard even when he is primarily meant, namely when at the end of the short "Preface" written by Horkheimer himself we read:

> The psychoanalytic revisionism of the various schools of thought, a revisionism which advocates allegedly Freudian exaggerations in contrast to a greater focus on so-called social factors, has not merely softened the greatest discoveries of Freud regarding the role of early childhood, of suppression, even the central concept of the unconscious.

This mispresents Fromm's views on psychoanalysis, but Horkheimer goes further when he writes, "but over and above that he [Fromm] suffered an attrition of critical acuity with his preoccupation with the trivial character of human understanding, remaining allied with social conformism." (Horkheimer 1996. Vol. 19, p. 19). This is a reproach made by Fromm's former colleagues, who cling fast to it in spite of all evidence to the contrary.

Horkheimer, Adorno, and later Marcuse and the supporters of orthodox psychoanalysis accused Fromm of "revisionism". As soon as this term is thrown into the ring, one thing becomes clear: the issue is no longer one of learning, but rather one of battles of belief. Revisionism, as is well known, is not an issue of learning. Quite the contrary: the primary task of learning is to review a theory, to improve it, to change it, and to discard it if necessary. At that time, however, battles of beliefs raged fiercely, driven by the desire for pre-eminence of interpretation, and naturally by vanity as well, and by a struggle for position, wealth, power and influence.

From today's vantage point it is clear that Horkheimer and Adorno – acting on the basis of timidity and opportunism – avoided a conflict with the psychoanalytic orthodoxy which was in the process of development. They also feared that the individual, without the resistance provided by the core drives which were Freud's starting point, might be defenseless and totally malleable in the face of manipulation. In the end, they found increasingly that Freudian pessimism was the only appropriate attitude given their view of the irreversibly painful and obtuse situation of human beings. Therefore, they rejected the illusory "idealism" and conformism" of Fromm, who in their eyes was still laughably bent on improving the world.

There is yet another historical mélange which heirs of the Frankfurt School have passed on down to the present day, as I was able to see incontrovertibly at an exposition at the University of Frankfurt just a few years ago: in contrast to most pictures painted by Horkheimer, Adorno and others, Theodor W. Adorno did not become a member of the Institute until 1938, not before that time.[3] It is also difficult to understand why both of the biographies presented upon Adorno's one-hundredth birthday, namely that of Detlev Claussen (2003) and that of Stefan Müller-Dohm (2003), ignore the pertinent literature about the constellation of topics concerning Fromm/Horkheimer/Adorno, and why Fromm is almost never mentioned in these publications.

The fact that his colleagues at the Institute, all of whom were not, after all, psychoanalysts, suddenly came to the defense of orthodox psychoanalysis against Fromm, was justly assessed by him as follows: "Partly this had to do with the influence of Adorno, whom I had criticized very sharply from the very beginning of his appearance in New York" – as Fromm wrote in a letter to Martin Jay (Fromm 1992, p. 254). In fact, Fromm and Adorno – quite apart from the many areas in which their convictions parted ways – simply disliked each other. Adorno had once secretly ridiculed Fromm in Frankfurt as a "professional Jew", while Fromm for his part detested Adorno's "aesthetic elitism". Moreover, both were highly narcissistic at this point in their lives, and both were courting Horkheimer's favors.

---

3 "In spite of his friendly and even collegial relationships with Horkheimer, Pollock, Löwenthal and Fromm, Adorno was not an official member of the Institute for Social Research either before or after he became a professor. His ideas were simply different from those of Horkheimer and the members of the Institute in many fundamental respects. Nevertheless Adorno continuously published articles intermittently in the Institute's journal from the first issue on." (Müller-Dohm 2003, p. 230)

Fromm keenly sensed Adorno's efforts to supplant him in Horkheimer's inner circle. And it is a fact that Horkheimer's correspondence from 1935 on clearly reveals that and how Adorno was seeking to squeeze others of the Institute in order to supplant them. At first it was Herbert Marcuse, but then he began to undermine Fromm's position of trust with Horkheimer in the form of subtle criticism. Because of its "lopsided assessment of authority, and due to its "middle-class, individualistic demand for more 'goodness'", for example, Adorno found that Fromm's essay of 1935 on *The Social Determinants of Psychoanalytic Theory* (Fromm 1935a) represented "in reality a threat to the basic line taken by the journal". In addition, he saw himself put in the

> paradoxical situation of being forced to defend Freud. It is both sentimental and directly in error, a mixture of social democracy and anarchism, and above all there is a painful lack of dialectical sensitivity. He makes things too easy on himself with his concept of authority, without which, after all, neither Lenin's avant-garde nor dictatorship are conceivable. I would urgently advise him to read Lenin. Astonishing, how allegedly infallible "Popes" level their criticisms at Freud! No, even if we and others on the left dare to criticize Freud, certain things are not permissible, like the simplistic argument about a "lack of goodness (Letter from Adorno to Horkheimer of 21 March 1936, quoted by Wiggershaus 1988, p. 299).

Horkheimer had always been an admirer of Adorno's genius and stylistic brilliance. He was also fascinated by Adorno's aggressiveness and his "hate-honed perspective on his own times" (Letter from Horkheimer to Adorno of 8 December 1936. Horkheimer 1995, Vol. 16) as he confessed in a letter to him. He felt that Fromm lacked this aggressiveness.

Adorno was successful, over the course of time, in appealing ever more effectively to Horkheimer's philosophic streak, with the result that Horkheimer grew increasingly disenchanted with the Frommian approach of linking psychoanalysis with the social sciences. Clearly a plotter to be feared, Adorno was able to write the following, eloquently and even brilliantly, to Horkheimer, for example on 23 March 1937:

> The position presently occupied by Fromm is of greatest importance; precisely for that reason, however, as it appears to me, it is exigent upon him to

be especially careful not to steamroll the relationships between psychology and society down to an Adlerian level. I find traces of this in the essay (Adorno's letter to Horkheimer of 23 March 1937. Horkheimer 1995, Vol. 16).

Horkheimer's growing skepticism about Fromm's revision of Freud, in which Fromm replaced the drive theory with one based on relationships, was – presumably without Fromm's knowledge – reinforced not only by Adorno, but also by the psychoanalyst Karl Landauer, with whom Horkheimer corresponded frequently until his tragic death in a German concentration camp in 1943. Landauer had voiced especially negative opinions about a book by Karen Horney and her psychoanalytic approach. Horney had permanently made herself an outcast among orthodox analysts with her best-selling books *The Neurotic Personality of Our Time* (Horney 1937) and *New Ways in Psychoanalysis* (Horney 1939). As her lover at that time and also influenced by her views, Erich Fromm was automatically put into the same boat with her.

Fromm departed from the Institute for Social Research "by his own choice" in 1939. The assertion that he was fired is just one more legend among the many told later. In the light of the research findings of Jay (1976), Bonss (1984) and Wiggershaus (1994), Fromm's role at the Institute for Social Research needs to be completely reassessed. For a long time it was the case that Marcuse's and Adorno's views of Fromm distorted the judgments of influential intellectuals to such a degree that even today it is still nearly impossible to get a hearing for a more factual evaluation (cf. in Internationale Erich-Fromm-Gesellschaft 1991 the comments of Rickert, Wehr, Bierhoff, Johach and Weber).

In his *Theory of Communicative Action*, Jürgen Habermas (1981) indeed attempted to return to the interdisciplinary approach of Critical Theory, but not to the cultural pessimism of Horkheimer and Adorno. Although he made various timid attempts at the time to rehabilitate Fromm as in the following quote, he did not persevere in them thereafter, as John Rickert (1986, p. 399) quite rightly summed up.

In distorting and subsequently neglecting his work, Fromm's critics have not only repressed the thought of one of the left's most passionate and penetrating spokesmen, they have also failed to benefit fully from the insights Fromm has to offer."

Psychoanalysis

Fromm's writings are permeated with a life-long, respectful, thorough, but also critical dialogue with the person and the thought of Sigmund Freud. As Fromm himself wrote in 1971 to Martin Jay: "I have never left Freudianism" (Fromm 1992, p. 251). Only in his later years did the magnitude of Erich Fromm's significance for psychoanalytic theory truly become clear. For a long time he was accused of "revisionism", and his approach was rejected. He was, in fact, even expelled from the International Psychoanalytic Association (IPA) in the 1950s. To be sure, this also shows that the psychoanalytic world for a long time resembled a sect more than a field of learning.

Fromm was merely ahead of his time with most of his "re-visions" and his departures from Freud; since then, the times have caught up with him again step by step. In addition, only through the posthumous publications made available by Rainer Funk did it become clear that Fromm, the largely unknown therapist, was ahead of his time in this area as well in many other respects. Here too, his positions have now been accepted for the most part. Fromm repeatedly undertook to re-calibrate the theoretical structure of Freud's thought. In my view, this was his great talent. By himself, he is not a great initiator or discoverer. But he is indeed the master of a holistic understanding which remains uncorrupted by interests or illusions; he presents a clear-eyed body of insights which are unhampered by specialized or ideological blinders. Fromm carries out philosophical anthropology with an empirical basis and a solid footing in therapeutic experience. He himself views this as his contribution to "a science of man".

In his book *The Legacy of Erich Fromm* (unfortunately still available only in English), Daniel Burston (1991) comes to the conclusion that Fromm from the beginning was always merely in a justifiable position of "loyal opposition" to Freud and that it was thanks to him that psychoanalysis opened itself to interdisciplinary perspectives.

The Freiburg analyst Johannes Cremerius wrote in the 1980s:

One of the curious aspects of this story is that Freud himself was relegated more and more to the camp of dissidents at the same time that the Psychoanalytic Institute of Berlin and then that of London increasingly donned the straitjacket of orthodoxy. For example, his third and final conceptualization of the psychic event, the formulation of structural theory of 1923, was not adopted by many analysts [a fact to which Fromm had also referred repeatedly]. They clung to the earlier positions of his theory and thus also to earlier forms of treatment techniques. In addition, these institutes instituted a rigorism of training which he, Fromm, resolutely countered with a bold, more liberal point of view. And finally (...) he did not hold fast to the basic principles of treatment techniques which he himself had promulgated between 1910 and 1914 (Cremerius 1986, p. 30).

To continue with Cremerius: psychoanalysis opened up in the forty years since Freud's death:

All are contained and tolerated under the same roof: the theory of Melanie Klein, the supporters of dasein analysis, the theories on the pre-oedipal phase of development and its meaning for the aetiology and therapy of neuroses, etc. – and this would also include and tolerate those who have exited from it by their own choice, such as the supporters of the cultural, interpersonal school of psychoanalysis (Horney, Fromm, Thompson, Sullivan et al.). Viewed from today's standpoint, the latter name appears far less removed from Freud's "foundational ideas" and far less "dissident" than those of other groups which remained under that same roof (Cremerius 1986, p. 32).

While the last part of this quote is quite true, it is simply inaccurate to say that the "Neo-Freudians" departed from the psychoanalytic society of their own free will. They did not do so; rather, they were ostracized and thrown out. After its promising beginning, unfortunately, the essay of Cremerius, after its very good depiction of the heterogenic situation which developed over the course of time within the Psychoanalytic Association, characteristically loses itself in the old reproaches of the "Frankfurt School" of adaptational psychology against the "Neo-Freudians".

In the last twenty years, however, a strong tendency has now finally become noticeable in the old trench warfare: there are many analysts who wish to bury the battleaxes, and to view the different perspectives as mutually enhancing rather than apodictic pronuntiamentos of truth. Tzvetan

Todorov, who has written a book about general anthropology which is well worth reading, distinguishes between two "subtraditions": The one, which can be traced back to Ferenczi, objects to Freud's "father orientation" and emphasizes the relationships which are formed in the "pre-oedipal phase between mother and child"; in reaching back to Bachofen's speculations about the "rights of the mother", it discovers conflict-free relationships at the wellspring of the life of the individual. No matter how deeply one manages to penetrate into the human spirit, one will never find a being in isolation but only a complex of relationships with other beings" (Todorov 1998, p. 54). He names Alice and Michael Balint as the most important representatives of this direction.

> The other subtradition has its origin in Erich Fromm's marxistic criticism of Freudian teaching and Freudians, of Karen Horney's social, culturalistic and feministic criticism, and finally of the interpersonal psychiatry of H.S. Sullivan. (...). These were then joined by certain psychologists of the "self" who also built up a close collaboration with the ethnologists. (...) Fromm also channeled attention to another aspect of the Freudian model: the recourse to the economic model [of the 19th century] (Todorov 1998, p. 55).

Although Todeorov is quite right in this, he fails to perceive that Fromm must legitimately be counted among the progenitors of both groups.

In point of fact, Fromm must also be regarded as a patriarch of the "self-psychology" which is so popular today and of which Heinz Kohut is regarded as the founder. From *Escape from Freedom* (Fromm 1941a) to his fully developed narcissism concept in *The Heart of Man* (Fromm 1964a), he – and many other psychoanalysts, – provided an abundance of ideas upon which Kohut later drew upon (allegedly on his own). The Kohut biographer Ralf J. Butzer writes about this as follows (Butzer 1997, p. 147):

> The general impression [with Kohut] is that self-psychology expresses fully new, never-before glimpsed aspects and that Kohut's thought is characterized by great originality. But a vague suspicion about this may well arise in the form of a question for persons acquainted with the psychoanalytic literature: is Kohut not acquainted with the groundwork-laying writings of famous theoreticians like M. Balint, W.R.D. Fairbairn, H. Guntrip or D.W. Winnicott, or does there a method to his silence about them?

Cremerius goes so far as to accuse Kohut of "intellectual theft" inasmuch as he helped himself to large portions from the works of Eissler and Karen Horney without naming the sources of his discoveries (Cremerius 1986, p. 30). This list could be lengthened with further names, including those of such classic authors as Ferenczi, Jung, Adler, Lou Salome, Otto Rank, Sullivan and – last but not least – Erich Fromm. As is illustrated by the distinction between "benign" (Fromm) or "non-destructive" (Kohut) aggression and "hostile destructivity" (Kohut), Kohut's findings are astonishingly similar to those of Fromm.

The Psychology of religion

The topic of religion has a large and important place in Fromm's works. Many of his critics were at a loss to understand Fromm's interest in religion. For the most part, they experienced it as his "regression to childhood" (Rattner) or even as a form of "counter-enlightenment" (Wiegand). The social climate from the 1960s to the 1980s made religion appear to many intellectuals as an anachronism which was to be quickly disposed of. They were clearly mistaken.

Fromm, the religious psychologist, has indeed something important to say. Until today, however, this has lacked either acknowledgement or an appropriate reception in the fields of both theology and religious studies. Fromm begins by building a viable synthesis of the religio-psychological ideas of Freud and Jung which he supplements with his own corrections and insights. He provides important impulses, especially with his character orientations, his concept of societal character, and his analyses of narcissism and/or group narcissism in the various religions. In addition, his psychological definition of religion brings a helpful new perspective on a phenomenon which is, as is well-known, difficult to define.

In contrast to what many critics have asserted, Fromm never abandoned his religio-critical positions – as he himself made clear in his early paper *The Dogma of Christ* (1930a). In 1963 he wrote in the preface to the first American edition of this essay:

> While I have not changed my views (…), today I would also emphasize the view (which I held then, as now) that the history of religion reflects the history of man's spiritual evolution (Fromm 1963a, p. viii).

Rather than being a defender of religion (a misunderstanding which is found repeatedly), Fromm's intention is to pass it on to others (like Ernst Bloch). He crosses out not a single jot or tittle of the criticism of religion voiced by Freud, Feuerbach or Marx – quite the contrary: he invariably agrees with it. But – in contrast to Freud – he regards religions as ambivalent phenomena in which constructive ideas are to be found, whereas Freud, as a person stamped by the rationalistic vision of knowledge of the second half of the nineteenth century, in Fromm's view had perceived only that which Fromm himself called "authoritarian religion".

Fromm was a post-metaphysical thinker. He systematically interpreted all ontological statements of all the mystics, theologians, founders of religions and philosophers in terms of the inner psyche. However, Fromm opposed only such projections which from his point of view had the potential to do damage. In Fromm's view, humanistic projections, which take into account the respectively possible status of knowledge, are realistic in orientation and therefore reasonable. According to Fromm humanist projections can help humans grow, and to be freer and happier. He studied the history of religions to find where authoritarian and where humanistic tendencies were to be found. In addition, he was a proponent of the feminist perspective inasmuch as he distinguished matriarchal and patriarchal religions long before the development of feministic theology or philosophy.

Astonishingly, there is not a single chair of religious psychology in Germany even today, and the psychology of religion remains a wallflower – even in my own discipline of religious studies. The dominance of the historical-philological disciplines plays just as much a role in this as the factual a-religiosity of the occupants of many chairs and their anxiety in the face of such topic areas. For this reason, I find it very good that it is possible here at the IPU to study psychoanalysis as a cultural science and that the psychology of religion plays a role in the process.

References

Adorno, Th.W., et al. (1950). The Authoritarian Personality, New York (Harper and Row).
Bierhoff, B. (1991). Erich Fromm und das Institut für Sozialforschung; Triebstruktur oder soziale Beziehungen. In: Wissenschaft vom Menschen/Science of Man. Münster (LitVerlag), pp. 55–81.

Bierhoff, B. 1993. Erich Fromm. Analytische Sozialpsychologie und visionäre Gesellschaftskritik. Opladen (Westdeutscher Verlag).

Bonss, W. (1979). Sozialpsychologie als neue Dimension materialistischer Theorie. Zum Verhältnis von sozialer Struktur und psychischen Verarbeitungsformen (Typescript 1979, 66p.). Retrieved from: http://opus4.kobv.de/opus4-Fromm/frontdoor/index/index/docId/24188 (March 19, 2015).

Bonss, W. (1984). Critical Theory and Empirical Social Research: Some Observations. In: E. Fromm. The Working Class in Weimar Germany. A Psychological and Sociological Study. Edited by Wolfgang Bonss. London (Berg Publishers).

Burston, D. (1991). The Legacy of Erich Fromm. Cambridge (Mass.) and London (Harvard University Press).

Butzer, R.J. (1997). Heinz Kohut zur Einführung. Hamburg (Junius Verlag).

Claussen, D. (2003). Theodor W. Adorno. Ein letztes Genie. Frankfurt am Main (S. Fischer Verlag).

Cremerius, J. (1986). Psychoanalyse – Jenseits von Orthodoxie. In: H.-M. Lohmann, Die Psychoanalyse auf der Couch. Frankfurt am Main (Fischer), pp. 27–45.

Friedman, L.J. (2013). The Lives of Erich Fromm. Love's Prophet. Assisted by Anke M. Schreiber. New York (Columbia University Press).

Friedman, L.J. (2013a). Erich Fromm – Die Biografie. Unter Mitarbeit von Anke M. Schreiber, Bern (Huber Verlag).

Fromm, E. (1930a). The Dogma of Christ. In: E. Fromm. The Dogma of Christ and Other Essays on Religion. New York (Holt, Rinehart and Winston) 1963, pp. 3–91.

Fromm, E. (1935a). The Social Determinants of Psychoanalytic Theory. International Forum of Psychoanalysis (9): 3–4, October 2000), pp. 149–65.

Fromm, E. (1937a). Zum Gefühl der Ohnmacht. Erich Fromm Gesamtausgabe in zwölf Bänden. Ed. by Rainer Funk. München (Deutsche Verlags-Anstalt und Deutscher Taschenbuch Verlag), 1999, (I), pp. 189–206.

Fromm, E. (1941a). Escape from Freedom. New York (Farrar and Rinehart).

Fromm, E. (1963a). The Dogma of Christ and Other Essays on Religion, Psychology and Culture. New York (Holt, Rinehart and Winston).

Fromm, E. (1964a): The Heart of Man. Its Genius for Good and Evil. New York (Harper and Row).

Fromm, E. (1966a): You Shall Be as Gods. A Radical Interpretation of the Old Testament and Its Tradition (1966a), New York (Holt, Rinehart and Winston).

Fromm, E. (1980a). The Working Class in Weimar Germany. A Psychological and Sociological Study. Edited and introduced by Wolfgang Bonß, London (Berg Publishers), 1984.

Fromm, E. (1992). Letter to Martin Jay. In: M. Kessler & R. Funk (Ed.). Erich Fromm und die Frankfurter Schule. Akten des internationalen, interdisziplinären Symposions Stuttgart-Hohenheim vom 31. Mai bis 2. Juni. Tübingen (Francke Verlag).

Funk, R. (1983). Erich Fromm. Bildmonographie. Reinbek (Rowohlt Verlag).

Funk, R. (2000). Erich Fromm – His Life and Ideas. An Illustrated Biography. New York (Continuum International).

Habermas, J. (1981). Theorie des kommunikativen Handelns. Vol.1: Handlungsrationalität und gesellschaftliche Rationalisierung, Vol. 2: Zur Kritik der funktionalistischen Vernunft. Frankfurt am Main (Suhrkamp).

Hardeck, J. (1990). Religion im Werk von Erich Fromm. Münster (Lit-Verlag).

Hardeck, J. (1992). Vernunft & Liebe. Religion im Werk von Erich Fromm. Frankfurt am Main (Ullstein).

Hardeck, J. (2005). Erich Fromm. Darmstadt (Wissenschaftliche Buchgesellschaft).

Horkheimer, M. (1995). Gesammelte Schriften in 19 Bänden. Edited by Alfred Schmidt and Gunzelin Schmid Noerr. Vol. 15. Frankfurt am Main (Fischer Verlag).

Horkheimer, M. (1996). Gesammelte Schriften in 19 Bänden. Edited by Alfred Schmidt and Gunzelin Schmid Noerr. Vol. 16. Frankfurt am Main (Fischer Verlag).

Horkheimer, M. (Ed.) (1932ff.). Zeitschrift für Sozialforschung. Reprint with an introduction by Alfred Schmidt. München (Deutscher Taschenbuch Verlag), 1980.

Horkheimer, M. (Ed.) (1936). Studien über Autorität und Fmilie. Paris (Felix Alcán).

Horney, K. (1937). The Neurotic Personality of Our Time. New York (W. W. Norton & Company).

Horney, K. (1939). New Ways in Psychoanalysis. New York (W. W. Norton & Company).

Internationale Erich-Fromm-Gesellschaft (Ed.) (1991). Erich Fromm und die Kritische Theorie. Vol. 2. Münster (Lit-Verlag).

Jay, M. (1976). Dialectic Imagination. The History of the Frankfurt School and of the Institute for Social Research 1923–1950. Boston (Little and Brown).

Johach, H. (1991). Erich Fromm und die kritische Theorie des Subjekts. In: Wissenschaft vom Menschen – Science of Man. Jahrbuch der Internationalen Erich-Fromm-Gesellschaft. Münster (LIT Verlag). 2, pp. 33–54.

Knapp. G.P. (1982). Erich Fromm (Köpfe des XX. Jahrhunderts, Vol. 97), Berlin (Colloquium Verlag).

Lévy, A. (2002). Erich Fromm. Humanist zwischen Tradition und Utopie. Würzburg (Königshausen und Neumann).

Müller-Dohm, S. (2003). Adorno. Eine Biographie. Frankfurt am Main (Suhrkamp Verlag).

Reich, W. (1976). People in trouble. New York (Farrar, Straus and Giroux).

Rickert, J. (1986). The Fromm-Marcuse debate revisited. In: Theory and Society (15), pp. 351–400.

Todorov, T. (1998). Abenteuer des Zusammenlebens. Versuch einer allgemeinen Anthropologie. Frankfurt am Main (Fischer-Taschenbuch-Verlag).

Wehr, H. (1990). Erich Fromm zur Einführung. Hamburg (Junius Verlag).

Wiggershaus, R. (1994). The Frankfurt School, Cambridge (Polity Press). German original: Die Frankfurter Schule. Geschichte – Theoretische Entwicklung – Politische Bedeutung. München (Deutscher Taschenbuch Verlag), 1988.

Erich Fromm: Lives and Voices, or Life and Voice?

Joan Braune

Abstract: Two sources, Lawrence Friedman's recent biography and Michael Maccoby's important 1994 essay on the "two voices" of Erich Fromm, present Fromm as torn between his roles as scholarly "scientist" and as revolutionary "prophet." Contra Friedman and Maccoby, who see the "prophetic" as impinging on Fromm's scholarly objectivity and rigor, I argue that Fromm's prophetic and scientific sides must be understood as fundamentally linked. Fromm's ethical-prophetic orientation and his theory of "prophetic messianism" are intellectually sophisticated. Fromm draws on philosophical traditions that privilege human flourishing (Aristotle, Spinoza, Marx) as the basis for ethical decision-making. Like Marxist Georg Lukács's "totality," Fromm's prophetic messianism not only doesn't limit his theoretical work – it opens up new vistas, through an encounter with reality that is both theoretical and practical.

Because the papers in this volume reflect Fromm's "expansive humanism" (Anderson 2007) in several ways, the theme of human agency or of putting humanity "back in the saddle," will be my focus. I believe Fromm's concept of getting "back in the saddle" should be explored with a focus on the meaning of Fromm's own way of exercising agency, as an activist and a public intellectual, in light of his work as a whole. Fromm's commitment to inter-subjectivity, social cooperation, and Marxist humanism (topics addressed in various ways by the some of the papers in this volume) is inseparable from his broad social-scientific, philosophical, and psychoanalytic project. By contrast with this holistic view, others have suggested a tension between Fromm's work as a scholar or a psychoanalyst on the one hand and as outspoken advocate of social change on the other. Lawrence Friedman's 2013 biography, *The Lives of Erich Fromm: Love's Prophet*, frequently contrasts Fromm as evidence-based, data-gathering researcher and Fromm as "prophet" (Friedman 2013), Michael Maccoby makes a similar point in an earlier essay "The Two Voices of Erich Fromm: The Prophetic and the Analytic" (1994), arguing that Fromm's work is characterized by a tension between the analyst and the prophet, and that Fromm's work is weakest when the prophetic predominates. Possibly Friedman and Maccoby define science in the contemporary, narrow sense of the term, wanting to reign in Fromm's philosophizing and get him to focus on gathering and analyzing empirical data. (Maccoby assisted on one of Fromm's most important empirical studies, his study of "social character" in a Mexican village, and he knows and appreciates Fromm's empirical and psychoanalytic work from the inside.) But more to the point and regardless of the question of the proper relationship between data and theory, Friedman and Maccoby show wariness towards Fromm's prophetic (inherently political) impulse and seem to conclude that Fromm's scholarly objectivity is threatened by his outspoken advocacy; it is this latter wariness that is of concern and interest to me here.

It is particularly important to address this matter at the present time, because as the first full-length English language biography of Fromm, Friedman's book has been highly influential and has been received at times too uncritically. Followers of Fromm's work easily get excited when a major new publication explores Fromm's work, and Friedman's biography is an important contribution to scholarship on Fromm. Some Fromm scholars have neglected to notice, however, that Friedman's biography is hostile to Fromm's project in many ways and generally dismissive (with limited explanation and argument) of nearly all of Fromm's key ideas, including his humanistic socialism, his interpretation of psychoanalysis, his reading of Jewish thought, and his strategy for social change. *The Lives of Erich Fromm* also tends to psychologize Fromm's radical socialist organizing as neurotic, while seeing it as encroaching on Fromm's scholarly objectivity.

Are we to understand Erich Fromm as a thinker of two "voices" (Maccoby) or many "lives" (Friedman), or can we understand Fromm's life and work as a coherent unity, both the public intellectual and socialist organizer on the one hand, and the scholar and therapist on the other? I argue that understanding Fromm's work requires taking it seriously as a whole and not discounting his work as a public intellectual and socialist (Marxist) organizer.

Marx, like Fromm, has frequently been accused of allowing the prophetic orientation of his work to overrun the scientific. Like the term "idealist" (an accusation Fromm has also suffered – Hansen 1956) or the more plainly derogative term "fanatic" (a charge not frequently made against Fromm, but also layered in political and religious purposes – Toscano 2010), the term "prophet" has multiple meanings and social functions, adapting itself to an array of contexts. Fromm's synthesis of the organizer and scholar stands in the same tradition as Karl Marx's own commitment to the unity of theory and practice. In the case of Marx, some use the term to approve or criticize Marx's "predictions" about the future development of capitalism (consolidation of wealth, globalization of markets, increasing impoverishment of workers, cyclically recurring economic crises). Others charge that Marx was too "prophetic" in the sense of an overheated hoary-headed moralist making uninformed condemnations of the exploitation of the poor by the rich, without a scientific understanding of how capitalism functions. Each depiction of Marx is problematic. Although Marx had an ethical critique of capitalism, his ethical critique need not be assumed to have weakened his scientific judgment. And although Marx did make statements about the future operation of capitalism (as well as hopeful or agitational assertions of its demise), Marx's critique of market fetishism and his nuanced, nonlinear philosophical understanding of causality from the time of his early doctoral dissertation, make Marx far less deterministic than today's capitalist economists, who are apt to ardently profess their objectivity.

Lawrence Friedman's recent biography of Fromm misunderstands Fromm's "prophetic" orientation in the very way that Marx is often misunderstood. Friedman sometimes interprets the prophet as one who makes predictions, and at other times as an overwrought moral critic issuing "jeremiads." Contrary to Friedman's sneering, Fromm has a careful and technical definition of the "prophet," according to which the prophet is neither an esoteric seer nor a nagging moralizer. The prophet does not make "predictions" and rejects determinism (cf. for example Fromm 1967b). Fromm considers Spinoza, Marx, and Rosa Luxemburg "prophets" and "alternativists" who rejected determinism. As a public educator and agitator, the prophet warns people about the likely results of particular courses of action, beginning from an informed understanding of present possibilities and an ethical commitment to social change, not mystical foresight.

The prophet's ethical commitment is a humanistic one. Fromm's humanistic ethics is neither voluntarism nor raw emotionalism, and he has no set of rules that descend from above, whether from God's will or from human institutions. Rather, Fromm's humanistic ethics is based upon a commitment to human flourishing. Like Aristotle, Aquinas, Spinoza, and Hegel, and others, Fromm believes – and he argues that Marx also believes – that human nature is in some degree knowable. Human nature is sufficiently knowable to outline basic human needs and desires, such as our sometimes competing needs for both love and autonomy. The individual is not simply subject to her human nature, however, but has agency and stands within a matrix of at least four different forces. Firstly, Fromm holds that we have a certain baseline, unchanging human nature, which includes such things as our fundamentally social orientation and our need to embrace "activeness" (perhaps a reference to Fichte's *Tätigkeit*, another concept linking the theoretical and the practical). Secondly, distinguished from this baseline human nature, there is the "social character" predominant in one's particular epoch (making our era one in which the "marketing personality" is becoming more prominent, for example, in contrast to the mindset of the early capitalist focused on saving of money and sexual Puritanism). Thirdly, in addition to the universal, unchanging human nature, and the particular modifications of human nature in each historical epoch, each person has a specific character and uniqueness, partly as a result of her past choices. Fourthly, most individuals retain free will to make certain crucial choices that will shape their future possibilities for thought, feeling, and action. Thus, the individual stands within a complex matrix of forces: human history and present social context, her own past (shaped by her environment, her genetics, and her own choices), and her present decision-making power. What is ethically required for Fromm is what leads to human flourishing, and the study of the human thus constitutes a crucial feature of political and ethical action.

Fromm's commitment to human flourishing is more than a negative restraint upon his research. One might argue in defense of Fromm's "prophetic" side, that instead of worrying that an outspoken thinker's value commitments will bias their results, we should worry about the danger of operating science without such ethical commitments. We might then turn to Max Weber's warnings about the rise of instrumental rationality (*Zweckrationalität*) or Hannah Arendt's concerns about Nazi bureaucrats who were so unconcerned about ethical ends that genocide became just another day's work. However, an argument in defense of Fromm needs to go further. Fromm's humanistic commitment does not merely constrain him, preventing his work from going awry; it opens him to new realizations. Value commitments do more than set boundaries to scientific research. Indeed, when impelled by hope and faith, values (and the real-world action they imply) *open up truths* hidden to the detached observer.

In Georg Lukács' *History and Class Consciousness* (which Fromm praises in *Marx's Concept of Man* [Fromm 1961b, p. 57]), Marxism is presented as "the standpoint of totality," a standpoint uniting theory and practice. Marxism according to Lukács is not encapsulated by any formulae or creeds but is the beholding of reality as a single process, an ongoing human making, in which all that is (including humanity itself) is a human product. Even apparently untouched nature (to whatever extent such a thing exists) is always perceived by human beings through the lenses of human history and of human understanding as shaped by that history. In his Paris Manuscripts, Marx can be seen to be making roughly the same point: "Since, however, for socialist man, the *whole of what is called world history* is nothing but the creation of man by human labor, and the emergence of nature for man, he, therefore, has the evident and irrefutable proof of his *self-creation*, of his own origins" (Marx 2004, p. 112).

Lukács' class-conscious worker understands herself and reality through self-creative revolutionary action, and paradoxically also acts as a result of her understanding of herself and reality. She unites herself with the universe and participates in moving the course of world history. She experiences unity with the whole and transcends the limits of individual existence. By attaining the standpoint of totality, the subject becomes the object (of her own knowledge and activity), and the object (subjugated humanity and nature) becomes the subject (agent of change). The non-committed, so-called neutral observer is blinded by the external viewpoint she adopts and cannot see the way in which social facts are connected in a larger whole, in which a change to any part of social reality results in a change to the totality.

Lukács' vision of the working class subject-object of world history belongs to a subterranean philosophical tradition with predecessors including Nicholas of Cusa, Giordano Bruno, and Benedict Spinoza. For such thinkers, the infinity of God or of nature would be the basis for a new humanism, in which limitless possibilities were open to those who could unite themselves by contemplation and activity with the boundless. This idea arises again in German idealism, including Hegel, and carries over into Marx. Fromm is keenly aware of this trajectory and himself stands within it, especially with regard to the credit he gives to Spinoza and also to an extent in his interest in Meister Eckhart, D.T. Suzuki's Zen Buddhism, and Walt Whitman's friend, Maurice Bucke, the author of *Cosmic Consciousness*.

Fromm's "prophetic messianism," which of course is related to his conception of the prophetic, is an even more specific emancipatory commitment and a way of understanding and talking about humanity's relationship to its past, present, and future. Messianism is an enduring intellectual commitment evident throughout Fromm's mature work from the 1950s to the 1970s, and the roots of its influence are even earlier, in 1920s Germany. Fromm's turn to Marx's early writings in the late 1950s and 1960s enabled him to see that this commitment was not peripheral to Marxism but lay at the heart of Marx's philosophy. Among the thinkers Fromm praises as prophetic-messianic are Meister Eckhart, Spinoza, Lessing, Fichte, Hegel, Goethe, utopian socialist Saint-Simon, Young Hegelians Moses Hess and Heinrich Heine, Karl Marx, and early socialist and anarchist thinkers after Marx, including Rosa Luxemburg and Gustav Landauer (Fromm 1961b, p. 54; 1992b, pp. 144–145; 1955a, p. 236).

As I argue in a contribution to a recently published book, *Reclaiming the Sane Society: Essays on Erich Fromm's Thought* (Braune 2014), Fromm's interpretation of socialism as the contemporary heir of prophetic messianism situates him within one camp of thinkers and distinguishes him from another. Fromm was aligning himself with a particular camp of thinkers, offering allegiance to the messianism of Hermann Cohen, Ernst Bloch, and others, while differentiating himself from others, including Gershom Scholem, Walter Benjamin, and Herbert Marcuse (Fromm 1976a, p. 126). Cohen held that humanity could make a choice for an ethical socialism by rational consideration of the alternatives. Fromm, although he had a deeper understanding of the unconscious through Freud, shared Cohen's view that this commitment was itself ethically obligated and that the person who wished to work for a better future for humanity was bound by an obligation of openness to hope and cultivation of hope. Fromm contrasted prophetic messianism with catastrophic (or apocalyptic) messianism. Catastrophic messianism envisioned the messianic age occurring as a result of a destructive rupture, arriving deterministically (at an appointed time) or voluntaristically (with a small group instigating a catastrophe to force change). Fromm saw catastrophic messianism evidenced in the pessimistic mood that swept over Germany after World War One and in the work of various thinkers including Gershom Scholem and Herbert Marcuse. The prophetic element to Fromm's thought is central to his most important intellectual contributions and is not a flaw as Friedman suggests or a different voice as Maccoby asserts. Messianism sits at the center of his work and anchors Fromm's insights, writings and actions in the world.

References

Anderson, K. (2007). Thinking about Fromm and Marxism. In: Logos Journal (6.3), pp. Retrieved from: http://www.logosjournal.com/issue_6.3/anderson.htm (March 19, 2015)

Braune, J. (2014). Erich Fromm's Socialist Program and Prophetic Messianism, Part II. In: S.J. Miri et al. (Eds.). Reclaiming the Sane Society. Essays on Erich Fromm's Thought. Rotterdam (Sense Publishers), pp. 74–91

Friedman, L. J. (2013). The Lives of Erich Fromm. Love's Prophet. Assisted by Anke M. Schreiber. New York (Columbia University Press).

Fromm, E. (1955a). The Sane Society. New York (Rinehart and Company).

Fromm, E. (1961b). Marx's Concept of Man. London (Continuum), 2004.

Fromm, E. (1967b). Prophets and Priests. In: E. Fromm. On Disobedience. Why Freedom Means Saying "No" to Power. New York (HarperCollins), 2010, pp. 13–40.

Fromm, E. (1976a). To Have or To Be? New York (Continuum), 2009.

Fromm, E. (1992b). On Being Human. New York (Continuum), 1994.

Hansen, J. (1956). A Psychoanalyst Looks for a Sane Society. Marxists Internet Archive. (Reprinted from Hansen, J. (1956). Fourth International, (17) 2, Spring, pp. 65–69). Retrieved from: http://www.marxists.org/archive/hansen/1956/xx/psych.htm (March 19, 2015).

Maccoby, M. (1994). The Two Voices of Erich Fromm: The Prophetic and the Analytic. Retrieved from: http://www.maccoby.com/Articles/TwoVoices.shtml (March 19, 2015).

Marx, K. (2004). Economic and Philosophical Manuscripts. Trans. T.B. Bottomore. In: E.Fromm. Marx's Concept of Man. London (Continuum).

Toscano, A. (2010). Fanaticism. On the Uses of an Idea. London (Verso).

Wiggershaus, R. (1994). The Frankfurt School: Its History, Theories, and Political Significance. Translation M. Robertson. Cambridge (MIT Press).

Erich Fromm's Legacy

Rainer Funk

A value-oriented science

The longer I occupy myself with the thought and writings of Erich Fromm, the more undeniable it becomes to me that Fromm's scientific legacy is the concept of the social character, as already expounded on by Michael Maccoby. This concept, however, is invariably used by Fromm in a judgmental, evaluative context, that is to say: the social character orientations are distinguished from one another by whether or not they contribute to the person's psychic development. For Fromm, we must ask whether character orientations contribute to a productive effect which promotes human and psychic development, or to a non-productive impact on the self-fulfillment of the person and thus impede psychic growth or even thwart it.

This humanistic-ethical dimension is a central aspect of Fromm's *scientific* legacy. Since the mainstream of scientific thought advocates value-free research, instruction and for the most part application as well – and for good reason: one need only remember what happens when science is kept on a leash by a political party, by the Mullahs, or by the business world's interest in monetary return – Fromm's value-oriented understanding of science is regarded by many as obsolete.

But even when Fromm's thought does indeed enjoy a good reception, it can be observed that there is a strong temptation to distinguish between a "scientific" Fromm and a religious, humanistic or spiritual Fromm. An attempt is made in such cases to separate one from the other, as if Fromm had spoken with two voices (Maccoby 1995). In his biography of Fromm's life and work, Lawrence Friedman (2013) is partly organized around trying to distinguish the "spiritual" or "prophetic" Fromm from in contrast to Fromm, the man of science.

Such interpretations (and mis-interpretations) of Fromm's value-oriented scientific understanding become unnecessary when an attempt is made to perceive Fromm's understanding of science as an independent scientific paradigm in which the value orientations of man and society are part and parcel of the object of scientific understanding. It is certain that the mainstream, still stamped today by altercations about freedom from value judgments in science, by relativism and constructivism in the behavioral sciences, and by an autocratic rule of the natural science paradigm, will not be convinced of this.

One indication that a value-oriented understanding of science in the social sciences in the meantime is no longer quite obsolete is the new discussion, however, has been set in motion above all by sociologists, concerning the issue of alienation and questions pertaining a "good life", a "good society" or "good politics" (cf. e.g. Ehrenberg 1998; Rosa 2010). Worth reading in this context is Kieran Durkin's book *The Radical Humanism of Erich Fromm* (2014) where he compellingly makes the case that a value-oriented social science is still thoroughly relevant today.

Now I wish to show the individual reasons why Erich Fromm arrived at this value-oriented concept of the human and social sciences. In doing so, I am not addressing here the Jewish tradition of thought from which Fromm came – that is, Jewish orthodoxy and Hasidism, with its visions of man. The value orientations which formed part of his life are clearly reflected here in Fromm's own dissertation "The Jewish Law" (Fromm 1989b), about which Jürgen Hardeck (1990; 2009) and – with great competence – Domagoj Akrap (2011) have already written (cf. also Funk 1987). Over and above this, Fromm's sociological dissertation from the year 1922 clearly imparts the sense of a particular interest which guided his insights and which acted as a determinant of Fromm's socio-psychological research throughout his life – that is, the question of what causes human beings who share in their practice of economic, social and cultural living to think, feel and act in a similar manner.

The socio-psychoanalytic approach

Shortly after he finished his dissertation, Fromm was introduced by Frieda Reichmann to Freudian psychoanalysis. The goal of psychoanalysis is to identify and make experiential the conscious and unconscious inner drives which cause the individual human being to think, feel and act in a certain manner.

Fromm's stroke of genius, which he conceptualized in the context of questions considered relevant at the Institute for Social Research in the early 1930s, was that he now brought together the sociological and psychoanalytical objects of understanding – i.e. society and the individual – by showing that the societal aspect, with its requirements regarding life, survival, and communal living must be represented in each individual human being in the form of a libidinal structure formation. Thus "every society has its own distinctive *libidinal structure*" (Fromm 1932a, p. 160), which can be studied by looking at the libidinal structure which causes large numbers of individuals to think, feel and act similarly. The study of this socially molded libidinal structure not only makes it possible to formulate statements about the impulses which are at work in a societal group but also explains why human beings passionately and gladly contribute whatever they *must* in the form of psychic and social acts of accommodation in order to bring about a successful communal life. Social requirements are thus internalized in this way and determine social drives in each of the many individuals. The problem caused by the insight that social drives, although socially caused on the one hand, stem from a libidinal structure formation on the other was not widely understood at that time.

The decisive point is the new determination of the relationship between the individual and society. In Fromm's socio-psychoanalytic approach, the two are no longer antipodes. Rather, society is present with its expectations in each individual in the form of libidinal impulses, and the individual cannot exist in any other way than as a social being. Fromm exemplified this approach for the first time in 1936 in his analysis of the authoritarian social character, published in the volume on *Authority and Family* of the Institute for Social Research, which has still not been translated into English down to the present day (Fromm 1936a).

There are numerous indications that Fromm was increasingly doubtful about the Freudian libido theory that he had used to explain the passionate strivings as libidinal drives caused by societal requirements. To be named here among others are Fromm's interest in matricentric cultures, his criticism of Freud's appraisal of the Oedipus Complex, and his criticism of Freud's view of women; also important, however, are Fromm's new contacts in the United States: with Margaret Mead and Ruth Benedict and their cross-cultural anthropological studies and with Harry Stack Sullivan, in whose view human beings are driven by an existential need for relatedness and not by the desire to satisfy libidinal wishes.

In the winter of 1936–1937 Fromm took time off for a few months to re-formulate his social psychoanalytic approach more accurately and to delve into the "basic principles" of Freud's libido theory, as he wrote in a letter to his Institute colleague Wittfogel: "I am trying to demonstrate that the urges which motivate social activities are not, as Freud supposes, sublimations of sexual instincts, rather products of social processes." (Letter to Karl August Wittfogel on 18 December 1936 – Erich Fromm Archive – cf. Funk 2013.) In this eighty-five-page-long paper, Fromm (1992e) states in detail his reasons for saying that most psychic structures are not only formed by the object relations of man but are also independent of libidinal drives.

Sullivan's relational approach naturally played godfather to Fromm's revision of psychoanalytic theory in the sense that the individual's underlying *psychic* problem is not the satisfaction of drives but rather the satisfaction of his or her need for relatedness. For Fromm, however, every person must always stand in a relationship not only with reality and with other human beings, as Sullivan made clear with his interpersonal and intersubjective approach. The hunger to be related to oneself and to the social group one belongs to arises with the same existential urgency from this relational approach.

Before I go into the implications of this specifically Frommian aspect of the relational theory paradigm, however, I want to say something about the fate which this stance met with. Fromm's colleagues at the Institute for Social Research, namely Horkheimer, Loewenthal and Marcuse, rejected his approach because it opened up the Freudian theory of drives to questioning. A submission for publication in the *Zeitschrift für Sozialforschung* was rejected, thus initiating Fromm's ostracism from the so-called "Frankfurt School". The fact that Fromm completed an English translation in addition to the German text shows how important this essay was to Fromm himself. After its publication was turned down, it remained lying in a drawer of Fromm's desk. The upshot was that this essay, which was so central to the development of Fromm's theories, was never published by him and was in fact forgotten by Fromm himself as he worked on the book *Escape from Freedom* (Fromm 1941a) and on a summarized version of his new approach entitled "Character and the Social Process" in the appendix to that book.

In the end, the essay turned up in that part of his estate which contained his manuscripts and letters from the years 1935 to 1949 and which he donated to the New York Public Library in the 1950s. The librarian there believed the author to be unknown. I discovered the manuscript there in December 1990. It was published two years later as a posthumous German text in 1992, and shortly thereafter in Spanish and Italian translations as well. The English version of the manuscript did not become available in printed form until 2010 (Fromm 1992e).

Implications of Fromm's socio-psychoanalytic approach

Now I want to speak of the implications by postulating some theses which go hand-in-hand with the socio-psychoanalytic approach developed by Fromm.

(1) I have already mentioned Fromm's *new determination of the relationship between the individual and society*. Rather than standing opposite each other, they are structurally joined, and this is the reason why Fromm could say the following in his essay of 1937: "Society is nothing but living, concrete individuals, and the individual can live only as a social human being" (1992e, p. 58).

In writing this, Fromm no longer takes societal institutions as a starting point for defining the object of sociological studies, namely society, but rather the many individual persons (which was certainly one reason for the poor reception of Fromm's thought in sociology). More important in my view, however, is that from the very beginning Fromm understands the individual as a socialized being. This is also reflected in his expansion of Sullivan's relational approach and its postulate of the necessity for a relationship with oneself; this led Fromm even at an early time to clearly formulate a "psychology of the self" (Fromm 1939b; cf. Fromm 1941a, pp. 115–120) in which the existential hunger for ties to a social group leads to the development of an individual psychic structure and thus makes every type of psychology a form of social psychology.

(2) Every person has an inevitable need for relationship with a social group. And the formation of every psychic structure must satisfy the genetically pre-programmed need for a relationship not only with persons of reference but also with the social group. It is my view that this *primary sociality of man* often receives too little attention in the reception of Fromm's thought, even though his thesis of *Escape from Freedom* is based upon man's existential fear at the thought of isolation.

Fromm expressed his ideas even more clearly in *Beyond the Chains of Illusion* (1962a, p. 126), where he wrote the following:

> For man as *human being* [that is to say, inasmuch as he transcends nature and is aware of himself and of death] the sense of complete aloneness and separateness is close to insanity. Man as man is afraid of insanity, just as man as animal is afraid of death. Man must enter into relationships with others, he *must* find union with others, in order to remain sane. This need to be at one with others is his strongest passion, stronger than sex and often even stronger than his wish to live.

The Fromm who speaks here is not only the sociologically trained psychoanalyst but also the Jew who was born in Frankfurt almost exactly thirty-six years after the Ghettoization law was finally lifted. Fromm had to be isolated in 1931 due to his tuberculosis illness, and he was forced to emigrate and experienced the stigmatization, the segregation, and the annihilation of some of his family's relatives by the Nazis.

Fromm's socio-psychoanalytic approach is based on a view of man that highlights his need for social attachment – an approach confirmed in turn by Bowlby, whose studies of attachment behavior were highly prized by Fromm. And this view undergoes further development in the socio-biological studies of which Mauricio Cortina will write about in one of the following chapters. These theories are developed in present-day research into relationships, the topic of Sonia Gojman's chapter.

(3) If we view Fromm's socio-psychoanalytic approach against the back-drop of our deep-rooted fear of social isolation and the psychic structures whose formation it makes necessary, a number of other implications with theoretical impact come into view. Freud's concept of *"primary narcissism"*, for example, and the notion that man is "primarily self-sufficient and only secondarily in need of others in order to satisfy his/her instinctual needs" was emphatically rejected by Fromm (1941a, p. 290) and was criticized by him point by point in one of his later writings (Fromm 1979a, pp. 43–54). The concept has also been quite clearly disproven by the studies of infants and attachment.

From the very beginning, every human person is a being in relation to reality, one who requires a bond with other individuals, to a social group, and to him- or herself for his or her interactional behavior, his or her group behavior, and his or her self-regulation. In this regard, the latter, that is, the relationship with oneself, has in my view and in that of Fromm himself nothing to do with narcissism (Fromm 1964a, pp. 62–94).

(4) However, this attachment behavior, which is guided by inherent affec-tive reactions and attachment patterns, is subject to a process of develop-ment and – as it takes shape – is dependent for long periods on relational experiences which take root via internalization processes in the *formation of psychic structures.*

It is precisely here that Fromm's socio-psychoanalytic approach takes effect, since it becomes important here to make a basic distinction between two different types of psychic structure formation, using their functions as criteria, namely:

➤ those types which help to lay the foundation for the *formation of in-dividual character* on the basis of quite individual circumstances and experiences in the first years of life (for example parental divorce, the birth of a sibling, an unusually empathic motherly reference person, etc.)

➤ and those types which help to lay the foundation for the *formation of social character* on the basis of circumstances and experiences which are shared with the social group (for example being forced to assume a position of either rivalry or cooperation)

In designating these types of psychic structure formation, Fromm built on and developed the Freudian concept of character in the sense understood by Karl Abraham and taught at the Psychoanalytic Institute in Berlin, where Fromm concluded his psychoanalytic training. After abandoning libido theory, Fromm appears to use the term "character structure" by and large as a synonym for the term "psychic structure".

(5) The formation of psychic structure or character goes hand-in-hand with a decisive change in the dynamics of relatedness: relational behavior becomes more and more independent of both real reference persons and of identification with the social group, since it is now guided by the internalized images of experiences and character orientations. That which we generally call "*autonomy development*" and "*the process of individuation*" always presuppose the development of a corresponding inner structural formation.

Fromm's primary interest consisted in measuring man's being related in everyday life in light of the question of individuation; he did so in two directions:

➤ firstly, it is necessary to identify the *progress* of the individuation process within a societal group and to determine how perception of the self and its convictions and values are basically *defined pre-individually* by the "We" of the collective, that is, by the tradition, by the bonds of the family, etc.

➤ secondly, it is necessary to find out whether the step from the pre-modern to the modern – that is, from the collective to the individual sensing of one's self – *can* be done or actually *is* done, but is counteracted *secondarily* by a social character formation by which the individual *prefer to be dependent on authorities or technical acquirements which lie outside himself and herself* and which – with regard to the psychic processes of development and individuation – have a *non-productive effect* and *alienate* the person from his own individual powers and possibilities

It is therefore not enough to focus attention only on the necessity for relatedness. Rather, one must also always keep the *type of relatedness* and the *quality of being related* in view. This is all the more true inasmuch as one can also develop relational qualities and character orientations on the basis of one's ability to imagine and the ability to be conscious of oneself – qualities and orientations unknown as such to his animal predecessors but which enable human beings to express their love for nature in a lyrical poem or also to develop a permanent readiness for cruelty and destructiveness – and to take pleasure in it. (The psychodynamics of cruelty and necrophilous destructiveness is the subject of Fromm's *The Anatomy of Human Destructiveness* – 1973a.)

(6) The study of character formation processes thus always goes hand-in-hand with an evaluative question, namely the question of what *impact* character formation has upon a human being and his or her potential for the development and the individuation as well as on the human living with others: is it *humanly productive or non-productive*?

We are quite familiar with such value-oriented scientific questions which focus on the individual. Most branches of psychology are guided by the concepts of what is healthy and what is pathological, and what allows the person to succeed or fail as a human being. Value-oriented science becomes far more complicated in the socio-psychoanalytic approach developed by Fromm, however, inasmuch as it takes two different structure formation processes as its point of departure.

(7) While it is true that the impact of the individual and of the social character should be humanly productive, the task of the social character consists first and foremost in contributing to stability and to the *successful outcome of a specific society*. This functional determinant has the result that the social character often does not contribute to the individual's psychic success but is rather directed towards a financial and social success which can often be achieved only *at the cost of a successful outcome on the part of the individual* – one need only think of the subservient authoritarian character type who is plagued by inhibitions and anxieties, or of those persons today who are ill from "burnout".

Thus productive or non-productive quality can differ between the individual and the social character, so that an inner psychic conflict arises between the orientations of the two character formation processes and can bring about *illness* as a result. Thus the conflict which Freud discussed between libidinous wishes and a culturally required renunciation of instincts is no longer present as such in Fromm's socio-psychoanalytic approach; its place is taken by the potential conflict between the orientations of the individual and the social characters and their respective productive or non-productive quality.

(8) Finally, it remains to be mentioned that Fromm's socio-psychoanalytic approach also has *consequences for character study*:

The major challenge for empirical social character research consists in the fact that the persons involved are aware of social character orientations inasmuch as they are ego-syntonic. That is to say that most orientations are accessible to such persons only in their rationalizations. No test person will admit to an affinity for beating children or of being attracted by what is lifeless and inanimate. The persons involved are not allowed to be aware of their true character orientation. Likewise a society built upon rivalry must suppress the awareness of how destructive it is, if there are to be only winners and losers.

The challenge therefore is as follows:

➤ *to develop methods* with which the *socially unconscious and suppressed* aspects of test persons can be studied empirically, and

➤ to ensure that the *researchers* are aware of their own social character orientation and its respective influence on evaluation

(9) An important prerequisite for this, in my opinion, is to make a *strict distinction* between the basic striving which is at work in a character and which Fromm called character *orientation* and the character *traits* which yield information only after recognition of the conscious or unconscious character *orientation* which is at work in them.

The instrumentalism of research must therefore be directed first and foremost to character orientation, since it is only this *orientation* which makes it possible to recognize the basic striving which is psychically at work. Work with behavioral observations, attitudinal studies and character traits, becomes socio-*psychoanalytic* in nature only when it focuses on character *orientation*. I believe that it is only in this way that one can do justice to the term *psychodynamic character study*.

(10) The term *"orientation of character"* is important in a socio-psychoanalytic approach in yet another sense: it is used by Fromm not only to

designate individual, non-productive social character orientations (the authoritarian character, the hoarding character, the marketing character, the narcissistic character, the necrophilic character, etc.) but also to designate the productive or non-productive quality of character orientation. What is decisive in both uses of the term "orientation" is that it designates both the direction and the directedness of striving – that is something which attracts me rather than a place where I am.

The above-named implications of Fromm's socio-psychoanalytic approach make it clear why Fromm advocates a value-oriented understanding of science – like that, by the way, which is fully a matter of course in medicine and in therapeutic psychoanalysis. To sum it up in a single sentence: if society, with its demands that every individual contributes to the successful outcome of society, is represented in the social character of the many individuals, then the conflict between what makes society successful and what make the person successful will be avoidable only if the conditions for living together in a society are also oriented toward the successful outcome of human beings. For Fromm (1955a, p. 72), it was the case "that mental health cannot be defined in terms of the 'adjustment' of the individual to his society, but, on the contrary, *that it must be defined in terms of the adjustment of society to the needs of man*".

For me, Fromm speaks only with *one* voice which goes against the mainstream of today's understanding of science, a voice which says: the successful outcome of man as man must be the value which science takes as its point of orientation.

References

Akrap, D. (2011). Erich Fromm – ein jüdischer Denker. Jüdisches Erbe – Tradition – Religion. Münster (LIT-Verlag).

Ehrenberg, A. (1998). La Fatigue d'être soi – dépression et société. Paris (Odile Jacob).

Friedman, L.J. (2013). The Lives of Erich Fromm. Love's Prophet, with assistence from Anke M. Schreiber. New York (Columbia University Press).

Fromm, E. (1932a). The Method and Function of an Analytic Social Psychology. In: E. Fromm. The Crisis of Psychoanalysis, New York (Holt, Rinehart and Winston), 1970, pp. 135–162.

Fromm, E. (1936a). Sozialpsychologischer Teil. In: Erich Fromm Gesamtausgabe in zwölf Bänden (GA). Ed. Rainer Funk. München (DVA and dtv), 1999, Vol. I, pp. 139–187. So far not translated into English.

Fromm, E. (1939b). Selfishness and Self-Love. In: Psychiatry. Journal for the Study of Inter-personal Process. Washington (The William Alanson Psychiatric Foundation), Vol. 2, pp. 507–523.

Fromm, E. (1941a). Escape from Freedom. New York (Farrar and Rinehart).

Fromm, E. (1955a). The Sane Society. New York (Rinehart and Winston Inc.).

Fromm, E. (1962a). Beyond the Chains of Illusion. My Encounter with Marx and Freud. New York (Simon and Schuster).

Fromm, E. (1964a). The Heart of Man. Its Genius for Good and Evil. New York (Harper and Row).

Fromm, E. (1973a). The Anatomy of Human Destructiveness. New York (Holt, Rinehart and Winston).

Fromm, E. (1979a). Greatness and Limitations of Freud's Thought. New York (Harper and Row), 1980.

Fromm, E. (1989b). Das Jüdische Gesetz. Dissertation [originated 1922]. In: Erich Fromm Gesamtausgabe in zwölf Bänden (GA). Ed. Rainer Funk. München (DVA and dtv), 1999, Vol. XI, pp. 19–126.

Fromm, E. (1992e). Man's impulse structure and its relation to culture. [originated 1937]. In: E. Fromm. Beyond Freud: From Individual to Social Psychoanalysis. New York (American Mental Health Foundation), 2010, pp. 17–74.

Funk, R. (1987). Von der jüdischen zur sozialpsychologischen Seelenlehre. Erich Fromms Weg von der einen über die andere Frankfurter Schule. In: R. Sesterhenn (Ed.). Das Freie Jüdische Lehrhaus – eine andere Frankfurter Schule. Munich and Zürich (Schnell and Steiner), pp. 91–108.

Funk, R. (2013). Erich Fromm and the Intersubjective Tradition. In: International Forum of Psychoanalysis, Abingdon (Routledge – Taylor and Francis), 22 (1), pp. 5–9.

Hardeck, J. (1990). Religion im Werk von Erich Fromm. Eine religionswissenschaftliche Untersuchung. Münster (Lit Verlag).

Hardeck, J. (2009). Erich Fromms Judentum und sein Verständnis der Religion. In: Fromm Forum (German Edition), Vol. 13, Tuebingen (Self-published), pp. 6–16.

Maccoby, M. (1995). The Two Voices of Erich Fromm: Prophet and Analyst. In: Society, 32 (5 July-Aug.), pp. 72–82.

Rosa, H. (2010). Alienation and Acceleration. Towards a Critical Theory of Late-Modern Temporality. Natchitoches (Northwestern University Press).

Erich Fromm's Impact on Humanistic Psychology

Helmut Johach

Abstract: Humanistic Psychology (HP) includes several psychological movements such as *Client-centered therapy*, *Gestalt therapy*, and *Theme-centered Interaction*. It is based on a "holistic" view of man emphasizing awareness of bodily expressions, creativity, a self-actualizing tendency and spiritual needs. Abraham Maslow, Carl Rogers, Fritz Perls and others called it a "third branch" in psychology setting it apart from orthodox Freudian theory and behaviorism. Erich Fromm is often considered as a founder of Humanistic Psychology because he was the first one who used the term "humanistic" to make a distinguishing mark from Freudian psychoanalysis. He wrote about a "self-actualizing tendency" in human life and said that therapy should be a "core-to-core-relationship" between two adult persons. Fromm was very influential in HP through his "humanistic" ideas but he remained a *psychoanalytic* therapist who tried to unveil the unconscious. So we can say that he never was in the center of the humanist movement, but he held a key position on its periphery.

Introduction

"Humanistic Psychology" is a generic term used to describe several psychological movements such as *Client-centered Therapy* (Carl R. Rogers), *Gestalt Therapy* (Fritz and Laura Perls), *Existential Therapy* (Rollo May), and *Theme-centered Interaction* (Ruth C. Cohn). These movements agree

111

in a view of man which emphasizes creativity, responsibility, self-actualization and psychological health. In the 1960s and 1970s, Humanistic Psychology was very influential in America and later on in Europe. Abraham Maslow and James F. Bugenthal, two important members of the *American Association of Humanistic Psychology,* called it a "third force in psychology" distinct from both traditional psychoanalysis and behaviorism (cf. Johach 2009, pp. 23–26).

Erich Fromm is often considered a founder of humanistic psychology, although he was never a member of the *American Association of Humanistic Psychology* nor was he ever present at the meetings. In the decade between 1955 and 1965 he used the term "humanistic" to delineate the difference between his own thinking and Freud's orthodox version of psychoanalysis. Twenty years earlier, in a paper on "Man's impulse structure and its relation to culture" (Fromm 1992e) he had made it very clear that he no longer agreed with Freud's biological libido theory and with his concept of "Todestrieb". Critical comments on Freud's "naturalistic" and "pessimistic" view of human beings were common to all humanistic psychologists. Fromm was one of the first authors in the United States who brought these views to the public. Nevertheless, he never gave up his fundamental psychoanalytic orientation.

Karen Horney, Harry S. Sullivan and Erich Fromm were called "Neo-Freudians" because of their revisionist interpretation of Freudian theory. It was very important that Fromm widened the psychoanalytical theory of character formation by historical, socio-economic and cultural factors. Humanistic psychologists consider human organism to be a "holistic" and an active center of biological, intellectual, emotional und social activities which are fostered by the world around us. Freedom to choose makes a difference to conditioned reflexes which are the basic explanation of human behavior according to naturalistic scientists. Man should also be free from social constraints. Fritz Perls and other "humanistic" psychologists transformed Fromm's critical category of "alienation" into a more rebellious or even an anarchist practice. Instead of adapting to social rules or roles, everybody should "do his own thing". This misinterpretation of Fromm's idea, under the slogan of "self-actualization", occasionally led to an excessive individualism (cf. Johach 2012).

Fromm was not only a psychological theorist, but also a reformer of practical therapeutic treatment. Following Sándor Ferenczi's variations in psychoanalytic "techniques," Fromm no longer made use of the couch but preferred a "face-to-face-relation" with his patients and a more "active" mode of therapy. He was convinced that the therapist should learn about his own feelings as well as of the patient. There should be a "central relatedness" (cf. Fromm 1992g, p. 104) between two adult persons instead of interpreting transference from the patient's childhood. Fromm was not the only one who criticized Freud's rule of "abstinence" in therapeutic treatment; most of his practical postulates were shared by humanistic psychologists.

It is worth noting that, in later years, Fromm went beyond the traditional frame of therapeutic treatment by proclaiming some way of "trans-therapeutic" psychoanalysis. Psychoanalysis should not only help people get free from neurosis in everyday-life but also show a way to become richer as a human being and more self-congruent by self-analysis outside of the therapeutic relationship. As Fromm suggested in *Psychoanalysis and Zen Buddhism* (Fromm 1960a), self-analysis and Buddhist meditation aim to could reach the same spiritual goals by different means. Many protagonists of Humanist Psychology were also convinced that spiritual needs were indispensable for human growth.

When he wrote the sections of *To Have or to Be?* (Fromm 1976a) which were published only after his death, Fromm said that he had decided against speaking of "humanistic" psychoanalysis because this attribute was adopted by a group of psychologists with whom he did "not agree" (Fromm 1989a, p. 64). Although there was some convergence, he could not share all assertions and practices of Humanistic Psychology. One key difference is the function of *unconscious* thoughts, wishes and emotions which Fromm tried to reveal, according with Freud and other psychoanalysts. In contrast to Fromm, some protagonists of HP declared that one could neglect the unconscious if awareness was extended beyond daily routine. In the following paper, I first will describe some biographical connections between Fromm and other founders of Humanistic Psychology, and then I will deal with what were the similarities and differences in their theories and practices.

Biographical Connections

Abraham Maslow (1908–1970) was a visionary psychologist and the main protagonist of the Humanistic Psychology Movement. In 1962, he called the *American Association of Humanistic Psychology* into being, assisted by Carl C. Rogers, Rollo May, Charlotte Buehler, James Bugenthal and others. He also was the editor of the *Journal of Humanistic Psychology* which has been published to the present day. He famously suggested in *Toward a Psychology of Being* (Maslow 1962), that psychologists and therapists should give more attention to a "health-and-growth-psychology" than to a "deficiency psychology" which has its focus on disturbances and faults impeding the development of a "fully functioning" person. Maslow was primarily a theorist and researcher, not a practical therapist. The most famous part of his writings is the "hierarchy of needs" which he described in his book on *Motivation and Personality* (Maslow 1954). It begins by fundamentally "physiological" needs like eating, drinking, sleeping, then moves to "higher" and "specifically human" needs like love, self-esteem and support by others, and ends with the "self-actualization" of persons wishing to fully realize their human capacities.

Maslow spoke of a "new humanistic world-view" represented by a "Third-Force-Psychology" that should widely differ from behaviorism and orthodox Freudianism. In his last publications, after having studied many accounts of "peak experiences", he announced the need for a "Fourth Psychology" which should extend to spiritual needs.

Abraham Maslow was influenced by Erich Fromm and other neo-Freudian therapists, but he was not analyzed. Between 1935 and 1940, he came to know and study with Alfred Adler, who at that time lived in New York. He had many conversations with Erich Fromm, Karen Horney and other psychotherapists who promulgated a more "culturalist" interpretation of psychoanalysis, and with the anthropologists at Columbia University, especially Ruth Benedict and Margaret Mead. At the same time, he became acquainted with Kurt Goldstein and Max Wertheimer, which were two representatives of Gestalt psychology. Like Fromm, they were Jews and left Europe because of the persecution by the Nazi regime. Kurt Goldstein was a psychiatrist and pioneer of a "holistic" brain research approach. In his famous book *The Organism. A Holistic Approach to Biology derived from*

Pathological Data in Man (Goldstein 1939), Goldstein spoke of a "self-ac-tualizing tendency" in the human organism – an expression which was taken over by Fromm, Maslow and Rogers. I do not know if Fromm ever met with Goldstein when both were living in New York, but I am sure that he knew his book and would have held the work in esteem.

Erich Fromm, in my opinion, was the first philosophically reflecting therapist in the twentieth century who made use of the term "humanistic" to point to a certain psychological position. In *Man for Himself* (Fromm 1947a, pp. 8–37) he wrote about "humanistic ethics" and in *The Sane Society* (Fromm 1955a, p. 22) and *The Heart of Man* (1964a, p. 15) he used the term "humanistic psychoanalysis" as a distinguishing mark from orthodox Freudian psychoanalysis. Abraham Maslow was very impressed by Fromm's books. In his own writings he referred to Fromm, especially to his idea of a *self-actualizing tendency* underlying human growth and productivity. Maslow's decision that the "Third Force" in psychology should be called "humanistic" was a tribute to Fromm.

Another pioneer of Humanistic Psychology was *Rollo May* (1909–1994) who was better known as a founder of "Existential Therapy". May started his career as a theologian who was influenced by Kierkegaard and Tillich. In the early 1930s he studied with Alfred Adler who at that time lived half a year in Vienna and the other time in New York. May began to practice as a therapist and, in the late thirties, he decided to contact Erich Fromm in order to be analyzed. In the beginning, it was a fruitful connection, but after some months, May felt uncomfortable. He said that Fromm was not empathizing sufficiently – when May e.g. was infected by tuberculosis Fromm did not mention that he had been infected too a few years earlier. Fromm was upset by the fact that May took notes from their therapeutic conversations and made use of them in his own writings. In 1943, the therapeutic connection was ended.

Some years later, Rollo May joined the teaching staff of the *William Alanson White Institute*. As colleagues, they could better get along with each other. May said that Fromm's contributions to the discussions of the staff were "refreshing" because Fromm went beyond therapeutic techniques and spoke with verve of the "meaning ground" of human life (cf. Friedman 2013, pp. 131–132). Nevertheless, the distrust resulting from his failed therapy did not cease totally. And there were theoretical differences between them, as May's therapeutic system was based more on existential philosophy than on "neo-psychoanalysis." Buber and Tillich were more important for him than Fromm. There was clearly a rivalry between Fromm and May, even if they respected each other as colleagues who shared a "humanistic" theoretical background.

A third founder of Humanistic Psychology, to whom Fromm referred several times, was *Carl R. Rogers* (1902–1987). Rogers began as a practical theologian; after his studies he worked in child guidance. Rogers' ideas had some connection with psychoanalysis, especially with the theories of Otto Rank who emphasized the problem solving capacities of the client and the importance of trust and security in therapeutic relations. In his first book *Counseling and Psychotherapy* (Rogers 1941) Rogers described his method of "non-directive" counseling which later on was widened to *Client-centered Therapy* (Rogers 1951). Rogers was never trained as a psychoanalyst and he did not deal with "the unconscious" and "transference" or "counter-transference" in therapy, but his work was clearly stimulated by the ideas of Rank and Buber concerning "lived experience" and the relation of "Me and You" in therapy.

In 1961, Rogers published his most influential book *On Becoming a Person* (Rogers 1961), in which he delineated his theory of the "self" as an organizing principle in the process of forming and reforming one's own capacities and actualizing tendencies. He made evident that there are core conditions of successful therapeutic intervening: congruence, empathy and unconditional positive regard. Later on, Rogers joined the *Center for Studies of the Person* in La Jolla, California and began to work with *Encounter Groups* (Rogers 1970) and partnership training. As he was also engaged in school reform and peace movement, he was one of the most prominent proponents of Humanistic Psychology in the United States in the late twentieth century.

I don't know if Fromm and Rogers ever had a meeting, but we know that Fromm took note of Rogers' therapeutic method because he commented on it. Vice versa, there are no indications that Rogers' practical and theoretical work was directly influenced by Erich Fromm. But he was influenced by Maslow who was a follower of Fromm. Certainly, Rogers and Fromm had some congruent opinions on personal growth as an *actualization of human potential*. They had correspondent ideas about therapy as a *core-to core-*relationship of two adult persons without regression to early childhood. But Fromm did not know Rogers' method very well and his comments on client-centered therapy were superficial. Finally, he disapproved of group therapy.

There are some German Jewish psychoanalysts who got into contact with Erich Fromm in America before they joined the humanistic movement in psychology. During his formative period in Berlin, Frederick S. Perls (1893–1970) was a follower of Wilhelm Reich. At the beginning of the Nazi regime, he went to Amsterdam and some years later he lived in Johannesburg as a training analyst of the *South African Institute of Psychoanalysis*. Laura Perls (1905–1990) who in Frankfurt had studied Gestalt psychology helped Frederick Perls write *Ego, Hunger and Aggression* (1969 [1942]), a book in which Freud's libido theory was criticized. Fromm knew this book and partly agreed with its unconventional interpretation of psychoanalytic theory. When Fritz and Laura Perls came to New York he gave support to them by referring some patients to them. Fritz Perls later on was asked if he would work as a training analyst at the *William Alanson White Institute*, but Perls did not accept this offer. Together with his wife and Paul Goodman, he established the *New York Gestalt Institute* based on the premise that an effective therapeutic method should not work merely as a "talking cure", but in a more "holistic" or "organismic" way, including bodily expressions. In the late sixties, Fritz Perls was very famous as a group-therapist and a "guru" at the *Esalen Institute* in Big Sur/California. Erich Fromm would have heard indirectly about Perls' later career, but he never met him again.

Ruth C. Cohn (1912–2010) was another German psychoanalyst who met Erich Fromm in New York. Born in Berlin in a Jewish family, she left Germany in 1933 and went to Zurich. While studying psychology, she was married, got a child and undertook training in psychoanalysis. In 1941, she immigrated to the United States with her young family. The *American Psychoanalytical Association* gave her no permission to analyze adults because she had no medical certificate, so she could work only with children. Her husband tried to complete his medical studies by a psychoanalytical training at the *Washington School of Psychiatry* which later was called *William Alanson White Institute,* and his training analyst was Erich Fromm. As the family situation was complicated and tensions were increasing, Ruth Cohn wanted to have a therapeutic meeting with her husband and Fromm, but

Fromm refused to do so. Her husband's analytical training was broken off, and she was divorced. Ruth Cohn later said that Fromm should have been more helpful in this situation. Although discussions with the couple were unusual at that time, the *William Alanson White Institute* was progressive in testing new methods. In spite of Fromm's refusal – as she saw it – Ruth Cohn was very impressed by the writings of Harry Stack Sullivan and the therapeutic engagement of Clara Thompson, and she admired Frieda Fromm-Reichmann who was practicing "intensive therapy" with psychotic patients at *Chestnut Lodge*. The neo-Freudian orientation of the *William Alanson White Institute* was very influential on Ruth Cohn's own therapeutic work.

In the 1960s, Ruth Cohn took part in the humanistic psychological movement in the United States and in the German speaking countries in Europe. She worked with Fritz and Laura Perls, Carl Rogers, Carl Whitaker and Virginia Satir in the *American Academy of Psychotherapists* and described their meetings in a book entitled *Lived History of Psychotherapy* (Farau & Cohn 1984). Her special method is called *Theme-centered Interaction (TCI)* which means that a group engaged in a discussion should not work in a merely theoretical or academic manner but in a more personal or even "therapeutic" way. She said that Erich Fromm never participated in the meetings of the "humanistic" psychotherapists but his writings were very influential by spreading humanistic thinking.

Fromm's Comments on Humanistic Psychology

As I said in the beginning, Fromm in his own writings between 1955 and 1965 used to speak about "humanistic psychoanalysis". He avoided the term "humanistic psychology". This is significant because Fromm always was a psychoanalytical thinker. Other therapists who primarily were trained in psychoanalysis later on changed their theoretical foundations, as Fritz and Laura Perls did as they helped found "Gestalt" psychology. It is not surprising that Fromm, in one of his late manuscripts which were published under the title *The Art of Being*, said that he had given up the attribute "humanistic" because this word "had been used by a group of psychologists whose assumptions I could not share" (Fromm 1989a, p. 64).

In a paper written as addendum to "Freud's Model of Man and its Social Determinants" (Fromm 1970d) and finally published in 2013 (Fromm 1977g), Fromm pointed out that Freud's theory of human motivation merely was based on "physiological" needs and drives, whereas Marx and Goldstein thought that the "realization of human potential" was the driving force in human life. He added that Maslow had "popularized" this idea in *Motivation and Personality* (Maslow 1954). Some years later, Fromm's comments on Maslow were more critical. In *The Anatomy of Human Destructiveness* he said that Maslow, when he was enumerating human needs unsystematically, "failed to derive them from their origin in human nature" (Fromm 1973a, p. 222). According to his theory in *The Sane Society*, there are five existential needs rooted in human nature: relatedness, transcendence, rootedness, identity and frame of orientation (Fromm 1955a, pp. 30–66). All needs can be satisfied in an alternative mode: relatedness by love or narcissism, transcendence by creativity or destructiveness etc. Fromm believed that Maslow was right when he points out human life as an actualization of human potential, but he falsely neglected alternative possibilities in human nature. Fromm came to the conclusion that Maslow's concept of self-actualization was "degenerated" and the "humanistic" movement gave "simple answers" to existential questions by a mixture of "psychoanalysis, group therapy, yoga and other ingredients" (Fromm 1991h, p. 143).

Obviously Fromm did not know what to do with practical "humanistic" psychology, as it was done in group therapy and encounter groups. He said that he was "very skeptical" about group therapy because he would not like to speak about inner problems "when ten other people were present." Perhaps group therapy might be a chance for young people who have similar problems and are not suffering very much, but it "can never be equivalent to psychoanalysis" (Fromm 1991d, pp. 106–7). Fromm added, with a self-ironic wink, that he was "an individualist" and "somewhat old-fashioned" (ibid.).

Erich Fromm's notes on Carl Rogers indicate a critical distance, too, although there was some kind of companionship. In *The Anatomy of Human Destructiveness*, Rogers is quoted as an opponent to B. F. Skinner (Fromm 1973a, p. 34fn.). We may conclude that Fromm regards him as an ally to his own criticism of behavioristic thinking. Surely we can say that Fromm and Rogers had a great deal in common, for instance their thinking about the client's self-actualization and a living therapeutic relation, but they did not know very much about each other. In his late lessons called *Therapeutic Aspects of Psychoanalysis*, Fromm says that "client-centered therapy" is a strange terminology because *every* therapy has to be "client-centered" (Fromm 1991d, pp. 97–8). If the therapist is too narcissistic to be concentrated on the client's person, he or she should better give up their job. But this comment fails to hit the heart of the matter. The question is *in what way* the therapist is centered on the client's person. I think that Fromm is mistaken when he says that according to Rogers the therapist should be "like a mirror" (ibid.). In fact, the therapist shall answer by his own resonance expressing the client's original feelings, so that he can better understand his situation. Fromm, in contrast to Rogers, says that he "hears" something "different" from the client's saying that is unconscious and maybe opposite to his accessible feelings (Fromm 1991d, p. 98). He makes use of dreams and associations to get into contact with the client's unconscious feelings, while Rogers is concentrated on feelings which are present "here and now". Fromm's method seems to be more analytical and leading to interpretations, and Roger's method is more empathic. Ruth Cohn said that she never worked with a therapist who was more "gifted to emotional understanding by his mere concentration on the client" than was Rogers (Farau & Cohn 1984, p. 289).

Concluding Remarks

There is a note on Fromm in an article on the Internet concerning Humanistic-Existential Psychology, which seems to describe him very adequately. The author writes that Fromm "saw himself as neo-Freudian in orientation", but he also "occupied a key position on the periphery of the humanistic movement" (Pioneers 2015). Surely, Fromm never was in the center of the humanistic movement, but he was in a key position on its periphery.

There are three facts characterizing Fromm's role as a precursor of Humanistic Psychology. First, is his transition from Freudian drive theory to Sullivan's *interpersonal theory* of human development and therapy. In the appendix of *Escape of Freedom*, Fromm made it very clear that human beings are *primarily* social beings, and not secondarily dependent on others when they want their needs and drives to be satisfied, as Freud was thinking (Fromm 1941, p. 290). Secondly, he had a concept of *human growth and self-actualization* which should be supported by interpersonal relations (Fromm 1947a, pp. 219–226). Thirdly, he labelled his fundamental assumptions as *"humanistic" views* in ethics and psychology (Fromm 1964a, p. 15). These positions are common to all humanistic psychologists. Fromm was the first one who pointed that out.

It is not surprising that some founders of Humanistic Psychology developed some resentment towards Fromm in the 1940s because he was self-confident, direct and at times impulsive. Nevertheless, they made use of his writings and held them in high regard. On the other hand, Fromm did not maintain close ties with Humanistic Psychology. He underestimated the potential of Humanistic Psychology, because he was and remained a psychoanalyst. Some Humanistic Psychologists, like Fritz Perls, were trained as psychoanalytical therapists and gradually changed their theoretical framework. Fromm thought that psychoanalysis, with some "revisionist" modifications, was a better basis of therapy and superior to Humanistic Psychology.

There is an anecdote of a discussion between Carl Rogers and Martin Buber at the University of Michigan in April, 1957 that illuminates the core issues. Rogers said: "Man is basically good." Buber added: "And evil." I think if Fromm would have been present at the discussion, he would have taken sides more with Buber, and less with Rogers, and Humanistic Psychology today would benefit from this corrective.

References

Farau, A., Cohn, R.C. (1984). Gelebte Geschichte der Psychotherapie. Zwei Perspektiven. Stuttgart (Klett-Cotta).

Friedman, L.J. (2013). The Lives of Erich Fromm. Love's Prophet, with assistance from Anke M. Schreiber, New York (Columbia University Press).

Fromm, E. (1941a). Escape from Freedom. New York (Farrar and Rinehart).

Fromm, E. (1947a). Man for Himself. New York (Rinehart and Company).

Fromm, E. (1955a). The Sane Society. New York (Rinehart and Company).

Fromm, E. (1960a). Psychoanalysis and Zen Buddhism. In: D.T. Suzuki and E. Fromm: Zen Buddhism and Psychoanalysis. New York (Harper and Row), pp. 77–141.

Fromm, E. (1964a). The Heart of Man. Its Genius for Good and Evil. New York (Harper and Row).

Fromm, E. (1970d). Freud's Model of Man and Its Social Determinants. In: E. Fromm, The Crisis of Psychoanalysis. New York (Holt, Rinehart and Winston), pp. 42–61.

Fromm, E. (1973a). The Anatomy of Human Destructiveness. New York (Holt, Rinehart and Winston).

Fromm, E. (1976a). To Have Or to Be? New York (Harper and Row).

Fromm, E. (1977g). My Own Concept of Man. In: Fromm Forum (English Edition) 2013, 17, pp. 5–10.

Fromm, E. (1989a). The Art of Being (originated 1974–75). New York (Continuum), 1993.

Fromm, E. (1991d). Therapeutic Aspects of Psychoanalysis. In: E. Fromm. The Art of Listening. New York (The Continuum Publishing Corporation), 1994, pp. 45–193.

Fromm, E. (1991h). E. Fromm, The Pathology of Normalcy. Contributions to a Science of Man. New York (American Mental Health Foundation), 2010, pp. 109–146.

Fromm, E. (1992e). Man's impulse structure and its relation to culture (originated in 1937). In: E. Fromm, Beyond Freud: From Individual to Social Psychoanalysis. New York (American Mental Health Foundation), 2010, pp. 17–74.

Fromm, E. (1992g). Dealing with the Unconscious in Psychotherapeutic Practice (originated 1959). In: E. Fromm, Beyond Freud: From Individual to Social Psychoanalysis. New York (American Mental Health Foundation), pp. 83–122.

Goldstein, K. (1939). The Organism. A Holistic Approach to Biology derived from Pathological Data in Man.

Johach, H. (2009). Von Freud zur Humanistischen Psychologie. Therapeutisch-biographische Profile. Bielefeld (transcript).

Johach, H. (2012). Individualismus und soziale Verantwortung. Kontroverse Tendenzen in der Humanistischen Psychologie. In: J. Straub (Ed.). Der sich selbst verwirklichende Mensch. Ueber den Humanismus der Humanistischen Psychologie. Bielefeld (transcript), pp. 85–120.

Maslow, A. (1954).Motivation and Personality. New York (Harper & Bros.).

Maslow, A. (1962).Toward a Psychology of Being. Princeton (D. Van Nostrand).

Perls, F.S. (1969). Ego, hunger and aggression. The beginning of Gestalt therapy. New York (Random House).

Pioneers (2015). Pioneers of Humanistic-Exististential Psychology: Erich Fromm 1900–1980. – Retrieved from: http://www.google.de/url?sa=t&rct=j&q=&esrc=s&source=web&cd =4&ved=0CD4QFjAD&url=http%3A%2F%2Fmoe.machighway.com%2F~cliffor1 %2FSite%2FEXSupplementalReadings_files%2F6146252-Pioneers-of-Humanistic -Existential-Psychology-Unknown-3.pdf&ei=iIPLVKiQJcPKaMqggWg&usg=AFQjCN GUDzd90vJjCrS1SaxTKZ3cqB-hpg&sig2=UWKwCJfZ5NAmqXIWX_uxXw&bvm =bv.84607526,d.d2s (March 19, 2015)

Rogers, C.R. (1941). Counseling and Psychotherapy. Newer Concepts in Practice. Boston (Houghton Mifflin).

Rogers, C.R. (1951). Client-centered Therapy. Its current practice, implications, and theory. London (Constable).

Rogers, C.R. (1961). On Becoming a Person. A Therapist's View of Psychotherapy. Boston (Houghton Mifflin).

Rogers, C.R. (1970). Encounter Groups. New York (Harper and Row).

Male to Gay Male Emotional Communication and Erich Fromm's Notions of Being "Centrally Related" to the Patient and "Mature Love"

Luis Jimenez

Abstract: This paper presents a brief reflection of some aspects of previous qualitative research, carried out by the author, on an exploratory study of the negotiation of male to gay male emotional needs within a Frommian clinical approach. In particular, Erich Fromm's notions of "central relatedness" as well "mature love" are also discussed in an attempt to link the role of such notions as part of a developing clinical analytic work with gay men. Part of the research findings showed that whilst for gay men issues of central relatedness and love are of paramount importance, in practice, their most common practical approach to negotiate their emotional needs was actually through "friendships" and "friendliness" as a key relational paradigm that enabled them negotiate their emotional needs with other men. The implications of the salience of connecting Fromm's contributions to clinical analytic work to further develop clinical work with gay men and sexual diversity in general are also emphasized.

"Center to Center Relatedness"

When I did my psychoanalytic training in Fromm's approach to psychoanalysis, I soon became aware of Fromm's relational notion of "center to center relatedness" (Fromm 1992g) as a key relational paradigm for conducting effective analytic work. This notion, which is part of Fromm's few published attempts at systematically describing his clinical "technical" approach with patients, and which he also admitted it was difficult for him to put into words (ibid., p. 24), conveys a sense of being related to the patient from "center to center" (...) that is "to be interested. (...) We are interested in another person, we listen attentively, we listen with interest, we think about the person and yet the other person remains outside" (...) Fromm also noted:

> Just as hard as it is to actually put into words the difference between experiencing my 'I' as an Ego, as an object, and the experience of 'I' as an active subject of my powers, in which I forget about myself, although I am most fully myself in the process of expressing myself (ibid., p. 24).

In these lines, Fromm seems to be trying to emphasize that such form of relatedness is quite specific but cannot be simply put into words because, as he also stated: " either you experience it or you do not". Fromm also noted that "the most convincing and natural symbol of what I am talking about is actually sexual love, because in the act of sexual love, whether you are a man or a woman, you forget yourself" (Fromm 1992g, p. 24).

Fromm then further clarified that he was only referring to the sexual act in its symbolic form, only as a symbol, given that he did not believe there is a one to one relationship between sexual behavior and the general characterological pattern. In other words, Fromm is emphasizing the difficulty in neatly describing this process-experience: "So I would say there is no description, which is adequate, there is only a description of certain aspects" (Fromm 1992g, p. 24).

Fromm also stressed that such approach to clinical work with clients needed to be practiced: "For me personally, Zen Buddhism has been a very effective way to overcome an attitude of judging, which stems from my own biblical background" (Fromm 1992g, p. 25), for, as he also noted: "This is one of the most important therapeutic experiences which we can give to the patient, because at that moment the patient does not feel isolated anymore (ibid., p. 26).

Similarly, Fromm also connected his notions of center to center relatedness with his notions of love and mature love. For instance, as Kellner (1992, p. 122) also observed, in *The Art of Loving* (Fromm 1956a, pp. 27ff.) the phenomenon of love essentially manifests a desire for union with one's opposite gender and, taking up a rather essentialist position on love and gender, he claims that love best fulfills the need for union between the masculine and feminine poles. Continuing in the essentialist mold, Fromm describes the masculine character

> as having the qualities of penetration, guidance, activity, discipline, and adventurousness; the feminine character [is defined] by the qualities of productive receptiveness, protection, realism, endurance, motherliness (Fromm 1956a, p. 31).

Fromm does qualify this by indicating that: "It must always be kept in mind that in each individual both characteristics are blended but with the preponderance of those appertaining to 'his' or 'her' sex" (ibid.).

Furthermore, in *The Art of Loving* (1956a), Fromm's depiction of mature love further explained that:

> The homosexual deviation from the norm comes about because the polarized union does not take place, and as a result the homosexual suffers from the pain of his unresolved dividedness, which moreover reveals an inability he shares with the average heterosexual who cannot love. (Fromm 1956a, p. 31)

As Kellner (1992, p. 122) has also observed in relation to Fromm's views on mature love there is something of a naturalistic essentialism in his views of men and women, for he indicates that homosexuals can never attain the profound union of masculine and feminine in love because they are bonded to the same sex (Fromm 1956a, p. 28). Such views indicate that Fromm's perspectives on men and women were deeply shaped by the prejudices of his cultural milieu and that like other male Critical Theorists he tends to take a heterosexual male point of view in analyzing gender and sexuality.

When, as a psychoanalytic trainee, I was trying to find my way in developing my clinical approach, in particular to work with issues of male to gay male emotional communication, I would then read these very important technical observations from Fromm, and, also noticed that, to me, his notion of central relatedness, one way or other (e.g., conceptually, metaphorically, rhetorically, clinically) were also closely and continuously linked to his other key notions about "love" and "mature love" as he would describe these in *The Art of Loving* (Fromm 1956a). In this sense, I kept wondering how Fromm could simultaneously sustain an idea of the analytic encounter as "core to core" relatedness, while at the same time proposing an idea of love that seemed to refer to all but that actually does not really include a gendered perspective that allows the differentiation between various types of desire and forms of love. For example, in his essay "Sex and Character" (Fromm 1948a) which Fromm wrote in response to the Kinsey report on sexual behavior, he frames his notion of "core to core relatedness" in the context of connecting sexual behavior and feeling toward our fellow men as an important subject matter of ethical judgment. Taking as an example the incest taboo, as symbolizing in our culture the inability to "love the stranger", that is, a person with whom we are not "familiar" and not related by ties of blood and early intimacy, Fromm observed that:

> Only if one can love "the stranger", only if one can recognize and relate one-self to the human core of another person can one experience oneself as a human being, and only if one can experience oneself as a human individuality can one love "the stranger". We have overcome incest in the narrow sense of the word, as sexual relations between members of the same family, but we still practice incest not in a sexual but in a characterological sense, in as much as we are not capable of loving "the stranger". Race and nationalistic prejudices are symptoms of incestuous elements in our contemporary culture (Fromm 1956a, p. 142).

In this paper therefore, I will describe some of my attempts at trying to understand and use Fromm's work as part of my clinical work with male and gay male clients. Some of these efforts led me, years later, to write an empirical PhD thesis on these issues (Jimenez 2002). This work involved an average of fifteen hours of in depth face-to face interviews per research participant, with a group of young gay men in Spain. My research findings showed that for most of these gay men, "friendship and friendliness" (as opposed to "center to center relatedness") was actually a more common and key relational/survival paradigm. This realization became more apparent to these men once they became more aware that a "center to center" type of emotional connection with others, whilst indeed very needed and important, was often not that easy to achieve both in their interpersonal relations with their families and with other key significant persons as well as in therapy. Such difficulties in trying to maintain some form of meaningful relatedness with others was in part linked to all sorts of cultural, social and political issues, beliefs and prejudices surrounding their work and lives as gay men at the time.

However, for the purposes of this paper and in the context of this first International Erich Fromm Research Conference, I will only reflect on a few elements of this process, namely some of my attempts to also try to connect Fromm's notions of central relatedness with notions of male friendship and friendliness as a way to also reframe and develop further some of the application of Fromm's notions in clinical work with heterosexual and gay men.

Abstinence, Empathy and Friendship in the Analytic Session

The way in which the analytic setting is structured usually gives issues of friendship and friendliness a somehow frustrated character. There are two individuals, the patient and the unknown "other"; the latter has to forego self-revelation, and exclusively focus on the patient's intimate experiences.

In this setting, a partnership of two develops where the common focus of each is the "other", the phantom construct of the patient undergoing therapeutic exploration and, eventually, some understanding and healthy progression.

From the standpoint of friendship (cf. Nardi 1999, 2000; Price 1999) the analytic partnership is usually seen as an asymmetrical, frustrated friendship, given that the therapist role is not aimed at becoming a "friend" of the patient (Rangell 1963). The "proper" analytic attitude is aimed primarily at eliciting, in a "friendly" manner, the accessing of profound emotional experiences, thoughts and other repressed memories in the patient, which later will also become manifest in transferential reactions. However, this seemingly friendly attitude on behalf of the analyst also retains a rationalized authority-like fashion, which is usually not part of an ordinary friendship between two equals (Grotstein 1989).

Within Erich Fromm's work, the issue of friendship-friendliness as such and as part of a relational communication paradigm with gay male clients is not mentioned as comprising an essential element of the analytic setting, but rather, the friendly attitude of the analyst toward the patient is framed in terms of the quality of the relatedness that is established between the analyst and the patient, where issues of empathy are central.

Fromm's early accounts on theory and technique, in which he compares his position on these issues to Freud's and Ferenczi's, are contained in his article "The Social Determinants of Psychoanalytic Therapy" (Fromm 1935a).

Marco Bacciagaluppi, in his article "Fromm's views on psychoanalytic technique", comments on the issues raised by Fromm in his 1935 paper:

> In this essay Fromm discusses the attitude of tolerance towards the patient recommended by Freud. Fromm maintains that, in contrast to this conscious attitude, Freud and his followers had judgmental attitudes at an unconscious level which confirmed the social taboos in bourgeois society. (...) Fromm points out that although Freud did see the analytic situation as characterized by truthfulness, he considered it as 'a medical therapeutic procedure, as it had actually developed out of hypnosis.' (...) Through detailed references to Freud's papers on technique, Fromm stresses that Freud recommended that the analyst should maintain an attitude of 'coldness' and 'indifference', using the surgeon as a model. Tolerance is 'actually the only positive recommendation Freud gives for the analyst's attitude' (...) Fromm also criticized the aim of the analysis, as defined by Freud, of winning back a part of the patient's capacity for work and enjoyment. Fromm points out that Freud presents this capacity as a biological entity, although it is actually a social requirement. 'The analyst in this sense represents a model' (...) What Freud is really doing according to Fromm, is to present the capitalistic character as a norm and to define as neurotic anything which deviates from this. Towards the end of his discussion, Fromm views Freud's disapproval of deviant followers as indirect evidence of his basic identification with social norms. Fromm also discusses at length Ferenczi's half-hearted opposition to Freud. He quotes approvingly Ferenczi's recommendations to show the patient 'unshakable goodwill', to acknowledge the analyst's mistakes and to avoid replacing one super-ego with another. He point out that Ferenczi substituted the 'principle of indulgence' in place of the 'principle of frustration' (Bacciagaluppi 1989, pp. 228–9).

In fact, as Bacciagaluppi comments, in Fromm's first published paper in English in 1939 he contended that the detached attitude, in his opinion, was the most serious defect in Freud's technique. For Freud's model of the surgeon and his coldness in feeling confirmed that he not only recommended analysts not to express emotions, but also not to feel them. Fromm in contrast wrote:

> The basic rule for practicing this art is the complete concentration of the listener. (...) He must be endowed with a capacity for empathy. (...) The condition for such empathy is the capacity for love. (...) Understanding and loving are inseparable (quoted from Bacciagaluppi 1989, p 232).

In his later work, Fromm also based this capacity for empathy on his favorite Terence humanistic premise: "There is nothing human which is alien to me". Fromm applied this premise as particularly applicable to the analytic setting by stating that: "The analyst understands the patient only inasmuch as he experiences in himself all that the patient experiences" (Fromm 1960a, pp. 332–333).

Furthermore, Fromm wrote on the "productive relatedness between analyst and patient", of being "fully engaged with the patient, fully open and responsive to him/her" and of "center to center relatedness". Thus, while Fromm agreed with Freud that the aim of psychoanalysis is that of making the unconscious conscious, he also widened the aim of psychoanalysis. Fromm actually differentiated between the medical or therapeutic goal of psychoanalysis and the goal of "well-being", and later he stated that the aim of psychoanalysis is "to know oneself". According to Fromm, this would involve undergoing psychoanalysis not as a therapy but as an instrument for self-understanding, that is to say, an instrument for self-liberation, an instrument in the art of living.

These Frommian notions, in terms of the relational qualities of the analyst and the role of the patient, also included a more direct and active approach for both partners of the analytic relationship. Thus, when Fromm spoke about the complete concentration of the listener which requires his capacity for empathy, he suggested that the analyst should not merely adopt and conform to Freud's rationalistic attitude of "evenly hovering attention" whereby the analyst "must bend his own unconscious like a receptive organ towards the emerging unconscious of the patient."

In this Freudian setting, the analyst's unconscious becomes, according to Fromm, a mere rational instrument, which formulates responses primarily using the language of ideas, not of feelings. Fromm, in contrast, suggested that the analyst should respond with his/her whole self. He contended that Freud's concept of the detached observer was fortunately modified by Ferenczi, who postulated that it was not enough for the analyst to observe and to interpret, and that he also had to be able to love the patient with the very love which the patient had needed as a child.

Fromm also acknowledged the contribution of Sullivan's idea comparing analyst's work to doing "participant observation", but he suggested a different name for what analysts do and who they are -"observant participants." Fromm later developed this idea further and ended up with a notion of the empathic analyst who "understands the patient only inasmuch as he experiences in himself all that the patient experiences" (Fromm 1960a, p. 112).

This notion, which draws initially on Ferenczi's empathic notion, was framed by Fromm as a non-erotic loving attitude, that is the result of "brotherly love" and which is the most appropriate attitude for the analyst.

Fromm considered that the analytic relationship takes place on two separate levels; the analyst not only must offer him/herself as an object for transference and analysis, but he must also offer him/herself as a real person, for the analyst is not only the detached observer of transferential and countertransferential exchanges, but also participates in the relationship as a real person. The emphasis on the real relationship, together with the discouragement of dependency, further supports Fromm's preference for the real relationship with the patient rather than one mostly mediated by transference.

Similarly, Fromm considered that, among the basic elements in the personality of the analyst, should be the necessity of being a good companion to the patient, in the sense that he/she has to be able to do what a good mountain guide does, who does not carry the patient up the mountain but sometimes tells him/her "this is a better road" and sometimes uses his hand to give him a little push, but "that is all he can do" (Fromm 1960a, p. 113).

In his article "Causes for the Patient's Change in Analytic Treatment" (originated in 1964) Fromm observed:

> Regarding the personality of the analyst I just want to make a few points. I think Freud already made one very important point, namely the absence of sham and deception. There should be something in the analytic attitude and

in the analytic atmosphere by which from the very first moment the patient experience that this is a world which is different from the one he usually experiences: it is a world of reality, and that means a world of truth, truthfulness without sham – that's all that reality is. Secondly, he (the patient) should experience that he is not supposed to talk about banalities, and the analyst will call his attention to it, and that the analyst does not talk banalities either. In order to do this, of course, the analyst must know the difference between banality and non-banality, and that is rather difficult, especially in the world in which we live. (...) I think another very important condition for the analyst is the absence of sentimentality: one does not cure a sick person by being kind either in medicine or in psychotherapy. Now that may sound harsh to some of you, and I am sure I will be quoted for ruthlessness towards the patient, for lack of compassion and authoritarianism and what not. Well, that may be so. It's not my own experience of what I am doing or my own experience with a patient, because there is something quite different from sentimentality, and that is one of the essential conditions to analyze: to experience in oneself what the patient is talking about. If I cannot experience in myself what it means to be schizophrenic, or depressed or sadistic or narcissistic or frightened to death, even though I can experience that in smaller doses than the patient, then I just don't know what the patient is talking about. And if I don't make that attempt, then I think I'm not in touch with the patient. (...) I think the result of this attitude is that indeed one is not sentimental with a patient but one is not lacking in compassion, because one has a deep feeling that nothing that happens to the patient is not also happening in oneself. There is no capacity to be judgmental or to be moralistic or to be indignant about the patient once one experiences what is happening to the patient as one's own. And if one doesn't experience this as one's own, then I don't think one understands it. In the natural sciences you can put the material on the table and there it is and you can see it and you can measure it. In the analytic situation it is not enough that the patient puts it on the table, because for me it's not a fact as long as I cannot see it in myself as something which is real (Fromm 1991c, pp. 599–600).

But, when I worked with gay male patients and also when I was doing my research on their negotiation of their emotional needs with other men (gay or heterosexual) these seemingly useful notions of empathy, friendliness and even "brotherly love" as part of a more comprehensive analytic setting did not always seem to quite fit Fromm's own published work with gay patients, especially in relation to voicing the specific emotional needs and the importance of friendship for gay men in a less heterosexually framed and non-pathologizing analytic framework.

In Fromm's own published work there are very few references to issues of friendship and its relevance in working with gay male emotional experiences and so during my training it was unclear to me what Fromm's actual emotional attitude was in dealing with gay male patients. However, when I was writing up my PhD research work on gay male emotional communication, Rainer Funk – Erich Fromm's literary executor – who very kindly provided bibliographic support throughout my thesis, also gave me access to a letter written by Fromm himself in 1970 to an American gay male scholar who was seeking his advice in relation to his dealing with him being gay, which shows at least part of Fromm's attitude towards these issues:

Dear Mr. X,

Thank you for your letter, which clarifies your previous communication considerably. I think that one must distinguish between two or three problems, one of your tendency to relapse into conformity, one of the obsession to think "what if..." and thirdly, your being homosexual.

Let me begin with the last point. Whether one can call homosexuality a sickness is questionable. This form of sexual behavior is so stigmatized by society, or at least has been until recently, that many people suffer from this stigmatization rather than from the fact of being homosexual.

One has to consider also whether you feel unhappy with your homosexuality and want very much to change it (and not for the reason of public opinion) or whether you feel more or less well with it.

So many different factors can cause homosexuality that it takes many pages to enumerate them. Sometimes it cures itself in the growth of a personality and sometimes it is almost impossible to change. In between there are many gradations but all I can recommend at this point is to get over your apparent shame or embarrassment about this and to ask yourself and to analyze how you really feel about it and to get rid of the fear of what other people feel or might think.

Even provided homosexuality is to be considered neurotic, it is certainly not a malignant symptom. There are many heterosexual people who are more unloving and remote than many homosexuals are. Don't misunderstand me please, in the sense that I am praising homosexuality. I happen to think that it is somewhat of a handicap in living, all I am suggesting is that you analyze your own horror of it and with it your own feelings of guilt, of dependency, or lack of standing on your own feet not only physically but psychologically and morally. (...)

As to your obsessional symptom, you can look at it in two ways: (a) what is the reason that you torture yourself by turning on these obsessional doubts. Is it escape, a kind of masochistic performance, self-hate or what else, and (b) how does this obsessional mechanism comes into existence? That is something one could analyze and a skilled analyst might possibly deal with that in a few weeks. But one cannot do it by letter.

As to the problem of your danger of conforming, what can I say? To swim against the stream is exceedingly difficult and if you do suffer, as most people do today, from a lack of experience of yourself as your own center, then the course of the temptation is very great. If you have the possibility of seeing an analyst in the X area then I would suggest Dr. X.

Now about reading, I recommend to get a book which I edited together with a philosopher, The Nature of Man, published in a paperback by the Macmillan Co. I suggest you read it as a whole and then you see what kind of philosopher interests you, and perhaps after you have read it you write me something about your response.

With best wishes,
Sincerely Yours,
Erich Fromm

One of the things that struck me while reading this letter is how Fromm acknowledges that, in his experience, there are many heterosexuals who are more remote and unloving than many homosexuals are. Yet as has been previously mentioned, in *The Art of Loving* Fromm contended that

the homosexual deviation is a failure to attain a polarized union, [by which he meant the biological union between the sperm and the ovum as being the basis for interpersonal creativity] (...) and "thus the homosexual suffers from the pain of never resolved separateness, a failure, however, which he shares with the average heterosexual who cannot love (Fromm 1956a, p. 34).

Thus, throughout my psychoanalytic training (Frommian orientation), it was very unclear to me why Fromm would actually state that only the biological union between sperm and ovum is the only valid basis for interpersonal creativity, and how a pregnancy involving a man and a woman does in itself guarantee a creative relationship also in the psychological sense.

Similarly, it was also unclear to me how the love between two men either straight or gay would be depicted by Fromm as conveying merely a failure of heterosexuality as well as their "pain of never resolved separateness". Why is a heterosexual man who cannot or does not want to get involved in a pregnancy with a female partner be considered by Fromm as a failure, and as suffering in the same way as gay men also from never resolved separateness? Why is the emotional and sexual union between two men depicted by Fromm as only conveying a failed reproductive heterosexual union and not as one capable of being a creative relationship in a psychic sense? What is the "handicap in living" that he sees in being a homosexual man?

On the one hand, in this letter, Fromm states that the idea of homosexuality as a sickness is questionable, but at the same time, by telling this gay man that, in his perspective, homosexuality is somewhat of a "handicap in living", I wondered: what part of Fromm's "whole self" (to use Fromm's own terminology) is actually responding to this gay man in the way he does? This, for me, seemed to be inconsistent with his often quoted Terence principle that "nothing human is alien to me" and that we all, as human beings in Western society, have not overcome our xenophobic and incestuous prejudices, for we have not learned to accept the other and the different in us as ours.

I was also aware that some therapists, especially male ones, possibly still feared adopting a friendly open attitude with a gay patient, because doing that could directly point to and question taken for granted assumptions about masculinity, emotional intimacy and homophobia; and so some analysts may still tend to refrain from becoming more relaxed and friendly. They could also be very self-conscious and repress their own countertransferential homophobic and/or heterosexist reactions towards issues dealing with male desire and intimacy. Adopting a genuinely open and friendly stance could be experienced by some almost as a compromise formation, i.e. a compromise between voice and silence that is often enacted through the deployment of merely "tolerant" or "politically correct" attitudes in order to appear as an "open" analyst, which really only highlights the obscurity with which these crucial issues used to be dealt with in Fromm's times (and perhaps still are dealt with this way nowadays?) in some analytic settings.

These anxieties and ambivalence during my psychoanalytic training remained key topics for further detailed reflection in clinical and supervision sessions, which may have further contributed to the perpetuation of con-tradictory and "pseudo-empathic," "analytic" attitudes, that often ensued when analysts expressed either Fromm's or other similar notions – mainly through biased/partly digested countertransference reactions – while working with gay patients; although obviously these aspects of our clinical practice are not ordinarily researched and published.

These type of questions were not addressed in Fromm's written work and since there are not, for the moment -so far as I am aware- published papers detailing Fromm's own work with gay men, and given also that there is not a reply by the gay man of the letter in reply to Fromm's own views on the "handicap in life quality" that he saw in being a homosexual man, these issues remained as unclear during my training as a psychoanalyst. Conse-quently, I felt a mix of ambiguity and sense of oddness in trying to integrate and incorporate all the very insightful views on Fromm's central relatedness and how to position myself in relation to Fromm's views on this matter, and what to do in my analytic practice with gay men.

I never met Fromm in person nor could I have ever met him to ask him all these questions, since he died way before I even started my psychoana-lytic training. Given I am also a gay person, such issues remain important for my clinical and my psychoanalytic teaching and research work. When I would share these questions with my professors, my supervisors, my work colleagues and in my own analysis at my training institute (IMPAC) which was funded by Fromm himself, the answers I would get ranged from sym-pathetic acknowledgement of the issues I was raising, to the need to also be more proactive and further develop and incorporate into our training these same issues by developing ad-hoc seminars and specific training as part of the training program. I am also aware that, before and after the offi-cial declassification of homosexuality as a pathological entity from the older versions of the DSM and later also from the ICD back in 1974 and later on since 1990, although it still retained several purported mental disorders (Hoffman et al. 2000) there has been a whole range of clinical and research efforts to address some of these issues ever since (American Psychoanalytic Association, 1992, 2000; American Psychological Association 2005; Glass-gold & Iasenza 2004; King et al 2007; Levounis et al 2012; Savin-Williams et al 2004; Szymanski & Kashubeck-West 2008; Russell 2006). I am also aware of more recent efforts to further revise the International Classification of Diseases so that there is finally a removal of sexual orientation-related disorders from the health care classification system. If successful, this move will contribute to the improvement of healthcare in the LGBT community, as The World Health Organization is currently revising the 10th edition of the ICD for the new edition due in 2017.

Finally, I am also aware of a range of very useful research and clinical work has been developed worldwide ever since, and hopefully, I would like to think work with gay male clients nowadays using a Frommian approach may have a clearer reframing and focus.

In my work with gay and straight men on how they negotiate their emotional needs as men, I still find myself very influenced by Fromm's very insightful notion of central relatedness, and I can see clearly how understanding and loving go hand in hand in professional clinical work not only with men but also with any patient in general. However, the difference for me is that nowadays I simply do not equate the notion of central relatedness with Fromm's notion of mature love in an exclusive heterosexual sense. In this way, I manage to also incorporate Fromm's insightful ideas into my clinical and teaching work. Therefore, the occasion of this first Fromm International Research Conference seems to me the perfect place to still highlight these issues in the collegial spirit to continue researching and developing Fromm's valuable work in contemporary clinical analytic work.

References

American Psychoanalytic Association. (1992). Position statement: Homosexuality (Rev.). Retrieved from: http://www.apsa.org/sites/default/files/2012%20Position%20State ment%20on%20Sexual%20Orientation%2C%20Gender%20Identity%2C%20 and%20Civil%20Rights.pdf (April 4, 2015).

American Psychoanalytic Association. (2000). Position statement on reparative therapy. Retrieved from: http://www.apsa.org/ABOUTAPSAA/POSITIONSTATEMENTS/REPARA TIVETHERAPY/tabid/472/Default.aspx (November 30, 2007).

American Psychological Association. (2005). Resolution on sexual orientation and marriage and resolution on sexual orientation, parents, and children. American Psychologist, 60, 494–496.

Bacciagaluppi, M. (1989). Erich Fromm's View on Technique. Contemporary Psychoanalysis 25 (2), pp. 227–243.

Fromm, E. (1935a). The Social Determinants of Psychoanalytic Theory. International Forum of Psychoanalysis. Oslo (Scandinavian University Press) 9 (3–4, October 2000), pp. 149–65.

Fromm, E. (1948b). Sex and Character. The Kinsey Report Viewed from the Standpoint of Psychoanalysis. In: D.P. Geddes and E. Curie (Ed.). About the Kinsey Report. New York (The New American Library), pp. 301–311.

Fromm, E. (1956a). The Art of Loving. An Inquiry into the Nature of Love. New York (Harper and Row).

Fromm, E. (1960a). Psychoanalysis and Zen Buddhism. In: D.T. Suzuki and E. Fromm. Zen Buddhism and Psychoanalysis. New York (Harper and Row), pp. 77–141.

Fromm, E. (1991c). Factors Leading to Patient Change in Analytic Treatment [originated 1964]. In: E. Fromm. The Art of Listening. New York (The Continuum Publishing Corporation), 1994, pp. 15–41.

Fromm, E. (1992g). Being Centrally Related to the Patient (originated 1959). In: R. Funk (Ed). The Clinical Fromm. Personal Accounts and Papers on Therapeutic Technique. Rodopi (Amsterdam & New York), 2009, pp. 7–37.

Fromm, E. (1994a). Love, Sexuality, and Matrarchy. About Gender. Ed. and with an introduction by Rainer Funk. New York (Fromm International Publishing Corporation), 1997.

Glassgold, J. M., & Iasenza, S. (2004). Introduction: Lesbians, feminism and psychoanalysis: The second wave. Journal of Lesbian Studies, 8(1/2), 1–10.

Grotstein, J. (1989). Of Human Bonding and of Human Bondage. The Role of Friendship in Intimacy. Contemporary Psychotherapy Review, 5 (1), pp. 5–32.

Hoffman, L. et. al. (2000). Homophobia. Analysis of a "Permissible" Prejudice. A Public Forum of the American Psychoanalytic Association and the American Psychoanalytic Foundation. In: Journal of Gay & Lesbian Psychotherapy, 4 (1), pp. 5–53.

Jimenez, L. (2002). Entendidos. A Study of Emotional Communication amongst Gay Men of Barcelona. Unpublished PhD Thesis. Goldsmiths College, University of London.

Kellner, D. (1992). Erich Fromm, Feminism, and the Frankfurt School. In: M. Kessler and R. Funk (Ed.). Erich Fromm und die Frankfurter Schule. Tuebingen (Francke Verlag), pp. 111–30.

King, M., Semlyen, J., Killaspy, H., Nazareth, I., & Osborn, D. (2007)A systematic review of research on counseling and psychotherapy for lesbian, gay, bisexual, & transgender people. Leicestershire, England: British Association for Counseling & Psychotherapy

Nardi, P. (1999). Gay Men's Friendships. Invincible Communities. Chicago (The University of Chicago Press).

Nardi, P. (2000). Gay Masculinities. Thousand Oaks (Sage).

Levounis,P., Drescher, J., Barber, M.,(2012) The LGBT Casebook. American Psychiatric Publishing

Price, J. (1999). Navigating Differences. Friendships Between Gay and Straight Men. New York (Haworth Press).

Rangell, L. (1963). On Friendship. Journal of the American Psychoanalytic Association, 11, pp. 3–54.

Rubin, L. (1985). Just Friends. New York (Harper & Row).

Russell, G.M. (2006), Different ways of knowing: The complexities of therapist disclosure. J. Gay & Lesbian Psychotherapy, 10(1):79–94

Savin-Williams, R. C, & Cohen, K. M. (2004). Homoerotic development during childhood and adolescence. Childand Adolescent Psychiatric Clinics of North America, 13,529- 549.

Szymanski, D. M., & Kashubeck-West, S. (2008). Internalized heterosexism: Clinical implications and training considerations. The Counseling Psychologist, 36,615–630.

Inspired by Erich Fromm

Sandra Buechler

Abstract: This paper discusses some reasons Erich Fromm's thinking is essential in analytic treatment and training today. Nevertheless, one frequently encounters resistances when presenting his ideas to candidates in psychoanalytic programs in the USA. Trends toward relativism have diluted the sense of purpose in psychoanalysis. This makes Fromm's passionate dedication to human freedom and self-actualization crucial. But, ironically, the postmodern sensibility often contributes to a rejection of Fromm's legacy. The paper offers suggestions about how Fromm's thinking, with its emphasis on authenticity, directness, intensity, full presence, and passionate purposefulness, can be fruitfully integrated into an interpersonal psychoanalytic approach.

When I began preparing for the conference that led to this book, I had a most unusual experience, which brought to mind questions about how Erich Fromm's influence operates. As I researched, I had the sensation that many of the concepts I have developed in the last thirty years or so were more indebted to Fromm than I had realized. Of course, I always knew I had been influenced by his thinking, but not to this extent. I would have expected it to be somewhat disconcerting to find out that "my" ideas were not very original, but, actually, it was immensely pleasurable. I felt as though I had, at last, found my home.

How does Fromm's influence work?

What does this say about how Fromm's influence works? How did I come to write about ideas that I thought were mostly my own, but were really so heavily indebted to him? Had I read these ideas years ago, squirreled them away, and "discovered" them without realizing where they came from? Or, imprinted by Fromm himself, did my analytic parents, my training analyst, supervisors, and teachers convey more of his ideas than I consciously knew, during my candidacy at White? I am aware that I read Fromm hungrily in college, and ever since. But when I wrote my papers and books I didn't realize how much of a debt they, and I, owe to him.

I think we can learn from this about how Fromm's influence generally works, although perhaps my experience is somewhat idiosyncratic. A few examples will have to suffice. I offer here a few of the ideas I now see were very similar to Fromm's in order to encourage a larger discussion of the contemporary relevance of Fromm in psychoanalysis.

1. *The way the analyst focuses is an expression of values, intentions, and feelings:* Reading Rainer Funk's paper, "Direct Meeting" I was struck by his description of how much Fromm expressed in his way of establishing eye contact. In Funk's words, "His gaze corresponded to his way of being interested in my inner life, my soul" (Funk 2009, p. 61). This reminded me of an experience of my own. As a candidate I volunteered to present a case to Alberta Szalita, in an all-day-long conference at the New York William Alanson White Institute. The day was unforgettable and formative for me. The unwavering intensity of her focus on me was palpable. I felt as though her eyes reached into my innermost being, and saw into me as one can see into clear water, to its very depths. Many years later, writing (Buechler 2008) about focus as an interpretation, and an expression of values, affects, and intentions, I credited Szalita as the source of my view about what focus can express. But now I wonder whether the idea really came from Fromm, and how that may have happened. Did Fromm influence Szalita to communicate through her focus, and did she then pass this on to me? I also wonder whether reading and absorbing Fromm helped prepare me to pick this up from Szalita. And I know that many who trained me were profoundly affected by Fromm. Perhaps they all contributed to pri-

ming me for the impact Alberta Szalita's riveted and riveting focus had on me, about thirty-three years ago, on a day I will never forget.

2. *The importance of attempting to "heighten the immediate reality and concreteness of the situation" as the patient talks about an experience:* Reading an article by David E. Schecter (2009), as I prepared for the conference, felt truly uncanny. He describes some of Fromm's methods for connecting the patient with immediate experience in words that recall to me some of the advice I have so frequently given supervisees. I can't count the number of times I have told them that it doesn't have much impact to develop a fine, abstract theory about the patient, with the patient. Experience is what changes people. I didn't realize how closely this connects with Fromm's teachings.

3. *The centrality of the analyst's courage:* Ruth M. Lesser (2009) described Fromm as expressing how much courage it takes to be an analyst. This has been a central theme in my own writing. Of course I knew Fromm wrote a great deal about human courage, but I didn't realize how much he referred to the analyst's courage.

4. *The importance of embracing the paradox that human beings express ourselves in characteristic patterns, and nothing human is alien to us all, but we are also very much individuals:* In much of Fromm's work I now see the effort to recognize patterns that recur in human beings, but also acknowledge each person's unique individuality. Holding the tension between these viewpoints has always challenged me in teaching the course on diagnosis at White. For years, I saw myself as finding my own way to deal with Sullivan's ideas about personality patterns and individuality. I didn't realize how closely my understanding of this issue follows that of Fromm.

5. I was certainly aware that *Fromm's emphasis on values* directly influenced my own writing, especially in my book (Buechler 2004) on *Clinical Values.* I knew that his attitude of cherishing truth deeply affected me. But when I have asked supervisees to voice "inconvenient truths" and become "radical truth tellers" I have not always consciously connected these ideas with Fromm, although I think I could have done so.

6. My belief that clinicians should aim for *relatively non narcissistic investments in our patients* now seems to me not unlike Fromm's way of ex-

pressing "central relatedness" (Fromm 2009, p. 18). In his words: "Then I do not think about myself, then my Ego does not stand in my way."

7. Consciously, I thought it was Edgar Levenson's influence that made me so careful at the outset of a treatment not to promise more than I know the work can deliver. But now I read Fromm's words, "When you come to me, I will be completely open to you, and I shall respond with all the chords in myself which are touched by the chords in yourself. That is all we can promise, and that is a promise we can keep" (Fromm 2009, pp. 26–27). Again, I ask, was Edgar influenced by Fromm? Or, did Fromm, Edgar, and I have some similar experiences that led all three of us to take this position?

8. My thinking about the *role of empathy in treatment* has evolved a great deal over time. I think it has circled closer to Fromm's. I love what Harold Davis wrote about Fromm. "His directness was a means of being in touch with a person without physically touching; the essence of empathy" (Davis 2009, p. 87).

Fromm's passionate promotion of passion in treatment was certainly known to me, and directly affected my work. His privileging of the power of human feeling has always very much appealed to me. His thinking about hope, his open promotion of biophilia, his distaste for cliché, canned interpretations, and sentiment, his compassionate humanism, his willingness to take positions, and stand up for what he believed in, his championing of freedom, have moved me all my adult life. What has surprised me, over these last months, is the specificity with which Fromm's ideas antedated so many of my own. I know that I did not consciously, deliberately fail to note how much Fromm affected my clinical writing and practice. I will continue to think about how this happened, because I believe that if I could understand it better, I might be able to contribute something about the process by which our analytic ancestors live on in us.

Teaching Fromm Today

In thinking about these issues, I posted a request on William Alanson White's listserv for reflections about experiences of teaching Fromm's work to candidates and others today. This is hardly a scientific inquiry. But I did get some interesting replies. Here are a few excerpts.

A graduate of WAWI wrote that when he taught at a small institute and assigned a paper by Fromm, "it's amazing how relevant and prescient his work still is..." But then he asked whether I think Fromm has become out of fashion.

Someone who is still a candidate and teaches a practicum has assigned students to read chapters from *The Art of Loving* (Fromm 1956a) and *The Sane Society* (Fromm 1955a). Her own attitude about Fromm is very positive, but she offered these thoughts about her current masters level counseling students. "They are all 'digital natives' and don't know life without a cell phone, texting, email, social media, etc." She goes on to say that this technology often does little to foster intimacy with others. "Some students can barely articulate a definition of interpersonal intimacy." She went on to speculate that Fromm's ideas about directness and his approach, with its immediacy of experience, may be particularly challenging for some students in their twenties today who are not familiar with, or comfortable with direct, immediate interpersonal interaction.

Emily Kuriloff, a graduate of WAWI, has recently published a book, *Contemporary Psychoanalysis and the Legacy of the Third Reich*. In it, she offers an appreciation of Fromm's contribution, in its humanism and ideas about the individual's agency, but also some criticism of his thinking. In her own words, Fromm leaves us a "choice" between going in the exalted direction of humanism or the much less exalted direction of surrendering to authority. She asks, "Where is Fromm's tolerance for the grey area that is so characteristic of a psychoanalytic awareness, the struggle back and forth that is itself transformative, and moreover, the mourning for what is always lost by virtue of one's having chosen?" (Kuriloff 2014, pp. 19–20). Kuriloff speculates that Fromm's WWII experiences contributed to this polarizing tendency.

Personally, I have noticed a trend in candidates toward looking for theory that tells them precisely how to react in sessions with their patients. They don't find this kind of concrete direction in Fromm. Some, as a result, reject his writing as too complicated, theoretical, and abstract. Perhaps ironically, others view him (along with the other interpersonalists) as too directive and superficial. In other words, candidates who want a script to read in sessions dismiss him as concentrating too much on underlying causes, but classically inclined analysts reject him for not working deeply enough.

Cortina's paper in this volume summarizes some of Fromm's contributions, and suggests some ways that current research in attachment theory, evolutionary sociobiology, and other recent research efforts could be utilized to correct some of Fromm's errors and supplement his theories. I think these ideas could prove fruitful.

If I had to name the most significant reason for a decline in Fromm's presence, at least, in my analytic neighborhood, it would be the meteoric rise in popularity of the relational school of psychoanalysis. Relational psychoanalysis is immensely attractive, particularly to the younger attendees at conferences in New York, and, increasingly, in many other locations throughout the world. It is hard to capture the reasons for its powerful appeal, but I do believe that (on the whole) the more an analyst identifies with the relational school the less likely they are to accord an important place in their thinking to Fromm.

A paper by Jay Frankel (1998) titled "Are Interpersonal and Relational Psychoanalysis the Same?" illustrates the relationalists' attitude. Frankel suggests that interpersonal analysts like Fromm harbor "a lingering positivism," even when we disavow it. In other words, we think we know objective reality, in contrast to the patient, and we feel relatively free to express it, without worrying about the patient's readiness to hear it, because of our confidence in the therapeutic value of authentic communication. In his words "the interpersonal approach creates what is often a challenging and confronting atmosphere in the treatment room, with a focus on clarity, directness, and honesty in communication" (Frankel 1998, p. 487).

I think many who hear this today, most especially those who are young and in an early stage of their careers, associate interpersonalism in general, and Fromm's writings in particular, with an authoritarian, patriarchal, old-fashioned, moralistic approach. In contrast, they see relationalists as, in his words, "more likely to be comfortable being 'playmates' and going with the flow of mutually, unconsciously directed self-state shifts, involving both patient and therapist" (Frankel 1998, p. 494). In other words, as I hear it, relationalists are better able to level the playing field between themselves and the patient, more aware of their own vulnerabilities and willing to admit them, more comfortable with being pulled into enactments, and better able to bear uncertainty. When I was in school, Fromm strongly appealed to a young person's appetite for freedom from authoritarian control, and for human equality and human dignity. Now those very appetites are motivating some to turn against Fromm! It is a remarkable phenomenon.

There is something hollow and sad, to me, in the effort many analysts expend to find a theory that will make them popular. Of course this occurs in every school of thought. But I have been to many meetings and conferences that rapidly become competitions for which analyst can reveal greater shortcomings, thus proving that he or she is actually the most humble. Grandiosity peaks through the thin veneer of humility. Some analysts try to prove that they have no vision of health. They just follow the patients' lead, expressing no values of their own. To me, this is the postmodern edition of the classical analyst's neutrality. On the contrary, I think we can't function without the inspiration that conviction can lend us. Passionate desires for our patients can center us and imbue our work with stamina and courage.

But my main argument when analysts profess they are not motivated by their own values is that I don't believe it is true. How we understand health shapes what we focus on, remember, and comment on, whether we know it or not. There is no such thing as value free treatment. When a patient spends five hours a day in hand washing rituals, do we make no judgment? Do we have no hopes, no direction? I believe that some who have dismissed Fromm for his passionate advocacy of living fully don't realize how they convey their own priorities in every session, in their tone, in their focus, in their manner, in their bodies, and in countless other ways. Personally, I think I give patients a better chance to know themselves if I am direct and open about my values so we can discuss the issues. Otherwise patients will still be influenced, but, perhaps, without an ability to formulate their own opinions. I see all analytic treatments as dialogues about what it means to live life as a human being. This dialogue is not always spoken in words. It may be expressed in the interest the clinician takes in the patient, the commitment to the work, or in many other ways.

What can we reply to some of the relationalist's other criticisms? In a discussion of Frankel's paper, Irwin Hirsch made the significant point that Frankel seems to be saying that Fromm was not empathic and nurturing.

If one speaks in terms of empathy, Fromm was empathically attuned to patients' wishes toward making the most of themselves, toward the desire for self-actualization. It is inaccurate, however, to conclude that Fromm was unaware of regressive and passive longings. (...) Fromm's attunement to symbiotic desires was acute and motivated him toward efforts to help patients combat the temptations of prolonged and comfortable regressive experience (Hirsch 1998, p. 506).

As for the issue of the common humanity of patients and their analysts, Hirsch says:

Many current analysts tend to view analyst and patient as more alike and human than otherwise. Hierarchies based on perceived respective health have diminished. Fromm and his socialist, humanistic colleagues should get partial credit for this shift in hierarchical attitude (Hirsch 1998, p. 521).

Again, I would suggest, values that Fromm championed, in his time, are being used as arguments against his merit now.

My Personal Integration of Fromm and Sullivan

I feel that Fromm provided, and still provides, a much needed antidote to the more removed aesthetic of the Sullivanian expert. For Fromm we are here, in our profession and, more generally, on this planet, to promote life passionately. I need Fromm. Very often he lends me courage and stamina. He provides a forceful ballast against my becoming too much of a cool, Sullivanian observer. On the other hand, I understand that Fromm can persuade me to be too forceful an advocate for fuller living, perhaps making it hard for some of my patients to express their depressive, hopeless, regressive urges.

Fromm is so different from Sullivan, that it is hard to integrate them into an interpersonal point of view. And yet, I think it is ultimately very fortunate that we can draw on both Sullivan and Fromm. Where Sullivan warns us to beware of evoking too much anxiety in the patient, Fromm challenges us to challenge our patients. Fromm exhorts us to have the courage to leave our own comfort zones, in order to help patients outgrow constraints that have limited their ability to fully live. He can be seen as an advocate of tough love. He adds a note of urgency. Clinicians should have a sense of purpose about our mission to overcome stagnation. Only honesty and directness are respectful toward the patient. Fromm had a vision of who the patient could become, and a passionate dedication to facilitating growth, as he understood it.

Sullivan's caution can be tempered by Fromm's zeal, and vice versa. Where Sullivan worried about whether a patient was ready to hear something, Fromm confronted, believing the truth really sets us free. I agree with Hirsch when he says that, "Analysis without a touch of Fromm's authenticity and romanticism is a far less rich enterprise" (Hirsch 1998, p. 510).

I have often played with the idea that Sullivan and Fromm recapitulate the old tension between Apollonian and Dionysian cultures. The cooler, more cognitive Apollonian approach emphasizes achieving greater clarity about one's interpersonal patterns, while the hotter, more passionate Dionysian empowers movement and accelerates change. For me, at least, one without the other is incomplete. And a re-examination within psychoanalysis of Fromm's often unacknowledged influence might help keep the tensions in productive dialogue.

References

Buechler, S. (2004). Clinical Values. Emotions that Guide Psychoanalytic Treatment. Hillsdale (Analytic Press).

Buechler, S. (2008). Making a Difference in Patients' Lives. Emotional Experience in the Clinical Setting. New York (Routledge).

Cortina, M. (2014). Fromm's View of the Human Condition in Light of Contemporary Evolutionary and Developmental Knowledge. Paper Presented at the International Erich Fromm Research Conference, Berlin, June 28, 2014 (enclosed in this book).

Davis, H. (2009). Directness in Therapy. In: R. Funk (Ed.). The Clinical Erich Fromm. Personal Accounts and Papers on Therapeutic Technique. Amsterdam-New York (Rodopi), pp. 85–91.

Frankel, J. (1998). Are Interpersonal and Relational Psychoanalysis the same? Contemporary Psychoanalysis 34, pp. 485–501.

Fromm, E. (1955a). The Sane Society. New York (Rinehart and Winston Inc.).

Fromm, E. (1956a). The Art of Loving. An Inquiry into the Nature of Love. New York (Harper and Row).

Fromm, E. (2009). Being Centrally Related to the Patient. In: R. Funk (Ed.), The Clinical Erich Fromm. Personal Accounts and Papers on Therapeutic Technique. Amsterdam-New York (Rodopi), pp. 7–37.

Funk, R. (2009). Direct meeting. In: R. Funk (Ed.), The Clinical Erich Fromm. Personal Accounts and Papers on Therapeutic Technique. Amsterdam-New York (Rodopi), pp. 59–71.

Hirsch, I. (1998). Further Thoughts about Interpersonal and Relational Perspectives. Contemporary psychoanalysis 32, pp. 501–539.

Kuriloff, E. (2014). Contemporary Psychoanalysis and the Legacy of the Third Reich. History, Memory, Tradition. New York (Routledge).

Lesser, R. (2009). There Is Nothing Polite in Anybody's Unconscious. In: R. Funk (Ed.), The Clinical Erich Fromm. Personal Accounts and Papers on Therapeutic Technique. Amsterdam-New York (Rodopi), pp. 91–101.

Schecter, D.E. (2009). Awakening the Patient. In: R. Funk (Ed.), The Clinical Erich Fromm. Personal Accounts and Papers on Therapeutic Technique. Amsterdam-New York (Rodopi), pp. 73–79.

Understanding Social Motivation for Encouraging Children's Development

Social Character Studies in Mexico

Sonia Gojman de Millán and Salvador Millán

Abstract: A group of psychoanalysts led the Seminario de Sociopsi-coanálisis to broaden their clinical perspective gained through work-ing with patients in the setting of a private practice. In this paper we describe participatory action research initiated by a community. We started by interviewing impoverished and economically disadvan-taged children, first from a miner's village and later on from a center for children living in the streets. A study on *Attachment and Social Character* of mothers and children as well as the systematic appraisal of the unconscious motivations in the individual's responses to the Social Interpretative Questionnaire are presented. We strive to bring the findings of our social character studies back to the communi-ties themselves. Our purpose is to support or foster possibilities for initiating participatory community-based action projects, aimed at transforming the quality of life and to confront the difficulties and obstacles that emerge on the path to change; furthermore we hope that our research will help to stimulate the development of childcare health policies.

When the inhabitants of Mexico City were shaken by the 1985 earthquake, people throughout the city – from every socio-economic class – responded in a spirit of impressive solidarity. Even though the official political leader-ship was largely absent, on the grass root and local level people still helped each other. These spontaneous reactions revealed existing latent psycholog-ical resources of the population that came to light in the face of the crisis.

Since then, the Seminario de Sociopsicoanalisis SEMSOAC has developed projects for working with people who live in difficult conditions, who usually don't have a chance to benefit from the deep understanding of human motivation that psychoanalysis can offer. We strive to bring the findings of our social character studies back to the communities themselves. Our aim is to support and foster possibilities for initiating participative action projects aimed at transforming the quality of life. Ultimately, our purpose is to help people confront the difficulties and overcome obstacles that emerge on the path to change.

We have been working on participatory community-based action projects for almost thirty years. Our efforts started by interviewing impoverished and economically disadvantaged children from a miner's village in order to study the development of their social character traits. The initial study was theoretical but led us to develop a nine-year participatory community-based action project.

A "Monthly Weekend Open School" in a Miner's Village

After we had applied the social interpretative questionnaire SIQ to the community, we started a monthly weekend project of an "open" community school, exploring the possibilities for change through the participatory action project.[1] We collaborated with the students, teachers and parents of the school, and gradually opened to the whole community. Community leaders, men and women, mining leaders, and members of the miners' union gradually became involved (See Gojman de Millán 1993).

The "open school" among many projects staged theater plays written and performed by the children and hosted handicrafts and painting classes for children and adults. A mothers' group formed to discuss everyday trepidations. This was later combined with a group that started separately, a handicrafts workshop group that would creatively recycle simple "waste" materials and used them to make things with practical applications. The

---

1 Actively participating were Cristina Barros, Carlos Diaz, Tomás Granados, Verónica Espinosa, Carolina Politi, Rafael Ruiz, José Escurdia, Galia Eibenshutz, Sara Burguete, Filiberto Valdiviezo and Sergio Cházaro.

two workshops were combined at the women's request; they felt their husbands would be less likely to object to their Sunday attendance if they returned home with something visible, material, and useful that they had done during the day. The men developed a silver smithing workshop, and finally an Alcoholics Anonymous self-help group was started.

After we discovered some children had hearing and vision problems that impeded their school progress, a Semsoac' member who was a language and hearing therapist worked with children with hearing impairment. We also initiated consultations with mothers that taught them to measure and recognize visual acuity and vision related problems in children. The mothers then volunteered to evaluate the children from the surrounding schools. The miners' union contributed a bus to bring children who needed glasses to Mexico City. We found a hospital that diagnosed them for a very low cost, and we contacted private schools willing to collect eye-glass frames discarded by their students and then donate them to the children who needed glasses.

Our work consisted of visiting the community once a month on Sundays and staying there for about eight hours. We worked with community members who positively surprised us with the extent of their willingness to do voluntary work. Members of our Seminar held two-hour weekly discussions, in which we examined each member's monthly activities during the community visits. At the end of our visits we discussed the meaning behind the children's paintings and the plays they created and performed in. We also examined our own emotional reactions and their meaning in relation to the community's gender battles, poverty and hopelessness.

We compared the initial children's responses to the questionnaire to those administered three years later (Gojman de Millán 1991). The outcome was unexpected. The children were apparently describing less – or experiencing less – maltreatment by their mothers. In the next session of the mother's workshop we asked them if they thought there had been any changes in their homes. Their straight answer was, "We have lowered the volume of our shouting at the children quite a bit, but what has definitely stopped has been the hitting."

Two of the mothers attended a congress on community action projects, where they shared their experiences. They said, "Through the doctors' visits we discovered that our problems were not only ours, that other women were facing the same kinds of problems and that we were not alone." Later on it was established a local "House of Culture," a government institution created to give space to the community for cultural related activities. An abandoned house, that was redecorated and rebuilt, was used for that purpose. In the end our participation came to a close, when political authorities took over the running of the building.

The Project "Artists for the Streets" in Mexico City

We started this project by administering the SIQ to the children and young adults who attended a "center for street children" (Gojman de Millán and Millán 2004; 2008). We also administered it to workshop instructors and board members of that center, in order to orient our participation in supporting the nonprofit organization called "Artists for the Streets," that was working with children at risk of becoming homeless or already being street children (Artistas por la Calle 2005).

Many children and young people survive on the streets of Mexico City by cleaning car windshields at traffic lights. The project made a permanent space, in an extremely poor suburb, for creative artistic activities for children and youth. It was open and available for them during the day for any time they wanted to attend. At this center the young people and children could do their laundry and get some food. They could also get involved in a variety of workshops in plastic arts, music, working with leather, and performing. When the staff members realized some of the attending girls were pregnant and others were adolescent mothers who carried their babies tied to their backs, they started a special room for babies and some of the mothers participated together in a singing lullabies workshop. Some of the children took part in a workshop fostering a circus spectacle that marched through and performed on the streets. A digital animation project using figurines made of plasticine clay entered into an international competition.

Every two weeks in two periods – in 2005 and in 2012 – SEMSOAC members participated in supervision and psychological counseling of the staff, and creating a safe space for therapeutic listening, which often took the form of crisis intervention. We held weekly meetings with the youth and separate with children. Since attendance was voluntarily, it was sporadic.

Some children came once and never returned. At every session we dealt with emotionally very difficult topics, which sometimes caused bizarre, aggressive and frantic behavior on the part of the attendees. The therapists dealt with the emotionally intense experiences in a once a month supervision sessions.

Social Character and Attachment in Mexico City and in an Indigenous Village[2]

In 1997 we started a research project based on two psychoanalytic theories that share an emphasis on relational processes that forge the psyche: the social character theory of Erich Fromm and the attachment theory of John Bowlby. The project (Gojman and Millán 2000, 2003) studied dyads (of mothers and their infants) from a middle class, urban, mestizo population in Mexico City, and from a rural, peasant Nahua population, from the Mountains of northern Puebla (Sanchez and Almeida 2005). The latter one was in collaboration with a forty-year-old community development project known as PRADE.

We shared our results with two institutions in Mexico City: the breast-feeding league and a natural delivery-training center that collaborated with us. In Puebla with PRADE in it's efforts to enhance the quality of life in the community and to support the local human rights commissions in the area, by providing them with the knowledge on the common manifestations of the psychological effects of mental fragmentation, resulting from adults and children's traumatic experiences.

Care giving quality and social character

We identified the prevailing social character orientations of mothers in the urban and rural groups and sorted them into five socio economic groups:

---

2 We are grateful to Teresa Villarreal for her constant support of the Seminario de Sociopsicoanalisis Attachment research project. We are also grateful to PRADE "Proyectos de Animación y Desarrollo" for the opportunity to participate with their organization which has conducted a permanent community development project of the Nahua.

middle-upper/upper, middle-middle, middle-lower, impoverished and very impoverished. Mothers' responses to the interview were written down and typed up by the interviewers. The typed interviews were then scored on the six scales specifically developed by SEMSOAC (Gojman de Millán et al. 2008) for detecting mothers' unconscious attitudes towards their lives and towards their children: (a) sensitivity to emotional needs, (b) lovingness, (c) joy of life, (d) attention to everyday survival needs of their children, (e) passive hopelessness and (f) active-violent hopelessness. We observed whether the individual responses showed a mother to be productive or unproductive and compared the two groups. Within each group, we juxtaposed the responses of the five socio-economic levels (Gojman de Millán et al. 2013).

As we read through the entire interview transcript, we identified and marked the elements that pointed to particular traits as defined in each scale, sometimes in subtle, yet meaningful ways. We then listed them together and we arrived at a point score ranging from 1 to 5, taking into account all the responses and representing them with one number.

Results

(1) The receptive orientation was predominant in both groups. In the urban group the receptive-productive orientation prevailed, and in the rural group the receptive-unproductive orientation was the most common.

(2) We found a statistically significant relationship between mothers' attitudes toward life and toward their children and their basic character orientation – whether productive or unproductive, looking at the urban and rural groups combined[3]

(3) We found significant relationships between basic productive-unproductive tendencies in mothers and the blindly coded attachment assessments[4]. Our results confirm that mothers with productive ori-

---

3 N = 70. Chi-squares varied between 45.316 and 4.015 df = 1, with a probability between .000 and .048.

4 We used three attachment instruments: The Adult Attachment Interview AAI (George et al. 1985; Gojman de Millán 2004; Gojman et al. 2014), videotaped Quality of Care Mother-infant interacting dyads (Ainsworth et al. 1974), and the Strange Situation laboratory procedure SSP (Ainsworth et al. 1978).

entations have babies with a "secure attachment pattern" more often than mothers with unproductive orientations [5]. Productive mothers tend to be more sensitive/cooperating in the treatment of their babies[6] and more frequently present Autonomous-secure transcripts as scored blindly on the Adult Attachment Interview.[7]

(4) Our results suggest that the daily material conditions of existence are closely related to the shared character orientations, especially the tendencies toward productive or unproductive orientations in the very impoverished mothers. Mothers fitting into "a very impoverished category", in the rural group, were almost exclusively unproductive even compared to mothers from the "impoverished" category, the vast majority of whom were productive. The contrast was even greater when we compared the very impoverished to the other socio-economic levels studied in this rural group.

On the other hand upper-middle and upper class mothers in the urban group were more likely to be rated unproductive than middle-lower and middle-middle income groups, although the results did not reach statistical significance. This finding points to our consideration that being able to count on economic resources beyond those required to fulfill basic, everyday life needs does *not* necessarily lead to a better quality of life or care giving. This is seldom consciously acknowledged.

We conducted a follow-up assessment of the children who were assessed on attachment when they were infants and are now eight or nine years old (Gojman, Millán, Gonzalez and Sanchez, in press). This follow-up involved a clinically systematized appraisal of their responses to the SIQ adapted for children from six to fourteen years and their responses to pairs of stories resembling those of Piaget's designed to explore cognitive moral reasoning, such as asking children to draw their family, and comment on their family history.

We are in the process of developing scales equivalent to the six, five-point scales used to score the mother's attitudes towards their lives and their chil-

---

5 Chi square = 7.349 df = 1 p < .006
6 Chi square = 16.144 df = 1 p < .000
7 Chi square = 10.353 df = 1 p < .001

dren. We code the children's responses to the SIQ on: joy of living, sensitivity to their own and others feelings and emotional needs, harmonious relations with parents and other authorities, sibling rivalry, passive hopelessness and active-violent hopelessness.

Conclusion

Our work as members of the Seminario de Sociopsicoanálisis[8] was aimed to widen our clinical perspective by applying socio psychoanalytic insights to understand the difficulties of everyday life of people in their community including, in particular, the raising of children in economically difficult conditions. We strove to participate in shared initiatives with these groups to develop practical, health enhancing, and developmental strategies for their children. The people have found these efforts stimulating. In the course of our study we realized that people are able to overcome hopelessness and resistance to change as they examine the common civil voluntary and creative alternatives available for them. We consider these findings a parallel benefit to the one offered to the individual in clinical practice when becoming aware of their unconscious motivations.

The SEMSOAC has made progress developing a methodology for conducting empirical studies of social character of women and children in México. The design of our research allowed us address and work with very diverse socioeconomic populations. We have developed special scales to detect character traits of mothers, and we are in the process of developing similar scales for their children. Individual responses to the SIQ have proven to be useful for discovering the effects of unconscious motivation accompanying people in their everyday life concerning behaviors that affect their children's development. Systematically assessing social character can become an excellent tool for stimulating the development of socially re-

---

8 The members who initiated the projects were: Sonia Gojman de Millán, Salvador Millán, Patricia González, Guadalupe Rosete and Guadalupe Sánchez. The members who joined over time were: Ana María Barroso, Carlos Sierra, Angélica Rodarte, Esmeralda Arriaga, María Eugenia Guzmán, Luz Angélica Quintero, Lucina Montes Juan José Bustamante, Mauricio Cortina, José Breton, Belinda Cruz, Isabel Cruz, Patricia Hurtado and Gerardo Hernández.

sponsible health policies, taking psychoanalytic insights out of therapeutic individual context into the social world as Fromm himself did so effectively.

Note

We are grateful to Bob Duckles who helped us editing this manuscript.

References

Ainsworth, M.D., Bell S.M. and Stayton D.J. (1974). Infant-Mother Attachment and Social Development. "Socialization" as a Product of Reciprocal Responsiveness to Signals. In: M.P.M Richards (Ed.). The Integration of a Child into a Social World. London (Cambridge University Press), pp. 99–135).

Ainsworth, M.D., Blehar M.C., Waters E, and Wall S. (1978). Patterns of Attachment. Hillsdale (Lawrence Erlbaum Associates).

Artistas por la Calle (2005). Nadie se dio cuenta nunca. Testimonios. Otras voces. México (CONACULTA).

George, C., Kaplan, N. and Main, M (1985). Adult Attachment Interview. Unpublished manuscript (3rd Edition 1995), Berkeley (Department of Psychology, University of California).

Gojman de Millán, S. (1991). Revaloración del cuestionario interpretativo en una comunidad minera después de tres años de trabajo comunitario (diseño experimental pre y post aplicación a la experiencia de trabajo de grupo). The Final Report to the National Council of Sciences and Technology (CONACYT) México.

Gojman de Millán, S. (1993). A Sociopsychoanalytic Intervention Project in a Mexican Mining Village. In: Wissenschaft vom Menschen – Science of Man. Yearbook of the International Erich Fromm Society, Muenster (Lit Verlag).

Gojman de Millán, S. (2004). Sistemas de calificación y clasificación de la entrevista de apego adulto (versión 7.2, agosto 2010). Unpublished manuscript, Semsoac México. [= Translation to Spanish of M. Main et al. (2002). The Adult Attachment Scoring and Classification System (Version 7.2, July 2003). Unpublished manuscript. Berkeley (Department of Psychology, University of California).

Gojman de Millán, S., and Millán, S. (2001). Attachment Patterns and Social Character in a Nahuatl Village. Socialization Processes through Social Character Interviews and Videotaped Attachment Current Methodology. In: Fromm Forum (English Edition). 5. (Self-published), pp. 38–42.

Gojman de Millán, S., and Millán, S. (2003). Integrating Attachment and Social Character Approaches to Clinical Training. Case Studies from a Mexican Nahuatl Village. In: M. Cortina and M. Marrone (Ed.). Attachment Theory and the Psychoanalytic Process. London (Whurr Publishers), pp. 179–203.

Gojman de Millán, S., and Millán, S. (2004). Identity in the Asphalt Jungle. International Forum of Psychoanalysis, 13 (4), pp. 254–263.

Gojman de Millán, S., and Millán, S. (2008). The AAI and its Contribution to a Therapeutic Intervention Project for Violent Traumatized and Suicidal Cases. In: H. Steele and M. Steele M. (Ed.). Clinical Applications of the Adult Attachment Interview. New York and London (The Guilford Press), pp. 297–319.

Gojman S., Millán S, Sanchez G and González P. (2008). Escalas para calificar a madres o cuidadores principales en las respuestas al cuestionario de carácter social. Manuscrito no publicado. Registro Público México, SEP_INDAUTOR # 032008-120511185300-01.

Gojman S., Millán S., Sanchez G., and González P. (2013) Caregiving and Social Character. Towards a systematization of the Clinical Assessment of Social Character Traits and Their Relation to Mothers' Care Giving Quality in Urban/Rural Mexican Samples. In: Fromm Forum. (English Edition) 17. pp. 35–46.

Gojman de Millán, S. Millán S., Carlson, E., González, P., Guzmán, M.E., Hernández, G., Rodarte, L.A., Sánchez, F., and Sánchez, G. (2014). La entrevista de apego adulto en Español. In: B. Torrez et al. (Ed.). La Teoría del Apego, investigación y aplicaciones clínicas. Psimática Editores. Capítulo 7.

Gojman de Millán, S., Millán as., Sanchez, G., González, P. et al. (in press). Attachment Research in Urban and Rural Mexico. Clinical and Social Implications. In: Ch. Herreman and S. Gojman de Millán (Ed.). Attachment across Clinical and Cultural Contexts. Accepted for publication by Routledge, the UK.

Sanchez, M.E. and Almeida, E. (2005). Las veredas de la incertidumbre. Relaciones interculturales y supervivencia digna. Puebla (Universidad Iberoamericana Puebla, Lupus Magíster).

Fromm's View of the Human Condition in Light of Contemporary Evolutionary and Developmental Knowledge

Mauricio Cortina

> Men work together, I told him from the heart,
> Whether they work together or apart
>
> *Robert Frost*

Introduction

Except for Freud, no other psychoanalyst made such an explicit, concerted and systematic effort to grapple with the human condition as Erich Fromm. Fromm called his view of the human condition his "concept or model of man" to get away from static and ahistoric concepts of human nature often used to justify power and privilege of the few over the many. Fromm saw human nature as being fluid and dynamic and always in the making, but also thought that some conditions are inherent to human nature and universal. He conceived the fluid and changing conditions as historical in nature and the inherent conditions as existential to the human condition. He first articulated this view in *Man for Himself* (Fromm 1947a) and later on in slightly different forms in many of his other books.

I will revisit here Fromm's view of the human condition and propose a different interpretation of the biological origins of the human condition. Fromm believed that human nature came about as a result of the combined effect of the relative loss of instinctual equipment and the dramatic enlargement of the neocortex. With the support of recent evolutionary and development literature I propose that human evolution was driven by a need to cooperate in ways that far surpass what is observed among our closely related ape relatives. Our instinctual equipment was not lost, as Fromm believed, but was gradually transformed to support the cooperative infrastructure of our species.

Fromm's view of the human condition

Over the expanse of almost fifty 50 years, a particular view of the human condition was a unifying theme in Fromm's work. He integrated a humanistic outlook (Cortina, in press) with a very bold biological speculation that he first expressed fully in *Man for Himself* (Fromm 1947a).

> The first element that differentiates human from animal existence is a negative one: the relative absence in man of instinctive regulation in the process of adaptation to the surrounding world. (...) The less complete and fixed the instinctual equipment the more developed is the brain and therefore the ability to learn. The emergence of man can be defined as occurring at a point in the process of evolution where instinctive adaptation has reached a minimum. But he emerges with new qualities which differentiate him from the animals: his awareness of himself as a separate entity, the ability to remember the past and visualize the future, and to denote objects and acts as symbols; his reason to conceive and understand the world; and his imagination through which he reaches far beyond the ranges of his senses. Man is the most helpless of all animals, but this very biological weakness is the basis for his strength, the prime cause for his development and his specifically human qualities (Fromm 1947a, p. 48).

The dynamism between minimal instinctual equipment and a large brain capable of learning, creating symbolic representations, and imagining past, present, and future produces several existential dichotomies that are built into the fabric of our humanity. Self-awareness, reason and imagination have disrupted the "harmony" which characterizes animal existence. Their emergence has made man into an anomaly, into a "freak of nature". As Fromm eloquently put it:

> He is part of nature, subject to her physical laws and unable to change them, yet he transcends the rest of nature. He is set apart while being a part; he is homeless, yet chained to the home he shares with all creatures. Cast into the world at an accidental place and time, he is forced out of it, again accidentally. Being aware of himself, he realizes his own powerlessness and the limitations of his existence. He visualizes his own end: death. Never is he free from the dichotomy of his existence: he cannot rid himself of his mind, even if he

should want to; he cannot rid himself of his body as long as he is alive – and his body makes him want to be alive. (Fromm 1947a, p. 49)

Adaptive flexibility was driven
by the need to cooperate during human evolution

Fromm was correct in identifying the dramatic expansion of the neocortex among our hominin ancestors as one of the major characteristics of our species, but Fromm was mistaken in thinking that there was no continuity between our species and other animals (we had "lost our home in nature" as he put it poetically) and that social character and cultural influences were the substitute for these missing instincts. We cannot fault Fromm for making this assumption. The prevailing concept of instinct when he was developing his view of human evolution was of instincts as fixed action patterns that were relatively immune to environmental influence, but this view of instinct does not hold true for social animals. This became clear when Bowlby developed attachment theory.

Bowlby showed that infants and young children's instinctive need for protection and care was exquisitely responsive to the quality of their mothers (instinctive) need to provide care and protection (Bowlby 1969; 1988). Another reason why Fromm thought our instinctive nature had become greatly reduced was based on the ethnographic data that supported the view that cultural rather than biological influences had a decisive role in molding human personality and human motivation. The relative lack of instincts in determining culture and personality was also supported by Fromm's Marxist version of the culture and personality school, in which the mode of production plays a fundamental role in determining social organization and social character types. This link was shown convincingly in the major research project in the Mexican village that Fromm undertook in collaboration with Michael Maccoby (Fromm & Maccoby 1970b). If a relative lack of instincts does not explain the adaptive flexibility in response to ecological and socioeconomic conditions, how else can we account for this remarkable adaptive flexibility?

I propose the following alternative explanation based on new research on human evolution that has accumulated in the last few decades. Severe

161

climate changes that took place in Africa during Pliocene -Pleistocene transition 2.5 to 1.8 million years ago (the beginning of the ice ages) produced prolonged droughts in Africa that drastically reduced the forest and river ravine environments that had been home to our hominin ancestors for the past four million years. These changes forced our hominin ancestors to find a mode of living in the open African savannah. To survive in this new environment they had to learn to cooperate at higher levels in order to scavenge for high caloric foods left behind by other predators and to protect themselves from these predators. The need for high levels of cooperation put strong selective pressures on the development of prosocial motives, particularly helping others, and wanting to share activities, as well as developing more effective modes of communications. Rather than having lost our instinctual equipment, the social instincts we share with other Great Apes (attachment and care giving bonds between mothers and young infants, affiliations of various sorts to group members, sexual bonds, and dominance hierarchies) have been *transformed* to support the highly cooperative nature our species (Suddendorf 2013; Tomasello et al. 2012).

To be clear it is not that chimpanzees and bonobos, our closest ape relatives, do not help or cooperate with their group members in many ways, it is that they cooperate and help almost exclusively from an individual-need perspective, and prosocially only when the costs of collaboration are not great. Collaborating from a "we" perspective in which the group members' collective welfare becomes important is *uniquely human* (Hermann et al. 2007; Tomasello & Carpenter 2005; Tomasello et al. 2012). The other major difference between human cooperation and the other Great Apes is one of scope. With the exception of territorial scouting expeditions and infrequent group hunting for small prey, chimpanzee collaboration is primarily limited to dyadic interactions (Mitani 2006; Tomasello et al. 2012). In contrast, human collaboration ranges from small-scale dyadic interactions to large-scale multinational forms of cooperation, and everything in between (for reviews see Suddendorf 2013; Tomasello 2009; Tomasello et al. 2012).

Prosocial instincts coevolved with socio-cognitive abilities to imitate, learn and communicate with others and with changes in the timing of development. Changes in the timing of development produced an extended childhood and adolescence, the most prolonged of any known species.

This extended period of development allowed our hominin ancestors time to assimilate the social competencies, cultural knowledge and communicative abilities necessary to collaborate effectively in small, but complex nomadic hunter gatherer groups (Bjorklund & Rosenberg 2005; Konner 2010).

I will begin describing this alternative model of human evolution by elaborating on what Fromm got right: the dramatic expansion of the neocortex (encephalization) among our hominin ancestors in the last two million years.

The social brain
and the expansion of the neocortex in primates

Robin Dunbar has been one of the main proponents of the most recent view that the enormous expansion of the brain – which in primates is centered on the neocortex – is primarily the result of the need of primate brains to compute complex social relations (Dunbar & Shultz 2007). A basic statement of the social brain hypothesis is that:

> Individuals living in stable social groups face cognitive demands that individuals living alone (or in unstable aggregations) do not. To maintain group cohesion, individuals must be able to meet their own requirements, as well as coordinate their behavior with other individuals in the group. They must also be able to defuse the direct and indirect conflicts that are generated by foraging in the same space (Dunbar & Schultz 2007, p. 1337).

The competing hypothesis is that the expansion of the neocortex in primates is driven by the need to solve ecological problems. Finding ways to survive in specific environments is of course essential, but the social brain hypothesis postulates that solving ecological problems is achieved by developing closer social bonds and collaborative strategies. In contrast, the earlier ecological explanations assume that these problems are solved individually through trial and error.

Two measures of social complexity, group size and the formation of long-term sexual bonds ("monogamy") have a very strong correlation with the expansion of the neocortex.[1] Correlation is not causation, and the strong correlation between neocortical expansion and social complexity could be a coincidence. To get an overall picture it is necessary to consider the energetic demands required by the brain to compute life in complex societies and solve ecological problems. Brain energy costs are eight to ten times more per unit mass than those of skeletal muscles. This large expenditure competes with other demands, such as the vast energy resources needed by mothers to feed immature infants. But constraints placed on brain size by these energy demands do not tell us what type of selective pressures drove the evolution of large brains in the first place. Using a sophisticated path analysis, Dunbar and Schultz (2007), show that these selective pressures are explicitly social.

In the next section I show how these explicitly social selective pressures are causally connected with the emergence of very advanced forms of cooperation during the course of human evolution.

Three steps toward the evolution of high levels of cooperation and prosocial motives

Michael Tomasello and his group at the Max Plank Center for Evolutionary Anthropology in Leipzig (Tomasello et al. 2012) and Benoit Dubreuil at the Université du Québec à Montréal (Dubreuil 2010) have proposed that the evolution of advanced forms of cooperation emerged in more than one

---

1 Brain size has to be measured in *relation* to body size to have any meaning. This measure is called the *encephalization quotient* (EQ). An EQ of 1.0 is the expected ratio between brain size and body size of a cat taken as the prototypical mammal. An EQ of less than I means that brain size is smaller than excepted and an EQ of more that 1.0 means that brain size is larger than expected in relation to body size. The EQ of humans is the largest of any land animal, 7.6, compared to 5.3 of dolphins, 4.8 of capuchin monkeys (that are the only other primate that is a full fledged cooperative breeder) and 2.5 for chimpanzees. Primates have achieved enlarged brains by expanding the neocortex, so a useful juxtaposition in primates is to compare the size of the neocortex in relation to the rest of the brain, the *neocortex ratio*. In anthropoid primates the mean social group size (a measure of social complexity) increases in proportion with the neocortex ratio. That is, the relative neocortex size in primates increases with mean group size. Together these two measures of brain expansion, the *encephalization quotient* and the *neocortex ratio* support the social brain hypothesis.

step during human evolution. Based on Tomasello's and Dubreuil's work, I propose a three-step model.

Step I:
Obligatory Cooperation and the emergence of "emotional modernity" (Pliocene-Pleistocene transition about 2.5 million to approximately 500,000 years Before Present (BP))

Climate produced severe droughts reduced the forest and river-ravine environments in many parts of Africa. To survive in the new open environment, small bands of nomadic foragers were forced to become dependent. Some refer to this step as the African Savannah hypothesis. The first Homo species fully adapted to this new environment is *Homo erectus* (*Homo ergaster* when referring to its African origin) appearing 1.8 million years BP. Home erectus is tall, with an anatomy adapted to walk and run long distances and a brain almost twice the size of previous *Australopithecine* species.

When meat was taken back to home base from scavenging expeditions or by hunting small prey, the meat would have had to be distributed to all the members of the group (probably no larger than thirty individuals) if collaboration and interdependence between group members was to work. This step required suppressing the dominance hierarchies which are the main form of social organization that characterizes primates and many other mammals. In species in which dominance hierarchies exist, high-ranking males and females use their power to claim preferential access to scarce food resources and sexual mates over lower ranking individuals.

According to Christopher Boehm the transformation toward a more egalitarian social structure was achieved by an inversion of dominance, in which group members acting as a collective exert dominance against alpha males (or females) who try to establish dominance over others (Boehm 1999). To support his hypothesis Boehm did a systematic examination of ethnographies of extant nomadic hunter-gatherer groups studied in the past eighty years all over the world. There are many cultural differences among these nomadic foragers that live in very different geographic environments, but they are all egalitarian when it comes to sharing food, particularly food obtained from hunting big game. As long as the groups remain nomadic, they will punish, shame and ostracize individuals who do not share or take advantage of this system of sharing.[2]

In researching material for *The Anatomy of Human Destructiveness* (1973a) Fromm became aware of the shift from dominance hierarchies to cooperation. Fromm quotes Service (Service 1966), who participated in a famous 1966 symposium *Man the Hunter* that gathered the leading experts of the day on hunter-gatherers:

> Hunter-gathering bands differ more completely from the apes in the matter of dominance than do other types of human society. There is no pecking-order based on physical dominance at all, nor is there any superior-inferior ordering based on sources of power such as wealth, hereditary classes, military or political office. (...) It seems that the most primitive human societies are at the same time the most egalitarian. This must be related to the fact that because of rudimentary technology, this kind of society depends on cooperation more fully most of the time than any other. Apes do not regularly cooperate and share, human beings do – this is the essential difference (Fromm 1973a, pp. 140–1).

An important part of step I is what Sarah Hrdy calls the emergence of "emotional modernity" (Hrdy 2013). By emotional modernity Hrdy means the beginning of a system of care for infants and young children in which other members of the group assist mothers in the care and feeding ("provision-

---

2 Some anthropologists specializing in hunter gathering societies have raised serious questions of using extant nomadic foragers as "models" to understand human social organization during the whole Paleolithic era (Kelly 2013). This criticism is valid, but somewhat muted by two factors. First, despite many cultural differences observed among nomadic hunter–gatherers around the world, the fact that they all remain fiercely egalitarian suggests that a nomadic foraging mode of subsistence favors an egalitarian-cooperative social structure. Second, and more importantly, the recent discovery in a cave in South Africa shows that the tools and artifacts found in the cave dating 40,000 years ago are almost identical to tools used by the San people who have maintained their nomadic hunter-gatherer form of subsistence in South Africa to the present day (d'Errico et al. 2012). This is the first direct evidence of cultural continuity among nomadic foragers that can now be traced backed to the late Stone Age in Africa. This is not the whole span of the Paleolithic of 2 million years, but is still quite impressive. At the very least this finding suggests that the life styles of extant nomadic hunter-gatherers can still be used cautiously in order to shed light on the evolution of Homo sapiens that first appear 200,000 years BP in Africa.

ing") of infants and young children, technically called cooperative breeding. Hrdy uses the term emotional modernity as a contrast to the cognitive and behavioral modernity[3] that appears much later in rudimentary form in Africa 100,000 years BP and more fully in Europe 60,000 years later.

We are the only Great Ape whose mothers allow others to take care or feed their infants (Hrdy 2009). This exclusive form of maternal care seen in the great majority of primate species is probably due a very high incidence of infanticide (Hrdy 1999; 2009). Only ten percent of species of birds and mammals have some type of cooperative care that combines different degrees of feeding (provisioning) and taking care of infants, technically called cooperative breeding (Hrdy 2009; 2005). This "it-takes-a-village-to-raise-a-child" type of sociality had profound effects on human evolution. Freed from the exclusive care and provisioning of infants, mothers could assist in foraging activities and provide more food for other members of the group. Being able to wean their babies earlier, hominin mothers were able to increase their fertility rates, roughly double that of chimpanzees. Finally being exposed to multiple adults and caregivers greatly accelerated infants' abilities to interact collaboratively and communicate with others, a phase that paved the way for the development of language and the ability to understand the minds of others (Hrdy 2009).

Another important step toward emotional modernity was the emergence of long-term pair bonding. With the exception of the gibbons (sometimes called "the small ape") humans are the only Great Ape whose males establish long-term pair bonding (monogamous) relations with females. In all the other Great Apes, sexual relations are limited in duration and are promiscuous. In the case of the gentle bonobos sexuality is used to smooth out social tensions of all kinds – which is why some call bonobos the "make love not war" ape (de Waal 2013). According to Chapais, the effects of establishing monogamous relations had cascading consequences for human evolution.[4] As males began to recognize their offspring as "one of their own",

---

3 Cognitive and behavioral modernity is defined by the use of symbols, sophisticated tools such as poisoned arrows, the use of nets to catch fish and traps to hunt animals, art in the form of cave paintings and sculpted figures, body paintings and musical instruments.

4 Chapais is not claiming that monogamy is normative among humans. Cultures have successfully adopted polygamy (one man many wives) and more rarely polyandry (one

they became more tolerant of other males, particularly males that developed long term relations with their daughters. Residence patterns began to change. Rather than leaving their natal group, females stayed in their local group and maintained these connections even when their siblings moved to a neighboring group. Greater familiarity among kin and non-kin begins to create social networks in surrounding groups (Apicella 2012).

The development of these social networks allowed for cooperative exchanges within and between groups of nomadic foragers. A study by Hill et al. of nomadic foragers across the world that included thirty-seven nomadic groups and a total 5067 individuals provided further evidence that monogamy does produce the type of social relations described by Chapais (Hill et al. 2011). Pauline Weissner, an anthropologist who lived for several years with the San people (commonly referred to as the "Bushmen") in the Kalahari Desert, was able to observe intergroup cooperation during a severe drought that threatened their survival. She found that the Bushmen had elaborate gift-giving exchanges, called *Hxaro*, that averaged sixteen stable partners, some of whom where kin and others where "adopted" kin. Some of these partners lived in groups 200 kilometres apart. This elaborate exchange system turned out to be crucial for their survival under those extreme conditions (Weissner 2002).

It is important to note that cooperative breeding and long term pair bonding (monogamy) are socio-biological adaptations that appear in other species of animals, which is why they should be included in step I, before the emergence of cultural evolution (step II). Cooperative breeding and monogamy are "pre-adaptations" to use the biological lingo.

Based on evidence coming from several lines of research, Benoit Dubreuil believes that these steps toward greater sociality among nomadic foragers ("emotional modernity") may have been present in *Homo Heidelbergensis*, (700.000 to 300,000 BP), an ancestor to Neanderthals and modern humans (Dubreuil 2010). The largest expansion of the prefrontal cortex[5] (up to 1100 to 1400 cm3) a size that is similar to or slightly larger

woman many husbands). Chapais' point is that the shift toward monogamy was a major change during human evolution.

5 This encephalization is particularly evident in the dorsolateral area of the prefrontal cortex, believed to regulate cooperation and functions like the inhibition of impulses and planning, (Dubreuil 2010).

than that of *Homo sapiens*, coincides with the appearance of *Homo heidelbergensis*. Human's control of fire and evidence of first campfires coincides roughly with this time period. As Richard Whrangham argues in *Catching Fire* (Wrangham 2009) cooking meat has a lot to do with this enormous expansion of the brain that develops in a relatively short period during the mid-Pleistocene period. It also has to do with the development of greater sociability, as campfires then and now have always been times when a group meets to eat together, converse and share stories.

Step II:
The emergence of cultural evolution, the transmission of cultural knowledge, shared social norms, social selection operating between and within groups, and the emergence of cognitive and behavioral modernity
(Mid to Late Pleistocene about 500,000 to 40,000 BP)

Cultural evolution is based on cultural knowledge being able to be transmitted from one generation to the next, on group behaviors being regulated through shared social norms and social reputations, and on selective pressures operating within and between groups. The result of all these changes acting together was the emergence of cognitive and behavioral modernity in our species 100,000 to 40,000 years ago.

A new form of inheritance

Humans are the only ape that deliberately teaches and learns from other group members, what Csibra and Gergely call the human capacity for natural pedagogy (Csibra & Gergely 2009). Natural pedagogy allows for cultural knowledge and skills to be transmitted from one generation to the next, the "ratchet effect" of culture (Tomasello 1999). The ratchet effect contributes powerfully to the enormous capacity for human inventiveness and to cultural diversity.[6] The transmission of learned knowledge interacts

---

6 This malleability and change is what makes human nature so diverse. The enormous

169

with gene-based inheritance. Heritability requires faithful transmission (Richerson & Boyd 2005). As long as cultural traits show stability over time (which many do) and phenotypic variation (which they also do) they are subject to selective pressures. The major differences between that gene-based and culturally-based inheritances are that the former is transmitted through DNA, whereas the latter is transmitted through learning and imitation. The other major difference is that they operate at vastly different scales of time. In large animals it might take a minimum of 10,000 years before a gene-based biological trait can become dominant (go to fixation in biological terms), whereas a cultural trait can become dominant in a matter of one generation.

The emergence of shared social norms
and the importance of social reputations

One of the main stumbling blocks in understanding how advanced forms of cooperation could have evolved during human evolution is the difficulty of understanding how natural selection solved the free rider problem. The free rider problem emerges when a common good that benefits all members (in economic terms a public good) is exploited by free riders, who benefit from the public good but do not contribute to it. Among nomadic foragers sharing meat from big game hunting among all group members is a public good. There is no single answer to the free rider problem and many proposals have been put forward. Punishing free riders and bullies is one answer and has been shown to be effective (Boyd, Gintis, & Bowles 2010). Punishment, however, can be very costly if it falls to just one or a few individuals, since the punished individual(s) can retaliate in kind which in turn can lead to a cycle of violence. A way to avoid the high cost of punishing free riders is to develop shared social norms that support cooperation. By internalizing shared social norms, the high costs of punishment are significantly diminished, since prosocial norms become enforced by shame, humiliation and ostracism and by the power that social reputations have in human societies

---

diversity and malleability have led some to view the concept of human nature as a myth (Buller 2005).

(Boehm 2012; Gintis 2003; Tomasello & Vaish 2013). There is a growing literature on the importance of social norms and their internalization in explaining how high levels of cooperation evolved in humans (Bowles & Gintis 2011; Boyd & Richerson 2005; Gintis 2004; Henrich & Henrich 2006).

This literature on social norms is consistent with Fromm's concept of social character, which describes how shared social norms are adapted to prevailing socio-economic conditions. Based on their systematic and exhaustive study of a Mexican village, Fromm and Maccoby show the historical and socio-economic origins of shared social norms and how they become internalized and how the process of internalization actually works (Fromm & Maccoby 1970b). Children as young as five years old are already concerned about their social reputations, a concern that is totally lacking in chimpanzees (Engelmann et al. 2010). For example, when a pre-schooler is put in an experimental situation where it is very tempting to cheat, all it takes is to have a familiar peer from preschool in the room to prevent cheating – an unfamiliar peer will not prevent cheating (Engelmann et al. 2010).

Shared social norms and social reputations regulate social life in small groups of nomadic foragers, and according to Tomasello these social norms lead to the emergence of "group mindedness" (Tomasello et al. 2012). This emerging form of group identity creates a sense of "we-ness" associated with group membership. The emergence of self-conscious emotions of shame, humiliation and guilt are linked with this sense of we-ness and the internalization of shared social norms. The internalization of shared social norms, the emergence of group mindedness and the significance of social reputations in regulating group life was the second major step toward emotional modernity during hominin evolution.

The emergence of selection operating at the level of groups

In the course of human evolution selective processes began to operate at the level of groups, with highly cooperative and cohesive groups having better chances of surviving than groups that were less cooperative and cohesive. Selection at the level of groups has been a controversial subject ever since George Williams wrote a brilliant critique of group selection showing that

171

concepts such as "selection for the benefit of a species" lacked rigor and precision (Williams 1966). Williams accepted that group selection was a theoretical possibility, but given the pervasive selective pressures operating at the level of individuals, Williams believed that in practice group selection was rare or nonexistent. Since William's critique there has been a rehabilitation of group selection theory based on a pluralistic and multilevel perspective in which selective pressures operate simultaneously at three different levels: genes, individuals and groups (Sober & Wilson 1998; Wilson & Sober 1994; Wilson & Wilson 2007).

Multilevel models of selection require specifying the trait selection is targeting. For instance, when the question is how altruism or cooperation could have evolved, the multilevel perspective shows that at the lower levels of genes and individuals, selfish or non-cooperative genes or individuals (such as the free riders) will prevail, but at a group level, groups with more cooperative and altruistic individuals will prevail over groups with fewer altruistic and cooperative individuals. Further precision requires a multilevel perspective to examine how selection operates at each level. Just averaging gene frequencies across groups over time (as the gene-centered and individual-centered approaches do) is very misleading, since it only informs us about the end product of what evolves and that selection has taken place. But it obscures what actually happens by not showing at what level selective pressures are having an effect or how these different levels are interacting (Sober & Wilson 1998).

Common or uncommon selection at the level of groups, however, may turn out to be (an empirical question that is still not resolved) many important researchers and thinkers working in the field of human evolution have come to think that several especially favorable conditions came together to make group selection, or cultural selection as some have called it (I think cultural group selection would be a better name), a very powerful agent during human evolution (Bowles & Gintis 2011; Boyd & Richerson 2005; Henrich & Henrich 2006; Sober & Wilson 1998; Tomasello et al. 2012; Wilson 2012). These favorable conditions were the cumulative effect of cultural knowledge in producing diversity and competition between groups and the effects of the internalization of shared social norms. Selective forces then begin to operate between cultures, ethnic groups, chiefdoms, kingdoms and states (Wilson 2012).

In *Social Character in a Mexican Village* Fromm and Maccoby (1970b) describe a process of cultural selection they called social selection that operates at the level of individuals and groups. Social selection is based on the selection of social character types (individuals that have internalized shared values and character traits) within the same society. Social character types that are better adapted to socio economic conditions usually prevail over less adapted types (Fromm & Maccoby 1970b, pp. 232–5). The concept of social selection expands cultural selection theory showing that selection operates *within* a society and not only *between* distinct cultural groups, corporations or nation states. Maccoby has given us many examples of social selection operating within corporations, governmental bureaucracies and non-profit organizations that are responding to changes from industrial-bureaucratic economies to service and knowledge based economies (Maccoby 1976; 1981; 2007).

The cumulative effects of cultural evolution lead to behavioral and cognitive modernity defined in the literature as the use of language, symbols, body paintings, cave paintings, sculptured pieces, musical instruments and advanced tools. It appears in rudimentary form in Africa 100,000 BP (McBrearty 2007; McBrearty & Brooks 2000) and more completely some 60,000 years later as seen in the Chauvet and Lascaux caves in Southern France and the Altamira cave in Spain.

Step III:
First human settlements, institutional building,
the reemergence of social hierarchies and rapid cultural change
(17,000 years ago to the present)

The first evidence of permanent human settlements appear during the "terminal Pleistocene" 17,000 to 11,500 BP in the Levante (now Israel). These settlements were based on an economy in which extensive hunting of large and small ungulates (hoofed animals such as deer) and rabbits became a main mode of subsistence (Yeshuran et al. 2014). The trend toward a sedentary life accelerated with the Neolithic revolution 10,000 BP characterized by the discovery of agriculture and the domestication of plants and animals.

As human settlements grew, life in groups could no longer be regulated informally through gossip, social reputations and shared social norms. It became necessary to build human institutions that control basic functions such a military defense against invading groups, as well as policing, judicial and governing functions. These institutions require a combination of vertical and horizontal forms of coordination and cooperation. With verticality comes a resurgence of dominance hierarchies, but this time transformed into the form of social hierarchies (Dubrueil 2010). Social elites that control these institutions can govern more or less despotically (the "return of the repressed" in Freudian terms) or can retain vestiges of our prehistoric yearnings for equality, dignity and fairness observed in existing nomadic foragers (Kelly 2013; Lee 1979), and, I think were also present during the prehistory of our species during the middle to late Paleolithic era.

As humans begin to create their own cultural and institutional environments to which they *must* adapt, a process of self-creation begins to emerge[7], which the Chilean biologist and philosopher Humberto Maturana called *autopoiesis*, from the Greek, *auto* = self, *poiesis* = creation, self-creation (Maturana & Varela 1973). Echoing a theme in Fromm's work, Loren Eisley expressed this idea in a beautiful essay, *Uncompleted Man* (Eisley 1971).

The evolution of childhood

High levels of cooperation and socialization would not have been possible if it weren't for changes in the timing of development that allowed children and adolescents time to develop the socio-emotional competencies and assimilate the cultural knowledge and technical skills needed to function in complex societies.

Evolution can have very large effects on development, either by accelerating or slowing certain developmental processes or milestones. These effects

---

7 The process of a species creating its own environment to which it must adapt is not unique to our species and is described in the evolutionary literature as niche construction (Fuentes 2012; Kendal et al. 2011). Beavers create their own dams, bees create their own hives, ants create elaborate underground cities, and spiders spin their own webs. What makes human niche construction different is that once these other species create their own niche, niche construction remains rather static. In comparison human niche construction based on cultural evolution is dynamic, pleomorphic, and becomes more complex over time.

on the timing of development are called heterochrony (from the Greek *hetero* = different. and *chronos* = time) and can have huge effects on the life cycle of a species (McKinney & McNamara 1991). The most important examples of acceleration of development in humans are the maintenance of fetal levels of rapid brain growth though the first year of life and the timing of weaning. In comparison with chimpanzees that wean their infants once they become nutritionally self-sufficient by the age of four or five, human nomadic hunter-gatherers wean their young by the time they are two and a half years old. The most important example of prolonging development during human evolution is the age at which sexual maturity is reached. Female chimpanzees mature by age ten, while human females in nomadic hunter-gatherer groups reach full sexual maturity six to eight years later. Weaning at a younger age and a very delayed sexual maturation makes for a very prolonged childhood and adolescence, the most prolonged of any known species (Konner 2010). Many believe that one major reason that changes in the timing of development were favored by natural selection was to allow for an extended period of developmental plasticity that facilitates children's ability to absorb the vast amount of accumulated cultural knowledge that is necessary to become a competent adult (Bjorklund & Rosenberg 2005; Gibbons 2008; Tomasello 1999).

A prolonged development came at a huge cost. Chimpanzees are nutritionally self-sufficient by the age of five. While there is significant diversity among different cultures depending on whether they are nomadic, horticultural, pastoral, agricultural or industrial societies, in most cases children remain nutritionally dependent on their families and communities until early or late adolescence. Infants and children need thirteen million calories before they reach nutritional self-sufficiency (Hrdy 2009, p. 101) and twenty-five percent of total metabolic resources go to meet the energy demands of a huge brain.

If these high costs were born by mothers alone, high levels of cooperation would probably have never evolved. This is why it seems likely that a very large neocortex, an extended period of development and cooperative breeding evolved together, so that the high costs of rearing immature infants and slowly developing children with a brain that consumes enormous energy could be spread around through cooperative breeding (D. F. Bjorklund & J. S. Rosenberg 2005; Gibbons 2008; Hrdy 2009). Cooking and consuming a high caloric meat and tuber diet is also an integral part of the story (Wrangham 2009).

The following diagram summarizes this model of human evolution:

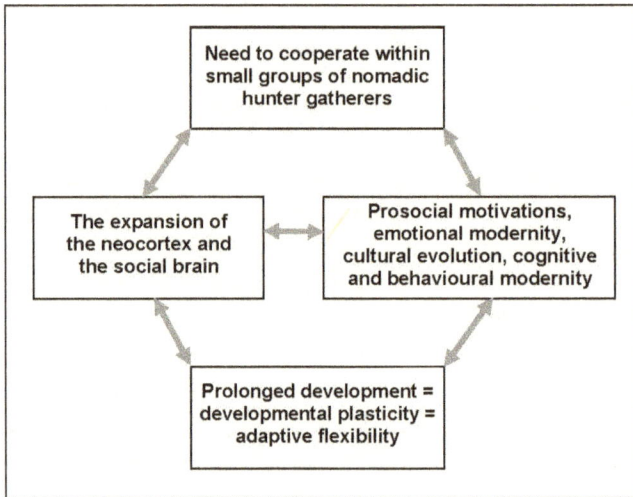

```
┌─────────────────────────────────────────────────────┐
│              ┌──────────────────────┐                │
│              │ Need to cooperate    │                │
│              │ within small groups  │                │
│              │ of nomadic hunter    │                │
│              │ gatherers            │                │
│              └──────────────────────┘                │
│                                                       │
│  ┌────────────────┐        ┌──────────────────────┐  │
│  │ The expansion  │        │ Prosocial            │  │
│  │ of the         │◄──────►│ motivations,         │  │
│  │ neocortex and  │        │ emotional modernity, │  │
│  │ the social     │        │ cultural evolution,  │  │
│  │ brain          │        │ cognitive and        │  │
│  └────────────────┘        │ behavioural modernity│  │
│                            └──────────────────────┘  │
│              ┌──────────────────────┐                │
│              │ Prolonged            │                │
│              │ development =        │                │
│              │ developmental        │                │
│              │ plasticity =         │                │
│              │ adaptive flexibility │                │
│              └──────────────────────┘                │
└─────────────────────────────────────────────────────┘
```

Research showing the emergence
of prosocial motivations early in the ontogeny of our species

Prosocial motivations show up very early in human development, before culture begins to have a large impact. Research shows that social norms do not begin to have an effect until the end of the second year of life, but most clearly by age three and four (Rakoczy & Schmidt 2013). The early expression of helping and cooperative motives and the desire to share experience with others supports the view that humans have developed a motivational infrastructure needed to develop high levels of cooperation that characterizes our species and prepares children to live within human-created cultural environments (For review of the literature on the development of prosocial motivations see Bloom 2013; Suddendorf 2013; Tomasello & Vaish 2013).

A generation of infant researchers has shown how infants and primary caregivers are socially engaged very early in development. The engagement is already evident by the second month of life and more clearly by the fourth month as shown in the charming "proto-conversations" between primary caregivers and their infants that have all the markings of a real conversation, except that infants can't speak words (Beebe et al. 2005; Stern 1985; Tomasello et al. 2005; Trevarthen 1979; Trevarthen & Aitken 2001; Tronick 2007; Warneken & Tomasello 2006; 2007; 2009). It is not surprising that social engagement takes the form of a conversation, since communication is its most important function (Cortina & Liotti 2010; Tomasello 2007; Trevarthen 1979; 1988) and prepares the ground for extensive cooperation and social learning needed to assimilate a huge amount of cultural knowledge (Boyd, Richerson, & Henrich 2011). For humans, this form of social engagement is the earliest expression of a social instinct to engage with others. Other primate species show rudimentary forms of this social engagement system and make eye contact, and face-to-face interactions soon after birth, but it disappears after a month or two, while in humans it continues to develop throughout life.

The work of Steven Porges has shown us the evolutionary origins of this social engagement system. The autonomic nervous system is comprised of the sympathic system that is a mobilizing system that prepares the organism for fight or fight reactions, and a parasympathic system that is a demobilizing system. One of the sub branches of the parasympathic system, the myelinated branch of the vagus nerve, in conjunction with cranial nerves involved in making eye contact and in facial expressions, developed in mammals, and especially in primates, to allow for emotional closeness (Porges 2011).

By the end of the first year of life an attachment to an exclusive parenting figure is fully developed. We share this social instinct to attach in moments of distress with other mammals and some species of birds (Bowlby 1969). The enormous significance of this attachment bond is that it provides a base of security for developing the capacities to self-regulate emotions and levels of arousal, (Sroufe 1996) and explore the material world (Bowlby 1988). A secure attachment is also the basis for developing cooperative relations and competencies needed for adapting to an expanding social world (Sroufe et al. 1999; Sroufe et al. 2005).

By fourteen months of age a new set of social motivations begins to emerge. Children engage in simple joined tasks or games like playing peeka-boo, and spontaneously helping strangers. Tomasello and colleagues at the Max Plank Institute in Leipzig have documented these spontaneous prosocial motivations (Hepach et al. 2013; Warneken & Tomasello 2007; 2009). It is impressive to watch these videotaped demonstrations of spontaneous helpful and cooperative behaviors with strangers in fourteen to eighteen month-olds who are not prompted by parents and have no immediate reward[8].

By the second year of life infants are engaging in a new form of "we-centered" interactions and infants show a strong desire to share experiences with others. When playful interactions are suddenly suspended by an adult, children expect and request that the adult continue the playful interaction (Warneken et al. 2006). Toddlers even turn instrumental tasks into a social game. The desire to share experience with others can also be seen by the simple gesture of pointing as a way to call attention of others to objects or situations of interest. This gesture to share something of interest is *unique to humans* (Tomasello et al. 2007).[9] All these developments prepare young children to internalize shared social norms and assimilate cultural values and begin to enforce social norms by age three (Rakoczy & Schmidt 2013). Three year olds enforce norms as if they were mandates ("you most do it this way" or "it is like this"), while five to seven year –old children are more flexible and use context to enforce social norms (Köymen et al. 2014).

As any parent who has raised a toddler knows, the presence of prosocial motivations in young children does not mean that they are always cooperative and helpful. Toddlers have not earned the reputation of "the terrible two's" (or "threes") for nothing. Sporadic selfishness, stubbornness, and resistance to share with siblings, peers and even with adults they love are normal parts of development. But parents' cooperativeness and helpfulness with their children strongly predicts how cooperative and helpful they will become with peers and teachers later in development (Sroufe et al. 2005).

Culture would not have taken root if it weren't for teaching and imi-

---

8 The videotapes illustrate, in ways that a verbal description fails to convey the importance of these prosocial instincts. You can see some of these videos by going to Michael Tomasello's website at: http://www.eva.mpg.de/psycho/videos/children_clothes.mpg.

9 Apes raised in captivity can learn to point to request something, but they never point to share an object of interest.

tation. Teaching is vertical, from adults to children, and horizontal, between siblings and peers. Learning occurs through deliberate teaching and through imitation (Tomasello, Kruger, & Ratner 1993). Apes may learn by imitation but adult apes do not deliberately guide learning as humans do (Tomasello 1999; Tomasello & Vaish 2013).

Humans are gifted imitators. In fact early in development they over imitate, even if the imitation may not be the most direct way to achieve a goal. If a two or a three year-old sees an adult turning on a light with her forehead, they will imitate this behavior even though it is clear that they can turn on the light with their hands (Horner & Whiten 2005; Nielson 2006; Suddendorf 2013). Over-imitation greatly facilitates absorbing ways of being and acting within different cultural settings.

Fromm's last effort to revisit the historical and biological conditions that determine human nature

In *The Anatomy of Human Destructiveness* (1973a) Fromm once again assumed that during the course of human evolution a split emerged between character-based passions rooted in socio-economic and cultural conditions and instincts based on our biological heritage. This split led him to include in *The Anatomy of Human Destructiveness* (Fromm 1973a) a list of character rooted passions: *rootedness*, (need for human relatedness), *unity* (need for coherence by developing our capacity for love and reason), *effectiveness* (the need to feel competent) and the need for *stimulation*. Of this list, only the need for a frame of orientation and devotion and the need for unity (based on developing our capacity for love and reason) can be considered uniquely human. The other items in the list, the need for rootedness, effectiveness and stimulation are present in other animals and have deep biological roots.

As I have tried to show, there is not a rupture between character-rooted passions that have their origin in socioeconomic, cultural and historical conditions *and* biological instincts. There is a gradual transformation of social instincts that support high levels of cooperation. But Fromm was on to an important idea when he focused on major changes in human evolution that had produced some uniquely human qualities that separate us from other animals. Some evolutionary changes occur quite rapidly and represent something new, such as the emergence of symbolic and imagistic abilities, language and the cultural transmission of knowledge.

Until the 1970's it was an accepted "fact" that evolution occurred through gradual change as the result of selective pressures favoring mutations better adapted to environmental conditions, that is, microevolution in contrast to rapid and sudden change (macroevolution). So when Stephen Jay Gould and Niles Eldridge introduced the concept of punctuated equilibrium to account for the non-gradual and rapid changes (in geological time scales of tens of thousands of years instead of millions of years) they observed in the paleontological record, it sent shock waves in the evolutionary world, (Gould & Eldridge 1977). It was believed that what appeared to be sudden change was due to deficiencies in the paleontological record. Gould and Eldridge challenged this belief and they were proven right. Punctuated equilibrium and macroevolution have now been accepted into the mainstream of evolutionary thinking (Eldridge 1995).

So while Fromm was right in thinking that human evolution had produced major changes that created unique qualities in human nature, he was wrong in thinking that these changes represented a rupture with our biological heritage. Major changes with new properties can be modelled as dynamic systems that have nonlinear effects. In these systems change is not linear and continuous but can be sudden (have nonlinear effects) and take on new *emergent qualities* that signal an organizational transformation of the system (Thelen & Smith 1994).

Conclusion

Were Fromm with us today I think he would have been delighted to hear about the paradigm change we are witnessing in seeing cooperative and prosocial motivations as being central components of understanding the evolution of our species. This new understanding would have supported what he and many of his contemporaries, such as the anthropologist Ashley Montague (Montague 1950) believed, namely, that Hobbs and Freud's pessimistic view of man as being selfish and brutish was one sided and wrong. Fromm's attempt to redefine human nature by emphasizing its more positive potential assumed a rupture between our biological and cultural heritage in which character rooted passion influenced by economic, cultural and parental influences had become a substitute for our missing instincts. As I have shown there are both continuities and discontinuities during human evolution –that are also observed during ontogenetic development (Sroufe et al. 2005). The discontinuities are best conceived as emerging properties (such as cultural evolution) that are rooted in social instincts that we share with the Great Apes. These social instincts were not lost; they were transformed to support high levels of cooperation. In addition to co-operative breeding and the emergence of monogamy and the internalization of shared social norms, one of the main mechanisms that led to this transformation was achieved by a prolonged period of development that allowed infants and children to become more receptive to environmental influences through learning and imitation.

I think that Fromm would also have been pleased to see that the new evolutionary paradigm has an unmistakably Marxist undertone – which as far as I know has not been conscious to the researchers and scholars who have advanced these views. The cooperative social organization of our species emerges as a response to ecological conditions (climate change in step I), and the emergence of permanent human settlements in step III due to efficient hunting and the invention of agriculture and the domestication of animals. In other words, how humans make a living (the mode of production) determines to a large extent the social organization. But that is not the whole story. With the emergence of shared social norms, (social character in Fromm's terms), cultural values and influences also begin to have a large impact during human evolution. A new bi-directional dynamic emerged between how humans make a living (the mode of production) and cultural influences mediated by the internalization of shared social norms and practices, a central thesis of social character theory. Updating Fromm's theories in light of these new developments in human sciences is vitally important as our species confronts new challenges to our survival in the twenty-first century and beyond.

References

Apicella, C.L. (2012). Social networks and cooperation in hunter gatherers. Nature 481, pp. 497–501.

Beebe, B. et al. (2005). Forms of intersubjectivity in infant research and adult treatment. New York (Other Press).

Bjorklund, D. F., & Rosenberg, J. S. (Eds) (2005). Origins of the Social Brain. Evolutionary Psychology and Child Development. New York (Guilford Press).

Bjorklund, D. F., & Rosenberg, J. S. (2005). The Role of Developmental Plasticity in the Evolution of Human Cognition. In: D. F. Bjorklund & B. R. Ellis (Eds.). Origins of the Social Brain. Evolutionary Psychology and Child Development. New York (Guilford Press), pp. 45–75.

Bloom, P. (2013). Just Babies. The Origins of Good and Evil. New York (Random House PPC).

Boehm, C. (2012). Moral Origins. The Evolution of Virtue, Altruism, and Shame. New York (Basic Books).

Boehm, C. (1999). Hierarchy in the Forest. The Evolution of Egalitarian Behavior. Cambridge (Harvard University Press).

Bowlby, J. (1969). Attachment (Vol. I). New York (Basic Books).

Bowlby, J. (1988). A Secure Base New York (Basic Books).

Bowles, S., & Gintis, H. (2011). A Cooperative Species. Human Reciprocity and It's Evolution. Princeton (Princeton University Press).

Boyd, R. et al. (2010). Coordinated Punishment of Defectors Sustains Cooperation and Can Proliferate When Rare. Science 328, pp. 617–620.

Boyd, R. et al. (2011). Rapid Cultural Adaptation Can Facilitate the Evolution of Large-Scale Cooperation. Behavior Ecology Sociobiology 65, pp. 431–444.

Boyd, R., & Richerson, P.J. (2005). The Origin and Evolution of Cultures. New York (Oxford University Press).

Buller, D.J. (2005). Adapting Minds. Evolutionary Psychology and the Persistent Quest for Human Nature. Cambridge (A Bradford Book. The MIT Press).

Cortina, M. (In press). The Greatness and Limitations Erich Fromm's Humanism. Contemporary Psychoanalysis.

Cortina, M., & Liotti, G. (2010). Attachment is About Safety and Protection. Intersubjectivity is About Social Understanding and Sharing. Psychoanalytic Psychology 27, pp. 410–441.

Csibra, G., & Gergely, G. (2009). Natural Pedagogy. Trends in Cognitive Science 13, pp. 148–153.

d'Errico, F. et al. (2012). Early Evidence of San Material Culture Represented by Organic Artifacts from Border Cave, South Africa. PNAS. 109, pp. 13214–13219.

de Waal, F. (2013). The Bonobo and the Atheist. In Search of Humanism Among the Primates. New York (W.W. Norton).

Dubreuil, B. (2010). Paleolithic Public Goods Games. Why Human Culture and Cooperation Did not Evolve in One Step. Biology & Philosophy 25, pp. 53–73. doi: 10.1007/s10539-009-9177-7.

Dunbar, R.L.M., & Shultz, S. (2007). Evolution in the Social Brain. Science317, pp. 1344–1347. doi: 10.1126/sceince.1145463.

Eisley, L. (1971). The Uncompleted Man. In: B. Landis & E. S. Tauber (Eds), In the Name of Life. Essays in the Honor of Erich Fromm. New York (Holt, Rinehart and Winston), pp. 130–142.

Eldridge, N. (1995). Reinventing Darwin. The Great Debate at the High Table of Evolutionary Theory. New York (Wiley).

Engelmann, J. et al. (2010). Five-Year Olds, but not Chimpanzees, Attemptto Manage Their Reputations. PLoS ONE 7 (10) e48433. doi: 10.1371/journal.pone.0048433Ferrari, P.F. et al. (2009). Reciprocal Face to Face Communication between Rhesus Macaque Mothers and Their Newborn Infants. Current Biology 19, pp. 1768–1772.

Fromm, E. (1947a). Man for Himself. An Inquiry into the Psychology of Ethics. New York (Holt, Rinehart & Winston).

Fromm, E. (1973a). The Anatomy of Human Destructiveness. New York (Holt, Rinehart and Winston).

Fromm, E., and Maccoby, M. (1970b). Social Character in a Mexican Village. Englewood Cliffs (Prentice Hall).

Fuentes, A. (2012). Race, Monogamy and Other Lies They Told You. Bursting Myths about Human Nature. Berkeley (University of California Press).

Gibbons, A. (2008). The Birth of Childhood. Science 322, pp. 1040–1042.

Gintis, H. (2003). The Hitchhiker Guide to Altruism. Gene-culture Coevolution, and the Internalization of Norms. Journal of Theoretical Biology 220, pp. 407–418.

Gintis, H. (2004). The Genetic Side of Gene-Culture Coevolution. Internalization of Norms and Prosocial Emotions. Journal of Economic Behavior & Organization 53, pp. 57–87.

Gould, S.J., & Eldridge, N. (1977). Punctuated Equilibrium. The Tempo and Mode of Evolution Reconsidered. Paleobiology 3, pp. 115–151.

Henrich, J., & Henrich, N. (2006). Culture, Evolution and the Puzzle of Human Cooperation. Cognitive Systems Research 7, pp. 220–226.

Hepach, R. et al. (2013). A New Look at Children's Prosocial Motivation. Infancy 18, pp. 67–90.

Hermann, E. et al. (2007). Humans Have Evolved Specialized Skills of Social Cognition. The Cultural Intelligence Hypothesis Science 317, pp. 1360–1366.

Hill, K.R. et al. (2011). Co-Residence Patterns in Hunter-Gatherer Societies Show Unique Human Social Structure. Science 331, pp. 1286–1289.

Horner, V., & Whiten, A. (2005). Causal Knowledge and Imitation/Emulation in Chimpanzees (Pan troglodytes) and Vhildren (Homo sapiens). Animal Cognition 8, pp. 164–181.

Hrdy, B.S. (1999). Mother Nature. Maternal Instincts and how they Shape the Human Species. New York (Ballantine Books).

Hrdy, S.B. (2005). Evolutionary Context of Human Development. In: C.S. Carter et al. (Ed.). Attachment and Bonding. A New Synthesis. Cambridge (The MIT Press), pp. 9–32.

Hrdy, B.S. (2009). Mothers and Others. The Evolutionary Origins of Mutual Understanding. Cambridge (The Belknap Press).

Hrdy, S.B. (2013). Development and Social Selection in the Emergence of "Emotionally Modern" Humans. In: C.L. Meehan & A.N. Crittenden (Eds). Origins and Implications of the Evolution of Childhood. Santa Fe (SAR Press).

Kelly, R. (2013). The Lifeways of Hunter-Gatherers. The Foraging Spectrum. Cambridge (Cambridge University Press).

Kendal, J. et al. (2011). Human Niche Construction in Interdisciplinary Focus. Philosophical Transactions of the Royal Society B: Biological Sciences 366(1566), pp. 785–792. doi: 10.1098/rstb.2010.0306.

Konner, M. (2010). The Evolution of Childhood. Relationships, Emotion, Mind. Cambridge (Harvard University Press).

Köymen, B. et al. (2014). Children's Norm Enforcement in Their Inteeractions With Peers. Child Development 85, pp. 1108–1122.

Lee, R.B. (1979). The Kung San. Men, Women and Work in a Foraging Society. Cambridge (Cambridge University Press).

Maccoby, M. (1976). The Gamesman. The New Corporate Leaders. New York (Simon and Schuster).

Maccoby, M. (1981). The Leader. New York (Simon and Schuster).

Maccoby, M. (2007). The Leaders We Need. And What Makes Us Follow. Boston (Harvard Business School Publishing).

Maturana, H., & Varela, F. (1973). Autopoiesis and Cognition. The Realization of the Living. In: R.S. Cohen & M.W. Wanofsky (Eds). Boston Studies in the Philosophy of Science No. 42. Dordech (D. Reidel Publishing Co).

McBrearty, S. (2007). Down With the Revolution. In K. Boyle et al. (Ed.). Rethinking the Human Revolution. Cambridge (McDonald Institute Monographs).

McBrearty, S., & Brooks, A.S. (2000). The Revolution that Wasn't. A New Interpretation to the Origin of Modern Human Behavior. Journal of Human Evolution 39, pp. 453–563.

McKinney, M.L., & McNamara, K.J. (1991). Heterochrony. The Evolution of Ontogeny. Plenum Press (New York).

Mitani, J.C. (2006). Reciprocal Exchange in Chimpanzees and Other Primates. In: P. Kappeler & C. van Schaik (Ed.). Cooperation in Primates. Mechanisms and Evolution. Heidelberg (Springer), pp. 101–113.

Montague, A. (1950). On Being Human. New York (Henry Schumna, Inc).

Nielson, M. (2006). Copying Actions and Copying Outcomes. Developmental Psychology 42, pp. 555–565.

Porges, S. (2011). The Polyvagal Theory. Neurophysiological Foundations of Emotions, Attachment, Communication, and Self-Regulation New York (W.W. Norton).

Rakoczy, H., & Schmidt, M.F.H. (2013). The Early Ontogeny of Social Norms. Child Development Perspectives 7, pp. 17–21.

Richerson, P.J., & Boyd, R. (2005). Not by Genes Alone. Chicago (The University of Chicago Press).

Service, E.R. (1966). The Hunters. Englewood Cliffs (Prentice Hall).

Sober, E., & Wilson, D.S. (1998). Unto Others. The Evolution and Psychology of Unselfish Behavior).

Sroufe, L.A. (1996). Emotional Development. The Organization of Emotional Life in the Early Years. New York (Cambridge University Press).

Sroufe, L.A. et al. (1999). One Social World. The Integrated Development of Parent-Child and Peer Relations. In: W.A Collins & B. Laursen (Eds). The Minnesota Symposia on Child Psychology 30. Relationships as Developmental Contexts. pp. 241–261.

Sroufe, L.A. et al. (2005). The Development of the Person. The Minnesota Study of Risk and Adaptation from Birth to Adulthood New York (The Guilford Press).

Stern, D.N. (1985). The Interpersonal World of the Infant. New York (Basic Books).

Suddendorf, T. (2013). The Gap. The Science of What Separates us from Other Animals. New York (Basic Books).

Thelen, E., & Smith, L. (1994). A Dynamic Systems Approach to the Development of Cognition and Action. Cambridge (MIT Press).

Tomasello, M. (1999). The Cultural Origins of Human Cognition. Cambridge (Harvard University Press).

Tomasello, M. (2007). Cooperation and Communication in the 2nd Year of Life. Child Development Perspectives 1, pp. 8–12.

Tomasello, M. (2009). Why we Cooperate. Cambridge (Boston Review Book).

Tomasello, M., & Carpenter, M. (2005). The Emergence of Social Cognition in Three Young Chimpanzees. Monographs of the Society for Research in Child Development 70 (1), pp. 46–72.

Tomasello, M. et al. (1993). Cultural Learning. Behavioral and Brain Sciences 16(03), pp. 495–511. doi:10.1017/S0140525X0003123X.

Tomasello, M. et al. (2005). Understanding and Sharing Intentions. The Origins of Cultural Cognition. Behavioral and Brain Sciences 28, pp. 675–735.

Tomasello, M. et al. (2007). A New Look at Pointing. Child Development 78, pp. 705–22.

Tomasello, M. et al. (2012). Two Key Steps in the Evolution of Human Cooperation. Current Anthropology 53, pp. 673–692.

Tomasello, M., & Vaish, A. (2013). Origins of Human Cooperation and Morality. Annual Review of Psychology 64, pp. 231–255.

Trevarthen, C. (1979). Communication and Cooperation in Early Infancy. A Description of Primary Intersubjectivity. In: M. Bullowa (Ed.). Before Speech. The Beginning of Human Communication. London (Cambridge University Press), pp. 321–346.

Trevarthen, C. (1988). Universal Cooperative Motives. How Children Begin to Know Language and Skills and Culture. Acquiring Culture. Cross-Cultural Studies in Child Development, pp. 37–90.

Trevarthen, C., & Aitken, K.J. (2001). Infant Intersubjectivity. Research, Theory, and Clinical Applications. Clinical Psychology and Psychiatry 42, pp. 3–43.

Tronick, E. (2007). The Neurobehavioral and Socio-Emotional Development of Infants and Children. New York (W.W. Norton).

Warneken, F. et al. (2006). Cooperative Activities in Young Children and Chimpanzees. Child Development 77, pp. 640–79.

Warneken, F., & Tomasello, M. (2006). Altruistic Helping in Human Infants and Young Chimpanzees. Science 311, pp. 1301–4.

Warneken, F., & Tomasello, M. (2007). Spontaneous Altruism by Young Children and Chimpanzees. PLoS Biology 5, pp. 1414–20.

Warneken, F., & Tomasello, M. (2009). Varieties of Altruism in Children and Chimpanzees. Trends in Cognitive Science 13, pp. 397–402.

Weissner, P. (2002). Hunting, Healing and Hxaro Exchange. A Long Trem Perspective On King Ju-Hoansi Large-Game Hunting. Evolution and Human Behavior 23, pp. 407–36.

Williams, E. (1966). Adaptation and Natural Selection. Oxford (Oxford University Press).

Wilson, D. S., & Sober, E. (1994). Reintroducing Group Selection to the Human Behavioral Science. Behavioral and Brain Sciences17, pp. 585–652.

Wilson, D.S., & Wilson, E.O. (2007). Rethinking the Theoretical Foundations of Sociobiology Quarterly Review of Biology, pp. 327–328.

Wilson, E.O. (2012). The Social Conquest of Earth. New York (Liveright Publishing Company).

Wrangham, R. (2009). Catching Fire. How Cooking Made Us Human. New York (Basic Books).

Yeshuran, R. et al. (2014). Intensification and Sedentism in the Terminal Pleistocene Natufian Sequence of El-Wad Terrace (Israel). Human Evolution 70, pp. 16–35.

Man as a Contradiction

Philosophical Ideas of Erich Fromm

Nikolai Omelchenko

Abstract: In his paper, the author argues that some of Fromm's ideas have the potential to answer bigger philosophical questions. Fromm's notion of the fundamental principle of individual relatedness to the world, in particular, allows us to understand the human nature much better. Fromm's way of seeing "man as full of contradictions" is provided with another argument. Sharing Fromm's interpretation of the human freedom, the author further discusses the problem of the original source of free will and makes the case that Fromm's understanding of love is productive for integrating contemporary theory of knowledge and philosophy of human beings. The author ultimately believes that the value of Fromm's theory lies, first of all, in the consistency of his humanistic vision.

Introduction

The humanistic doctrine of Erich Fromm significantly influences contemporary philosophical anthropology, ethics, social and political philosophy. In Russia, the study of Fromm's views started in the seventies of the last century (cf. Egorova 2004). In that period Fromm's philosophical work and diagnoses of social reality met with a severe ideological criticism. Moreover, his philosophical interest in human beings was characterized as an unscientific anthropologism (cf. Schwartzman 1971; Dobrenkov 1972; 1974; Kurkin 1983). Ten years later a number of papers and monographs presenting Fromm's ideas in a more objective manner appeared, but his own works were essentially unknown. The next stage of studying his work was undoubtedly triggered by the publication of some of his works in Russia. For example, Pavel Gurevich published eight volumes of Fromm's works. According to Irina Egorova, those publications which were accompanied by analytic introductory articles, insightful commentaries, is when the serious study of Fromm's legacy began in Russia (cf. Verchenov 1980; Rutkevich 1991; Gurevich 1992; 1994). In my view, at present we can observe a revival of interest in Fromm's work (for example: Egorova 2004; Dobrenkov 2006; Zaripov 2012).

I was first exposed to Fromm's ideas when his books were published in Russian. As a member of International Erich Fromm Society (from 1993 on), I participated with my paper "Ecological Crisis and the Need for a New Metaphysics" in an International Symposium in Osnabrück (Omelchenko 1996) and with my paper "Philosophy as a Productive Orientation" in an International Conference in Magliaso (Omelchenko 2006).

1. On the Definition of the Human Soul

First of all, I would like to concentrate on Erich Fromm's understanding of human essence which stimulates the debate on the topic in the field of philosophy. His studies tell us that being connected to the surrounding world is an *essential* need of humans (see Fromm 1955a, pp. 22–66). This statement supports the assumption that the human essence (understood by me as comprising of mind, soul, spirit) is seen in *relation to*, or to be more precise, as an ensemble of the (inner and outer) steady universal relations of an individual to the world.

Hegel seems to express a similar opinion, when he writes that "everything that exists is in relation, and this relation is the truth of any existence" (Hegel 1974, p. 301). If any object essence is seen in relation, then we have a chance to catch the human essence which is after all in our mind (soul).

Now let us turn to the components of the human soul.

(1) An individual is a representative of all humankind. An ensemble of the steady and universal relations between people makes up a fragment of human essence. If we try to clearly imagine an individual ab-

solutely isolated from society, we would be very soon aware that such an individual would cease to exist as a human being. Such absolute loneliness is equal to nothingness. Thus, an aggregate of the steady universal relations among living people, as well as between past and future generations, forms one of the components of the human essence (logos).

(2) There are steady relations inside the human body. These are neurodynamic regularities in the brain, mechanical, physical and chemical, physiological, genetic, and many other steady correlations in human corporeal organization. Such structures influence each other and form a general inner "pivot," i.e., the human inner logos. Moreover, there is an interaction of outer and inner correlations, which is a condition of the human essence too.

(3) An aggregate of the steady universal relations between society and nature makes up yet another fragment of the human essence.

From this point of view, one may represent thought (mind, soul, spirit) as a *relation* between the human being and the surrounding world on the one hand, and as a human *relation* to the self (i.e., self-reflection phenomenon) on the other. These *relations* become visible and audible due to human language. The human mind is then located not only in the brain but at the same time beyond the bounds of the brain, between the human body and outside reality.

According to this approach, the human soul is located not only within the human body but also beyond its limits: between the individual and society, between the individual and the Cosmos. Having gotten thus far, we need now to understand the complexity of the question "what is the human soul," as well as "what is its place of stationing."

It turns out that the human soul has an extra-spatial and timeless character. It is in fact infinite and thus incapable of final definition. The final, exhaustive definition of a soul would mean its death, at least in theory. That is why, in particular, we can give no final definitions to the human being. The human soul's infinity constitutes its immortality. In other words, the human being includes an immortal principle. Thus human nature itself presents a unity between the mortal and the immortal. In a sense, one may say that the human soul is entelechy of the infinite universe; it is a microcosm and cannot be entirely determined by social processes and structures.

2.   Man Is Contradiction

In his works, Fromm discussed an important question: is it possible to speak of the human nature or essence in general, and if 'yes', how then can we define it? He rejected an "anthropological relativism" which refused to acknowledge the existence of any human essence and described human beings as products of their cultural conditions. Fromm, like many other scholars, began with an assumption that human nature does exist.

Fromm considered human nature as a combined product of historical evolution and certain innate mechanisms and laws. Human nature has such invariable factors as necessity to satisfy physiological needs and necessity to avoid moral loneliness. Man's inalienable rights of freedom and happiness are founded in inherent human qualities: his striving to live, to expand and to express the potentialities that have developed in him in the process of historical evolution (Fromm 1941a, p. 244).

At the same time Fromm mentioned the difficulty in finding a satisfactory definition for the human nature. If one assumes a certain *substance* as constituting the essence of man, one is forced into a non-evolutionary, unhistorical position which implies that there has been no basic change in man since the very beginning of his emergence. Such a view is difficult to square with the fact that there is a tremendous difference to be found between our most undeveloped ancestors and civilized man as he appears in the last four to six thousand years of history. On the other hand, if one accepts an evolutionary concept and thus believes that man is constantly changing, what is left as an alleged "nature" or "essence" of man? (Fromm 1964a, pp. 83–4).

Fromm believed that the dilemma can be solved by defining the essence of man not as a given quality or substance, but as a *contradiction inherent in human existence*. This contradiction is to be found in two sets of facts. On the one hand, man is an animal, yet his instinctual equipment, in comparison with that of all other animals, is incomplete and not sufficient to ensure his survival unless he produces the means to satisfy his material needs and develops speech and tools. On the other hand, man has intelligence, like other animals, which permits him to use thought processes for the attainment of immediate, practical aims; but man has another mental quality which the animal lacks. He is aware of himself, of his past and of his future, which is death; of his smallness and powerlessness; he is aware of others as others – as friends, enemies, or as strangers. Man transcends all other life because he is, for the first time, *life aware of itself.* Man is *in* nature, subject to its dictates and accidents, yet he *transcends* nature because he lacks the unawareness which makes the animal a part of nature – as one with it. Man is confronted with the frightening conflict of being the prisoner of nature, yet being free in his thoughts; being a part of nature, and yet to be as it were a freak of nature; being neither here nor there. Human self-awareness has made man a stranger in the world, separate, lonely, and frightened (Fromm 1964a, p. 84). In this discourse, you may hear existential motives.

According to Fromm, the contradiction he has described so far is essentially the same as the classic view that man is both body and soul, angel and animal, that he belongs to two worlds in conflict with each other. What Fromm wants to point out here is that it is not enough to see this conflict as the essence of man, that is to say, as that by virtue of which man is man. It is necessary to go beyond this description and to recognize that the very conflict in man *demands a solution* (Fromm 1964a, p. 84).

We agree with Fromm that the mentioned contradiction in itself requires a solution, and basically there are both regressive or progressive solutions. At any new level man has reached, new contradictions appear which force him to go on with the task of finding new solutions (Fromm 1964a, p. 87).

In my turn, I would like to demonstrate the ontological foundations for another fundamental contradiction in the human existence.

According to the Bible, when Moses wondered about His name, God answered: "I am that I am" (Ex 3, 14). In philosophy's language, this reply means: "I am Being." In other words, God's name is Being. God Himself informed all people about it. His mystery is a mystery of the essence of nature, cosmos, life, human being; His characteristics are properties of infinite being, i.e., of rational-irrational essence of the universe.

This metaphysical interpretation of God invites to remember Parmenides' categories of being and non-being. Now let us make the following comparisons:

God and devil,
being and non-being (nothing),
life and death,
good and evil,
love and hatred,
beauty and ugliness,
truth and falsehood,
"yes" and "no,"
affirmation and negation,
creation and destruction.

One may meet such a logic in Heidegger's works: "'Nothing' is more original than the No and negation"; "The No does not come into being through negation, but negation is based on the No, which derives from the nihilation of Nothing"; "Nothing is the source of negation, not the other way about" (Heidegger 2000, pp. 217, 220). Using the religious terminology, one may explain these quotations: "Devil preceded the No and negation"; "Devil is the source of negation," and so on.

Of course, a special thorough research of these oppositions is required. Obviously, we will be able to get very interesting results. But now we can note that truth, good, love and beauty acquire the single ontological foundation in metaphysical being which, in terms of religion, is named as God. Thus, God is being, life, good. Devil is nothing, death, evil. Being and non-being, life and death, good and evil constitute two opposite principles of the human nature and cosmic order.

We find a support for such a discourse in Fromm's works: his *biophilic ethics* have their own principle of good and evil. Good is all that serves life; evil is all that serves death. Good is "reverence for life" (in terms of Albert Schweitzer), all that enhances life, growth, unfolding. Evil is all that stifles life, narrows it down, and cuts it into pieces (Fromm 1964a, p. 36).

3. Escape from "the Unbearable Lightness of Being"

Fromm's *Escape from Freedom* (1941a) is still greatly appreciated in Russia. In particular, it is rather popular among those intellectuals who like dictatorship. Such sociologists have a very simple argument: people did not bear freedom, did not stand the test of freedom, so we need a new "iron hand," new dictatorship. They are mistaken, however, concerning Fromm's ideas, in spite of the note that his "book is devoted mainly to freedom as a burden and danger" (Fromm 1941a, p. 83).

According to Fromm (1941a, pp. 43, 23), the main theme of his book is as it follows. Man gains freedom in the sense of emerging from the original oneness with man and nature and becomes an "individual." Freedom, though it has brought him independence and rationality, has made him isolated and, thereby, anxious and powerless. This isolation is unbearable and the alternatives he is confronted with are either to escape from the burden of his freedom into new dependencies and submission, or to advance to the full realization of positive freedom which is based upon the uniqueness and individuality of man.

In short, freedom has a twofold meaning for modern man: he has been freed from traditional authorities and has become an "individual," but at the same time he has become isolated, powerless, and an instrument of purposes outside of himself, alienated from himself and others (Fromm 1941a, p. 229). Obviously, the problem of freedom also discloses a contradictory nature of man.

In Fromm's view (1941a, p. 23), the escape from freedom has a totalitarian character, and so it is a pitiful and mean action not representing genuine human existence. Fromm is not defending dictatorship but arguing that understanding of the reasons for the totalitarian flight from freedom is a premise for any action which aims at the victory over different forms of tyranny.

As for me, I believe that freedom is the human essence, or attribute. It means that the human ceases to be human without freedom. In antiquity, slaves were called as 'speaking tools'; they had no right to be humans. Therefore, freedom is a natural condition for human beings. For instance, man himself cannot cease to breathe, or "to escape from his own breath." Just so man himself cannot escape from his own freedom, he escapes from "the unbearable lightness of being," according to successful expression of Milan Kundera (for example, from loneliness or individual weakness).

Fromm speaks approximately in the same terms:

> Once the primary bonds which gave security to the individual are severed, once the individual faces the world outside of himself as a completely separate entity, two courses are open to him since he has to overcome *the unbearable state of powerlessness and aloneness* (Fromm 1941a, p. 133 [my italics – N.O.]).

According to Fromm's viewpoint, the physiologically conditioned needs are not the only imperative part of man's nature. There is another part just as compelling, one not rooted in bodily processes but in the very essence of the human mode and practice of life: the need to be related to the world outside oneself, the need to avoid aloneness. Feeling completely alone and isolated leads a man to mental disintegration, just as physical starvation leads to death (Fromm 1941a, p. 40).

Fromm believes that there are various paths for a man to grow to "positive freedom." He can relate spontaneously to the world in love and work, in the genuine expression of his emotional, sensuous, and intellectual capacities; he can thus become one again with man, nature, and himself, without giving up the independence and integrity of his individual self. The other route open to him is to fall back, to give up his freedom, and to try to overcome his aloneness by eliminating the gap that has arisen between his individual self and the world. This second route is an escape from an unbearable situation which would make life impossible if it were prolonged. This path of escape, therefore, is characterized by its compulsive character, like every escape from threatening panic; it is also characterized by the more or less complete surrender of individuality and the integrity of the self (Fromm 1941a, p. 133).

Fromm explains that positive freedom consists of the spontaneous activity of the total, integrated personality. Freedom as the realization of the self implies the full affirmation of the uniqueness of the individual. Positive freedom also implies the principle that there is no higher power than this unique individual self, that man is the center and purpose of his life; that the growth and realization of man's individuality is an end that can never be subordinated to purposes which are supposed to have greater dignity (Fromm 1941a, pp. 220, 224, 225).

Now I would like to discuss the question of the deep source of the human free will which is, for Fromm, *freedom of choice.* In his opinion, "the problem of freedom of choice cannot be solved unless one considers that unconscious forces determine us, though leaving us with the happy conviction that our choice is a free one" (Fromm 1964a, p. 90).

Let us assume that humans depend on unknown powers. However, if they are aware of them, the situation will change a little since then humans will depend on well-known powers. In other words, man always depends on something. Therefore, his behavior, his choice and motivation are determined by certain factors and these are not free. Moreover, in the surrounding world with the cause-effect links, it is impossible to find the human willing and practical action that would be in a miraculous way free from the principle of determination. For man, it remains to conclude a certain convention with those realized powers, to submit himself willingly to them and declare himself to be free.

But how in that case can one give a satisfactory interpretation of free will? In my view, the next solution is possible. In fact, my free will, my wanting means demonstration of my mental and physical condition, of inner state of my mind and body. The confessions of my "I" are revelations of my unconscious being. For instance, if I say that I want to go to a doctor, it will mean that my body or mind gives me the signal of its unsatisfactory condition, and my "I" speaks, transmits this signal coming from the depths of my organism and mind. My "I" expresses my mood *autonomously* and *freely*, I adequately reproduce that which is required for my personal system. My "I" would not be free if I declared my wish to go to a doctor under pressure of my relatives or friends who noted a pale color of my face.

Thus, free will does not mean an absence of any determination of my "I" when I express my wish. My "I" is found to be really free since I express *my and only my* inner state. By this, my "I" can absolutely know nothing about original, latent causes of the very organism to visit a doctor. My will can be mistaken or be a usual caprice. In this sense, free will does not presuppose cognition or realization of necessity.

Of course, my own will can depend on unconscious powers; cosmic logos or transcendent God are able to influence my inner state, and I cannot know about it. But here it is very important that my will is identical with my physical and mental state, and so my will is free and autonomous. Free will is a spontaneous impulse proceeding from my own mind or body. We have always free will that is an ability to manifest our inner states as living creatures in the infinite universe.

In my view, the human free will as a spontaneous impulse is primary, and the procedure of choice from available possibilities is secondary, derivative from this inner impulse of mental or physical condition of an individual.

4. Love as a Heuristic Principle

Fromm notes that in contemporary society emotions in general are discouraged. While there can be no doubt that any creative thinking – as well as any other creative activity – is inseparably linked with emotion, it has become an ideal to think and to live without emotions. To be "emotional" has become synonymous with being unsound or unbalanced. By the acceptance of this standard the individual has become greatly weakened; his thinking is impoverished and flattened. On the other hand, since emotions cannot be completely killed, they must have their existence totally apart from the intellectual side of the personality; the result is the cheap and insincere sentimentality with which movies and popular songs feed millions of emotion-starved customers (Fromm 1941a, p. 210).

I believe that horror, hatred, love, respect, and other feelings are a kind of human relation to the surrounding world. Any emotional relation to objects participates in understanding of these objects. The so-called "pure cognition," i.e., cognition without feelings, does not exist. Our feelings influence our cognitive processes. They are able to promote finding the truth or misrepresenting the facts, and, moreover, our feelings themselves are a type of human cognition.

In my view, if "dread reveals Nothing" (in terms of Martin Heidegger), then love opens Being. Love is a natural property of the human soul coinciding with one's cognitive abilities and having an effect on the process and result of knowledge. Love is the most optimal relation for understanding of the world and human being. Only love can help to achieve a heuristic success. It means, for example, that only a mother who loves her children is able to understand them.

The history of philosophy has many manifestations of the idea that love paves the road for reason to things and people. The contemporary intellectual situation also makes it important to consider love as a heuristic principle, as an epistemological category. From this viewpoint, only those who love humans will be able to know the truth about them.

According to Fromm, *"love is union* with somebody, or something, outside oneself, *under the condition of retaining the separateness and integrity of one's own self"* (Fromm 1955a, p. 31). This is a very interesting rational definition, but it does not adequately represent that human emotional relation which we call love.

The experience of love does away with the necessity of illusions. There is no need to inflate the image of the other person, or of oneself, since the reality of active sharing and loving permits us to transcend our individualized existence, and at the same time to experience ourselves as the bearers of the active powers which constitute the act of loving.

Love is one aspect of what Fromm has called the productive orientation: the active and creative relatedness of man to his fellow man, to himself and to nature. In the realm of thought, this productive orientation is expressed in the proper grasp of the world by reason. In other words, *the truth is opening to love.*

In Fromm's view (1955a, pp. 31–2), productive love always implies a syndrome of attitudes; that of *care, responsibility, respect and knowledge.* If I love, I care – that is, I am actively concerned with the other person's growth and happiness; I am not a spectator. I am responsible, that is, I respond to his needs, to those he can express and more so to those he cannot or does not express. I respect him, that is, I look at him as he is, objectively and not distorted by my wishes and fears. I know him; I have penetrated through his surface to the core of his being and related myself to him from my core, from the center, as against the periphery, of my being. By the way, the identity between "to love" and "to know" is contained in the Hebrew *jadoa* and in the German *meinen* and *minnen.*

In a word, love accompanies the deepest revelations of being. Being lays down one indispensable condition for its revelation – the thinker's love. By this, being reminds us about its *ordo amoris* (Max Scheler). Nothing but reason filled with love is able to discover the essence of being. Therefore, to see the truth, reason must observe the surrounding world with love. In other words, the truth of being reveals itself towards loving reason.

Obviously, falling in love with knowledge is an additional condition for a heuristic success. The very word "philosophy" is symbolic: in order to know the truth, it is important to love – not formally but really – wisdom, knowledge. People tend not to believe in love, however as they do not see it. It appears that this human relation, this feeling is rare in the world of people, and that is why we smile with skepticism when we hear of love, in particular of love connected to knowledge.

Philosophy as love for wisdom is in itself wisdom in the sense that it understands that it is not a certain container for *veritas rerum*, but is just a sincere love to the truth of being. One may say it is possible to contemplate wisdom only in the case when one truly loves it. In other words, philosophy as love for wisdom teaches love, including love to itself. Apparently, *love to philosophy* is an indispensable condition for its understanding.

Conclusion

In this paper, I tried to present some of Fromm's philosophical ideas including that of the contradictory character of human nature, which is discovered looking for the solution of the problem of freedom. The fundamental principle of individual relatedness to the world allows us to understand human nature much better. Fromm's conception of love is productive for making a contemporary theory of knowledge that is an integral part of the philosophy of human being.

Fromm's doctrine combines psychological and philosophical conceptions and conclusions. The most important value of this doctrine lies in its steady humanistic intention. The ideal of free development of personality is a supreme principle of Fromm's psychological analysis. The disclosing of the unique human faculties is possible only in this humanist way.

References

Dobrenkov, V. (1972). Kritika neofreidistskoi kontseptsii Erikha Fromma [Criticism of Neofreudist Conception of Erich Fromm]. Moscow (Znanie).

Dobrenkov, V. (1974). Neofreidizm v poiskakh "istiny" (Illyuzii i zabluzhdeniya Erikha Fromma) [Neofreudism in the Search of "the Truth" (Illusions and Delusions of Erich Fromm)]. Moscow (Mysl).

Dobrenkov, V. (2006). Psikhoanaliticheskaya sotsiologiya Erikha Fromma: uchebnoe posobie [The Psychoanalytical Sociology of Erich Fromm. Textbook]. Moscow (Alfa-M).

Egorova, I. (2004). Filosofskaya antropologiya Erikha Fromma [The Philosophical Anthropology of Erich Fromm]. Dissertation. Institute of Philosophy, Russian Academy of Sciences. Moscow. – Retrieved from: http://www.dslib.net/religio-vedenie/filosofskaja-antropologija-jeriha-fromma.html (March 19, 2015).

Fromm, E. (1941a). Begstvo ot svobody. [Escape from Freedom], translated by Grigory Shveinik and Galina Novichkova. Moscow (Academic Project), 2007.

Fromm, E. (1955a). The Sane Society. New York (Rinehart and Winston Inc.).

Fromm, E. (1964a). Dusha cheloveka. Eyo sposobnost k dobru i zlu. [The Heart of Man], translated by Vladimir Zaks. Moscow (Respublika), 1992.

Gurevich, P. (1992). Vidnyi myslitel XX stoletiya [A Distinguished Thinker of the XX Century]. In: E. Fromm. Dusha cheloveka. Eyo sposobnost k dobru i zlu. [The Heart of Man], translated by Vladimir Zaks. Moscow (Respublika), pp. 5–12.

Gurevich, P. (1994). Razrushitelnoe v cheloveke kak taina [The Destructive in Humanity as a Mystery]. In: E. Fromm. Anatomiya chelovecheskoi destruktivnosti [The Anatomy of Human Destructiveness], translated by Emilia Telyatnikova. Moscow (Respublika), pp. 3–14.

Hegel, G.W.F. (1974). Entsiklopedia filosofskikh nauk [Encyclopedia of Philosophical Sciences]. In 3 vols. Vol. 1. Science of Logic, translated by Boris Stolpner. Moscow (Mysl).

Heidegger, M. (2000). What Is Metaphysics? In: S. Luper (Ed.) Existing. An Introduction to Existential Thought. Mountain View, CA (Mayfield Publishing Company), pp. 215–27.

Kurkin, B. (1983). Gumanisticheskaya utopia E. Fromma [E. Fromm's Humanistic Utopia]. In: Voprosy filosofii [The Questions of Philosophy]. No. 2, pp. 85–94.

Omelchenko, N. (1996). Ecological Crisis and the Need for New Metaphysics. In: M. Zimmer (Ed). Von der Kunst, umweltgerecht zu planen und zu handeln. Osnabrück (Selbstverlag), pp. 71–9.

Omelchenko, N. (2006). Philosophy As a Productive Orientation. In: Fromm Forum (English edition). Tuebingen (Selbstverlag). Vol. 10, pp. 44–6.

Rutkevich, A. (1991). "Anatomiya destruktivnosti" E. Fromma ["The Anatomy of Destructiveness" of E. Fromm]. In: Voprosy filosofii [The Questions of Philosophy]. No. 9, pp. 56–69.

Schwartzman, K. (1971). "Gumanisticheskaya etika" E. Fromma ["The Humanistic Ethics" of E. Fromm]. In: Voprosy filosofii [The Questions of Philosophy]. No. 6, pp. 89–100.

Verchenov, L. (1980). Sotsialnaya teoriya Erikha Fromma: nauchno-analiticheskyi obzor [The Social Theory of Erich Fromm: A Scientific-Analytic Review]. Moscow (INION RAN).

Zaripov, D. (2012). "Zdorovoe obschestvo" kak proekt voploscheniya idei pozitivnoi svobody (politiko-filosofskaya kontseptsiya Erikha Fromma) ["The Sane Society" as a Project for Realization of the Ideas of Positive Freedom (Political and Philosophical Conception of Erich Fromm)]. Dissertation. Moscow. – Abstract available: http://www.docme.ru/doc/235163/«zdorovoe-obshhestvo»-kak-proekt-voploshheniya-idej-pozitivnoj... (February 4, 2015).

Social Character
and Social Unconscious

Erich Fromm's Discovery and the Problems of Today

Tatiana Panfilova

Abstract. In the Soviet Union Fromm was primarily known as a social thinker. He was highly appreciated for his adherence to socialist principles, his interpretation, in Marx's spirit, of ideology as "false consciousness" as well as his creative reformulation of Marx's concept of man. Furthermore, Fromm's concept of social character gained a lot of attention in the USSR. Through elaborating the idea of social unconscious Fromm warned his readers against modern democracy, consumerism and the power of technocrats. Unfortunately his warnings were ignored by the Soviet and Russian leaders. Nevertheless, Fromm's ideas remain valid today.

I will look at Fromm's work from the familiar to me point of view of a Russian scholar. In the Soviet Union Fromm's works became popular in the sixties, the period when I first became exposed to them. At the time, however, Fromm's books were not translated into Russian from English. I, among many others, read them in the original language at the library.

Although Fromm was well-known as a neo-Freudian psychoanalyst he was considered a social thinker first of all. His elaboration of the socio-psychological mechanisms of modern society in Marx's spirit and more importantly his creative interpretation of Marx's concept of man, made him popular among Soviet and Russian scholars. At the time Marx was officially recognized in the Soviet Union as a political economist who had worked out the revolutionary theory of overthrowing capitalism. Marx's concept of man was in the background but according to Fromm it deserved far more attention especially its social aspect, that is, man's connection with society. Thus, inspired by Marx, Fromm developed a theory seeing man as a social product. He developed the concept of social character playing a role of an intermediary between the economic base and the ideological superstructure. At the same time, Fromm drew readers' attention to the humanistic aspect of Marx's theory. I was one of those readers.

It doesn't mean that I fully agree with Fromm. I find contradictions in the view of human nature that he presents as potentially existing in all of us. It does not seem to go together with the concept of social character, in my view. However, I admit that dialectically speaking contradiction is a source of development. My subsequent intellectual development was affected by this contradiction on the one hand, and the achievements of Fromm's social and socio-psychological thoughts, on the other hand. Fromm's works seemed to have reviewed well-known theories. His ideas gave the reader a chance to look more analytically and critically at the changing world. What made his ideas so attractive was that they were rather flexible and easily applicable to the new circumstances. What seemed very relevant was that he encouraged examining ideological postulates from a humanistic angle.

Although Fromm harshly criticized the Soviet Union's policies and ideology, his criticism was not ignored. One of the reasons for that was that he also criticized the United States' policies and ideology just as severely. Another reason was that his criticism concerning Russia coincided to a considerable extent with the internal criticism existing within the country. In spite of the widespread opinion that the Soviet frame of mind was ideologically homogenous, the public recognized the flaws of the Soviet style of life and voicing such opinions during discussions on the social and human problems was usual. It does not mean that critical attitude to some aspects of Soviet life turned the general public into the enemies of the Soviet system. The purpose of this criticism was to improve the situation in the country in order to make further advancements in the areas of social justice and social security as well as creating more employment opportunities and a universal access to higher education. Fromm's books presented a similar vision of what social betterment should look like. He embraced socialist principles at the same time objecting when they were violated. He saw these principles as being more socially constructive in comparison with bourgeois values.

The views of Soviet scholars on ways to improve the world situation differed from Fromm's position but his theories were still very useful and instructive, especially his interpretation of ideology as "false consciousness" following Marx's ideas. Marx's diagnosis of the causes of world socio economic problems was well known, but it was difficult to realize that in the Soviet Union there was a discrepancy between the socialist principles declared and the actual Soviet ideology. At the same time the idea of replacing the Soviet ideology with the ideology of liberalism was met with opposition. Soviet intellectuals differed in opinions. Some among them were those who repudiated socialist principles and accepted the ideology of liberalism. They became dissenters. Others insisted that the ideology of liberalism did not fit the Soviet Union and the socialist principles should be strengthened. I joined the second trend in accordance with Fromm's adherence to the idea of socialism.

Fromm's work helped us better understand the dangers of confusing the ideological system with actual real life as it was lived in society. Fromm helped to differentiate between the official ideological system as a sort of "false consciousness" and the set of ideas as an expression of the distinctiveness of a particular society. The concept of "false consciousness" refers to the consciousness of the elites who consider "their way of organization and the values that are implied in it as being in 'the best interests of man'" (Fromm 1962a, p. 116). The ideas defining the nation that Fromm talks about are a manifestation of real spiritual and intellectual social life of the nation.

Fromm demonstrated that when two opposite ideological systems operate side by side none of them could be entirely correct. The reason for this was that ideologists from each camp presented their point by distorting the facts and arguments made by their opponents. Under such circumstances mutual understanding was and is impossible.

Following Marx, Fromm rejected all ideologies. He preferred Marx's radical point of view which suggested "go[ing] to the roots" in order to grasp what constitutes a human being and what is humane. At the same time Fromm showed that going to the roots was very difficult if not impossible because social alienation does not allow people to embark on such journeys of self-scrutiny. Nevertheless, Fromm did his best to show how the modern situation, more precisely the alienation of contemporary societies, can be overcome. He started by criticizing American democracy, demonstrating that modern democracy had turned into an official ideology and degenerated into a form of human deprivation.

Fromm was not the first thinker in the European tradition who critiqued democracy. Oswald Spengler regarded democracy as a feature of the so-called "civilization" that he considered to be a culture in decay. Spengler showed that the democracy of the 20th century created a system in which money meant getting access to political power. That stood, of course, in start contrast to what democracy was supposed to be. Modern democracy, as Spengler stressed, is destroyed by the money- power connection.

It seems that Fromm took Spengler's conclusions into account while analyzing the world situation after the WWII. In his book *The Sane Society* (1955) Fromm stresses that "the functioning of the political machinery in a democratic country is not essentially different from the procedure of the commodity market" (Fromm 1955a, p. 166) and that the professional politicians use the method which looks like the method of high pressure advertising. No wonder that his estimation of such features of democracy as universal suffrage is not purely positive. He writes in *The Sane Society*: "Under these circumstances universal suffrage becomes a fetish" (Fromm 1955a, p. 165).

These passages were written in the middle of the previous century. Now it seems pretty obvious that democracy has become a fetish, or I would even say "an idée fix" just as is the idea of human rights. I spoke about these questions at the XVII International Forum of Psychoanalysis held in Mexico-city in 2012. I would like to stress that this transformation of democracy took place because of the "socially conditioned filter" as a mechanism of social unconscious enumerated by Fromm in *Beyond the Chains of Illusion* (1962a, p. 125). The idea of democracy, just as with the idea of human rights, was ideologically transformed into a dead framework. Now both frameworks are recognized as legitimate and uncritically accepted. Life manifestations must fit these frames to be recognized as real or true otherwise they will be artificially forced into them. This situation will probably remain the same as long as alienated society exists and until the elite of the globalizing world regards its own interests as the best interests of the humanity.

So we can ascertain that Fromm warned us against modern democracy as a manifestation of an alienated society. Unfortunately during the so called "perestroika" (reconstruction), Soviet authorities yielded the temptation to appear democratic and liberal. Following the advices of their American counselors, Soviet and then Russian leaders tried to establish a democratic government by placing national resources at their supporters' disposal. However, the vital problems of the country were ignored. As a result the country experienced destruction rather than the reconstruction of the nation's social life. New social institutions that can be considered foreign to Russian society were established but they don't function properly.

To tackle these problems authorities resorted to promoting the ideology of consumerism combined with liberalism. Fromm warned us against consumerism beforehand. He pointed out the negative consequences of this phenomenon, especially its destructive impact on the human psyche. He criticized the Soviet Union of the sixties as a "have" state based on the "possession" principle. Fromm considered this principle to be bourgeois and criticized the Soviet government for deviating from Marxism.

I fully agree with Fromm's evaluation of consumerism. But we must distinguish between consumerism as a style of life and as a mode allowing people to satisfy their needs. In the sixties there was a conviction among the Soviet people that certain needs haven't been met and that they need to get access to more basic goods. Thus, an introduction of the "have" principle into the Soviet life was to some extent relevant. Unfortunately, the following Soviet leaders didn't take Fromm's warning into consideration. During the "perestroika" the basis of consumers' society was established. After the collapse of the Soviet Union this tendency was strengthened. The corresponding type of social character developed in Russian society side by side with the establishment of the free market and "democracy". So we stepped back from the declared socialist ideals to bourgeois ones. Instead of developing more progressive principles promoted by Fromm we stepped back to the principles of the past that were already very well developed in capitalist countries. This retreat was officially explained by the fact that Russia was technologically less advanced and technological development required the capitalist approach to the means of production and to the productive forces. People as a new productive force had to be equipped with computers and to be capable of using them.

The socio-psychological problems arise: what kind of social character corresponds with a computerizing world and does this type of social character promote the humanization of the world? These are the burning problems that the world is currently facing. There are no ready answers in Fromm's books but his ideas give us a good starting point.

Fromm was worried about the seemingly ruling principle of the modern world fetishizing technology according to which everything must be done using technology if it is possible. The consequences of following such a principle seems not to worry the technocrats even if subscribing to such technologically fixated life might lead to the annihilation of humanity. Fromm insisted that technology itself is not bad, it has to be used responsibly and should serve human beings. Both economic and technological development must be the means of human development.

The wide availability of computers around the world makes this problem far more urgent than it was in the late sixties, when Fromm wrote *The Revolution of Hope* (Fromm 1968a). One wants to ask if a modern person serves a computer that symbolizes here technology or technology is serving people. Fromm would answer in a humanistic voice that a computer must help people to develop themselves and do so while maintaining contact with other people. In fact the situation is more complicated. We encounter a problem of a new social character corresponding to the computer reality. I propose to call this type of social character the "information character". A person of this character is capable of perceiving, processing and sending information without digesting it as if a person is not a subject of the process but a means of transmission. This means that subjectivity is lacking and social alienation is deepened in the era of globalization.

According to Rainer Funk's conception (Funk 2006) modern social character can be called a "I-am-me orientation" and it is characterized by a "kaleidoscopic" perception and thinking. A person of such character needs permanent outer stimulation and outer integrators. This description confirms that subjectivity is lost nowadays.

The world situation is uneasy and today humanism appears to be old-fashioned. The Russian government follows the world tendency of dehumanization. It pursues the liberal course of the economy destructive of the country and the people who live there. Fromm's legacy is appreciated highly by supporters of socialism but they are not the ones who determine current policies. Even the system of education in Russia is oriented towards consumerism. There is no room for Fromm's humanistic views in contemporary Russian education. Nevertheless, those who share Fromm's ideals do their best to bring his ideas to the young generation. The most famous books by Fromm are translated into Russian and published and thus, are available to a wider public, including students. This is vitally important, because Fromm's concepts of social character and social unconscious are still valid and useful for analyzing modern society and cultural changes taking place in it.

References

Fromm, E. (1955a). The Sane Society. Greenwich (Fawcett Publications)..
Fromm, E. (1962a). Beyond the Chains of Illusion. New York (Pocket Books)..
Fromm, E. (1968a). The Revolution of Hope. Toward a Humanized Technology. New York (Harper and Row).
Funk, R. (2006). The Psychodynamics of the Postmodern I-am-me Orientation. In: Fromm Forum (English Edition) (Self-published) 10, pp. 52–61.

Fromm, Marx, and Humanism

Kevin B. Anderson

Abstract: Fromm's early work connecting Marx and Freud as part of the Frankfurt School has gotten inordinate attention, while his later work interpreting Marx as a humanist, democratic, and anti-totalitarian thinker has received short shrift in recent decades. This paper will examine works like *Marx's Concept of Man* (1961a) and *Socialist Humanism* (1965a) in terms of their context, their impact, and the controversies they stirred up with Cold War liberals like Sidney Hook and the young Richard Bernstein. Fromm's differences with Marcuse over humanism are also explored. In addition, this paper discusses Fromm's correspondence with the Marxist feminist and humanist Raya Dunayevskaya and his connections with Eastern European dissident Marxists. Fromm's persistent dialogue with Marx during the last two decades of his life had a wide impact on the 1960s generation and beyond. At a time when the crisis of capitalism has led to a new interest in Marx, this after the collapse of the Soviet Union, it also speaks to us today.

Erich Fromm is often underestimated by critical social theorists and philosophers, who characterize him as a liberal idealist, or as a popularizer who lacked rigor, in contrast to other members of the Frankfurt School like Theodor Adorno. None deny, however, that it was Fromm who first introduced the Frankfurt School to a form of Freudian Marxism that was at the root of all of their subsequent efforts to theorize "authoritarian personalities."

By the 1950s, with publications like *The Art of Loving* (1956a), Fromm seemed to be entering the American mainstream, perhaps even moving from Marxism to Cold War liberalism as so many others were doing in that period. That was what Marcuse seemed to suggest in his *Eros and Civilization* (1955), which led to a sharp exchange with Fromm in the left-liberal journal *Dissent*. However, a closer look at Fromm's writings in this period shows a far different picture. That same year, in *The Sane Society*, Fromm began to put forward a humanist interpretation of Marx's thought, extolling Marx's humanism as one of the major "answers" to the "decay and dehumanization behind the glamour and wealth and political power of Western society" (Fromm 1955a, p. 205).

By 1961, in his *Marx's Concept of Man*, Fromm foregrounded his Marxist humanist position, writing that Marx's "theory does not assume that the main motive of man is one of material gain; (...) furthermore, the very aim of Marx is to liberate man from the pressure of economic needs, so that he can be fully human" (Fromm 1961b, pp. 4–5). Fromm rooted such notions firmly in the notion that Marx stood for the abolition of the capitalist mode of production, not its reform via higher wages and the like:

> His criticism of capitalist society is directed not at its method of distribution of income, but its mode of production, its destruction of individuality and its enslavement of man, not by the capitalist, but the enslavement of man – worker and capitalist – by things and circumstances of their own making (Fromm 1961b, p. 49).

Fromm's (and Marx's) notion of human emancipation is predicated on a vision of a new society, not as a distant or imaginary utopia, but as a real possibility that exists as a tendency inside the very structures of capitalist society itself. For the first time since the Neolithic revolution subjected laboring populations to unremitting toil in order to achieve a surplus product that helped to create the first class societies, the vast productive apparatus created by capitalism makes possible – for the future – sharply reduced hours of labor alongside material abundance. This possibility is of course conditioned by the danger that the system might first annihilate humanity in nuclear war or irrevocably damage the global ecological system.

With *Marx's Concept of Man*, Fromm probably did more than any other writer to introduce Marx's 1844 *Economic and Philosophical Manuscripts* to the English-speaking public, also bringing the notion of socialist humanism to the fore. *Marx's Concept of Man* consists of a ninety-page introductory essay by Fromm, Tom Bottomore's translation of 110 pages from Marx's *1844 Manuscripts*, twenty-three pages from other texts by Marx (primarily *The German Ideology* and *The Critique of Political Economy*), and forty pages of reminiscences from Marx's contemporaries.

One point needs to be underlined here. Despite the widely repeated claim that Fromm expresses in his introduction a preference for the young Marx over the "mature" Marx of *Capital*, Fromm makes no such statement anywhere in the book, or later on for that matter either. This is one of the most persistent myths in the Marx scholarship, but in fact the most prominent radical thinker who saw the writings of the early Marx as far superior to his later ones was not Fromm but Jean-Paul Sartre, who extolls the *1844 Manuscripts*, noting that they were written before what the French existentialist philosopher terms the "unfortunate meeting with Engels" (Sartre 1949, p. 248).

In response to *Marx's Concept of Man*, some of those on the left who had chosen the Western camp in the Cold War now renewed their attacks upon Fromm, whom they already detested for his critiques of the U.S. nuclear arsenal. They resented and resisted as well the whole new view of Marx as a radical humanist that Fromm was presenting.

Earlier in the same year, 1961, Fromm had stirred up the Cold War liberals with several searing attacks on nuclear weapons, in some of which he characterized U.S. Cold War attitudes toward the Soviet Union as an example of extreme paranoia. In response, Cold War liberals like the former leftist and academic Marx specialist Sidney Hook, a neoconservative *avant la lettre*, launched a series of savage attacks in the liberal journal *New Leader*, accusing Fromm of opposing Western "readiness to defend freedom against Communist aggression" in favor of appeasement. Not only was he an appeaser, Hook added, but Fromm should also "recognize that his position on defense makes the triumph of world Communism easier, and justif[ies] it as the lesser evil" (Hook 1961a, p. 13). In their exchange, Fromm wrote that Hook's response "is a good summary of the current clichés on the problem of disarmament" (Fromm 1961c, p. 10). Some months later, Fromm's book against nuclear weapons appeared, entitled *May Man Prevail?* (Fromm 1961a). At this point, *New Leader* ran another scurrilous attack, "Fromm's Logic of Surrender," written by a future neocon, Martin Peretz (1962).

Fromm's was not the first attempt to launch a discussion of the *1844 Manuscripts* in the U.S. Marcuse had analyzed them with more philosophical depth in his *Reason and Revolution* (Marcuse 1941), although he did not make a category out of humanism. My intellectual mentor Raya Dunayevskaya continued the philosophically grounded discussion in her *Marxism and Freedom* (1958), a volume that did center on Marx's humanism, which she sharply differentiated not only from the oppressive social reality but also the reigning ideologies of Soviet Union and Maoist China. Dunayevskaya's was also the first book to include an English translation of two of the most important *1844 Manuscripts*, "Private Property and Communism" and "Critique of the Hegelian Dialectic." A full but somewhat flawed English edition of the *Manuscripts* appeared in 1959 in a small edition from Progress Publishers in Moscow. These previous discussions and translations on the *1844 Manuscripts* had touched off some discussion within leftist or academic circles, where they had begun to make an impact.

Fromm's standing as a public intellectual and his popular form of presentation – honed in books like *Escape from Freedom* (Fromm 1941a) or *The Sane Society* (Fromm 1955a) – helped to spark a far wider discussion of the young Marx in the English-speaking world, not only among the broad intellectual public, but also in mass media outlets like *Newsweek* that rarely discussed Marx, let alone in positive terms. This made *Marx's Concept of Man* one of the most widely read collections of Marx's writings ever published.

An important and sadly still relevant part of Fromm's own contribution to *Marx's Concept of Man* is his critique what he terms "the falsification of Marx's concepts" in the mass media and even among most intellectuals. He adds pungently that "this ignorance and distortion of Marx are more to be found in the United States than in any other Western country" (Fromm 1961b, p. 1).

The first falsification, Fromm writes, involves portraying Marx as a crude materialist who "neglected the importance of the individual" (Fromm 1961b, p. 2). Fromm refutes this, holding, as mentioned above, that "the very aim of Marx is to liberate man from the pressure of economic needs, so that he can be fully human" (ibid., p. 5).

What Fromm sees as a second "falsification" of Marx, one carried out by both Western intellectuals and Stalinist ideologues, is the erroneous identification of Marx's thought with the single-party totalitarianism of the

Soviet Union and Maoist China. During the Cold War, this led most leftist or liberal intellectuals to take sides with either the West (for example, Albert Camus or the U.S. Cold War liberals) or the Soviet Union and its sphere (for example, Jean-Paul Sartre or Georg Lukács) as the supposedly lesser evil.

Significantly, Fromm rejects and moves beyond this framework, as he sharply differentiates "Marxist humanist socialism," on the one hand, from "totalitarian socialism," on the other (Fromm 1961b, p. viii). He characterizes the latter as actually "a system of conservative state capitalism" (ibid., p. vii). Again, this critique on Fromm's part has importance for today, in the light of the many attempts to tie the collapse of the Soviet Union to the "death" of Marxism.

While orthodox Marxists – and a bit later, of course, anti-humanist ones like Louis Althusser – surely had a lot of objections to Fromm's book, they were not the first to take the field against it. Instead, Cold War liberals like Hook led the attack once more. Here again, if one judges the general thrust of *Marx's Concept of Man* by the kind of opposition it stirred up, the book is an example of how far in relative terms Fromm had moved to the left, this was at a time when McCarthyism still retained a strong grip on U.S. intellectual life.

In one of the attacks on *Marx's Concept of Man*, the young philosopher Richard Bernstein went so far as to dismiss Marx's *1844 Manuscripts* as "a series of jottings" (Fromm 1961b, p. 29). Such statements do not stand the test of time very well. More tellingly, Bernstein, who later achieved international recognition as a pragmatist philosopher with close ties to Habermas, prefigures, in his attack on Fromm, later Habermasian and post-structuralist critiques of Marx. For Bernstein also warns that Fromm's talk of human "self-realization" in Marx is a "dangerous" form of "absolute humanism" that "as history has taught us... can by subtle gradations turn into an absolute totalitarianism" (ibid., p. 30). Thus, it was for the very reason that Marx might be a humanist that his thought was dangerous, even totalitarian! What was at issue here, of course, was Bernstein's rejection of any attempt to transcend [*Aufheben*] the capitalist order. Any such attempt, it evidently seemed to Bernstein at this juncture, would lead straight to Stalin. The tone of that 1961 review – by a scholar who later moved somewhat to the left – also suggests the extent to which the stench of McCarthyism still wafted over even liberal and progressive sectors of American intellectual life.

Hook, an originator of the "Hegel and totalitarianism" school who had ignored Marx's *1844 Manuscripts* in his acclaimed *From Marx to Hegel* (Hook 1936), and who had launched violent attacks against Marcuse's *Reason and Revolution* when it appeared in 1941, pontificated in an even more hostile review of *Marx's Concept of Man*: "To seek what was distinctive and characteristic about Marx in a period when he was still in Hegelian swaddling clothes (...) is to violate every accepted and tested canon of historical scholarship" (Hook 1961b, p. 16).

None of these attacks seriously dented the impact of *Marx's Concept of Man*, however. For by now the ground was shifting toward a wider appreciation of the totality of Marx's writings and toward the new type of radicalism of the 1960s that would attack not only economic exploitation, but also alienation and the oppressions of race, gender, and later, sexuality.

Fromm followed up *Marx's Concept of Man* with an edited book, *Socialist Humanism: An International Symposium*, published in 1965 with one of America's largest publishing houses at the time, Doubleday (Fromm 1965a). For several years afterwards, this volume was the only widely circulated book on socialism in the U.S. It comprised essays by some thirty-five noted intellectuals, among them over a dozen from within Eastern Europe, most of them philosophical dissidents, but also a few who hewed more toward the party line. In most cases, these Eastern European philosophers were appearing in English for the first time. The more dissident Eastern European Marxist humanists included several who would become prominent in the upheavals of the 1960s in the Eastern bloc, most notably the Prague Spring of 1968. Among the intellectuals from what was then Czechoslovakia were the Marxist humanists Karel Kosík and Ivan Svitak, while Poland was represented by Bronislaw Baczko as well as the more pro-party Adam Schaff, the latter a personal friend of Fromm. What was then Yugoslavia had a particularly large representation, with a number of figures from the dissident philosophers of the Praxis group, among them Mihailo Markovic, Gajo Petrovic, and Rudi Supek. From Western Europe, North America, and Australia the volume drew upon Marxist philosophers like Marcuse, Dunayevskaya, Lucien Goldmann, Ernst Bloch, and Eugene Kamenka. As Fromm himself acknowledged in his introduction to the volume, it lacked very much representation from the Third World, although it did contain essays by the left-wing Gandhian Nirmal Kumar Bose and by Leopold

Senghor, the president of newly independent Senegal, who espoused a decidedly non-revolutionary form of socialist humanism.

Interestingly, Fromm rejected a contribution on the young Marx by Louis Althusser, whose attacks on humanism and characterization of the young Marx as not yet Marxist fell far outside the perspectives of the book. In this way, Fromm helped delay by several years the entrance of the French anti-humanist philosopher into the English-speaking world. The French Communist Party member Althusser replied quite aggressively to this affront, writing several letters of complaint to the Polish Communist Adam Schaff, who had recommended him to Fromm. Althusser also penned several private essay-length accounts of this episode, which were published posthumously under the title *The Humanist Controversy* (Althusser 2003). In another interesting turn, Fromm's old antagonist Hook's hostility to Marxist humanism was evidently so great that he crossed the Cold War divide to write an essay in praise of Althusser's interpretation of Marx, this at a time when Hook was supporting Richard Nixon (Hook 1973).

In his introduction to *Socialist Humanism*, Fromm also spelled out more of his notion of socialist humanism, going to great lengths to show its identity with earlier forms of humanism:

Humanism has always emerged as a reaction to a threat to mankind: in the Renaissance, to the threat of religious fanaticism; in the Enlightenment, to extreme nationalism and the enslavement of man by the machine and economic interests. The revival of Humanism today is a new reaction to this latter threat in a more intensified form – the fear that man may become the slave of things, the prisoner of circumstances he himself has created – and the wholly new threat to mankind's physical existence posed by nuclear weapons (Fromm 1965a, p. viii).

But where there was identity, there was also difference.

In the latter sense, Fromm also stressed the core differences between socialist humanism and earlier forms of humanism:

Socialist Humanism differs in an important respect from other branches. Renaissance and Enlightenment Humanism believed that the task of transforming man into a fully human being could be achieved exclusively or largely by education. Although Renaissance Utopians touched upon the need for social

215

changes, the socialist Humanism of Karl Marx was the first to declare that theory cannot be separated from practice, knowledge from action, spiritual aims from the social system. Marx held that free and independent man could exist only in a social and economic system that, by its rationality and abundance, brought to an end the epoch of "prehistory" and opened the epoch of "human history," which would make the full development of the individual the condition for the full development of society, and vice versa. Hence he devoted the greater part of his life to the study of capitalist economics and the organization of the working class in the hopes of instituting a socialist society that would be the basis for the development of a new Humanism (Fromm 1965a, p. viii).

This was not the whole story, however.

Marxism also had to be differentiated along a humanist versus crude materialist axis, with the latter not really Marxist in Fromm's eyes:

> Marx was misinterpreted both by those who felt threatened by his program, and by many socialists. The former accused him of caring only for the physical, not the spiritual, needs of man. The latter believed that his goal was exclusively material affluence for all, and that Marxism differed from capitalism only in its methods, which were economically more efficient and could be initiated by the working class. In actuality, Marx's ideal was a man productively related to other men and to nature, who would respond to the world in an alive manner, and who would be rich not because he had much but because he was much (Fromm 1965a, p. ix).

To many, then and since, such lofty goals, articulated in such a ringing fashion, were at best utopian and at worst, completely outdated or even dangerous.

Some of these kinds of criticisms of socialist humanism found their way into the book *Socialist Humanism* itself. For example, Marcuse's essay expressed considerable doubt about the socialist humanist project in terms of the emancipation of real human beings from alienation and exploitation:

> Marxian theory retains an idea of man which now appears as too optimistic and idealistic. Marx underrated the extent of the conquest of nature and of man, of the technological management of freedom and self-realization. He did not foresee the great achievement of technological society: the assimilation of freedom and necessity, of satisfaction and repression, of the

aspirations of politics, business, and the individual. In view of these achievements, socialist humanism can no longer be defined in terms of the individual, the all-round personality, and self-determination (Marcuse 1965, p. 101).

Thus, the success of twentieth century capitalism, of the ever deeper penetration of its commodity fetishism into popular consciousness, of its Fordist high wages, etc., meant that the old revolutionary humanist ideal that underpinned Marx's thought had been superseded by the historical development of capitalism into so subtle a form of domination that even conceptualizing humanism in Marxian terms had become impossible. While he did not go the full distance of someone like Adorno and his notion of the totally administered society, Marcuse in this essay exhibited more than a flavor of that kind of thinking, as also seen in his book published the year before, *One-Dimensional Man*. (An unpublished Marcuse essay from this period on humanism, expressing a similar ambivalence, has recently turned up [Marcuse 1962]).

It was while putting together *Marx's Concept of Man* in 1959 that Fromm began his thirty-year correspondence with Dunayevskaya, which contains an interesting Marxist humanist discussion of gender. In 1976, while working on her *Rosa Luxemburg, Women's Liberation*, and *Marx's Philosophy of Revolution*, Dunayevskaya writes to Fromm concerning the "lack of camaraderie between Luxemburg, Lenin, and Trotsky." Referring to Luxemburg, she asks: "Could there have been, if not outright male chauvinism, at least some looking down on her theoretical work, because she was a woman?" Fromm responds:

> I feel that the male Social Democrats never could understand Rosa Luxemburg, nor could she acquire the influence for which she had the potential because she was a woman; and the men could not become full revolutionaries because they did not emancipate themselves from their male, patriarchal, and hence dominating, character structure. (Fromm's letter appears in Dunayevskaya 1985, p. 242; Dunayevskaya's letters to Fromm from this period appear in Anderson and Rockwell 2012, pp. 208–10.)

Fromm's life and work centered on how human beings could realize their full humanity, not only in psychological terms, but also politically and philosophically. Always searching for a pathway out of the alienated world of capitalism, he played a major role in the discussions of Marx and of socialist humanism in the U.S. and internationally.

References

Althusser, L. (2003). The Humanist Controversy and Other Writings. François Matheron (Ed.) Trans. by G. M. Goshgarian. London (Verso).

Anderson, K., and Rockwell, R. (Eds.) (2012). The Dunayevskaya-Marcuse-Fromm Correspondence, 1954–1978. Dialogues on Hegel, Marx, and Critical Theory. Lanham (Lexington Books).

Bernstein, R. (1961). Fromm's Concept of Marx. New Leader. 44 (21), pp. 29–30.

Dunayevskaya, R. (1958). Marxism and Freedom: From 1776 until Today. Amherst (Humanity Books), 2000.

Dunayevskaya, R. (1985). Women's Liberation and the Dialectics of Revolution. Reaching for the Future. New Jersey (Humanities Press).

Fromm, E. (1941a). Escape from Freedom. New York (Farrar and Rinehart).

Fromm, E. (1955a). The Sane Society. New York (Rinehart and Winston Inc.).

Fromm, E. (1956a). The Art of Loving. An Inquiry into the Nature of Love. New York (Harper and Row).

Fromm, E. (1961a). May Man Prevail? An Inquiry into the Facts and Fictions of Foreign Policy. New York (Doubleday).

Fromm, E. (1961b). Marx's Concept of Man. New York (Frederick Ungar), 1966.

Fromm, E. (1961c). Paranoid or Hysterical Thinking. New Leader 44 (22), pp. 10–12.

Fromm, E. (Ed.) (1965a). Socialist Humanism. New York (Doubleday).

Hook, S. (1936). From Hegel to Marx: Studies in the Intellectual Development of Karl Marx. New York (Reynal and Hitchcock).

Hook, S. (1961a). Escape from Reality. New Leader 44 (22), pp. 12–14.

Hook, S. (1961b). Marx and Alienation. New Leader 44 (39), pp. 15–18.

Hook, S. (1973). For Louis Althusser. Encounter 41 (4), pp. 86–92.

Marcuse, H. (1941). Reason and Revolution: Hegel and the Rise of Social Theory. New York (Oxford University Press).

Marcuse, H. (1955). Eros and Civilization. New York (Beacon Press).

Marcuse, H. (1962). Humanism and Humanity. In: Ch. Reitz (Ed.). Crisis and Commonwealth. Marcuse, Marx, McLaren. Lanham (Lexington Books), 2013, pp. 289–295.

Marcuse, H. (1964). One-Dimensional Man; Studies in the Ideology of Advanced Industrial Society. Boston (Beacon Press).

Marcuse, H. (1965). Socialist Humanism? In: E. Fromm (Ed.). Socialist Humanism. An International Symposium, Garden City. New York (Doubleday and Co. Inc.), pp. 96–105.

Peretz, M. (1962). Fromm's Logic of Surrender. New Leader. 45 (5).

Sartre, J.-P. (1949). Materialism and Revolution. In: J.-P. Sartre. Literary and Philosophical Essays. Translation by Annette Michelson. New York (Collier), 1962, pp. 198–256.

Erich Fromm and Critical Theory in Post-War Japanese Social Theory

Its Past, Present, and Future

Takeshi Deguchi

Abstract: Erich Fromm has been one of the most influential social theorists in Japanese social sciences, especially in sociology and social psychology and the adoption of his theory reflects the socio-cultural structure of post-war Japan and its historical changes. In this paper, I will examine Fromm's social theory in relation to Japan's post-war swift rehabilitation and rapid economic growth and discuss the remarkable role that it played by the 1970s in critical analysis of Japanese society. I will discuss Fromm's popularity and influence in Japan, examining its theoretical features from the view point of Critical Theory, since in Japan Fromm's theory is considered to have its roots not only in American sociology and social psychology but also in German Critical Theory (the Frankfurt School). As a result of Japan's economic success and status as an affluent consumption society, however, postmodern relativism and cynicism prevailed in the world of thought through 1980s and 1990s and consequently Fromm was forgotten. This story of Fromm in Japan is not over, however, for we will discuss how neo-liberal reforms are breaking the fetters of an outdated Japanese-style management regime and giving people the freedom for self-realization. This "pseudo positive freedom," of course, creates again the social pathologies of escapes from freedom Fromm discussed in 1940s. Fromm's normative anthropology of human freedom is thus recovering its popularity and has a great theoretical potential for critiquing today's neo-liberal reforms.

Introduction

This study examines the role that Erich Fromm's social theory has played in Japanese sociology since the end of the Second World War and discusses its potential for criticizing contemporary neo-liberal capitalism. Nearly all theories applied by the social sciences in Japan, including sociology, originated overseas. Japanese social scientists appropriated Western social theories and explored their own society with the help of these theoretical frameworks. Erich Fromm's social theory was adopted enthusiastically by "critical sociologists" in Japan immediately after the end of the Second World War in order to identify sociocultural elements that facilitate the emergence of fascist dictatorships. By "critical sociologists", I refer here to those who have been strongly influenced by the Critical Theory of the Frankfurt School, although they did not use the term "critical sociology" or "critical sociologists" to refer to themselves (Hidaka 1958; Miyajima 1980; Shoji 1977; Tanaka 1972). Interestingly, Erich Fromm, though outside the mainstream of the Frankfurt School, was for some time more influential in Japan than Max Horkheimer and Theodor Adorno, the authors of *Dialectic of Enlightenment* (2002), which is considered the *magnum opus* of Critical Theory (Deguchi 2013).

However, the situation changed drastically during Japanese capitalism's period of stable economic growth beginning in the early 1970s. Critical sociologists in Japan have paid less attention to Fromm's social theory since then, believing that it has lost its potential for criticism due to structural changes in the capitalist system. These sociologists have reached the conclusion that Fromm's theoretical resources have been completely exhausted. In contrast, my intention here is to re-examine their opinion and demonstrate the unexhausted theoretical richness of Fromm's work.

To introduce my discussion, I would like to describe briefly the present study's methodological approach in two ways. First, the purpose here is not restricted to *theoretical* or *philological* reconstruction of the influence of Fromm's theory on Japanese sociology; rather, I would like to focus on the *practical* and *sociological* backdrop against which his theory gained wide acceptance. Second, I will pay much attention to the concept of "reason" in order to contrast Fromm with the critical theorists of the Frankfurt School. So far, comparative research on the relationship between Fromm and Horkheimer or Adorno has remained superficial in that it has been limited solely to investigating differences in their interpretation of Sigmund Freud's psychoanalytic theory – especially its biological element, libido. In contrast, I will review Fromm's place in the intellectual history of Critical Theory itself, encompassing theoretical developments from its first generation (Horkheimer and Adorno) through the second and third generations (Jürgen Habermas and Axel Honneth) (Deguchi 2010; 2011).

Having completed this methodological preface, I will now move on to my primary subject. First, I will elucidate the relationship between Fromm and post-war Japanese critical sociologists. Next, I will examine the concept of reason in Fromm and in the critical theorists in terms of how it addresses our relationships to others and to our inner nature (psychological drive), and I will demonstrate the uniqueness of Fromm's perspective. Then, I will put Fromm's views aside briefly and take a look at the changes in Japanese capitalism, in order to explain why Fromm has been unpopular among Japanese critical sociologists since the early 1970s. Finally, I will return to Fromm's original theory, and with the help of Honneth's critical analysis of neo-liberalism, reappraise its theoretical potential in the age of neo-liberal society.

Fromm and Post-War Critical Sociology in Japan

Dialectic of Freedom or Vestiges of Feudalism?

Escape from Freedom was introduced relatively early in Japan and enjoyed wide readership among Japanese critical sociologists, providing guidance for their analysis of Japanese society (The Japanese translation was published in 1950, while that of *The Dialectic of Enlightenment* was published in 1990). The first point to be noted is that there are significant differences between the results of sociological research on fascism conducted by Fromm and by Japanese critical sociologists. Before turning to a closer examination of this point, I would like to describe Fromm's original theoretical proposition of modern freedom in terms of a "dialectic of freedom", a concept introduced by Axel Honneth in characterizing Fromm's *Escape from Freedom* as contrasted with Horkheimer and Adorno's *Dialectic of Enlightenment* (Honneth 2006). The dialectic of freedom can be defined as a contradictory process in which the freedom made possible by modernization is undermined and destroyed by freedom itself. Fromm investigated the mechanisms of the rise of National Socialism (as an instance of escape from freedom) in terms of the dialectical contradiction of modernization itself. In his view, modern freedom was a negative freedom, emancipating people from bonds such as hierarchy of status, the traditional family system, guilds and village communities; however, that same emancipatory power also evoked in people's minds a sense of isolation, angst and powerlessness as the cost of independence. As a result, people eventually chose to give up their freedom and obey a new authoritarian dictator, or accepted traditional oppression because it promised them protection and security.

In contrast to this process, Japanese critical sociologists investigated Japanese fascism and found its causes in the traditional, pre-modern feudalism, which continued in Japanese society and which they referred to as "vestiges of feudalism". In Fromm's view, however, the phenomenon of escape from freedom could never have occurred in such a "half-traditional" society as pre-war Japanese society, where a variety of old and feudal ties remained very strong and provided people with protection. Nevertheless, despite this great difference in the explanation of fascism's causes between Fromm and Japanese critical sociologists, Fromm's social theory was popular in Japan from the 1950s through the 1960s. To explain this fact, we must turn to the sociological context in which Fromm's social theory enjoyed wider readership among Japanese intellectuals.

Escape from Freedom after the Second World War in Japan

First, we must note the time lag between the German society that Fromm used as his primary object of research and the Japanese one to which his theory was applied by critical sociologists. Let us return to Fromm's analysis in *Escape from Freedom* (Fromm 1941a). According to Fromm, Germans enjoyed freedom just after the First World War ended, but it came as a result of the collapse of an imperial regime and the subsequent turbulence in the social order and traditional values that the former imperial authority had secured. This political and sociological situation, combined with the economic depression that Germany suffered due to the post-war reparations required by victorious nations, made the nation a hotbed for National Socialism.

In Japan as well, freedom was given after the breakup of the imperial dictatorship. In this sense, the historical situation concerning freedom and democracy in the Weimar Republic is comparable to Japanese society. However, only after the Second World War did Japan begin to enjoy freedom and democracy. Therefore, the main proposition of escape from freedom is more applicable to *post-war* Japan, after its fascist period – not to a time period during which popular discomfort with freedom may have led to the emergence of authoritarianism, as in Fromm's theory. In addition, beginning in the late 1940s, as the Republic of China was founded, the Cold War intensified and the Korean War broke out, the Japanese government followed *gyaku-kosu* (reverse course) and implemented reactionary policies. These political circumstances after the war made the truths of *Escape from Freedom* more relevant to Japan than they had been under imperial fascism before and during the war. In this context, Fromm's message on the need to develop from negative freedom to positive freedom touched the heartstrings of liberal and critical intellectuals. In fact, the research on the Japanese social character conducted by Rokuro Hidaka, translator of *Escape from Freedom*, aimed not only at elucidating the causes of imperial fascism before and during the Second World War but also at foreseeing the possibilities of a *post-war* anti-democratic dictatorship (Hidaka 1958)[1].

Fromm and the Frankfurt School

Escape from Freedom and Dialectic of Enlightenment

As Axel Honneth demonstrates, *Escape from Freedom* shares a motif of dialectical self-erosion of modernity with *Dialectic of Enlightenment*. I will

---

1   His investigation is directed particularly towards possibilities that the democracy transplanted in Japan from the West might die out. He explained the current people's social character categorised into five cases: the social character of plebeian, the subordinated, citizen, the mass and revolutionary subject. Needless to say, the plebeian and subordinated subject, or pre-modern traditional subject, had been the main carrier of imperial dictatorship.

explore this point further in terms of the difference in the concept of reason between Fromm and the authors of *Dialectic of Enlightenment* and *The Communicative Theory of Action* (Deguchi 2002).

The dialectic of enlightenment is a paradoxical process by which enlightening reason, which controlled both the inner nature (our psychological drive) and outer nature (the environment) and built up rational civilization, also dialectically produces barbarism or violent domination. In this sense, it might be said that dialectics of freedom and the dialectic of enlightenment are referring to the same negative social phenomenon in which the emancipation process erodes itself and evolves into violence in the modern age. However, of the two, only Fromm's theory could have a positive and hopeful perspective on the future of reason and its emancipatory potential. One reason for this is that Fromm avoids a "categorical mistake", a term used by Habermas in criticizing the theoretical impasse that Horkheimer and Adorno reached. Specifically, Fromm distinguishes reason from "intelligence", which he describes as equivalent to the instrumental and enlightening reason of Horkheimer and Adorno. Intelligence, or instrumental reason, can be seen, in Fromm's view, as a pathological and alienated form of reason. On the contrary, reason in Fromm is not instrumental but serves a communicative and emancipatory function.

Reason, according to Fromm, relates the independent self to others by the capacity of comprehending or understanding, and consequently, enables one to build inter-subjective relationships between the self and others without losing one's independence. If reason fails in realizing inter-subjective relationships, its ability turns into the instrumental and unproductive power of domination or subordination between the subject and the object. In other words, Fromm finds the emancipatory ability of reason at the inter-subjective relational level just as Habermas does. In Fromm's theory, this philosophical consideration is built on a foundation of psychological observations on sadism and masochism, which are two different types of "alienated" attitudes of the self towards others that arise when one gives up one's independence and falls into symbiotic relationships.

Let us now attempt to extend the discussion into Fromm's sociological concepts of negative and positive freedom. *Negative* freedom is a state in which people have emancipated themselves spontaneously and gained independence from existing social bonds. This situation can be viewed as an objective prerequisite for actively exercising one's ability of reason. However, people can enjoy *positive* freedom only when they develop reason fully and consequently attain individual independence and inter-subjective relatedness to others. This fact sheds light on the issue that I raised previously, namely why Fromm's social theory was popular in Japan despite the great difference in the causes identified for fascism between Fromm and Japanese critical sociologists, and why Fromm, though outside the mainstream of the school, was more influential than Horkheimer and Adorno. It appears that Fromm's dialectical thought of freedom enabled Japanese sociologists and intellectuals to think of Japanese society in the late 1940s as not only being in a critical state of emergency but also as being at the key moment when Japanese society satisfied at last the objective prerequisites for reason realizing itself. Negative freedom is a threat to freedom itself, but dialectically, it also promises hope at the point of hopelessness.

Communicative Reason or Natural Reason

I will now shift my focus away from Horkheimer and Adorno to Habermas. After Fromm's prominence faded in Japan, Habermas's writings, especially *The Structural Transformation of the Public Sphere* (1992) and *The Theory of Communicative Action* (1984), attracted a growing interest among critical sociologists. Fromm and Habermas's writings have two things that *Dialectic of Enlightenment* (Horkheimer & Adorno 2002) lacks: a relatively positive evaluation of the potential of reason and a perspective on reconstructing a democratic society on the basis of reason. *Escape from Freedom* goes beyond performing a psychological analysis of National Socialism to propose a psychological prerequisite for the rebirth of democracy, namely the simultaneous attainment of individual independence and inter-subjective relatedness to others. Habermas's two writings, in contrast, examine the formation of social evolution towards the modern civil society and formulate a historical and sociological prerequisite for democracy. Despite these differences both Fromm and Habermas conduct critical and thorough investigations of mass society and attempt to identify the normative potential of reason.

We cannot simply compare Habermas and Fromm as a whole, as Habermas's communicative theory covers a wide variety of disciplines including philosophy, sociology, linguistics and psychology. Therefore, I will here focus solely on the difference in their concepts of reason: communicative reason in Habermas and "natural reason" in Fromm. Habermas assumes that reason demonstrates its ability exclusively in the "ideal speech situation", in which those involved aim at mutual understanding and agreement through verbal communication without compulsion. In this theoretical framework, one's inner nature or psychological drive is dissipated in the verbal communication process, and consequently, repressed inner psychology is treated only as a theme of "distorted communication". As a result, in Habermas' communicative theory, the motivational power of latent inner emotions matters little.

In contrast, Fromm adopts the Spinozist monistic concept of reason and nature, which is different from the Kantian dualistic concept typically seen in Horkheimer, Adorno and Habermas. On the basis of the dynamism of potency and power, Fromm makes clear the close relationship of reason, emotions and inter-subjective relatedness to others. In Fromm's view, emotional experiences and the productive or unproductive use of reason are inseparably related to each other and motivate people to build relations with others. People who have a potency of actively using reason can simultaneously attain an independent and inter-subjective relatedness to others, but those who cannot productively use their ability of reason and fail in relating themselves to others suffer emotional experiences such as isolation and angst, and ultimately have a feeling of decrease in power, i.e. "powerlessness". They then have a psychological desire to compensate for this negative feeling of powerlessness by building dominating or subordinating relationships with others, that is, through sadistic or masochistic relationships.

We can conclude this discussion as follows. First, Horkheimer and Adorno pay attention to the dialectical bonding of reason and the inner nature or psychological drive, but do not consider the inter-subjective and emancipatory aspect of reason. Second, in contrast, Habermas develops the communicative concept of reason and finds an emancipating potential in the inter-subjectivity of verbal communication, but in his theory, emotion or inner nature takes a backseat because his reason is inter-subjective, dualistic and separated from inner nature itself. Finally, in contrast, Fromm links the inner emotional nature with the motivational power of reason as partners in building inter-subjective relationships with others.

Fromm in Japanese Rapid Capitalist Modernization

Rapid Economic Growth and the Theory of Alienation

Let us leave our theoretical considerations for a moment and go back to the description of the sociological context in which Fromm was accepted in Japan. After the political crisis of military dictatorship in the early 1950s, Japan's swift rehabilitation and economic growth from the late 1950s through the 1960s demonstrated the usefulness of Fromm's well-known concept of alienation. During this period, Japan experienced an unprecedentedly rapid economic recovery, to the extent that, by 1968, its GNP ranked second in the world. This rapid capitalist modernization frees people from the traditional bonds of intermediate communities, atomizing people from co-existence into individual separate existence, and at the same time, changes human beings into depersonalized parts organized into a huge mechanical system. Those who fall victim to alienation experience themselves as parts of an abstract system and have a psychological sense of isolation and powerlessness, losing inter-subjective relationships with other people.

Extending this perspective from the psychological level to the micro-societal level in its foreign economic policy, the Japanese government and its bureaucracy took the initiative in social and economic development and protected companies in "the convoy system" against economic threats coming from overseas; simultaneously, in its domestic economic policy, the same technocratic state bureaucracy improved and expanded the social capital and infrastructure needed for the development of a capitalist system and eliminated excessive competition inside Japan. This coalition of technocratic state bureaucracy and a capitalist system made possible Japan's remarkable economic growth. It is possible to describe this situation with Habermas' concept of "colonization of the life world by bureaucratic and capitalist systems". In other words, Fromm's concept of alienation was referring to the subjective and emotional side of this objective capitalist reality.

Fromm's Decline in Affluent, Postmodern Society

Japan progressed into a period of stable growth of capitalism, in contrast to the Western capitalist countries' experience of a long economic recession. The 1973 oil crisis, triggered by the Yom Kippur War between Israel and Arab countries in the Middle East, however, struck a blow against Japan's economy and ended the post-war pattern of rapid growth. Through the 1970s and 1980s, in an affluent consumption-based society, the so-called *Nihon teki keiei* (Japanese-style management) or *Kaisha shakai* (company-oriented society) was established, drawing the majority of workers into a company system that guaranteed them secure lifetime employment, along with stable seniority, salary and advancement policies and substantial intra-company welfare. It is true that this Japanese-company-oriented society was established by the state technocratic bureaucratic and capitalist system, and that in this sense, Japan can be seen as a "totally administrated society" in terms of Critical Theory. Yet most workers enjoyed having their affluent and secure lives protected by the Japanese style of management and employment practices. Also, within the Japanese company system, people enjoyed "self-realization" through good teamwork. One typical example is the Japanese-style quality control circle, in which workers, particularly in the manufacturing industry, discuss quality control in the workplace and propose improvements, thereby becoming participants in bottom-up management. This method was a key to the strength of the Japanese manufacturing industry.

Generally speaking, critical discourses lost their popular support due to the notable successes of Japanese-style management and company-oriented systems in building an affluent and secure society. This situation continued until the end of the bubble economy in the early 1990s. During this period, in place of critical sociology, postmodernism arose with its heavy dose of relativism and cynicism. Against this backdrop, Fromm and his social theory based on his normative concept of freedom fell into oblivion even among sociologists.

Fromm in the Future

Globalization and Neo-Liberal Reform in Japan

After the collapse of the bubble economy, neo-liberal reforms ensued in Japan, about fifteen years delayed relative to their implementation by Western capitalist countries. In 2001, principles of competition and privatization were proposed in the fields such as medical services, nursing care, welfare and education. In addition, with globalization affecting Japanese companies, opportunities for regular employment have been decreasing, while the number of non-regular positions has been rapidly increasing, and non-regular workers are vulnerable to layoffs. In this changing context, marked by great economic pressure from global markets, various neo-liberal reforms have aimed to restructure the aspects of Japanese-style management and employment practices that impede free competition. In conjunction with the spread of neo-liberal ideology, discourses concerning self-realization and personal responsibility are permeating not only the ruling class but also the general populace. Through internalizing belief in self-realization and personal responsibility, people have begun to experience themselves as entrepreneurs marketing themselves. Here we could comment on the relevance of Fromm's concept of "marketing orientation" or "personality market" in his *Man for Himself* (Fromm 1947a). However, I would like to turn to the theoretical connection between Fromm and the critical theorists, especially Axel Honneth (Honneth 2004; Honneth & Hartmann 2006).

Honneth, part of the third generation of Critical Theory, argues that the self-realization that emancipated individuals from traditional bonds experience is changing into dialectically institutionalized expectancy, which functions as an ideology for reproducing the economic system itself. Within the loop of self-realization and institutionalized expectancy, people experience increasing inner emptiness. As a result, compelling self-realization, referred to as "organized self-realization" in Honneth's discussion, destroys emotional relatedness or social solidarity, and consequently, the prevalence of crime, deviant behavior, mental illness and harmful addictions, including dysfunctional behaviors in intimate relationships such as domestic violence or child abuse, will greatly increase. We can refer to this neo-liberal ide-

229

ology of organized self-realization as "pseudo-positive freedom", because people can enjoy truly *positive* freedom only when they develop reason fully and consequently attain individual independence and inter-subjective relatedness to others. Neo-liberal ideology is a seemingly *positive* freedom, but in reality, it functions as a *negative* freedom and destroys intersubjective relatedness or social solidarity among people.

Criticizing Organized Self-Realization as Pseudo-Positive Freedom

In order to reappraise Fromm, we must go back to the proposition of escape from freedom. Both economic regression (due to the global price competition) and neo-liberal reforms (whose purpose is to restructure the secure employment system) have destroyed the social safeguards maintained in the post-war era. As a result, new social pathologies, such as intimate partner violence and motiveless murders of apparently random victims that were previously seldom if ever observed in Japanese society have attracted great interest. Fromm divided the mechanisms of escaping from freedom into three patterns: authoritarianism (sadism and masochism), destructiveness and automaton conformity. The first two patterns are applicable to the social pathologies that have become more common in contemporary Japanese society. In the process of individualization and expanding gender equality, domestic violence has become an increasingly serious issue. As psychological diagnosis says, the perpetrator and the victim of violence are in many instances co-dependent. This violent addiction can be explained by Fromm's inquiry into the symbiotic relationship between sadistic and masochistic personalities. As for motiveless murders, it is often said that these criminals have lost any recognizable relationship with others and are isolated from every social bond, with the result that their last hope is for the death of those around them as well as themselves. This interpretation is consistent with Fromm's theory of destructiveness in that the perpetrators want to destroy not only the victims but also themselves.

The growth of such social pathologies in everyday life and the present political climate are causes for despair about the future of peace and democracy in Japan. My pessimism is reinforced whenever I hear the Japanese Prime Minister, associated with the conservative right-wing, claim loudly that we must break away from the post-war regime, namely the regime under Japan's "no-war" Constitution. However, on the other hand, I am encouraged to note that, this year, *The Art of Loving* (Fromm 1956a) was discussed in a series of four lectures on a nationwide educational TV program, and that many Japanese are still being moved by Fromm's words. There was space for Fromm's insights and focus on freedom in Japan in the 1950s, and a need to return to his theories today in a nation facing political and cultural crisis.

References

Deguchi, T. (2002). Erich Fromm: Kibo naki jidai no kibo [Erich Fromm: Hope in the Hopeless Age]. Tokyo (Shin'yo Sha).

Deguchi, T. (2010). Axel Honneth no shoninron to hihanriron no sasshin). [The Recognition Theory of Axel Honneth and the Renewal of Critical Theory]. Gendai shakaigaku riron kenkyu [The Journal of Studies in Contemporary Sociological Theory] 4, pp. 16–28.

Deguchi, T. (2011). Hihanriron no tenkai to seisinbunseki no sassin [The Development ofCritical Theory and Renewal of Psychoanalysis]. Shakaigaku hyoron [Japanese Sociological Review] 61(4), pp. 422–438.

Deguchi, T. (2013). Critical Theory and its development in post-war Japanese sociology. Pursuing true democracy in rapid capitalist modernization. In: A. Elliott et. al. (Ed.). Japanese Social Theory. From Individualization to Globalization in Japan Today. Abingdon (Routledge).

Fromm, E. (1941a). Escape from Freedom. New York (Farrar and Rinehart).

Fromm, E. (1947a). Man for Himself. New York (Rinehart and Company).

Fromm, E. (1955a). The Sane Society. New York (Rinehart and Winston Inc.).

Fromm, E. (1956a). The Art of Loving. An Inquiry into the Nature of Love. New York (Harper and Row).

Habermas, J. (1984). The Theory of Communicative Action. New York (Beacon Press).

Habermas, J. (1992). The Structural Transformation of the Public Sphere. Cambridge (Polity Press).

Hidaka, R. (1958). Ideorogi Shakaishinri Shakaitekiseikaku. [Ideology, Social Psychology and Social Character]. In: R. Hidaka (1960). Gendai Ideorogi [Contemporary Ideology]. Tokyo (Keiso Shobo), pp. 3–20.

Habermas, J. (1987). The Theory of Communicative Action. Vol. 2. Cambridge (Polity).

Honneth, A. (2004). Organized self-realization. Some Paradoxes of Individualization. European Journal of Social Theory. 7 (4), pp. 463–478.

Honneth, A. (2006). "Die Frucht vor der Freiheit" [Escape from Freedom]. In: A. Honneth and Institute for Social Research (Ed.). Schluesseltexte der Kritischen Theorie [Key Texts of Critical Theory]. Frankfurt.

Honneth, A. and Hartmann, M. (2006). Paradoxes of Capitalism. Constellations 13–1, pp. 41–58.

Horkheimer, M., and Adorno, T. (2002). The Dialectic of Enlightenment. Stanford (Stanford University Press).

Miyajima, T. (1980). Gendai shakaiishiki ron [Contemporary Theory of Social Consciousness]. Tokyo (Nihonhyoron Sha).

Shoji, K. (1977). Gendaka to Gendaishakai no riron [Modernization and the Theory of Modern Society]. Tokyo (University of Tokyo Press).

Tanaka, Y. (1972). Shiseikatushugi hihan [Critique against Privatization]. In: Y. Tanaka (1974). Shiseikatushugi hihan [Critique against Privatization]. Tokyo (Chikuma Shobo), pp. 35–89.

Fromm's Critique of Consumerism and Its Impact on Education

Burkhard Bierhoff

Abstract: This paper presents some dimensions of Erich Fromm's analytical social psychology that can be related to consumer capitalism. In view of the limits of growth, the destructive consequences of the consumerist lifestyle are increasingly evident. A sane consumption is something we must develop. This new consumption would promote sustainable development as a counterweight to the commoditization of the consumer and of the world. The social character approach describes the social adaptation of the psychic powers of man to economic needs. At present this adaptive process has transformed education and learning, creating students who can be easily used by the economic system and who will be perfect consumers. To curtail a potentially meaningless life, production and consumption must be limited and cut to a reasonable level. More people must change their way of life. Erich Fromm's approach presents reasons why consumerism is a dead end for human development and he outlines life-saving solutions that involve change in our education systems.

Introduction

I am going to discuss Erich Fromm's criticism of consumerism and its consequences for education. The relation between consumerism and education needs to be considered and studied from both perspectives. On the one hand, most members of the consumer society are educated in such manner to be ideal consumers who will try to reach the standards set by the consumer society without questioning them. On the other hand, consumerism has such an effect on people that they voluntarily aim to acquire a certain type of education which strengthens the consumerist culture. The question is what causes people to overconsume? Fromm thought the concept of social character explains how the psychic powers of man draw him to fulfilling the social and economic needs and functional requirements of a consumerist society.

These issues are becoming widely discussed but, in my view, most recent publications concerning consumption and education do not offer deeper insights to those to be found in Fromm's writings from the 1940s through to the 1970s. In recent decades consumerism as a social phenomenon has increased therefore our understanding of what education and learning should look like and what their tasks should have been altered. Instead, education seems to be providing easily malleable workers who will smoothly fulfill their economic role. The development of neoliberal capitalism and the postmodern life can be easily criticized through the framework of analytic social psychology and the concept of social character and social development. Numerous authors as for example B. Benjamin Barber (2007), Zygmunt Bauman (2007) and Justin Lewis (2013), published extensively on the topics of consumerism and consumer capitalism (For a summary of selected aspects of mass consumption and lifestyles in consumer capitalism see: Bierhoff 2013.).

These contributions do not generally address Fromm's approach, but focus primarily on the topic of commoditization. These publications do not, however utilize the stance of analytical social psychology and do not propose an equivalent for the concept of social character, although they come to similar conclusions as Fromm did in the past. What matters to us is that Fromm's understanding of society is not out-dated and is still valid. For example Fromm's book *To Have Or to Be?* can be read as addressing the problem of climate change. The most complex social diagnosis done by Fromm can be found in *Escape from Freedom* (1941a), *The Sane Society* (1955a) and *To Have Or to Be?* (1976a). In these books Fromm has formulated his concept of the social character, he has analyzed the mechanisms of escape, studied the marketing character, and has asked the question regarding health and normalcy and has described the manipulation of regular citizens by anonymous authorities. In his later work titled *To Have Or to Be?* (Fromm 1976a) he presents the contradiction of the having mode as opposed to the being mode as capturing the core of his studies.

Consumerism as a Way of Life

Erich Fromm saw capitalist society as defined by two ways of life, in its non-productive variant life under capitalism is determined by alienation, passivity and destructiveness. In its productive variant it is characterized by reason, care, interest and love. The original element of his social diagnosis is that he turned his attention simultaneously to the social character of the members of society as well as to the socio-economic structure.

Fromm has used the term consumerism as a synonym for consumer behavior, but without elaborating on it systematically. The following features of the consumerism can be found in his works:

(1) Consumerism represents the socially desired high consumption (over-consumption) of goods and services in an economic system, which needs people whose major life target is to consume.

(2) Consumerism generates in consumers the attitude of possessing the world in a passive and receptive manner; this attitude turns the world into a world of consumable objects. "What is essential for modern consumption is that it is perceived as an attitude or, to put it more correctly, as a character trait. (...) The world in its richness is transformed into an object of consumption" (Fromm 1990a, p. 83).

(3) A specific feature of consumerism is a social character, which has, due to its traits, a penchant for excessive consumption. Its character dynamic drives the consumerist person to turn objects and people into consumable and replaceable objects, to turn the whole world into consumption articles.

(4) The consumerism has its roots in the character traits like envy and greed, which lead to a forced consumption of objects and services. "There is a kind of consuming that is compulsive and that arise from greed, a compulsion to eat, buy, own, use more and more" (Fromm 1983b, p. 5).

(5) Consumerism leads to an alienated experience and a limited view of

the world. Through consumption the human makes contact with the world of humans and objects but in an alienated manner. Thereby the consumer reduces the world to objects that match with his desires, in order to use them without being really deeply interested in them. As Fromm puts it, "Consumption is the alienated form of being in contact with the world by making the world an object of one's greed rather than an object of one's interest and concern" (Fromm 1990a, p. 83).

(6) Consumerism has used the sexual satisfaction in order to make people lose the attitude of dispensation. At the same time, consumerism has submitted sexual behavior to marketing in order to increase sexual attractiveness and the saleability on the personnel market. As a whole, the permissive sexual behavior stimulates directly and indirectly the need for consumption. From argues that "The present sexual behavior is part of general consumerism" (Fromm 1991a, p. 48) and "Historical development has shown that sexual liberation served the development of consumerism and if anything weakened political radicalism" (Fromm 1979a, p. 135).

(7) Consumerism leads to a pathogenic syndrome of boredom, chronic depression, fear and loss of consciousness, associated with the desire for belonging through demonstrative consumption, self-improvement and image cultivation. At the same time, consumerism weakens the engagement for political actions in the community, makes people passive and determines them to an optional contact, which protects against closeness.

(8) Consumerism is like a drug, although compared to the abuse of alcohol and other drugs, it does not limit people's ability to work and their social obligations. While consumerism determines a compensatory shopping, its increase in compulsive buying can be considered an addiction not related to substances.

Pathologies of Consumer Capitalism

Erich Fromm considers the capitalism of the 20th century as ruled by consumerism. Even if Fromm has never used the term "consumer capitalism", the designation matches the Frommian perspective. Fromm wrote: "Twentieth-century capitalism is based on maximal consumption of the goods and services produced as well as on routinized teamwork" (Fromm 1976a, p. 5). This capitalism has been designated as consumer capitalism. Undoubtedly it has its roots in the consumerist structures of mass consumption with greed and insatiability being major traits helping to create and expand markets for the sale of mass-produced goods.

Two features of capitalism Fromm considers to be typical: (1) the disciplined work with its assembly lines and the bureaucratic routine and (2) the emergence of leisure time in which people consume products of the consciousness industries and consumer durables. Both are connected in a dialectical unity. Since Fromm wrote these contradictions have further developed and the transition to the knowledge-based society and the nature of work has changed. This change is considered by Fromm to be a very significant one. In the current era, especially since the World War I, a radical hedonism has penetrated our modern way of life. One of the major goals of people is to experience "unlimited pleasure". This strengthens the pervasiveness of the consumption of commodities and services. The consumer lifestyle is based on a contradiction: rigorous work discipline and an ideal of laziness. This way of alienated disciplined work is made bearable with the receiving of a salary, which is the condition for free consumption. During the consumption process people are compensated and calmed for experiencing limitations in their work life. In order to participate in the constant consumption patterns and to continue buying, a pressure is created to ensure that an individual will show up to paid work.

In *The Sane Society* (1955a) Fromm compares this situation to the pathology of normalcy. Fromm understands a social defect as a non-productive attitude and perception that is shared and practiced by most members of a society, who usually do not realize the pathology of conformity and the limitation on personal growth that it imposes. If all members of a society have the same psychological limitations, then these are ignored in the common social context, but they are perceived as normal and apparently healthy. One of such social defects is the visibility of competition oriented behavior, which is considered to be normal by the so-called dog-eat-dog society. Such a defect is, in general, not connected to suffering, but is seen as diffusing non-well-being and as allowing people to escape from compensatory activities. Such character traits that are shared by the most consumers are considered by Fromm as a pathogenic way of life and in this case he speaks about a sick human being in a sick society.

Already in 1976 Fromm after looking at the data he was surprised that no direct measures were taken by policy makers to tackle the situation of passivity: "While in our private life nobody except a mad person would remain passive in view of a threat to our total existence, those who are in charge of public affairs do practically nothing, and those who have entrusted their fate to them let them continue to do nothing." (Fromm 1976a, p. 10) Today (2014), the situation has further sharpened socially and ecologically all around the world. No reforms have been proposed or decisive actions have been taken to alter the existing state of affairs. No radical decisions have been made either with regard to alleviating poverty and hunger in the world or in relation to tackling depleting resources and our rapidly changing climate. Fromm calls for *"a radical change of the human heart"* (ibid.). The crisis can only be resolved through "drastic economic and social changes" (ibid.).

On the basis of theoretical considerations and empirical findings as well as everyday observations, Fromm sees very clearly that radical hedonism cannot lead to happiness and well-being. Fromm argues: "We are a society of notoriously unhappy people: lonely, anxious, depressed, destructive, dependent – people who are glad when we have killed the time we are trying so hard to save" (Fromm 1976a, pp. 5–6).

The reasons for ignorance lie in the lacking of carefulness, and indifference towards life and disinterest in the well-being of other people. Through the compensatory self-deception and the permanent intervention of cultural antidotes like television and computering, people are put into a state of malaise and of the pathology of normalcy. Their vitality and initiative is being stolen from them. Since their character becomes indifferent and passive, they are activated by marketing superficially for activities that do not turn into productive activities.

The Primacy of the Economy and Its Consequences

In the first place Fromm mentions the radical change of economic behavior, which "became separate from ethics and human values" (Fromm 1976a,

p. 7). The economy seemed like an autonomous machine that served for its own logic of the exploitation of work forces and for the generation of profits, without considering the human will and the human needs. The economic system did not develop according to the question Fromm asked: *"What is good for Man?"*, but subordinated the human well-being to economic growth. Until today the economic complex is governed by the question: *"What is good for the growth of the system?"* (ibid.).

People are submitted to this system as work force and consumers and form a social character that is determined by "egotism, selfishness and greed" (Fromm 1976a, p. 7). According to Fromm, these traits are determined by the life conditions and cannot be considered as natural, innate drives. The current economic system with the way of life it generates "is based on the principle of unlimited consumption as the goal of living". (1976a, p. 6) Social progress is measured by quantity: the more produced, the better.

In *To Have Or to Be?* Fromm highlights the difference between two modes of existence: having and being. The having is oriented to quantities. Also the consumption in its widest form is based on having. "Consuming has ambiguous qualities: It relieves anxiety, because what one has cannot be taken away; but it also requires one to consume ever more, because previous consumption soon loses its satisfactory character. Modern consumers may identify themselves by the formula: *I am = what I have and what I consume"* (Fromm 1976a, p. 27). The forced consumption is considered by Fromm to be a pathological phenomenon, which he compares with being an alcoholic and a drug addict. The difference consists in the fact that the consumption of alcohol and drugs affects the social functioning, but the purchase and consumption belongs to the desired cultural activities and averagely leads to no limitations of the social functioning.

In human relations the having mode of existence leads to competition, social isolation, man against each other and social fear, fear of loss, greed, insecurity, and inability to build lasting relationships. Basic greed, an unsatisfied need for affection, for getting presents and entertainment can be stimulated at any time with inter-human comparison (what does he have and what do I have) or by advertising. This greed is a socially generated attitude, which allows to produce more and more, in order to maintain the mass production through an expanding line of products with an artificially generated demand.

"Being" as a Solution?

In the being mode greed and envy are missing since the identity of a person does not depend on having or private property. Wanting to have or possess something is not precondition for enjoying something. What Fromm means becomes clear when one perceives the difference between material and immaterial needs and their satisfaction. I can enjoy nature without possessing it. I can relate to other people and enjoy common activities which Fromm calls a "productive activity" and "shared enjoyment" (Fromm 1976a, p. 91, 115). Fromm also asks about the barriers that prevent this lived orientation towards the being. Here the character structure must be analyzed, namely the marketing orientation described by Fromm, to find a productive way to cope with the reality.

From Fromm's point of view, change character can take place from two perspectives. The change can be stimulated through economic needs and survival problems, which in order to be faced need new character orientations. Another route is through changes in human relatedness and a consolidation of the community life with manageable decentralized structures. Fromm considers the need to subordinate the economy to the needs of people, since the limitlessly aggressive expansion of consumption threatens the human surviving. It must be integrated again in a relation that serves to the human well-being. Such a change also supports a reasonable and sustainable consumption, which leaves the meaningless life of overconsumption behind. In summary, Fromm's argumentation goes along the following principal lines:

➤ "to subordinate economy to the needs of the people, first for our sheer survival, second for our well-being" (Fromm 1976a, p. 164)

➤ "production must serve the real needs of the people, not the demands of the economic system" (ibid., p. 160)

➤ "a radical change in the economic system is necessary: *we must put an end to the present situation where a healthy economy is possible only at the price of unhealthy human beings.* The task is to construct a healthy economy for healthy people. *The first crucial step toward this goal is that production shall be directed for the sake of 'sane consumption'* (ibid., p. 176)

➤ "Sane consumption can take place only if an ever-increasing number of people *want* to change their consumption patterns and their lifestyles" (ibid.)

➤ the goal is to overcome "the empty life of consumption" (ibid., p. 198)

The Importance of Education

The question of change also centrally concerns the education process. Education is a function of the society through which the social character is formed, which matches the given social conditions and structures. The educational system is not only a reflex of social relations but it is also a field where actors are reflexively creating new forms of education. The former education of the machine era, learning through technology and the following of authoritarian instructions will not secure the future. If affection and empathy grow in the human relations and during the education process, the changeability of human relations and dynamics of the self-consolidation can occur and spiritual bases of a new society can be built.

In an authoritarian society that is determined by dominance and submission, a character is functional, which is inhibited, controls its impulses and shows obedience when it is on the side of the powerless mass. In a consumer society individuals are freed from external limitations. Consumption should allow the expression not only of prosperity but also of individuality. However, the individuality is generated according to the patterns of commoditization. While in the authoritarian state the individual flees to the protection of authorities in order to avoid feelings of powerlessness and insecurity, in consumerism the individual seeks refuge in the experience of conformity. The economic conditions and functional requirements lead on the psychological level to pressure, uncertainty and powerlessness. The powerlessness of the individual

> leads either to the kind of escape that we find in the authoritarian character, or else to a compulsive conforming in the process of which the isolated individual becomes an automaton, loses his self, and yet at the same time consciously conceives of himself as free and subject only to himself (Fromm 1941a, p. 240).

The field of education has been explored in terms of analytical social psychology only in a rudimentary form. This is not the place to reconstruct Fromm's approach in detail. A special feature of Fromm's approach is that he does not describe education as the "cause" for the formation of character. Education only imparts given necessities of the economic and social structure into the character of the children by educational methods and educational practices.

In this sense, education is to be understood as a social function:

> The social function of education is to qualify the individual to function in the role he is to play later on in society; that is, to mold his character in such a way that it approximates the social character, that his desires coincide with the necessities of his social role. (Fromm 1941a, p. 284).

Man is not only determined by the requirements of economic and social conditions, but also by what Erich Fromm calls "human nature". This nature, however, is not infinitely adaptable because it is not biologically determined. As Fromm puts it: "While it is true that man is molded by the necessities of the economic and social structure of society, he is not infinitely adaptable" (Fromm 1941a, p. 285) – "(...) *although character development is shaped by the basic conditions of life and although there is no biologically fixed human nature, human nature has a dynamism of its own that constitutes an active factor in the evolution of the social process*" (ibid., p. 287).

The central question for the social tasks of education seems to be whether a socially initiated liberal development could actually be stopped and dismantled through following educational activities. When parents and teachers in the process of education increasingly develop empathy, is the result a developmental dynamism towards further changes in this direction? What are the social conditions under which ideas and abilities can become an autonomous change factor that exceeds the compulsive conformity and offers a way out of the destructive culture of having?

Even if man can not be completely described with the marketing orientation, where do the transformational impulses in the character structure come from? Fromm argues that "The marketing orientation, however, does not develop something which is potentially in the person." (Fromm 1947a, p. 77) Fromm may be wrong here, because the skills that are carried to market are more than pseudo-skills and exceed their monetary value. Certainly Fromm is right when he says about the marketing orientation: "(...) the very changeability of attitudes is the only permanent quality of such orientation. In this orientation, those qualities are developed which can best be sold" (ibid.).

To this the special combinations of productive and non-productive traits in the character orientations are added, which are also to be taken into account. The marketing orientation like the other character orientations can be described as an ideal type and is not representative for the individual characters. Overall, the marketing orientation shows an emptiness, "which can be filled most quickly with the desired quality" (Fromm 1947a, p. 77). Elsewhere Fromm admits that the marketing character can change more easily than, for example, the hoarding character, because it is a character not as strongly tied to possession.

> As pointed out in the earlier discussion of the "marketing character", the greed to have and to hoard has been modified by the tendency to merely function well, to exchange oneself as a commodity who is – nothing. It is easier for the alienated, marketing character to change than it is for the hoarding character, which is frantically holding onto possessions, and particularly its ego. (Fromm 1976a, p. 200.)

Lloyd deMause, who was appreciated by Fromm, has described changes in the educational structure that have taken place in modern times. The so-called "individualized psychoclass" has spawned a new educational mode, which he described as "empathic" and "helping" – and not as merely "socializing". His program for the change of education is: "What we need now is *some way for the more advanced psycho-classes to teach childrearing to the less evolved parents*, a way to end child abuse and neglect quickly enough to avoid the global holocaust that is awaiting us" (deMause 2002).

DeMause pleads for

> a vast world-wide program to end child neglect and abuse and raise all our precious children with respect (...). Only by reducing dissociation to a minimum through empathic parenting can we avoid inflicting the self-destructive power we now have available to us. (...) Free universal training centers for

parents may be a radical new notion, but so once was the idea of free universal schools for children. Our task is clear and our resources sufficient to make our world safe for the first time in our long, violent history. All it takes now is the will to begin (deMause 2002.)

I think Erich Fromm would have agreed with this statement.

In my opinion it is essential to promote human productivity by changing the way of life – away from consumerism to awareness and simplicity on the basis of downshifting. This culture change needs to be connected to transformations in education that move us to prioritize empathic care and unconditional affective attention.

Educational Reform and Productive Relatedness

In his introduction to the book by Father Wasson *You are my brother,* Erich Fromm described the educational concept of the orphanage, which was run by Wasson. Fromm first emphasized that these children are burdened by the circumstances:

> they are orphans; their background is one of extreme poverty and broken homes; and they live in an institution. I would say that was enough to make very maladjusted children out of them (Fromm 1975f, p. 6).

It is all the more amazing that these children do not fit into this scheme. So there must be special conditions in the organization of life in the home and in the concept of education.

Erich Fromm pointed out that there were the following four principles in his view that enabled the success of Father Wasson: "the principle of absolute security and at the same time of realistic responsibility; of self-management; and of stimulation (Fromm 1975f, p. 7).

The special feature Fromm mentioned is that the old principles of education are not simply replaced by new ones, but a new system was established, with new patterns of relationships with loving relatedness and without bureaucratic attitude. Fromm emphasized that the important point here is that Father Wasson has not tried to change one factor but that he has brought together a number of principles which, in their conjunction, make it possible for his family of more than 1,000 children to react as it does (Fromm 1975f, p. 8).

Other authors such as Stanley Greenspan and Barry Brazelton emphasized a series of seven needs that must be met for optimal child development (see Brazelton/Greenspan 2000):
(1) stable caring relationships
(2) physical protection with security and stability
(3) stimulating experiences that correspond to the individuality
(4) developmentally appropriate experiences
(5) experience of limits, clear structures and reasonable expectations
(6) stable supportive communities and cultures
(7) protecting the future.

The new education program refuses to structure education solely on the basis of economic efficiency. Education is not the promotion of economic productivity and economic growth. This destructive productivity based on quantification and commoditization, ends in destruction. The promotion of human productivity relies on criteria such as developed by Wasson, Fromm and Greenspan. Particularly important is the combination of unconditional affection in the maternal love and paternal requirements and encouragements. And there should be no suppression of spontaneity and vitality of the child so that his productive forces can grow. Education can help to bring forth a free man.

The problem to be solved in the education structure is to establish stable and irreversible changes that match the social-economic conditions. In reciprocal intensification a more productive education with attention and empathy for human development is accompanied by supportive structures. The theoretical starting point is an understanding of education as not merely a response to social conditions and functional requirements, but involving a relative autonomy with its own dynamics of development. The social context in which people act is always a socially constituted framework. The human responses that are found in the confrontation with social norms and values are changing this frame.

This process of change can be described with the concept of social character. The social character is a descriptive concept that concerns the dimensional compatibility of man and society. Its function is to bring people in accordance with society, so that the human energies can be used in the social contexts, for example, in the industrial work process or in the symbol-processing activities of the knowledge-based society. Social character is socially productive insofar as it establishes the humans as productive forces. This productivity, however, is socially immanent and not system-exceeding productivity. The human productivity that Fromm sees connected with the nature of man or that results from this nature is to be understood as a productivity beyond the existing limitations of a given society.

While the social immanent productivity can be described by the social character, human productivity that exceeds the established reality is assigned to individual characters and is to be understood as social-transcending. As long as only small changes occur in a society with a stable environment there is no pressure to develop inventive solutions. This is quite different in a society that is undergoing rapid changes.

In the globalized world, there are serious survival problems faced by human being associated with the risk of exterminism. Exterminism means the destruction of liveable structures in a final stage of the industrial civilization all over the world, including environmental degradation and loss of biodiversity. It describes the danger of the extermination of our ways of life and cultures and indeed of humans themselves by the consequences of the ecological crisis. Detraditionalization creates space for new views of the problems that are at first in the background, but then emerge and are dealt with. The direct view to the changing reality of situations and configurations evaluates them as problematic. With Fromm also can be said that the existing social character in times of change and crisis becomes fragile and is transformed from the cement of the social relations into an explosive. In a situation of radical change the social character is no longer functional and can no longer guarantee the further development of social relationships within the present socio-technical and socio-economic structures. A dramatic societal situation of upheaval can arise.

Such a social situation can prefigure new character traits which previously stood in the background. In such situations, new attempts will take place to find solutions and ways of life which in turn may be reflected in a new or at least modified social character. Since the social character fulfills a predominantly integrative function, the emerging character traits – in the framework of social character – are redirected to the predetermined structures of social order. In the framework of the individual character, it is not about adaptive social integration, but the development of the personality in the sense of autonomy and relatedness. The meaning of this understanding of the education and the upbringing of children and adolescents should be described in the following three ways.

First, there are situations that are paradigmatic and set new standards. These innovations result from the special nature of productive individuals who create new educational concepts on a practical level. As examples, Alexander S. Neill and Father Wasson can be mentioned, who have built new unusual institutions. Other examples of unusual conceptualizations are Albert Schweitzer and Erich Fromm who have reached the hearts of the people presenting effective approaches as the biophilous ethics, which is connected to the joy of growth, and loving human relatedness, empathy and mindfulness, reason and love, comprehending knowledge and helping care. In addition to the disillusioned mode of experiencing the reality and to the willingness to truth and self-reflection there is an active engagement at its core.

On the other hand, there are cross-institutionalizations, concerning, for example, the promotion of peace and the respect for human rights. Institutions are acting against social and educational occupations and irrational authorities, which are often associated with forms of physical, sexual and psychological violence. Child protection centers and refuges for victims of violence are to be mentioned. The parenting centers described by Lloyd deMause are part of it. They are to be understood as institutionalized assistance for distressed families and individuals and can be expanded to protection-seeking children, advice-seeking parents, old people, asylum seeking people, sick persons, the homeless, at all marginalized people in precarious situations that threaten life or human dignity.

While these two levels of ground-breaking *initiatives* of especially productive people who are pioneering, and human support-giving *institutions* are already established and indispensable to the spectrum of the helping social structure, the third level is still underdeveloped. This level of change would act structurally against the conditions of material and educational poverty, includes measures of the political and economic system, and encompasses the corporate management and the areas of science, technology and work, as well. There are approaches that try to link the social structures to humanistic values, but their success is minimal, because at this level the power and capital concentration is greatest. In addition, the sphere of maintaining power and system integration is not within the reach of the actors of the everyday world. In contrast, the other two levels of initiatives and institutions are part of the sphere of influence available to everyday actors.

Conclusion

The way out from consumer capitalism can only be successful if people freely decide which needs they want to satisfy. Will people choose the needs that keep people in the rat race of the forced consumerism as opposed to the needs which, if satisfied, make people more active, more alive, more happy and free and which contribute to the well-being and to the human growth? Steps to freedom are also supported by work which gives working people room to decide and to act responsibly, allowing them to build a decent society and active community. As compared to this, a monotonous and boring work makes people subaltern and drives them to compensatory consumption activities. The same applies to unemployment, poverty and social exclusion. Transfer incomes preventing poverty will be necessary to protect people against different risks. If there is not enough paid labor as a reliable source of regular income there are still lots of public interest activities in the community that are useful to acquire a peaceful and meaningful atmosphere for human encounters and unconditional love and support for outcasts, women, children and elderly people at material and non-material levels. On an overall basis system of prevention, family-supporting services, and parenting centers are to be implemented in every community to attain these goals. Education plays an important role in building lasting relationships with the care and affective support of the family, other groups and individuals. In a time of great transformations the need for new educational ideas increases that encourage humane behavior and civil commitment in the community. People will then become more and more susceptible to ideas which stimulate their involvement in the community life and encourage to enjoy a full and rich life. The current social character does not yet offer any solution for survival in a post-growth society. So people have to create alternative forms of interaction, work and education by themselves in order to survive.

Research and theory on social character has to call for the emergence of new traits and character orientations, which are formed by the individuals in the personal examination on life and to create a new balance between our own standards and the economic and social requirements. The current consumer-oriented social character inhibits the confrontation with the ecological crisis by calming down people in virtual worlds or in efficiency-oriented cultures of learning, working and doing business so that they experience exploitation and alienation. We find in this area, a hidden discipline that makes the thinking and action conformist – a multioptionality which can easily be confused with freedom, but ultimately does not mean much more than arbitrariness. In addition, social character research has to consider the changes in the socio-economic and technological basis of the society, which can promote ideas and alternative concepts of life, accompanied by new demands on the people as a productive force.

Finally it is not possible to simply dismiss the impression that in the last decades a great number of new topics and ideas arise that form a counterweight to the consumer capitalism and neoliberalism and reconsiders the way of life in the so-called affluent societies with a shift to communality and sustainability combined with the will to establish a hierarchy of universal norms of social justice and integrity of creation. The people, however, can only decide on a sane consumption and a sustainable way of life if they are inspired by a new vision, for example, of a "sustainable prosperity" (Duane Elgin). They must then take advantage of the possibilities that science and technology will offer to develop the productive forces in production and consumption to reduce precariousness and to promote a life in harmony with the love of nature, conservation of biodiversity and the well-being of all creatures. This is just the kind of sane society Fromm called for, and we have much work to do to make it a reality.

References

Barber, B. (2007). Consumed! How Markets Corrupt Children, Infantilize Adults, and Swallow Citizens Whole. New York (Norton and Company).

Bauman, Z. (2007). Consuming Life. Cambridge (Polity Press).

Bierhoff, B. (2013). The Lifestyle Discourse in Consumer Capitalism. Social Change Review 11(1), pp. 85–101. Retrieved from: http://www.degruyter.com/view/j/scr.2013.11. issue-1/scr-2013-0007/scr-2013-0007.xml (March 19, 2015).

Brazelton, T.B.; Greenspan, S.I., (2000). The Irreducible Needs of Children. What Every Child Must Have to Grow, Learn and Flourish. New York (Perseus Books).

deMause, L. (2002). The Emotional Life of Nations. New York (Karnac – Other Press). – http://psychohistory.com/books/the-emotional-life-of-nations/(March 19, 2015)

Fromm, E. (1941a). Escape from Freedom. New York (Farrar and Rinehart).

Fromm, E. (1947a). Man for Himself. New York (Rinehart and Company).

Fromm, E. (1955a). The Sane Society. New York (Rinehart and Winston Inc.).

Fromm, E. (1975f). Introduction. In: U. Bernath and E.D. Campbell (Eds.). You Are My Brother. Father Wasson's Story of Hope for Children. Huntington (Our Sunday Visitor, Inc.), pp. 6–8.

Fromm, E. (1976a). To Have Or to Be? New York (Harper and Row).

Fromm, E. (1979a). Greatness and Limitations of Freud's Thought. New York (Harper and Row), 1980.

Fromm, E. (1983b). Affluence and Ennui in Our Society. In: E. Fromm. For the Love of Life. Ed. by Hans Jürgen Schultz, New York (The Free Press), 1986, pp. 1–38.

Fromm, E. (1990a). The Revision of Psychoanalysis. Boulder (Westview Press), 1992.

Fromm, E. (1991a). The Art of Listening. New York (The Continuum Publishing Corporation), 1994.

Lewis, J. (2013). Beyond Consumer Capitalism. Media and the Limits to Imagination. Cambridge (Polity Press).

Social Character and its Significance for the Art of Living

Rainer Otte

Abstract: In Fromm's writings, philosophy and psychoanalysis are closely intertwined. The same holds true for Sigmund Freud's self-analysis, giving birth to the psychoanalytic framework in the 1890s. Today, psychoanalytic insights are indispensable whenever philosophers examine the knowledge of oneself or the art of living. The discussion is challenging for both sides. Ehrenberg's theory of *The Exhausted Self* poses fundamental questions: Does autonomy still promise liberation and insight or has it turned out to be a pathological agent promoting widespread depression, burnout and borderline symptoms? Erich Fromm's contributions help us understand the dynamics of the *False Self* (Winnicott) and its relationship to the socio-economic backgrounds of people. Fromm's philosophy focuses on a critical art of living instead of postmodern self-fashioning.

Social character and its significance for the art of living connects two paradigmatic features of Erich Fromm's thinking. Social character points out to a framework integrating psychoanalysis and sociology. The art of living sees individual and social practice in a broader perspective. What contributes to a good and meaningful life? Can we create a just and sane society? Do our values appeal to our own insights or do they put us in chains, as ideologies tend to do? These questions are often addressed by philosophers, and in this this paper we will discover Fromm as a philosopher.

At first, however, we should ask why a psychoanalyst could be inclined to enter the field of philosophy at all. Sometimes psychoanalysis and philosophy were happily married and sometimes they were happily divorced. Freud's psychoanalysis started off as a self-analysis and it was a philosophical project to a certain degree. In his letters to Fliess, Freud confessed, that working as a medical doctor seemed to be a detour (Freud 1985, p. 165 and 190). But Freud changed his views later on. He looked at philosophers as tourists who needed a Baedecker to travel through life. The pride to have one or to write such travel guides appeared a little bit narcissistic (Freud 1999c, p. 123). Freud himself kept the philosophical dimensions of his beginnings secret. Others followed him (see: Anzieu 1990). Biographers of Freud like Ernest Jones also played down the whole philosophical matter (Jones 1960; Bernfeld & Bernfeld-Cassirer 1981, pp. 142–7).

Freud kept his distance from philosophy. He felt uncomfortable in the world of rationalist theories or foggy introspective phantasies (Freud 1999a, p. 406). Many philosophers, so he admitted, could well be outstanding characters. But the psychoanalyst has to find out the subjective motivation of any philosophical system. He might come across hidden problems behind the logical surface. Thankfully he would receive some inspirations, but only as a matter of further scrutiny.

To cut a long story short: while philosophers play with interesting problems seldom will they find reliable solutions. After all, reading philosophical books evoked a mysterious suffering in Freud. Especially with regard to Nietzsche and Schopenhauer, he developed a painful double-phantasy (cf. Otte 2011, p. 113; Gödde 1991). Philosophical conceptions of the unconscious or of the drives, the interpretation of dreams and the parapraxis in daily life anticipated psychoanalytic insights. But never did Freud accept them as Baedeckers for psychoanalysis.

Fromm did not suffer from these ambivalent attitudes towards philosophy. His psychoanalytic practice has always been ambitious in a philosophical sense. He wrote in a grounding essay on therapeutic practice: "I would say this is the hope for the human race, that in fact truth makes us free" (Fromm 2009, p. 8). Truth has no separated philosophical and psychoanalytic realms. Does a liberating spirit ask through which door it is allowed to come in?

Fromm, like many philosophers, asked: "Who am I?" This is not a rhetorical question, though we tend to give rhetorical answers. Fromm suggests that "It sounds like a full statement, but is actually a dissociated statement, because we are not aware of the affective experience, which exists and yet does not come into our awareness" (Fromm 2009, p. 10). Rationalization is the-merry-go-round of self-deception. The center may be peaceful, but you are never in it, moving in circles and arriving nowhere.

Does philosophy advocate this self-deception, blinded by big ideas? Karen Horney, Fromm's colleague and a friend for many years, warned in her book on self-analysis:

> The upshot of these considerations is the banal truth that if you want to analyze yourself you must not study only the highlights. You must take every opportunity to become familiar with this stranger or acquaintance that is yourself (Horney 1978, p. 182).

In the last decades, philosophers rediscovered historically existing connection between philosophy and psychoanalysis. *The Art of Living* became one of the most important topics with chart-climbing book written by both philosophers and psychologists. And some of these books and discussions involve more than a little bit of psychoanalytic seasoning. Fromm would not have been taken by surprise. He understood humanist ethics as an applied science of the art of living (Fromm 1947a). But how much of psychoanalysis is contained in that philosophical art?

Take Martha Nussbaum's ground laying book *The Therapy of Desire*: Her study of ancient Hellenistic ethics puts out amazing connections between philosophy and medicine:

> Philosophy heals human diseases, diseases produced by false beliefs. Its arguments are to the soul as the doctor's remedies are to the body. (...) Correctly understood, it is no less than the soul's art of life (Nussbaum 1994, p. 14).

These words do not advertise rationalization or set Baedeckers up for sale.

Evidently, we have to translate a little bit. Ancient concepts like "nature" appear to be value-laden to us. We can never be sure to find the correct psychoanalytic term for the word "greed", which plays its role in Fromm's psychoanalysis and in his critique of modern consumerism. Imagine the concept of "ataraxia", meaning the happy stillness of passions. Man enjoys a transparent self-awareness and grasps surprising sides of reality. Should we understand it in terms of Freud's nirvana principle and accept that the death instinct works behind its back (See: Freud 1999b, p. 373; Fromm 1979a, p. 102–103)?

The trouble with these translations goes far beyond terminological matters. We will come across many unquestioned assumptions. They force us to evaluate and even to reinterpret parts of our theoretical framework. This is a crucial point of every demanding philosophical activity.

Is it worth the effort? "The problem of mastering, or at least accommodating, the passions was seen both in Greek and in early modern ethics as absolutely central to philosophy's goal of teaching how to live", says philosopher John Cottingham in his book *Philosophy and the Good Life* (Cottingham 1998, p. 6). For him, psychoanalysis is the last act of this drama. Nobody understands the play if they only strolled in during that act.

Many authors are influenced by Pierre Hadot. He showed that some ancient philosophies included a therapeutic practice with daily exercises (Hadot 1991). *Having* a self was not what philosophers were looking for. *Being* a self was the challenge to become what you are. It will never be a gift that you take away with a smile. The philosophical self is a productive creation, Alexander Nehamas stressed in his book *The Art of Living* (Nehamas 2000, p. 18). It is inconsumable. The psychoanalytic art of living, Mari Ruti explains, is linked to creative activity. Nothing is done until you do it, nothing is clear until you try to understand it: "What it means to become a person (...) is far from self-evident" (Ruti 2009, p. 38). This art does not imply high ideals of the self or rigid practices.

Michel Foucault invented many influential terms and phrases, but *the care of self*, for example, must be rightly understood. The self is not an atomistic spirit hiding in the depth of man's mind. The self is the relation to the others and vice versa (cf. Schmid 1991, p. 244). Techniques of the self constitute a subject for himself as well as in the public and political spheres. The government of the self and the government of the others could therefore never be separated (Foucault 2012, p. 64). Tensions in everyday life indicate that clearly: Anyone who wants to tell the truth and feels anxious to do so will make that experience. Taking over a personal risk to utter what seems the right word shows him in the field of power. He will calculate the effects of his speech at the very first beginning and will perhaps modify what he has to say.

Fromm is not mentioned in these books by name, but his topics are central to them. Fromm and Foucault would agree that we missed the point if we restricted our self-analysis or the care of the self to our hidden private life. The art of living can hardly be an attempt to forget in which world we are all living together. My lifestyle is not my castle. For decades, we have witnessed attempts to suggest this and to create a market for soulful wellness. Fromm was a fierce critic of that spiritual business or transcendental product placement. He called it "the great shams" (Fromm 1989a, p. 11). Locking men in this well-furnished seclusion will not cure the ills of modern or postmodern times.

The topic of this section is dedicated to social character. Man is a *zoon politicon*, as Aristotle said, being a private individual as well. The two sides show a worrying dialectic today. Take an example: "Productive work calls for primary focus on reality external to one's self", stated a paper on stress and burnout published by the International Labor Organization. (Freudenberger 2011) Symptoms are spreading globally. The *European Working Conditions Survey* confirmed a strong growth of professional diseases associated with them. A study of the German Federal Chamber of Psychotherapists established that the number of workers and employees who were unfit to work due to burnout increased by fourteen times from 2004 to 2011 (cf. Bundespsychotherapeutenkammer 2012).

Many business-philosophies and codes of enterprise say that democratic leadership has been implemented. They claim to follow the ideas of humanistic management and acknowledge the worker or employee as a partner who will be heard. If it were so, this might be a good first aid to cure these ills. Obviously, burnout, depression and stress-related diseases are still spreading.

That seems to be exactly what we have to expect, if we follow medical sociologist Alain Ehrenberg. He launched a thesis named *The Exhausted Self*. Ehrenberg analyzed the changing faces of autonomy in our modern socioeconomic contexts: Being associated with freedom in the past, autonomy has become the duty of today and a source of increasing depression and psychiatric disorders (cf. Ehrenberg 2012, p. 26).

Societies experience negative consequences of deregulation. Among them are ones which change dominating norms and the relevance of the authorities. Interpersonal relationships have become porous and unreliable.

The individual self has to – but hardly can – compensate for the missing coherence.

These demands are fostering the contemporary disorders of narcissistic personalities. Autonomy changes from a promise into a disease-causing agent. Concurrently, philosopher Axel Honneth stated that individual self-realization came under the wings of rigid institutionalized expectations (cf. Honneth 2010, p. 207). These ideals of the selves will be reactive ones. They give rise to the ever-growing feelings of emptiness, of being superfluous and of losing one's own personal distinguishing marks. But should we call it, what Ehrenberg and Honneth are writing about, a self?

We must introduce more precise distinctions. Think of Winnicott's concept of the *false self*, defined by its lack of spontaneity and originality. People lead a mechanical life of emotional disengagement (Winnicott 1984). Winnicott assumed that this *empty self* is a hiding-place, where the self could find protection (cf. Fonagy et al. 2004, p. 202). Fonagy and colleagues spoke of the *disintegrated self*: patients lose the feeling of being the real author of their actions and thoughts (Allen et al. 2011, p. 356).

In a philosophical sense, it would be pointless or a misuse of words to talk of autonomy in these cases. The term is derived from the Greek words *autos* meaning self and *nomos* meaning law or governance (cf. Beauchamp & Childress 1989, p. 67). The *false self* and all kinds of forced autonomy simply do not play in this league.

What would Fromm have said about these discussions of today? His critical mantra goes like this: In non-productive character orientations, the demands of the "social role must become 'second nature', i.e., *a person must want to do what he has to do*" (Fromm & Maccoby 1970b, p. 18). Individuals strive to be what others want them to be. They will be aware of their alienated self as a nice or an awful packing and see themselves only from the outside (cf. Fromm 1992g, p. 96).

Being a self has to do with the freedom to be productive. Autonomy intends, in a Kantian sense, that man is his own purpose (Fromm 1947a, p. 7; Kant 1965, p. 50). The art of living is the practical dimension of the productive character. As a crucial experiment, it serves as a critical instance in the sense of Spinoza: *Veritas est index sui et falsi* (Spinoza 1976, p. 92). Fromm held that insights unconnected to practical issues to be a waste of time (cf. Fromm 1976a, p. 170). The art of living strives for the opposite and dares to do so.

References

Allen, J.G. et al. (2011). Mentalisieren in der psychotherapeutischen Praxis. Aus dem Englischen von E. Vorspohl. Stuttgart (Klett-Cotta).

Anzieu, D. (1990). Freuds Selbstanalyse und die Entdeckung der Psychoanalyse. 2 Vol. München/Wien (Verlag Internationale Psychoanalyse).

Beauchamp, T.L., and Childress, J.E. (1989). Principles of Biomedical Ethics. 3rd Ed. New York/Oxford (Oxford University Press).

Bernfeld, S.; Bernfeld-Cassirer, S. (1981). Bausteine der Freud-Biographik. Einleitung von I. Grubrich-Simitis. Frankfurt (Suhrkamp).

Bundespsychotherapeutenkammer (2012). BPtK-Studie zur Arbeitsunfähigkeit. Psychische Erkrankungen und Burnout. BPtK, Klosterstr. 64, D – 10179 Berlin. Retrieved from: www.bptk.de. (March 19, 2015)

Cottingham, J. (1998). Philosophy and the Good Life. Reason and the Passions in Greek, Cartesian and Psychoanalytic Ethics. Cambridge (Cambridge University Press).

Ehrenberg, A. (2012). Das Unbehagen in der Gesellschaft. Aus dem Französischen von J. Schröder. Frankfurt (Suhrkamp).

Fonagy, P. et al. (2004). Affektregulierung, Mentalisierung und die Entwicklung des Selbst. Aus dem Englischen von E. Vorspohl. Stuttgart (Klett-Cotta).

Foucault, M. (2012). Die Regierung des Selbst und der anderen. Vorlesung Collège de France 1982/83. Übersetzt von J. Schröder. Frankfurt (Suhrkamp).

Freud, S. (1985). Briefe an Wilhelm Fließ. Ungekürzte Ausgabe. Ed. by J. Moussaieff Masson. German by M. Schröter. Frankfurt (S. Fischer).

Freud, S. (1999a). Das Interesse an der Psychoanalyse. Gesammelte Werke VIII, pp. 389–420.

Freud, S. (1999b). Das ökonomische Problem des Masochismus. Gesammelte Werke XIII, pp. 369–383.

Freud, S. (1999c). Hemmung, Symptom und Angst. Gesammelte Werke XIV, pp. 111–123.

Freudenberger, H.J. (2011). Stress and Burnout and Their Implications in the Work Environment. Retrieved from: http://www.ilo.org/iloenc/part-i/mental-health/mood-and-affect/item/268-stress-and-burnout-and-their-implication-in-the-work-environment (March 19, 2015).

Fromm, E. (1947a). Man for Himself. New York (Rinehart and Company).

Fromm, E. (1976a). To Have Or to Be? New York (Harper and Row).

Fromm, E. (1979a). Greatness and Limitations of Freud's Thought. New York (Harper and Row), 1980.

Fromm, E. (1989a). The Art of Being [originated 1974–75]. New York (Continuum), 1993.

Fromm, E. (1992g). Dealing with the Unconscious in Psychotherapeutic Practice [originated 1959]. In: E. Fromm, Beyond Freud: From Individual to Social Psychoanalysis. New York (American Mental Health Foundation), pp. 83–122.

Fromm, E. (2009). Being Centrally Related to the Patient. In: R. Funk (Ed.), The Clinical Erich Fromm. Personal Accounts and Papers on Therapeutic Technique. Amsterdam-New York (Rodopi), pp. 7–37.

Fromm, E., & Maccoby, M. (1970b). Social Character in a Mexican Village. Englewood Cliffs (Prentice-Hall) 1970. Reprinted with an introduction by Michael Maccoby, New Brunswick (Transaction Publishers), 1996.

Gödde, G. (1991). Schopenhauer als Vordenker der Freudschen Metapsychologie. Psyche. Vol. 45, pp. 994–1035.

Hadot, P. (1991). Philosophie als Lebensform. Geistige Übungen in der Antike. Berlin (Gatza).

Honneth, A. (2010). Das Ich im Wir. Studien zur Anerkennungstheorie. Frankfurt (Suhrkamp).

Horney, K. (1978). Self-Analysis. London (Routledge & Kegan Paul).

Jones, E. (1960). Der Leben und Werk von Sigmund Freud. Bd. 1: Die Entwicklung zur Persönlichkeit und die großen Entdeckungen 1856–1900. Übersetzt von Catherine Jones. Bern/Stuttgart (Huber).

Kant, I. (1965). Grundlegung zur Metaphysik der Sitten. Hamburg (Meiner).

Nehamas, A. (2000). Die Kunst zu leben. Sokratische Reflexionen von Platon bis Foucault. Aus dem Englischen von M. Haupt. Hamburg (Rotbuch).

Nussbaum, M. (1994). The Therapy of Desire. Theory and Practice in Hellenistic Ethics. Princeton (Princeton University Press).

Otte, R. (2011). Sigmund Freud. In: Ch. Niemeyer (Ed.). Nietzsche-Lexikon. 2nd Edition. Darmstadt (Wissenschaftliche Buchgesellschaft).

Ruti, M. (2009). A World of Fragile Things. Psychoanalysis and the Art of Living. Albany (State University of New York Press).

Schmid, W. (1991). Auf der Suche nach einer neuen Lebenskunst. Die Frage nach dem Grund und die Neubegründung der Ethik bei Foucault. Frankfurt (Suhrkamp).

Spinoza, B. de (1976). Die Ethik nach geometrischer Methode dargestellt. Übersetzung O. Baensch. Hamburg (Meiner).

Winnicott, D.W. (1984). Ich-Verzerrung in Form des wahren und des falschen Selbst. In: D.W. Winnicott. Reifungsprozesse und fördernde Umwelt. Frankfurt (Fischer), pp. 182–199.

Erich Fromm
in Hebrew Bible Research

With a Side Glance at Religious Studies

Jan Dietrich

Abstract: Erich Fromm, the author of *You Shall Be as Gods* and many other well-known works, not only made references to the Hebrew Bible in his writing but also provided lengthy interpretations of the biblical texts themselves. In this paper, I aim to evaluate the influence of the works of Erich Fromm on how exegetes and other scientists interpret the Hebrew Bible. In the conclusion of this paper, I call for further research on the possible applications of Erich Fromm's ideas on Hebrew Bible interpretations. I suggest that Erich Fromm's ideas could help to solve problems of the psalms, vengeance and violence in the Bible, and I also claim that the application of Fromm's model of social character could contribute (from a psychodynamic perspective) to ongoing research on Israel's religious history as well as our understanding of religious symbol systems in general.

The Impact of Erich Fromm on Hebrew Bible Studies

Erich Fromm was a psychotherapist and author of socio-psychoanalytical and philosophical books on a wide range of topics. He achieved the height of his reputation in the 1940s, 1950s and early 1960s, though his influence declined in later years (on Fromm's rise and fall as a famous intellectual, cf. McLaughlin 1998). Fromm was not a Hebrew Bible scholar; however, in his youth, he was trained in the Hebrew Bible and the Talmud by Rabbinic scholars such as Ludwig Krause and Nehemia Anton Nobel. Later, whilst studying at Heidelberg University, Fromm continued his Jewish studies under the supervision of the Chassidic Salman Baruch Rabinkow and became influenced by the ideas of the Neo-Kantian thinker Hermann Cohen. He also completed a dissertation on Karaite Judaism under the supervision of sociologist Alfred Weber, the younger brother of Max Weber (On these early biographical aspects see, cf. Funk 2000a, pp. 6–58; Akrap 2011, pp. 33–70; Friedman 2013, pp. 3–27.).

Taking these early biographical facts into account, it is no surprise that Fromm not only referred to the Hebrew Bible in his socio-psychoanalytical and philosophical works but also provided lengthy interpretations of the biblical texts themselves. Although Fromm's impact on Hebrew Bible scholars and Hebrew Bible research is less than one might expect, it is still present, and, in the following paper, I aim to evaluate how Fromm's works influenced exegetes and other scientists in their interpretations of the Hebrew Bible. I will conclude the paper with a call for further research on the possible applications of Erich Fromm's ideas on Hebrew Bible interpretation.

The work of an important scholar impacts an academic field in various ways: firstly, it might prompt the writing of PhD dissertations or other secondary literature works that outline, reiterate and critically evaluate its ideas. Secondly, it might be the subject of critical reviews in academic journals or other types of literature. Thirdly, it might be cited or used as a basis for discussion in other scholarly articles or books. And, finally, it might serve as a catalyst or a guide for further research in a given area. Let us now explore each of these in relation to Erich Fromm's work.

The Impact of Erich Fromm's Bible Studies on Dissertations and Similar Secondary Works

Erich Fromm's contributions to the study of the Hebrew Bible prompted the writing of dissertations and similar secondary works, the majority of which outline and evaluate his interpretations of the bible and other religious topics. The following list comprises dissertations and books on these topics (but not research articles; an example of a recent article is Schimmel 2009; cf. also Gertel 2014):

➤ Jon Stanley Glen (1966). Erich Fromm. A Protestant Critique. Philadelphia (Westminster Press)

➤ Rainer Funk (1982). Erich Fromm. The Courage to Be human. With a Postscript by Erich Fromm. New York (Continuum); German edition 1978

➤ Joerg Jeremias (1983). Die Theorie der Projektion im religionskritischen Denken Sigmund Freuds und Erich Fromms, Dissertation. Universität Oldenburg

➤ Juergen Hardeck (1992). Vernunft & Liebe. Religion im Werk von Erich Fromm. Frankfurt am Main und Berlin (Ullstein)

➤ Svante Lundgren (1998). Fight Against Idols. Erich Fromm on Religion, Judaism and the Bible. Frankfurt am Main (Peter Lang).

➤ Domagoj Akrap (2011). Erich Fromm – ein jüdischer Denker. Jüdisches Erbe, Tradition, Religion. Münster (LIT-Verlag).

Given that Erich Fromm was neither a scholar in Hebrew Bible studies nor religious sciences, at first glance, this list may appear impressive. Although all of the above dissertations and books deal in part with Erich Fromm's views on the Hebrew Bible, not one work, however, is written by an Old Testament/Hebrew Bible scholar nor focuses exclusively on the Hebrew Bible. Moreover, none of the above authors explicitly applies Fromm's insights to the Hebrew Bible. For this reason, we could argue that the impact of this list on Hebrew Bible research itself and its scientific community is relatively small.

Erich Fromm's *You Shall Be as Gods* (1966) in Book Reviews by Hebrew Bible Academics and Other Scholars

Alongside his books and articles that include references to or interpretations of the Hebrew Bible, Fromm's main work on the Old Testament and its Jewish and Christian traditions is his monograph *You Shall Be as Gods: A Radical Interpretation of the Old Testament and Its Tradition*, which was published in 1966 in New York. In this book, Fromm presents his thoughts on "authoritarian" and "humanistic" religions by interpreting the bible's history of ideas about God and Man. Here he presents his thoughts on negative theology and his view that it was already present in the Hebrew Bible. Furthermore, he explores Man as a maker of history, Man's ability and reluctance to engage in revolution, the prophet's critique of adultery as alienation, the idea of the Sabbath, and the messianic hope for peace. He also introduces his concept of X-experience, presents his interpretation of sin and repentance, and propounds a new psychodynamic classification of the psalms, which includes an appendix on the function and meaning of psalm 22 in the passion of Jesus.

Upon publication, this book did not escape the attention of Old Testament scholars, especially from the United States, and the number of reviews it received demonstrates the influence it exerted (at least in its first years – hence the overviews presented in this paper are not exhaustive). In general, most Old Testament scholars were skeptical. They criticized Fromm for combining historical-critical insights and the application of hermeneutics too easily and in such a way that neither was recognizable in its own right. For example, Eugene H. Maly, once Professor of Sacred Scripture at Mount St. Mary's Seminary in Cincinnati, Ohio, expressed the following view in *Catholic Biblical Quarterly*:

> the entire picture rests on an interpretation of the Hebrew Bible that can be termed at best eclectic and at worst eisegetical. (...) Rather than an interpretation of the OT the book is an interpretation of certain passages which are manipulated to support a preconceived hypothesis (Maly 1967, pp. 620–1).

In his review for the *Pittsburgh Perspective*, Donald E. Gowan, Professor Emeritus of Old Testament at Pittsburgh Theological Seminary, recognizes Fromm's knowledge and insights:

> This is a well-written work, clearly and carefully done; it was written by a man who knows his source material well, so does not contain the kind of blunders which often appear when men who are not biblical scholars interpret the Bible in terms of their own specialties; and it contains some excellent insights into man's predicament, based, no doubt, on Fromm's own special field of competence, yet very often in full accord with the Bible's understanding of man (Gowan 1967, p. 29).

Gowan, however, accuses Fromm of imposing his own line of thoughts on the Old Testament scriptures:

> The impression which this work makes on an OT specialist is that we have here no interpretation of the OT, but a scheme whose origin has nothing to do with the Bible at all, into which a few Bible stories and rabbinic sayings have been fitted. The result of doing so has been in almost every case to make them say something their authors did not want to say (Gowan 1967, p. 32).

He criticizes Fromm's main idea – namely, that Man's task is the Becoming of God – by identifying biblical accounts that Fromm fails to mention:

> The result to which Fromm comes is not something unknown to the biblical authors; it is clear that some of them had already considered some such position (though obviously in a much less sophisticated form), and had rejected it. This is what is meant by Isa. 14:1–21, Ezek. 28:1–19, 31:1–18, and Dan. 4. Fromm is certainly correct in finding in the OT a real exaltation of humanity; man is, for the OT writers 'almost God,' but for them the 'almost' is an indispensable part of the affirmation. They do not take the final step with Fromm, not because evolution has not progressed far enough, but because they *have* considered that possibility and have concluded that to take it would be to destroy their humanity. (...) The reviewer must conclude, then, that this very interesting book is not really an interpretation of the OT and its tradition, but a philosophical statement with illustrations from religious traditions. For if the theism of the OT and Judaism is done away with, its humanism is gone as well (Gowan 1967, pp. 32–3).

Fromm's book was not only reviewed by Old Testament scholars; academics from other disciplines also criticized his method of imposing his own ethical views on the scriptures. Irving Block, Professor emeritus of Philosophy at the University of Western Ontario in London, Canada, expressed the following critique in the orthodox Jewish journal *Tradition*:

> What is puzzling about Fromm's exegesis is his selectivity: he selects some things from the Bible to illustrate his view, but ignores others that do not fall in line. Or if he does not ignore them he calls them "archaic" – arguing that the final editor, an ancient humanist, who left the archaic passages in the

text for some reason or other (p. 89). Fromm appears to assume the following: Since humanism is good and authoritarianism is bad, and all admit the Bible to be essentially good, therefore the Bible must be essentially humanistic and all traces of authoritarianism must be due to earlier "bad" influences (archaic). This kind of reasoning needs no comment (Block 1968, p. 133).

However, as a thinker himself, Irvin Block recognizes the significance of Fromm's own insights:

> Yet there are some good features of the book. Fromm's discussion of idolatry is the best and, I think, the finest description of the Jewish notion of idolatry in English. (...) However, to utilize it [radical humanism; J.D.] as a tool in interpreting and understanding the Torah and Judaism is as clear an example of *elbonoh she Torah* – the willful misuse of Torah – that one might find (Block 1968, p. 137).

As late as 1999, Rabbi Elliot B. Gertel expressed a somewhat similar view in the journal *Judaism*:

> Like Jewish homiletics of all ages, Fromm's interpretations of Scripture range from brilliant insights into the plain meaning of the Bible to shameless forcing of the biblical text, in Fromm's case, to fit psychoanalytic dogmas. (...) But Fromm's best insights into the bible more than compensate for any forced characterizations we might encounter. *You Shall Be As Gods* contains many important interpretations of biblical texts; and there is not a knowledgeable Jewish preacher who at one time or another has not cited Fromm's brilliant defense of the Sabbath in *The Forgotten Language* (Gertel 1999, p. 431).

On page 437, Gertel (1999) reminds the reader of Petuchowski's evaluation of Fromm's *The Art of Loving* (cf. Petuchowski 1956) and adds: "Jakob J. Petuchowski could refer to *The Art of Loving* as "Erich Fromm's Midrash on Love." Fromm is capable of distorting the Bible in some of his midrashim" (cf. also Schimmel 2009, p. 12.).

Arthur Hertzberg, a conservative Polish-American Rabbi, even makes claims about Fromm's psychological motivation for writing the book. According to Herzberg, Fromm desperately needed the book as a form of self-defense in order to prove to himself and others that his own worldviews were not heretical but within the wider stream of Jewish thinking. (Akrap 2011 and Schimmel 2009 also aim to present Erich Fromm as a Jewish thinker and not a heretic.) In the journal *Book Week*, Hertzberg states:

> The Bible deserves to be taken seriously and to be confronted in all its complexities. Precisely because quotations from it, from the Talmud, and from Hasidic sources come fluently to Fromm's pen, he creates the illusion that a sane, contemporary mind has now produced a new understanding of the Jewish past. What he has really done is a piece of *ex-parte* pleading, a lawyer's brief in defense of his own present before the bar of his own past. Like Paul before him, he seems to want to believe that he is not a rebel but an heir – but to go further with this thought would mean to turn the tables on Fromm and analyze him as he has attempted to analyze the biblical God (Hertzberg 1967, p. 5).

Reviews of Fromm's *You Shall Be as Gods* (Fromm 1966a) also appear in other theological and religious scientific journals (cf. e.g. Isaak 1967; Thornton 1967; Hay 1967; Midgley 1968; Duba 1968; Maître 1981). Instead of exploring these in more detail, let us now turn to the question of whether Fromm's work impacted on scholarly contributions (beyond review articles) to the Theology of the Old Testament and other literary and hermeneutical Hebrew Bible studies.

Fromm's Impact on Scholarly Contributions to the Theology of the Old Testament and Other Literary and Hermeneutical Hebrew Bible Studies

A scholar could be said to impact a given academic discipline if his/her work is cited and discussed in main works by other scholars in the field. In this respect, we have to acknowledge that, although Fromm's work is present, it is not as significant as one might expect. On a few occasions, Fromm's works are cited in passing references by major scholarly papers in the field of Old Testament Theology. For example, Walter Brueggemann, Professor emeritus of Old Testament at Columbia Theological Seminary and one of the leading American theologians on Old Testament theology, occasionally builds upon Erich Fromm's insights in his own monographs. In his book *Interpretation and Obedience* (1991), Brueggemann writes about alienation in sexuality and economics and, in this context, also mentions *Escape from Freedom* (Fromm 1941a) and *The Anatomy of Human Destructiveness* (Fromm 1973a) in a footnote (Brueggemann 1991, p. 257 fn 7). In another of his books, *Biblical Perspectives on Evangelism*, Brueggemann cites Fromm's *Escape from Freedom* during a passage in which he explores Psalm 78's emphasis on the god of life and compares this to modern society's love of death (Brueggemann 1993, p. 124). Similarly, during a passage in *Theology of the Old Testament* that centers on interpersonal relationships, John W. Rogerson, Professor emeritus of Old Testament at Sheffield University, briefly claims that "human beings share characteristics that can be classified with various personality types or traits", which he follows with a footnote reference to Fromm's *Man for Himself* (1947a) (Rogerson 2010, p. 64).

Other Old Testament scholars occasionally quote and build upon Fromm in journal articles. For example, in an article on Old Testament's reception history, Bernhard Lang, Professor emeritus of Old Testament and Religious Science at Paderborn University, examines Kant and Schiller and interprets the fall as a fortunate event that allowed humanity to begin to develop its own capacity for reason. During this passage, Lang mentions Fromm's *You Shall Be as Gods* as a follower of this idea of the Enlightenment (Lang 2014, pp. 313–4 with fn. 30).

Aside from Old Testament Theology, Fromm's work also received a limited amount of attention from the representatives of hermeneutical approaches to the Hebrew Bible. Uwe Steffen's book *Jona und der Fisch. Der Mythos von Tod und Wiedergeburt* devotes two pages to outlining Fromm's view in Fromm's *The Forgotten Language* (1951a) (Steffen 1985, pp. 28–9). The book *The Hebrew Bible in Literary Criticism*, edited by the poet Alex Preminger and the Hebrew Bible scholar Edward L. Greenstein, centers on all forms of literary comments on the Bible and therefore also cites extensively Fromm's *The Forgotten Language* (1951a) in its chapter on the book of Jonah (Preminger & Greenstein 1986, p. 470) and from Fromm's *You Shall Be as Gods* (1966a) in its chapter on Psalms (Preminger & Greenstein 1986, pp. 534–5). More recently, Roger E. van Harn and Brent A. Strawn edited the book *Psalms for Preaching and Worship: a lectionary commentary*. In a passage on Form-Criticism and the Lament Psalms, they present various theories to explain the shift from petition and complaint to confession of trust and vow of praise in the Lament Psalms. Here, it is not only the old theory of the oracle of salvation and newer theories that are mentioned; we also find a passage that presents and appreciates Erich Fromm's psychodynamic approach in *You Shall Be as Gods* (Harn & Strawn 2009, pp. 9–12). Overall, we have to acknowledge that Fromm's impact on Old Testament Theology and other literary and hermeneutical approaches does not amount to more than passing references of varying lengths. For this reason, I would now like to examine Fromm's impact on descriptive and historical-exegetical Hebrew Bible studies.

Erich Fromm's Impact on Descriptive and Historical-Exegetical Hebrew Bible studies

Erich Fromm is not usually regarded as a scholar interested in descriptive historical clarification for its own sake. In his book *The Right Chorale: Studies in Biblical Law and Interpretation*, Bernard M. Levenson, Professor of Classical and Near Eastern Studies and of Law at the University of Minnesota, refers briefly to Fromm's *You Shall Be as Gods* in a passage on non-philological and non-historical-critical attempts to restore meaning to the biblical text (Levenson 2008, p. 14 with fn 10). Even though experts do not regard Fromm as a scholar concerned with mere description and clarification, it is evident that exegetical contributions do occasionally appeal to Erich Fromm's works, albeit mostly in the form of passing references (we will discuss the few exceptions later in this paper). This is primarily because the majority of scholars only refer to Fromm's later works and explicit references to the Bible and do not consider Fromm's earlier works presenting his socio-psychodynamic model as applicable to historical research. (In the last section, I will refer back to this point and try to show how Fromm's model might be used in historical research on biblical and other historical texts.)

Rüdiger Lux, Professor emeritus of Old Testament at the University of Leipzig, also includes a chapter on the history of research in his book on Jonah. In a subchapter on the history of the psychology of religion, he briefly outlines Fromm's views in *Man for Himself* (1947a) as well as *The*

Forgotten Language (1951a) (Lux 1994, p. 26). In the final chapter of his book *Myth and History in the Bible*, Giovanni Garbini, Professor emeritus of Semitic studies at the University of Rome, writes the following:

> The new religion deletes any trace of myth; with the well-chosen expression of Hermann Cohen, we could define it a "religion of reason"; the complex philosophical elaboration of this scholar, together with the interpretation of the Hebrew Bible offered by Erich Fromm in a fascinating book [*You Shall Be as Gods*; J.D.], are somehow the best comment to the over-hasty description of the Sadducees written by Flavius Josephus: "the Sadducees (...) affirm that men have the power of choice between good and evil and that, according to his own will, each one goes towards the former or the latter" (Garbini 2003, pp. 138–9).

While Erich Fromm's works are only mentioned in passing in the aforementioned books, they are addressed in more detail by psychologists interested in the Hebrew Bible as well as biblical scholars willing to apply psychological approaches to the biblical texts. Fromm only features minimally in the footnotes of Drewermann's opus magnum *Tiefenpsychologie und Exegese* (cf. Drewermann 1991. Vol. 1, p. 32, 257, 262; Vol. 2, p. 587). Albert Rabin, once Professor of psychology at Michigan State University, examines Fromm's works extensively in his book *Psychological Issues in Biblical Lore: Explorations in the Old Testament*. He does so in three ways. Firstly, when addressing the Bible's contemplations of death, Rabin cites Fromm's *Man for Himself* regarding Man's capacity to contemplate his own death (Rabin 1998, p. 38). Secondly, when dealing with the Bible's Song of Songs, Rabin again refers to *Man for Himself* (1947a), this time citing its view on love (Rabin 1998, p. 48). Thirdly, when discussing dreams in the Hebrew Bible, Rabin cites Fromm's *The Forgotten Language* (1951a) on several occasions (Rabin 1998, pp. 172, 176, 179).

In his book *Psychological Biblical Criticism*, Andrew Kille, an American writer and teacher educated in theology and Bible studies, engages at length with Erich Fromm's ideas (Kille 2001, pp. 109–24). He compares Fromm's interpretation of the Eden narrative in *You Shall Be as Gods* with Lynn Bechtel's interpretation in which the Eden narrative represents the individual's process of maturation and transition from childhood via adolescence to adulthood (Kille 2001, p. 114). Although Kille acknowledges that

Fromm's work lives up to Paul Ricœur's criteria for adequate psychological explanations, he ultimately prefers Bechtel's interpretation to Fromm's, since, in Kille's opinion, Fromm's theory "ignores details that do not fit. His theory is predominant; he subordinates the text to theory" (Kille 2001, p. 120); and, for this reason, he prefers Bechtel's interpretation. In this way, Kille takes up a criticism presented in the above review articles on Fromm's *You Shall Be as Gods*. In his critique, Kille continues to state that,

> Although both Fromm and Bechtel agree that the traditional 'sin and fall' model for interpreting Genesis 2–3 is misleading, Fromm's exegesis still owes much to that very model. He asserts that the act of disobedience entails no cosmic alteration in human nature or the world, but that the essence of the tale is still to be found in disobedience/rebellion and punishment by a jealous God (Kille 2001, p. 122).

A full appreciation and application of Fromm's *To Have Or to Be?* (1976a) is found in an article on *Haben oder Sein? Anmerkungen zur Anthropologie des Buches Kohelet* by Rüdiger Bartelmus, Professor emeritus of the Old Testament at the University of Greifswald. In this article, Bartelmus applies Fromm's differentiation of attitudes behind Man's actions as *to have* or *to be* to the understanding of the anthropology of the book of Ecclesiastes. In the face of death as man's destiny, Ecclesiastes presents two different attitudes: Man can aim to *have* (to have things, to have work to do, a frantic activeness as a way of striving after wind) or Man can try to *be* (to rejoice, to enjoy, to relish as a way of living in accordance with Man's share in this world) (cf. Bartelmus 1990.)

More recently, I took up Fromm's emphasis on Hebrew *emunah* (steadfastness, veracity), which can be found in several of Fromm's works – for example, *Man for Himself* (1947a) and *To Have Or to Be?* (1976a) – and I applied Fromm's view of *The Art of Loving* (1956a) to "the art of friendship", which can be found in the Old Testament and ancient Near Eastern sources. My aim was to demonstrate that friendship should also be regarded as an art of living that builds intensively upon trustworthiness, steadfastness, and veracity *(emunah)* (cf. Dietrich 2013a).

In the next section, I will examine whether Hebrew Bible studies could benefit from a further application of Fromm's Ideas.

Possible Benefits for Hebrew Bible Studies from a Further Application of Fromm's Ideas

Erich Fromm and the Psalms

It could be suggested that Fromm's genre criticism could be applied to the problem of the change of mood in the lament psalms. Writing in 1998, Svante Lundgren remarks that such an application has not been undertaken:

> If Fromm thought that his analysis of the different moods in which the psalms were written would influence biblical scholarship he was wrong. In no major commentary on the Psalms written after 1966 is his theory even mentioned. The classification of the psalms is still made in the footsteps of Gunkel, and no non-theologian is allowed to disturb that. Nobody can expect Fromm's classification to become the standard one or to replace Gunkel's, but as an additional theory one might expect it to be mentioned, discussed, and criticized. But the exegetical reaction was silence (Lundgren 1998, p. 150–1).

However, more recently (as described above), Roger E. van Harn and Brent A. Strawn took up Fromm's "genre criticism" in their book *Psalms for Preaching and Worship*, since, in their opinion, Fromm's "genre-criticism" helps to shed light on the change of mood in the many psalms of lamentation (Harn & Strawn 2009, pp. 9–12). Although presenting insightful ideas, these authors unfortunately fail to combine Fromm's ideas with modern performative explanations. Such a connection could help to further explain the so-called *Stimmungsumschwung*, as it could effectively combine psychodynamic and performative approaches without needing to build upon problematic explanations such as the oracles of salvation. In the following section, the psalms continue to play a role as I address the problem of violence in the Hebrew Bible.

Erich Fromm and the Problem of Violence in the Hebrew Bible

Since Jan Assmann's book *The Price of Monotheism* (2010), there has been an ongoing discussion surrounding the inherent intolerance of monotheism in its differentiation between true and false. This debate recently re-emerged on the German webpage *perlentaucher.de* and in the subsequent publication *Die Gewalt des einen Gottes* (cf. Schieder 2014). This might raise the question of whether and how Erich Fromm's differentiation between authoritarian and humanistic religions might fit into the ongoing debate about violence and intolerance in the Old Testament. There are two points I would like to make here. Firstly, we must remember that, in his essay *Im Schatten des Sinai*, Peter Sloterdijk takes up Exodus 32 as an example of Israel's intolerant and totalitarian view (Sloterdijk 2013). But he was not the first to do this. In his 1983 work *Die Theorie der Projektion*, Jörg Jeremias already called Erich Fromm's perspectives on idolatry intolerant and appealed to Exodus 32 as the most violent example of intolerant monotheism. Fromm, according to Jeremias, never escaped the typical "Jewish intolerance" towards polytheistic religions and its images (Jeremias 1983, pp. 325–404).

Secondly, I would like to suggest that one could take up Erich Fromm's emphasis on *different attitudes* behind official doctrines and deeds in an attempt to expose the overly "idealistic" nature of the ongoing discussion (in the sense that it is Man's ideas that govern history) and in an attempt to demonstrate that Fromm's differentiation between authoritarian and humanistic religion runs through all existing societies and religions, including monotheism. From this perspective, Fromm's "fight against idols" might be worth considering (whilst avoiding a flat identification with the Old Testament fight against idolatry and images). Furthermore, the application of Fromm's differentiation between defensive and malignant aggression might help to solve the problems of violence in the psalms of revenge. In this case, Fromm's differentiation could reveal that the Psalmist's wishes for revenge are more defensive than malignant: It is the ongoing "enemy" attacks the Psalmist attempts to fight, which expresses his wish for "revenge" in situations of an ongoing attack (On the so-called Psalms of revenge, cf. e.g. Zenger 1994; Dietrich 2013b).

In the final section, I will address Erich Fromm's theoretic model in an attempt to deepen our understanding of religious symbol systems, including the Hebrew Bible's.

The Legacy and Application
of Erich Fromm's Socio-Psychoanalytic Model

The perspectives and approaches of the so-called 'non-orthodox Neo-Freudians', such as Erich Fromm, Karen Horney, or Harry Stack Sullivan, all emphasize the importance of inter-personal relationships and cultural and social circumstances as exercising major influences on the self. It is particularly evident with regards to Fromm's concept of social character (cf. Funk 1998) that cultural and social influences and dependencies on Man's mind play a major role; and, with the rejection of Freudian libido-theory, Fromm's focus on psychic needs as well as psychic mechanisms, are open-ended with regard to finding various historical expressions in culture and society. (On these psychic needs and mechanisms that are open-ended for historically divergent cultural and social actualizations and forms, see below). Therefore, I would like to argue that, pertaining to psychoanalytic models, Fromm's concept of social character complements cultural-historical, social-historical, and religious-historical research – including Hebrew Bible research – more than other psychoanalytic models. (In this way, Fromm's theoretic model is not affected by the critique of Drewermann's depth analysis by Lohfink & Pesch 1987. On sound historical-psychological approaches in regard to New Testament scriptures, see Berger 2003; Gemünden 2009.)

In recent years, the history of religion has re-emerged as a main discipline within Hebrew Bible studies. In these instances, evolutionary thinking has come back in full by the name of religious history of ancient Palestine/Israel (e.g. Albertz 1994; Keel & Uehlinger 1998) as well as pertaining to religious history in general (e.g. Bellah 2011), thereby including theoretic approaches and models from related sciences (on some of these, see below). In these instances, Fromm's differentiation of steadfast character orientations could be effectively applied not only to Ecclesiastes (as Bartelmus (1990) did commendably) but also to numerous biblical books and extra-biblical sources, which would not only apply *To Have Or to Be?* (Fromm 1976a), but, by utilization of Fromm's model of non-orthodox social psychoanalysis, would also include his differentiation of character orientations. So, although some may not wish to appeal to Fromm's concrete interpretations of biblical texts, we could instead appeal to his theoretical model to provide new insights. In doing so, however, we should be aware of frameworks that resemble Fromm's. In recent decades, various theoretical models and approaches to reveal attitudes and mentalities in history and society have been developed. In historiography, this includes the so-called *history of mentalities* by Lucien Febvre and Marc Bloch; in sociology, this includes the concept of *habitus* by Pierre Bourdieu; and, in cultural anthropology, this includes the classical definition of religion by Clifford Geertz.

According to Geertz' definition in his *Religions as a cultural system*, a *religion* is

(1) a system of symbols which acts to

(2) establish powerful, pervasive, and long-lasting moods and motivations in men by

(3) formulating conceptions of a general order of existence and

(4) clothing these conceptions with such an aura of factuality that

(5) the moods and motivations seem uniquely realistic (Geertz 1993, p. 90).

It is clear that Erich Fromm's socio-psychoanalytic model identifies similar aspects and that, from the perspective of psychodynamic sociology and the differentiation of social character orientations, it might effectively complement Geertz' approach and other approaches mentioned above. While these frameworks have the potential to focus on reflective as well as non-reflective attitudes and mentalities, Fromm's psychodynamic approach can contribute by examining socially shared unconscious aspects of habitūs, mentalities, orientations and "long-lasting moods and motivations" (Geertz 1993, p. 90). Furthermore, his theoretic model helps to explain how these shared, long-lasting and socially conditioned character orientations come into being[1] and how they are maintained[2]; and it does so without referring

---

1 With his model, Fromm wished to show the way in which social circumstances enter the human mind (and, in turn, influence the religious symbol system), in this way solving problems of Marx' concept of basis and superstructure. Fromm's model is not a crude form of Marxism but is open to the fact that ideas are important factors (though not the most important factors) in governing history.

2 Geertz'"aura of factuality" arises because, according to Fromm, socially conditioned and shared, long-lasting moods and character orientations help people to think and do what they have to think and do, according to culture's and society's expectations.

back to instinctual drive theories, which are less insightful regarding history's divergent developments and cultural as well as social variability. In my article *Religion und Gesellschafts-Charakter*, I aimed to show how Fromm's socio-psychoanalytic model is connected to his non-orthodox thinking about the human condition with its psychic needs and socially shared character orientations. I also aimed to apply this model to the history of religions in exegesis and religious studies. The following diagram indicates how Fromm's model could be applied to religious symbol systems in general and in the Hebrew Bible (cf. Dietrich 2000, p. 200):

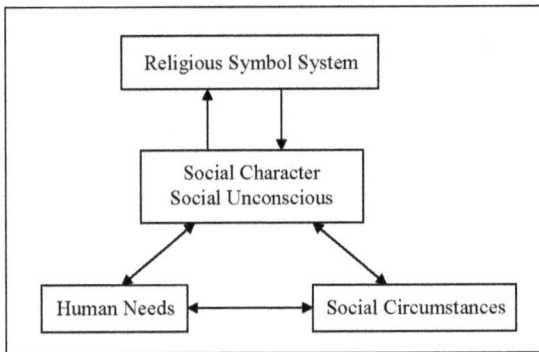

According to Fromm, Man is not determined by Freudian drives as instinctual sources, but (alongside basic physiological needs such as hunger, thirst, sleep, and sexuality) by psychic needs that find diverging expressions as passionate strivings in history's different cultures and societies. First and foremost, these include the need for relatedness, the need for rootedness, effectiveness, identity experience, and for a frame of orientation and an object of devotion.[3] As these strivings find various expressions in history and become long-lasting attitudes conditioned by society's cultural, social, and economic systems, important components of Man's longings become social character orientations shared by many members of the group or even

---

3 For a critical evaluation of Fromm's view of the human condition, cf., e.g., Thomson 2009, pp. 25–49, esp. 45-9. In any case, "Fromm's philosophical anthropology was closely tied to his interpretation of the Old Testament" (Burston 1991, p. 94).

the given society. These psychodynamic (i.e. conscious as well as preconscious and unconscious) character orientations find their expression in the given culture's religious symbol systems. In this way, religion is not only the expression of Man's conscious feeling, thinking and acting but also an expression of man's unconscious but socially dependent character orientations. In regard to expressions of the social unconscious, religious symbols can, according to Fromm, do three things. Firstly, they can elude the linguistic community's verbal filter in giving symbolic expression to experiences for which everyday language has no words. Secondly, they can elude the community's filter of logic in giving expression to "un-logical" ways of feeling and thinking found in associations and emotions. And, thirdly, they can express and also elude society's taboos in giving expression to otherwise unapproved moods and orientations; for example, on special feast days or in "secret" (e.g. apocalyptic) scriptures. Religion might, therefore, provide unveiled expression to experience – even preconscious and unconscious experience – but it might also provide veiled, concealed and "domesticated" (that is, socially conditioned) expression of suppressed experiences via psychic mechanisms such as rationalization, repression, transference, or reaction formation that are open-ended to different historical formations. In this way, religion is never a direct expression of society, as Marx and Engels claimed, but is always mediated through Man's mind, including his unconscious ways of striving and thinking in a way that religion is influenced by but also retroacts on society and social character. Two of my previous articles, *Religion und Gesellschafts-Character* and *Cultural Traumata in the Ancient Near East* provide historical examples taken from texts of the Hebrew Bible and from the ancient Near Eastern cultures.

Conclusion

Over the course of his life as a therapist, scholar, and writer, Erich Fromm was influenced by the ideas and texts of the Hebrew Bible and by the ways in which his Jewish teachers taught him the scriptures. His main work on the Hebrew Bible, *You Shall Be as Gods* (Fromm 1966a), received several reviews by Old Testament and other scholars, the majority of which criticized his anachronistic merging of historical and hermeneutical aspects. Fromm also made many references to the Hebrew Bible in other works, and these works have also received attention in the form of passing references or sporadic applications by Hebrew Bible scholars. In general, however, it is fair to say that his impact on Hebrew Bible studies, especially in today's academic community, is minimal. Nevertheless, even if some scholars doubt the scientific fruitfulness of Fromm's own interpretations of and references to the Hebrew Bible, it could be argued that his own competence as a Jewish specialist in sociology and psychoanalysis could help to further Hebrew Bible studies from a socio-psychodynamic perspective. This could be possible on different levels: While some of Fromm's individual psychodynamic insights may help to solve particular exegetical or theological problems (for example, problems of the psalms, of vengeance and violence in the Bible), his non-orthodox sociological-psychoanalytic model might foster studies in religious history, thereby contributing a socio-psychodynamic perspective to the scientific community's "thick descriptions" of historical mentalities, socially bound forms of habitus, and long-lasting moods and orientations that all find expression in religious symbol systems, including the Bible's.

References

Akrap, D. (2011). Erich Fromm – ein jüdischer Denker. Jüdisches Erbe, Tradition, Religion, Münster (LIT-Verlag).

Albertz, R. (1994). A History of Israelite Religion in the Old Testament Period. 2 Volumes. (Old Testament Library). Louisville (Westminster Knox Press).

Assmann, J. (2010). The Price of Monotheism. Stanford (Stanford University Press).

Bartelmus, R. (1990). Haben oder Sein? Anmerkungen zur Anthropologie des Buches Kohelet. In: Biblische Notizen 53, pp. 38–67.

Bellah, R.N. (2011). Religion in Human Evolution. From the Paleolithic to the Axial Age. Cambridge (Harvard University Press).

Berger, K. (2003). Identity and Experience in the New Testament. Minneapolis (Fortress Press).

Block, I. (1968). Radical Humanism and the Bible. Review article of Erich Fromm, "You Shall Be as Gods: A Radical Interpretation of the Old Testament and Its Tradition". Tradition. A Journal of Orthodox Jewish Thought 10, pp. 131–7.

Brueggemann, W. (1991). Interpretation and Obedience. From Faithful Reading to Faithful Living. Minneapolis (Fortress Press).

Brueggemann, W. (1993). Biblical Perspectives on Evangelism. Living in a Three-Storied Universe. Nashville (Abingdon Press).

Burston, D. (1991). The Legacy of Erich Fromm. Cambridge (Harvard University Press).

Dietrich, J. (2000). Religion und Gesellschafts-Charakter. In: R. Funk et al. (Ed.). Erich Fromm heute. Zur Aktualität seines Denkens. München (Deutscher Taschenbuch Verlag), pp. 187–202.

Dietrich, J. (2013a). Die Kunst der Freundschaft. In: B. Bierhoff and H. Johach (Ed.). Humanismus in der Postmoderne. Rainer Funk zum 70. Geburtstag. Pfungstadt (Selbstverlag), pp. 141–52.

Dietrich, J. (2013b). Schadenfreude und Rachegedanken in den Sprüchen und Psalmen. In: A. Grund et al. (Ed.). Ich will dir danken unter den Völkern. Studien zur israelitischen und altorientalischen Gebetsliteratur. Gütersloh (Gütersloher Verlag), pp. 80–92.

Dietrich, J. (2014). Cultural Traumata in the Ancient Near East. In: E.-M. Becker et al. (Eds.). Trauma and Traumatization in Individual and Collective Dimensions. Insights from Biblical Studies and Beyond (Studia Aarhusiana Neotestamentica 2). Göttingen (Vandenhoeck & Ruprecht), pp. 144–60.

Drewermann, E. (1991). Tiefenpsychologie und Exegese. 2 Volumes. Olten (Walter-Verlag).

Duba, A.D. (1968). Review of Erich Fromm, "You Shall Be as Gods: A Radical Interpretation of the Old Testament and Its Tradition". In: The Princeton Seminary Bulletin 61, pp. 77–8.

Friedman, L.J. (2013). The Lives of Erich Fromm – Love's Prophet. New York (Columbia University Press).

Fromm, E. (1941a). Escape from Freedom. New York (Farrar and Rinehart).

Fromm, E. (1947a). Man for Himself. New York (Rinehart and Company).

Fromm, E. (1951a). The Forgotten Language. An Introduction to the Understanding of Dreams, Fairy Tales and Myths. New York (Rinehart and Co.).

Fromm, E. (1956a). The Art of Loving. An Inquiry into the Nature of Love. New York (Harper and Row).

Fromm, E. (1966a). You Shall Be as Gods: A Radical Interpretation of the Old Testament and Its Tradition. New York (Holt, Rinehart and Winston).

Fromm, E. (1973a). The Anatomy of Human Destructiveness. New York (Holt, Rinehart and Winston).

Fromm, E. (1976a). To Have Or to Be? New York (Harper and Row).

Funk, R. (1982). Erich Fromm. The Courage to Be human. With a Postscript by Erich Fromm. New York (Continuum).

Funk, R. (1998). Erich Fromm's Concept of Social Character. In: Social Thought and Research. Vol. 21, pp. 215–29.

Funk, R. (2000a). Erich Fromm: His Life and Ideas. An Illustrated Biography. New York (Continuum).

Funk, R. (2000b). Psychoanalyse der Gesellschaft. Der Ansatz Erich Fromms und seine Bedeutung für die Gegenwart. In: R. Funk et al. (Ed.). Erich Fromm heute. Zur Aktualität seines Denkens. München (Deutscher Taschenbuch Verlag), pp. 20–45.

Garbini, G. (2003). Myth and History in the Bible. Journal for the Old Testament. Supplement Series 362.

Geertz, C. (1993). Religion as a Cultural System. In: C. Geertz. The Interpretation of Cultures. Selected Essays. London (Fontana Press), pp. 87–125.

Gertel, E.B. (1999). Fromm, Freud, and Midrash. Judaism 48, pp. 429–439.

Gertel, E.B. (2014). Fromm, Erich. In: Encyclopedia of the Bible and its Reception 9, pp. 769–771.

Gemünden, P. von (2009). Methodische Überlegungen zur Historischen Psychologie.

Exemplifiziert am Themenkomplex der Trauer in der Bibel und ihrer Umwelt. In: B. Janowski and K. Liess (Eds.). Der Mensch im alten Israel. Neue Forschungen zur alttestamentlichen Anthropologie und ihren altorientalischen Kontexten (Herders Biblische Studien 59), Freiburg (Herder Verlag), pp. 41–68.

Glen, J.S. (1966). Erich Fromm. A Protestant Critique. Philadelphia (Westminster Press).

Gowan, D.E. (1967). Book Review of Erich Fromm, "You Shall Be as Gods: A Radical Interpretation of the Old Testament and Its Tradition." Pittsburgh Perspective. 8, pp. 29–33.

Hardeck, J. (1992). Vernunft & Liebe. Religion im Werk von Erich Fromm. Frankfurt am Main und Berlin (Ullstein).

Harn, R.E. van; Strawn, B.A. (Eds.) (2009). Psalms for Preaching and Worship. A Lectionary Commentary. Grand Rapids (Erdmans).

Hay, D.M. (1967). Review of Erich Fromm, "You Shall Be as Gods: A Radical Interpretation of the Old Testament and Its Tradition." Theology Today 24, pp. 244–5.

Hertzberg, A. (1967). Yahweh on the couch. In: Book Week. Vol. 8, pp. 4–5.

Isaak, E. (1967). Mystical Humanism. Review of Erich Fromm, "You Shall Be as Gods: A Radical Interpretation of the Old Testament and Its Tradition." Commentary. 43, pp. 99–101.

Jeremias, J. (1983). Die Theorie der Projektion im religionskritischen Denken Sigmund Freuds und Erich Fromms, Dissertation. Universität Oldenburg.

Keel, O., and Uehlinger, Ch. (1998). Gods, Goddesses, and Images of God in Ancient Israel. Edinburgh (T&T Clark).

Kille, A. (2001). Psychological Biblical Criticism. Minneapolis (Fortress Press).

Lang, B. (2014). Three Philosophers in Paradise: Kant, Tillich and Ricœur Interpret and Respond to Genesis 3. Scandinavian Journal of the Old Testament. 28, pp. 298–314.

Levenson, B.M. (2008). "The Right Chorale". Studies in Biblical Law and Interpretation (Forschungen zum Alten Testament 54). Tübingen (Mohr Siebeck).

Lohfink, G., and Pesch, R. (1987). Tiefenpsychologie und keine Exegese. Eine Auseinandersetzung mit Eugen Drewermann (Stuttgarter Bibelstudien 129). Stuttgart (Katholisches Bibelwerk).

Lundgren, S. (1998). Fight Against Idols. Erich Fromm on Religion, Judaism and the Bible. Frankfurt am Main (Peter Lang).

Lux, R. (1994). Jona. Prophet zwischen Verweigerung und Gehorsam. Göttingen (Vandenhoeck & Ruprecht).

Maître, J. (1981). Book Review of Erich Fromm, "Vous serez comme des Dieux. Une interprétation radicale de l'Ancien Testament et de sa tradition." Archives de sciences sociales des religions 52, p. 228.

Maly, E.H. (1967). Book Review of Erich Fromm, "You Shall Be as Gods: A Radical Interpretation of the Old Testament and Its Tradition." Catholic Biblical Quarterly 29, pp. 619–21.

McLaughlin, N. (1998). How to Become a Forgotten Intellectual. Intellectual Movements and the Rise and Fall of Erich Fromm. Sociological Forum 13, pp. 215–46.

Midgley, L. (1968). The Divinity in Humanity. Review of Erich Fromm, "You Shall Be as Gods: A Radical Interpretation of the Old Testament and Its Tradition." Dialogue. A Journal of Mormon Thought 3, pp. 134–8.

Petuchowski, J.J. (1956). Erich Fromm's Midrash on Love. The Sacred and the Secular Forms. Commentary 22 (6), pp. 543–549.

Preminger, A.; Greenstein, E.L. (Eds.) (1986). The Hebrew Bible in Literary Criticism. New York (Ungar).

Rabin, A. (1998). Psychological Issues in Biblical Lore: Explorations in the Old Testament. New York (Springer).

Rogerson, J.W. (2010). A Theology of the Old Testament. Cultural Memory, Communication, and Being Human. Minneapolis (Fortress Press).

Schieder, R. (2014). Die Gewalt des einen Gottes. Die Monotheismusdebatte zwischen Jan Assmann, Micha Brumlik, Rolf Schieder, Peter Sloterdijk und anderen. Berlin (Berlin University Press).

Schimmel, N. (2009). Judaism and the Origins of Erich Fromm's Humanistic Psychology. The Religious Reverence of a Heretic. Journal of Humanistic Psychology 49, pp. 9–45.

Sloterdijk, P. (2013). Im Schatten des Sinai. Fußnote über Ursprünge und Wandlungen totaler Mitgliedschaft. Frankfurt am Main (Suhrkamp).

Steffen, U. (1985). Jona und der Fisch. Der Mythos von Tod und Wiedergeburt. Stuttgart (Kreuz Verlag).

Thomson, A. (2009). Erich Fromm. Explorer of the Human Condition. London and New York (Palgrave Macmillan).

Thornton, E.E. (1967). Review of Erich Fromm, "You Shall Be as Gods: A Radical Interpretation of the Old Testament and Its Tradition." Pastoral Psychology 18, pp. 58–9.

Zenger, E. (1994). Ein Gott der Rache? Feindpsalmen verstehen. Freiburg (Herder Verlag).

I wish to thank Sarah Jennings (Aarhus) for improving my English.

Erich Fromm: "To Be" instead of "To Have" as a Model for the Justice of Distribution

An Inquiry on Fromm's Reference to Meister Eckhart

Dietmar Mieth

Abstract: The ambivalence that accompanies becoming wealthy is widely acknowledged. Wealth only is valuable if it can be put to good use, or, in other words, when it is used responsibly. Like Meister Eckhart in the later Middle Ages Erich Fromm also (*To Have Or to Be?*) pointed out that the alternative to the lack of distribution of goods is not merely a spiritual understanding of poverty but an ethical understanding of what responsibility should come together with being wealthy/rich. Wealth is, in this understanding, the capacity to distribute. In a religious approach, which Fromm maintains even as an agnostic, he proposes with Meister Eckhart to imitate the "divine" capacity of a distribution without making differences between the possible recipients, who all have the same dignity (cf. Mieth 2012a). For Fromm (like for Eckhart) "to be" is seen as a process of "detachment" as a promotion of a "productive character" which leads life and intellect to a real freedom and to the capacity of Being as an openness to Giving. In the actual discussion about the global dimension of poverty, philosophers search for the foundation of so called "positive duties". In the case of Fromm, we have an example of a humanistic foundation of such positive duties in the orientation of human character. The normative answer to the questions raised by Fromm's cultural, sociopsychological analysis is offered, in my opinion, by Alan Gewirth's *The Community of Rights* (1996), in which the correlation of liberal, social and economic rights is demonstrated.

Fromm writes: "Biblical ethics are not primarily concerned with wealth and poverty as such but with the social relations between those who are powerful and those who are powerless. (...) God appears in the bible as the God of justice and the God of compassion" (Fromm 1966a, p. 185).

"All knowledge of the other is based on shared experience. In cannot understand in another that which I do not experience in myself (...)." If I know only my customers, "I know myself only as the *social man*". *I must become an "universal man".* This concept of a *universal man* Fromm found in Maimonides (cf. Fromm 1966a, pp. 166–7). Fromm's ethical concept is related to Freedom, Justice and Compassion. In his book *To Have Or to Be?* (Fromm 1976a) he tried to find a spiritual key for a better distribution in an unjust world and in unjust societies. My conviction is that this key lies on the one side in Fromm's analysis of the negative assimilation and socialization of men in a post-industrial world, leading to a total economization of all behavior. The "having" character is a name for an inwardness according to Fromm that is the source of a wrong orientation. This inwardness Fromm labels "to have" orientation. It corresponds to an outwardness of "wealth". I will take Meister Eckhart's work, read and quoted by Fromm, as presenting a concept of wealth understood as inwardness which expresses not "to have", but "to be"– to be as God. By this I am joining the radical interpretation of the Old Testament by Fromm.

The ambivalence that accompanies acquiring wealth is widely acknowledged. Wealth only is valuable if it can be put to good use, or, in other words, when it is used responsibly. Similarly to Meister Eckhart in the later Middle Ages Erich Fromm (*To Have Or to Be?*) pointed out, that the alternative to the lack of distribution of goods is not merely a spiritual understanding of poverty but an ethical understanding of what responsibility should come together with being wealthy/rich. Wealth is, in this understanding, the capacity to distribute.

In a religious approach, which Fromm maintains even as an agnostic, he proposes together with Meister Eckhart to imitate the "divine" capacity of distribution without making differences between the possible recipients, who all have the same dignity. For Fromm (like for Eckhart) "to be" is seen as a process of "detachment" as a promotion of a "productive character" which leads life and intellect to a real freedom and to the capacity of Being as an openness to Giving. There is considerable interest in Meister

Eckhart (1260–1328) worldwide, even within the context of non-Christian approaches to religious experience. Through his connections to Jewish and Islamic philosophy and mysticism Meister Eckhart's legacy continues to live on in these traditions. Declared atheists, too, are fascinated by his thought, at least those with a certain interest on religion. A representative example is Erich Fromm whose book *To Have Or to Be?* (Fromm 1976a; cf. also Frederking 1994) is well-known. The chapter on Meister Eckhart is relatively brief, and refers to my works for further detail. Yet Fromm, a declared humanistic psychologist, actually read Meister Eckhart daily over a period of twenty years, more frequently than he read Karl Marx or Sigmund Freud, two major authors that he read regularly in addition to reading the Bible. I had the opportunity to spend an intense working weekend with Fromm in Locarno in 1975. He impressed me greatly (see Mieth 2001), and from then on we began correspondence on Eckhart which lasted for quite a while. Unfortunately, Fromm's deteriorating health did not allow him to conduct any further studies. Despite our consensus in reading Meister Eckhart we remained divided on the question of God. Fromm read Eckhart agnostically, I read him theologically, from a Christian perspective (cf. Mieth 2002, pp. 99–112).

Meister Eckhart is, in my opinion, writes something that essentially can be seen as presenting a compendium of knowledge and experience of the Judeo-Christian Bible with the assistance of philosophical interpretation. In accordance with his title, *magister sacrae scripturae*, he was a *Meister*, an expert on the Holy Scriptures, an exegete, an interpreter of scripture. In fact, Eckhart was both an exegete and a philosopher, since he considered it essential to interpret the Holy Scriptures "with the natural arguments of the philosophers" (see Meister Eckhart, *Expositio sancti Evangelii secundum Iohannem*, n.2, LW III, p. 4). His approach was twofold: to open the Bible to the highest form of scientific knowledge – in the tradition of his teacher Albert the Great – and to interpret it with the subtlest type of philosophical thought. The reverse is also conceivable: to retranslate the subtlest form of philosophical thought and the broadest forms of human knowledge about the world into the language of faith, i.e., given these intellectual possibilities, and given these possibilities in knowledge, to revert to an authentic, existentially fundamental experience. Faith and its "virtues," hope and love, are to be taken seriously.

All creatures say God's name, but lose themselves in the incomprehensible, the ineffable. For God does not answer to names, even if it is permissible to call on him with the name which holy persons have used to call on him. God remains unspeakable and unnamable in the clarity of his ground. Similarly, the human soul is also unspeakable and wordless, where it is grasped in its own ground (see Pr. 77, DW III, pp. 337–8; = Sermon 49, CMW, p. 263). God and the soul are so completely one that there is no longer a counterpart. The unspeakability of God contrasts with his essence as self-revelation, as the one who "shares Himself most of all" (Pr. 9, DW I, p. 149 = Sermon 67, CMW, p. 343), who totally emanates from himself. It can also be grasped by distinguishing God from himself, as Eckhart tries to do in his famous sermon on poverty: God works and shares himself; the Godhead, by contrast, remains silent. The person contemplating God, not as relation but in himself, must become "godless", "free of God" (see Pr. 52, DW II, p. 493: "gotes ledic" = Sermon 87, CMW, p. 424 as well as Pr. 77, DW III, p. 344; Sermon 49, CMW, pp. 262–4), must look into a silent desert. There, where knowing and willing can no longer comprehend themselves reflexively as knowledge of knowledge or as loving will, being is in itself, is the "negation of negation" (see, for example Pr. 21, DW I, p. 361–2 = Sermon 97, CMW, p. 467–8), that is, the "purum nihil" of contingent creature-liness. In this passage Eckhart is wordy, using language in an expressive way in order to talk about circumstances where there is no longer a word. In this sense he goes beyond his theories of relation – relation through the language of creation, through the language of birth, through the language of self-assurance. He surpasses the conception of happiness in seeing God that was still important to Augustine (see the conclusion to the model sermon on the nobleman, DW V, 118, p. 13–4 = CMW, 562).

Eckhart's Scholastic contemporaries criticize him for allegedly wanting to draw God too deeply into the human being, because the entering "spark of the soul," to the extent that it emanates from God but does not remain in the human being, is "uncreated"; on the other hand, they admonish him for allegedly approaching blasphemy, because even blasphemous talk about God affirms God indirectly. This misconstrues Eckhart's processual theories of relation. For even if God is conceived as unrelated, as relationless, this still involves a relation from the perspective of the human being, that no longer involves the criterion of consciousness. Only someone seeking a relationship can actually comprehend the termination of a relationship. Through this termination all intentions and goals are thwarted. What is to be strived for is a being, living, and knowing that no longer requires a goal and a why: "If a man asked life for a thousand years, '*Why* do you live?' if it could answer it would only say "I live because I live"" (Pr. 5b, DW I, p. 92 = Sermon 13b, CMW, p. 110). This indifference has revitalized the dialogue with Zen Buddhism. Indifference can also be understood as the immersion in nothingness as representative of the Absolute. Eckhart clearly knows the silent desert of the Godhead, but does not draw these conclusions; today they are occasionally drawn for him.

In Eckhart's conception of a fulfilled relationship between God and the human being there is definitely the "two in one" (Pr. 86, DW III, p. 484 = Sermon 9, CMW, p. 86), difference and identity at the same time. For God is "alius, non aliud" ("another, but nothing other than reality"), if it is real. Eckhart calls the distinction between God and world "undifferentiatedness" or "indistinction" ("distinctio per indistinctionem," see LW II, p. 489 as well as Fischer 1974, pp. 124–6). This is because, in the Dominican's opinion, it is not a categorical but a "higher" distinction, unlike a distinction between two things, which are differentiated on the basis of a "distinguishing mark" ("principium diiudicationis"). It is far more radical: undifferentiated, indistinct in being, suspended into but separate from nothingness, a nothingness that would be all individually existent being as created in itself ("purum nihil") if being did not continually flow into it "on loan." Eckhart is striving for the "breakthrough" to a union without a difference in consciousness, but without the medium of consciousness: it is even more compelling than this "analogy," distinction through indistinction, identity and difference, a "two in one." Eckhart does not strive for a mediated but a direct union. For this union the simple working of the working – God as pure working, the human being introduced into this working as a worker – is more decisive than seeing God (see Sermon 86, DW III, pp. 482–6 = Sermon 9, CMW, pp. 83–90).

Experienced-ness as knowing of the conditions of character

The path leading from religious experience to moral experience is described within the context of Eckhart's theory of divine justice. Justice is one of the identities of God. If God would lose this identity he wouldn't be of interest anymore. Without justice, God cannot be recognized by man:

> The just are determined by justice at such a rate, that if God were not just they would not care a fig for God: they are so firmly committed to justice and so thoroughly self-abandoned that they do not care for the pains of hell or the joys of heaven or anything at all. Indeed, were all the pain of those in hell, men or devils, and all the pain that has been suffered or ever will be suffered – were all this "to be set beside justice, they would not care a jot, so firmly do they stand by God and justice. (...) Whoever understands about the just man and justice understands all that I am saying (Pr. 6, DW I, pp. 103–5 = Sermon 65, CMW, p. 329).

This correlation of religion and moral in the divine origin doesn't mean that religious institutions and rules are allowed to dominate ethics. Eckhart attributes an eminent role to philosophy. That becomes clear when he conscientiously explains his approach in his famous sermon on Mary and Martha:

> Life experience gives the finest understanding. Life experience understands better than experience of delight and light (can do). Whatever, except God, man can experience in this body, is truly given by life experience. And in some ways this experience seems clearer than eternal light seems to be. For the experience in the eternal light enables to perceive oneself and God, not oneself apart from God; life experience in contrast makes one perceive oneself, apart from God. When one identifies oneself and nothing more, it is easier for him to tell what is like and unlike (right or wrong). This may be proved by comparing St. Paul and the pagan masters. St. Paul in his ecstasy saw God and himself in spiritual fashion, in God, but not each single virtue was precisely present in his vision, and that derived from the fact that he had not practiced them exercising virtues. By exercising virtues, the (pagan) masters got hold of such profound discernment that they recognized the nature of each single virtue more clearly than Paul or any saint in his first rapture (Pr. 86, DW II, p. 482–3 = Sermon 9, CMW, p. 84).

We can see how important the word "practice" – or creating life-experience here is. Eckhart insists with his description of the figure of Martha on the necessity of life experience or to be experienced by practice and by habituating in practice. We can here understand Eckhart as a theologian of process and a "metaphysical pragmatist".

And Eckhart continues in this sermon on Mary (Magdalen) and Martha (seen as her sister in Bethanien) a little later:

> Three things especially are needful in our works: to be orderly, understanding, and mindful. "Orderly" I call that which corresponds in all points to the highest (principle). "Understanding" I call knowing nothing temporal that is better. "Mindful" I call feeling living truth joyously present in good works. When these three points are one, they bring us just near and are just as helpful as Mary Magdalenas (contemplative) joy in the wilderness (Pr. 86, DW III, p. 486 = Sermon 9, CMW, p. 87).

Eckhart's definition of wealth

In his definition of wealth (cf. for the following reflections: Mieth, 2012a) Eckhart gives priority to the application of rich to God:

> Rich is whatever has all things without lack. I am a man and I am rich, but I am not therefore another man (...) no one is rich but God alone, who embraces in simplicity all things in Himself (Pr. 47, DW II, p. 398 = Sermon 23, CMW, p. 156).

Richness and giving are for Eckhart the same. At the highest level of richness/wealth, the characteristic of God's kingdom, distribution not preservation, is available. God is a gift. His real name is charity (mercy). Therefore, he not only can but he must, following his own nature, always give, and this is the second point about riches (cf. Sermon 23, CMW, p. 156). "Giving" is therefore the second definition of 'wealth', after having without lack" (DW II, 399, 2). God's giving is without restitution:

> the third point about riches is, that one gives without expecting any return, for he who gives in exchange for anything is not really rich. Therefore God's

richness is shown in this, that He gives all His gifts for nothing (Sermon 23, CMW, p. 156).

Perfect wealth implies remaining rich despite constant giving. In the end, this is not only true for God. Humans can participate in this wealth/richness too, if they give without reservation, and if this giving is not accompanied by any wanting or self-reference. Giving does not happen on the basis of an approach towards-which [oriented towards something], but happens in the opposite direction, emerges from something, a from-which orientation: from including oneself in the fulfilment of God's will (cf. Pr. 62, DW III 59 = Sermon 55, CMW, pp. 289ff.).

God is Therefore the "Rich Man" of the Gospel

The Latin sermon VII (LW IV, p. 75ff. to Lk 16,19) is similar to Pr. VIII to Lk 14,16: *Homo quidam fecit coenam magnam*, (to Lk 14,16, cf. LW IV, p. 90). In these Latin Sermons as well as in the German Pr. 80, DW III, pp. 378–88 = CMW 94, pp. 455–7 (to Lk 16,1) Eckhart draws a connection between the "homo quidam" and God. For Eckhart, the "homo quidam" can alternatively be a reference to "the Godhead and to every delicate soul" (cf. CMW 94, p. 455). But God is the only subject in which wealth is originally and completely existing. God is the origin of wealth – in the understanding of a reigning principle.

The "Modistic" grammar of his contemporary Thomas of Erfurt (1972) – later taken up programmatically by Charles Peirce! – stipulates that a word can be transferred from a particular context to another context in order to bring out the richness of its meaning (cf. the related observations of Stephan Grotz (2003)).

God's Wealth/Richness and the Kingdom of God

The central thesis of Eckhart about the kingdom of God among humans is: the kingdom of God is in you (cf. Pr. 68, DW III, p. 140,2: "daz rîche gotes ist in uns" = Sermo 69, CMW p. 352ff.: "the kingdom of God is within us"). The kingdom of God is the richness of the inner man. Inner richness concurs with the concept of real poverty. Inner richness is the positive side of the negative articulation: the threefold negation in poverty: not knowing, not willing, not having (see later on).

In his reception of the biblical message of the "kingdom of God", Eckhart maintains a psychological interpretation of "regnum Deum intra vos est" (Lk 17,21), as does Luther, amongst others, instead of the social interpretation: the realm/Kingdom is "amongst you", that is, constitutes a new social beginning. The Kingdom of God in the soul is an individualization of the biblical message: "I have a power in my soul which is ever receptive to God" (CMW 68, p. 352). This kind of individualization grants a distance from religious and political institutions (cf. Vinzent 2012). The door is then opened for a so called "mystical" interpretation.

Distance to institutions is derived from the distance to the "world", seen as "mundus" ("pure contingent reality") and as "society." The three worldly realms are mundus, flesh, and devil: " der werlt rîche sol man überwinden mit der armuote des geistes" (the wealth of the world shall be overcome with the poverty of spirit, Pr. 33, DW II, pp. 150ff. = CMW 81, pp. 401–2). This is not available for religious communities. Eckhart's anti-individualism is from the same strength as his Individualism of the inner man and the soul. The presence of Jesus Christ in the soul is also seen as a "communitarian" gift. I have exposed this element in a book about *Christ – the Social in Man* (Mieth 1972).

But Eckhart is not a "communitarian, "he is a universalist. God's wealth and his universal Kingdom belong together, once more what is at stake is the person's inner being, which indeed is accessible to anyone, independently of their status (cf. Pr. 38, DW II, p. 232,4 = Sermon 29, CMW, p. 178).

The inner radicalness of the transformation from inner wealth into poverty and social distribution, radical like the conception of God as a gift, is often expressed by Eckhart, when he is explaining the meaning of "The Lord's prayer." We therefore find in Eckhart's comments on the Lord's Prayer [Our Father]: "thy will be done" which presupposes the relinquishment will of one's own, indeed any intention of one's own (cf. also Pf, pp. 414–5). In Eckhart's prayer we read: "I was saying my Paternoster... that when we say 'Thy kingdom come, thy will be done', we are praying to God to deprive us of ourselves" (cf. Sermon 12, CMW, p. 102).

The Realm and Wealth of the Soul, the "Inner City"

"Rich" as an indication of man is related to *adelig* ("noble", "aristocratic") and *wirdekeit* ("honor", "dignity", cf. *The Nobleman*, CMW, p. 557ff.; cf. Sturlese's *Homo divinus* – the divine man). The analysis about richness is connected with Eckhart's doctrine of grace: grace accompanies one in becoming, while it is already "fundamentally" there. There is no distinction between grace in creation and grace in salvation (cf. Pr. 21, DW I, p. 367 = Sermon 97, CMW 97, p. 468). God's love starts not in history at a specific time, but exists before time is starting, "when we were not" (Sermon 12, CMW, p. 100).

The relation between rich and noble can be seen in the sermon *Homo quidam nobilis* (Lk 19,12). The given richness by God's distribution without reservation is on the level of anticipation of the real being of man. On the other side is the "becoming rich" as a necessity to transform the empirical status of man into the status of "being", which is at the same time the prefect status. Eckhart describes the way of becoming:

> This man returns *richer*, than when he set forth. Whoever had gone out of himself like that would be given back to himself in a truer sense; and all things, just he had fully abandoned them in multiplicity, will be entirely returned to him in simplicity, for he finds himself and all things in the present "now" of unity. And the man who went forth thus would return much *nobler* then when he had departed. This man now dwells in unhampered freedom and pure nakedness, for he needs undertake and take nothing small or great – for whatever belongs to God belongs to him (Pr. 15, DW I, 245 = Sermon 51, CMW, pp. 270ff.).

In the background are the promises of Jesus in Mk 10,29.30 and Lk 18,29.30: The gain [benefit] of giving without reservation, the wholehearted giving is reached already *in this worldlife* not only later in the eternal life!

In the same manner in which Eckhart speaks of the inner kingdom he speaks also of the inner city (cf. Sermo VIII, LW IV, 90: *A view of the city* (civitas). The mentioned city (Naim) is a parable of the secure soul, which is a "holy city", since it is blessed by God (cf. Sermo XXXVI, Lk 7,11–12, p. 313; cf. Pr. 18, DW Pr. 18 = Sermon 36, CMW), also on Lk 7,14: the city (Naim) is ordered, secured and sheltered. This is an inner purification, illumination and unification. Eckhart develops the "power of inner liberation" not the political power (cf. Mieth 2009).

The Interrelation between Wealth and Poverty

"Alliu rîcheit und armuote und saelicheit liget an dem willen." "All wealth and poverty and bliss depends on the will" (Pr. 36, DW II, 201 = Sermon 39, CMW, p. 222). "For the truly perfected man should want to be so dead to self, so lost in God to his own form and so transformed in God's will, that his entire blessedness consists in unknowing of himself and all things, and knowing only God, willing nothing and knowing no will but God's will" (BgT, DW V, 22 = Book on Divine Comfort, CMW p. 530). On Our Lord's Prayer: "thy kingdom come, that I may possess nothing I prize and regard as wealth but You, who are all riches" (CMW p. 531). Doing the will of God means willing without a why. We have to realize where we come from and not to make a plan where we want to go!

> Ob dich got naeme von innerlîcher armuote und begâbe dich mit rîcheit innerlîche. (Pr. Pr. 49, DW II, 446). There is another thing you should have. It is this: if God were to take you away from inner poverty and invest you inwardly with riches and with grace and were to unite you with Himself as much as your soul could endure this, you should hold yourself free of these riches and give the glory to God alone, just as your soul remained empty when God created it from nothing into something (CMW 89, p. 438).

The German sermon (Sermon 62, CMW and in German Pf. 55) may be a "collatio", very close to the *Talks of Instruction*, and according to Wackernagel (1876, pp. 156ff.) it can also be taken as an "after-dinner speech" or a table talk (Quint 1955, p. 515). It orients itself with Mk 10,29.30, as we have seen, where the receipt is spoken of already in this lifetime. In the end, the message concerns one's religious way through life: follow the first step and its direction, do not make a plan, but simply go ahead step by step. The beginning determines the direction, not the end. As a matter of principle, Eckhart argues from the ideal beginning, never towards a teleological planned ending. He prefers the light of the morning to the star of the evening.

What Eckhart means by "poor" is well known and discussed. We will find it for instance in the *Book of Divine Comfort*:

> Poor in spirit means as the eye is poor and bare of color yet receptive for all colors, so is he poor in spirit who is receptive of all spirit, and the spirit of all spirits is God. The fruit of the spirit is love, joy and peace. Bareness, and poverty, having nothing and being empty transforms nature; water makes water run upward and perform many other miracles (DW V, p. 29 = CMW p. 535).

Most known is the *sermon on poverty* (Pr. 52, DW II, p. 486ff. = Sermon 87 CMW, pp. 420–425): to be poor is on the highest level explained as no knowing, no having, no willing. "No", in Middle German "Niht", here is adverbal, not the object "nothing" (therefore I do not follow Walshe's translation and, Kurt Ruh, the best scholar on mysticism in Germany, acknowledged my translation). The no to knowing, having, willing on one's own means the quality of a consciousness free of having, without willing, without knowing, and of an attitude which follows the inner drive which is conceived from a notion of radical freedom.

The battle against empirical poverty under the neighbors is based in the unity of being. In the Sermon about Elisabeth of Thueringen, Eckhart came to the conclusion:

> Outwardly, in the eyes of the world, this woman dwelt in riches and glory, but inwardly she worshipped true poverty. And when her outward comforts failed her, she fled to Him to whom all creatures flee, setting at naught the world and self. In that way she transcended self and scorned the scorn of men, so that it did touch her and she lost none of her perfection. Her desire was to wash and rend sick and filthy people with a pure heart (Pr. 32, DW II, p. 147 = CMW 52, p. 278).

We will find this also in the figure of Martha:

> temporal work is as noble as any communing with God, for it joins us to Him as closely as the highest that can happen to us except the vision of God in His naked nature (Pr. 86, DW III, p. 488 = Sermon 9, CMW, p. 87).

Eckhart on Equality of Humans (cf. Mieth, 2014a)

Equality for Eckhart is initially seen in relation to the (gracious) equality of God and humans, then in relation to charity (cf. Pr. 4, NL p. 50; Pr. 9, NL p. 110); to man and woman [husband and wife]: Pr. 6, NL 82, pp. 2–7; and to master and servant: Pr. 27, NL p. 308 (cf. Mieth 2013a). Often we will find a dialectic of oneness and equality: the "two in one":

> If a man might and knew how to make a cup completely empty and keep it empty of whatever might fill it, even air, assuredly that cup would lose and forget its own nature, and emptiness would bear it aloft (in the heaven). So too, being bare, poor, and void of all creatures carries the soul to God. Likeness, too, and heat are causes of ascent. Likeness we ascribe to the Son in the Godhead, heat and love to the Holy Ghost. Likeness in all things, more especially and firstly in the divine nature, is the birth of the one, and likeness of one, in one and with one is the origin and source of the flowering, ardent love. One is beginning without any beginning. Likeness is beginning begotten of the One alone, getting its being, and it being-a-beginning, from and in the One. It is the nature of love to arise and flow out of two as a one. One as one is not love; two as two is not love; but two as one must produce natural, willing, ardent love (BgT, DW V, 30 = *Book on Divine Comfort,* CMW p. 535).

And again:

> When I and you are once embraced by the eternal light, that is one and two in the same moment. Two in one is a fiery spirit, standing over all things, yet under God, in the circle of eternity (...) then one becomes two, two is one: light and spirit, these two are one in the embrace of the eternal light (Pr. 86, DW III, p. 486 = Sermon 9, CMW, p. 86. For my reconstruction of the text, see Mieth (1969), p. 200, note 266).

Nothingness (Poverty) and Plenitude (Wealth) – the two Sides of the Same Divine Realm

Eckhart's describes rich and poor from different perspectives: someone who is poor outwardly, can be rich inwardly. Whoever is poor outwardly, cannot be poor enough inwardly (see above: Thomas Aquinas). Someone who is rich outwardly, can be hampered inwardly – and then he is not truly "rich". Someone who is rich inwardly, does not have to be poor outwardly. "Having, as if you did not have" (cf. Saint Paul: 1 Kor 7,29–32). From having coming to being: so goes the title of a book by Erich Fromm, in which he made a nice reference to my approach. But someone asked: what benefit is it for poor people, if they *are* more? This question is posed by Gonsalv Mainberger (1977). My answer to this critical question: If the rich *are* more, the poor will *have* more. That is Eckhart's social approach.

Eckhart integrates richness and poverty in his "idealist" view: poverty and wealth are both taken on their ideal ranks – or viewed "in essence" ["fundamentally"/"in principle"/"at heart"], that is, "in spirit" – and on this highest level they are not opposed, but identical. The background to this is the doctrine of the higher reality of so called transcendentals. Eckhart often refers to the example of justice. Justice in itself is not an empirical fact but a transcendental reality which is the fundamental condition and the starting point for a reflection about justice in institutions and in doing well. On the transcendent level of being God has a commitment to justice: he cannot be else than just (cf. Flasch 2010, pp. 52–5; Mieth 2013b).

As we have seen, for Eckhart the first application of the term "rich" is based on God's plenitude (fullness). This means "rich in principle", in Latin *in principio*, in the beginning of all beginning. Eckhart's internal conception of the kingdom of God places this kingdom in every individual soul. This concept promotes a religious individualization. Included in this individualization is the natural and spiritual equity of all humans (cf. Gal 3, 28). Typical for Eckhart is the possibility to exchange the terms "noble", "rich" and "divine" and their spiritual implications in relation to man (Sturlese 2007). Therefore, the stages of poverty of the spirit and of being rich are under the same criteria, the "absolute no" to any adherence.

Some General Remarks
on Eckhart's Fundamental Social Engagement

Eckhart maintains a constructive tension between belief and intellect (cf. Mieth, 1972). There is not a concurrence between them. The intellect has the obligation to accept that the belief does not exist because it has constructed it with its own instruments. On the other side the belief must be open for an intellectual disclosure. Belief will be disclosed by intellectual understanding – understanding by a reason which is placed in the heart of man. Belief will also be disclosed by natural science who delivers "parables" for a deeper understanding (cf. In Joh. n.2–3, LW III, p. 4 and n. 45, LW IIII, p. 37 and n. 361, LW III, p. 307).

Eckhart teaches the unity of grace. Grace is God's nature, in German "Barmherzigkeit", a word which needs to be translated with the "mercy" and "charity" at the same time. The unity of Grace is available from its start point in the heart of the Godhead. This unity stems from the grace of creation to the grace of salvation to grace as an individual support to develop the dispositions and to enforce the ongoing spiritual process. For Eckhart's new "philosophy of Christianity" (Flasch 2010) is in my opinion constitutive of the Christology, this means the transformation of all human nature by the incarnation, so that humaneness and the Divine cannot be separated.

Starting with these presuppositions Meister Eckhart proposes breaking from the attachment to goods to the real richness in the realm of grace, which is distribution without loss. He clarifies this from several perspectives: freedom, poverty and detachment. This corresponds to the utopia of the expropriated existence, i.e., of a mode of existence that does not accept economic structures as valid and needs structures as definitive. It is not a matter of the abolition of physical conditions, nor of the ascetic life, but of the incompleteness of human striving, like a wound that remains open until a true, and not a supposed, healing process ensues. This striving or permanent breaking through is stimulated by Christian hope. The reference to Christ reveals the expropriated or property less existence as fulfilled existence. The infinite extension of the human way, which is announced in the conception of permanent breaking through, is not grounds for resignation, but for hope and commitment. The reference to Christ reveals the expropriated existence as a social and action-oriented existence.

Christocentric anthropology logically encompasses the solidarity and socialization of human beings in Christ (Mieth 1972). Through the exposure of human self-realization – at the expense of or under the forensic inclusion of the moral responsibility of other human beings – the social existence replaces the ownership and personal structure of the person of individual means and individuality. Eckhart exposes self-realization in the sublime forms of piety and the *Do et des* relationship between human beings. The trend to sexual permissiveness with calculation of the consequences for the partner is one such form of private self-fulfillment, an equation with two unknowns, both being assumed as known in the blindness of supposed self-determination: the inaccessible self and the self of the other. The social is not simply the accumulation of self-determining, self-reliant individuals but an indeterminate system of relationships between and in human beings. Eckhart's thesis is that this system of relationships first attains its ultimate perspective in Christ, because Christ is the foundation of solidarity for the human race. Christ is the social in the human being, both from the perspective of his permanent expropriatedness as well as from the perspective of his human solidarity. He reveals the breakthrough character of human existence together with its meaning and its purpose.

Eckhart's orientation toward social action is already evident in the dynamism that this approach produces with regard to autonomy, the breaking through economic structures, and sociality. The dynamics of structure become a postulate of action for Meister Eckhart. This does not make the case for a rhetorical activism; an alienation of the human in over activity would not fulfill this orientation towards action as human "inwardness." The orientation toward action is the incarnation itself because it offers orientation and itself constitutes action, to the point that for Eckhart "incarnation" encompasses all the actions of Christ. Action on the basis of an autonomous faculty of reason impelled by the motivational power of faith is "inward," is not an outward drivenness induced by needs. Eckhart has illustrated this clearly in the figures of Martha and Elizabeth. The inwardness of acting is not, on the other hand, a quietist category. It simply distinguishes rational social "action" from mere "behavior," in that the human being acts not on the basis of inner distance (*"bei* den Dingen, nicht *in* den Dingen") but "as if possessed," driven by short-term goals and expectations which he or she does not control but which control him or her.

Conspicuous is Eckhart's exclusive naming of love as the orientation for action. Love is more closely specified, however; it is neither a category of the needs structure nor a category of the just balance between giving and receiving. Love is essentially "social" love, i.e., "expropriated" or unpossessing love, a love free of motivation, not a category of acquisition or entitlement, not a category of eros as a sophisticated form of the extension of the individual identity through the other. In this love Christ replaces the individuality of the human being; it is the love of the human being who has become truly incarnate, truly human, who already exists as a social being, and therefore unquestionably acts socially. The question is naturally justified whether this love of the truly incarnate human being is not a utopia, just as the expropriated existence is a utopia. For Meister Eckhart true human incarnation is actually existent. The existing reality is not the orienting standard, but rather the promised hope, the motivational power of faith, and the ultimate form of love, which is revealed in the incarnation of Jesus Christ. It is not that which is that serves as orientation for acting, but that which is to be. On the other hand, that which is to be is a reality already anticipated in Christ. Thus, the utopia is not an illusion; the future has already been imparted to the human being. What is to be is *within* the human being. Eckhart's comprehension of Christ as the social in the human being appears as we have seen above to be an interpretation of Paul's words that the human being no longer lives as "I" but as Christ (Gal 2, 20). This is how God reveals the process of becoming human in Christ.

But what has this to do today with an opaque, anonymous financial system, loss of responsibility in individuals and in politics (*bonum commune*, community of rights). Can we retreat and withdraw into spirituality? Can we take some spiritual admonitions and make them political: wealth is for distribution; it is assumed by Christian faith that there is an equality of participation to goods. For Eckhart this is clear, an important quotation from him reads:

> Whoever could exist in the nakedness of the nature, free from all mediation, must have left behind all distinction of person, so that he is as well disposed to a man who is across the sea, whom he never set eyes on, as the man who is with him and is his close friend. As long as you favor your own person more than a man you never have seen, you are assuredly not right and you have never for a single instant looks into this simple ground (Pr. 5b, CMW 13b, p. 109).

Eckhart's Christology is behind this (ibid., p. 108): "God not only became man, but he took on human nature". When humanness is integrated in God's birth in the world, than human dignity with all its implications of the rights and obligations of men, is assumed to be equal for all humans. Eckhart anticipates Kant, who sees, "human dignity as the absolute value", but it is, as he says, "even harder." Therefore, we can suggest as a conclusion: mysticism is an inner concept of social as universal. Our reading of Meister Eckhart has (hopefully) demonstrated that the experience of God and the inner-directedness of human beings do not signify a disregard of social dimensions. Remarks such as Thomas a Kempis's "Lerne deine Umwelt verachten, um dich an deine Innenwelt hinzugeben" (to have contempt for the human environment and to cultivate only the inner life) are not to be found in Meister Eckhart. On the contrary, whoever attempts "Gott zu finden in Innerlichkeit und Verzückung" (to find God in inwardness and rapture) will not find him. Rather it is a question of how those around us and our environment have their foundation and their continuation in us ourselves. Concentration of this type – called *innicheit* – is always meant comprehensively here, i.e., in the sense that the concentration at the middle of the circle also reaches the circumference of the circle at the same time.

Eckhart's ethics and social theology cannot be directly interpreted politically. Socialist-oriented interpretations prove inadequate because they employ presumed historical motivations which cannot be convincingly established in Meister Eckhart. Eckhart's motivation is indicated clearly enough in his own words: to experience God and to become human through this experience, not for oneself but for others. "Gott und ich, wir sind eins im Wirken, er wirkt und ich werde" (God and I are one in this operation: He works and I come into being. – Pr. 6, DW 1, p. 114 = Sermon 65, CMW p. 332).

Yet a specific social-therapeutic approach is inherent in Eckhart's fundamental ideas. Today we are also exceedingly aware that the adverse condition of human coexistence cannot simply be alleviated through structural and institutional changes. Necessary are human beings who choose to live differently so that life goes differently. Eckhart's sermon is thus directed against our mentality (whether we choose to call it a practical-materialist or a capitalist mentality makes no difference). This sermon against our mentality is just as provocative today as in the cities of the Middle Ages, Several indications: Eckhart exposes all motivations of humankind, including all objectified values, whether intellectual or material, as mere "appearance" or "pretense" in comparison to real human being as a preparedness for continual rethinking or changing. Eckhart exposes our tendency to act as a superficial appropriation of our world and ourselves and preaches committed detachment or abandonment instead. Eckhart exposes our mentality of achievement in the subtlest of areas, for example, in the area of piety, as an unsuccessful attempt at self-union and world-union. Finally, Eckhart exposes the seemingly justified demands of our "I" as attempts to erect a boundary of self-righteousness for our love.

In the actual discussion about the global dimension of poverty, philosophers search for the foundation of so called "positive duties". In the case of Fromm, we have an example of a humanistic foundation of such positive duties in the orientation of human character. The normative answer to the questions asked in Fromm' s cultural, sociopsychological analysis is, in my opinion, Alan Gewirth's *The Community of Rights* (1996), in which the correlation of liberal, social and economic rights is demonstrated.

References

DW = Deutsche Werke; Pr. = Predigt = Sermons with Arabic Numbers;
LW = Lateinische Werke; Sermons with Roman chiffres;
CMW = *The Complete Mystical Works of Meister Eckhart*. English translation by Maurice Walshe. New York (Crossroads Herder), 2008. Sermons with Arabic Numbers.
Pf. = Pfeiffer, F. (Ed.) (1857). Meister Eckhart Pfeiffer (= Deutsche Mystiker des 14. Jahrhunderts, Vol. 2). 4th Edition. Göttingen (Vandenhoeck & Ruprecht), 1924.
NL = Niklas Largier (1993). Meister Eckhart. Werke in zwei Bänden. Berlin (Bibliothek Deutscher Klassiker). (Pr. with Arabic Numbers identical with DW)
BgT = *Daz buoch der goetlichen troestunge*

Fischer, H. (1974). Meister Eckhart. Freiburg (Verlag Karl Alber).
Flasch, K. (2003). Meister Eckhart's "Beati pauperes spiritu"-Interpretation. In: G. Steer and L. Sturlese (Eds.). Lectura Eckhardi. Predigten Meister Eckharts von Fachgelehrten gelesen und gedeutet. Stuttgart (Kohlhammer), pp. 182–99.
Flasch, K. (2010). Meister Eckhart, Philosoph des Christentums, München (C.H. Beck).
Frederking, V. (1994). Durchbruch vom Haben zum Sein. Erich Fromm und die Mystik Meister Eckharts. Paderborn (Schöningh).
Fromm, E. (1966a): You Shall Be as Gods. A Radical Interpretation of the Old Testament and Its Tradition. New York (Holt, Rinehart and Winston).
Fromm, E. (1976a). To Have Or to Be? New York (Harper and Row).
Gewirth, A. (1996). The Community of Rights. Chicago (Chicago University Press).
Grotz, S. (2003). Zwei Sprachen und das eine Wort. Zur Identität von Meister Eckharts Werk. In: Vivarium, Leiden. 41(1), pp 47–83.

Mainberger, G.K. (1977). Mahnmal in verwüsteter Landschaft. Review E. Fromm. *To Have Or to Be?* In: Neue Zürcher Zeitung. Zürich 7(5), p. 66.

Mieth (1969). Die Einheit von vita activa und vita contemplativa in den deutschen Predigten und Traktaten Meister Eckharts und bei Johannes Tauler. Regensburg (Friedrich Pustet Verlag).

Mieth, D. (1972). Christus – das Soziale im Menschen. Texterschließungen zu Meister Eckhart. Düsseldorf (Patmos-Topos).

Mieth, D. (2001). Meister Eckhart, Karl Marx und die Gottesfrage. Aus dem Briefwechsel zwischen Dietmar Mieth und Erich Fromm. In: Fromm Forum 5, pp. 44–49.

Mieth, D. (2002). Religiöses Erleben ohne Erlebnis. Die X-Erfahrung bei Erich Fromm und die Zeichen der Gewissheit bei Meister Eckhart. In: Fromm Forum (German Edition). (Self-published) 6, pp. 24–29.

Mieth, D. (2009). Meister Eckhart. The Power of Inner Liberation. In: A.K. Giri (Ed.). The Modern Prince and the Modern Sage. Transforming Power and Freedom. New Delhi (Sage), pp. 405–428.

Mieth, D. (2012a). Meister Eckhart on Wealth. In: Medieval Mystical Theology 21 (1), pp. 233–54.

Mieth, D., Müller-Schauenburg, B. (Eds.) (2012b). Mystik, Recht und Freiheit. Religiöse Erfahrung und kirchliche Institutionen im Spätmittelalter. Stuttgart (Kohlhammer).

Mieth, D. (2013). Meister Eckhart's God. In: A. Kasher and J. Diller (Eds.). Models of God and other Ultimate Realities. New York (Springer).

Mieth, D. (2014a) Human Dignity in late medieval spiritual and political conflicts. In: M. Duewell, J. Braavig, R.Brownsword, Dietmar Mieth (Eds.) The Cambridge Handbook of Human Dignity, Interdisciplinary Perspectives. Cambridge University Press, pp. 74–84.

Mieth, D. (2014b). Meister Eckhart. Einheit mit Gott (A Selection of German and Latin Texts). Düsseldorf (Patmos). New Edition.

Quint, J. (1955). Meister Eckhart. Deutsche Predigten und Traktate. Regensburg-München (Pustet).

Springer, K.-B. (2013). Eckhart als Vikar von Thüringen und Prior von Erfurt. Zum ordenshistorischen Kontext. In: D. Gottschall (Ed.). Meister Eckharts Erfurter Reden in ihrem Kontext. Meister-Eckhart-Jahrbuch Vol. 6. Stuttgart (Kohlhammer), pp. 1–40.

Sturlese, L. (2007). Homo Divinus. Philosophische Projekte in Deutschland zwischen Meister Eckhart und Heinrich Seuse, Stuttgart (Kohlhammer).

Thomas of Erfurt (1972). Grammatica Speculativa. Edited and translated by G.I. Bursill-Hall. The Classics of Linguistics Vol. 1. London (Lonfmans).

Vinzent, M. (2012). Salus extra ecclesiam, Meister Eckhart Institutionenskepsis. In: D. Mieth and B. Mueller-Schauenburg (Eds). Mystik, Recht und Freiheit. Stuttgart (Kohlhammer), pp. 158–168.

Wackernagel, W. (Ed.) (1876). Altdeutsche Predigten und Gebete, Basel (Schweighauserische Verlagsbuchhandlung).

Walshe, M. (2008). The Complete Mystical Works of Meister Eckhart. New York (Crossroads Herder).

Erich Fromm in China – Overview of the Reception of his Thinking (1961–2014)

A Preliminary Study. Poster Presentation

Manfred Zimmer

弗洛姆 "创发性的爱" 新论

张和平

（西北师范大学 学报编辑部，甘肃 兰州 730070）

[摘 要] 弗洛姆为了解决现代西方社会人与人之间存在的严重问题，提出了他的 "创发性的爱" 的理论。这一理论后既强调爱的合理性质，又为建立人与之间和谐、友爱、完满的美景提了具有一定启发性的探索。这对于我们了解和建立人际之间的良好关系，建立和谐社会，具有重要的启发意义。但弗洛姆的这一学说也存在着马克思《关于费尔巴哈的提纲》中批判过的抽象、空洞、直观的局限，这一局限决定了弗洛姆学说的本质特征。

[关键词] 弗洛姆；"创发性的爱"；人际交往

[中图分类号] B712.5　[文献标识码] A　[文章编号] 1001-9162(2005)01-0015-06

亨里希·弗洛姆（Erich Fromm）1900 年 3 月 23 日生于德国美因河畔的法兰克福，他成长于一个正统的犹太家庭，父亲纳夫特里·弗洛姆（Napatoli Fromm）和祖先罗若都是虔诚的犹太教的拉比。1980 年 3 月 18 日，弗洛姆在距离 80 岁生日很近在瑞士的穆拉尔托逝世。

正如有的学者所言，他是一位具有艺术才能和魅力的德国人。他不虽有马尔堡的犀利激进，但不蹲弗洛伊德那样易怒激烈，但他需有为数不多的……

论，人类生存的理论为基点"。人超越自己的生命时迷惘合一，还弱与他人合源相统，是任何时代，任何文化中的人都必须解决的问题。关于这一点，不论是存在原始中的意始人，看管生羊的牧边民族、埃及的农夫，那尼基商人，罗马士兵、中古僧侣，日本武士，现代职员以及工厂中的工人，都是同样的，因为这是像力人的本性的。解决这一问题的最理想、最生效的办法 "在于人与人之间的结合，在于人同他人的融合，在于爱" 。（P22）

Revised version of the contribution to International Erich Fromm Research Conference. International Psychoanalytic University Berlin / Germany, June 26 - June 28, 2014.

Abstract

Erich Fromm is highly regarded in the Chinese academic field. This preliminary paper reports the major findings of an extensive data gathering project in China that gives us a basic outline of the trends in the reception of Fromm. We conducted several literature searches between June 2012 and May 2013 using different online databases, mostly China Knowledge Resource Integrated Database KNS (CNKI). This paper offers a categorization of the more than 800 contributions of Chinese authors, discusses the most important results, compares Fromm's very extensive reception in China to other countries and makes suggestions for future projects.

While we initially expected Fromm to be invoked for criticism of Western capitalism, his views on how to cope with "the predicaments of modern man" are mostly used to underpin critical comments on mis-management in China itself. In this way Fromm is used as a source of inspiration and creativity in theoretical matters as well as in practical questions, and also to comment on the spiritual and emotional development of the individual in modern China. There are, furthermore, extensive Chinese debates on Fromm's concepts of "social character", "the nature of man", "escape from freedom", "alienation", "Marxism as humanism" and "the art of love" and there is an interesting reception of Fromm's concepts of psychoanalysis and social psychology in literature and art studies. Fromm's humanistic and humanistic-ethical contributions are particularly appreciated with reference to their importance for theory and practice – even though there is a fair amount of criticism of Fromm in China as well.

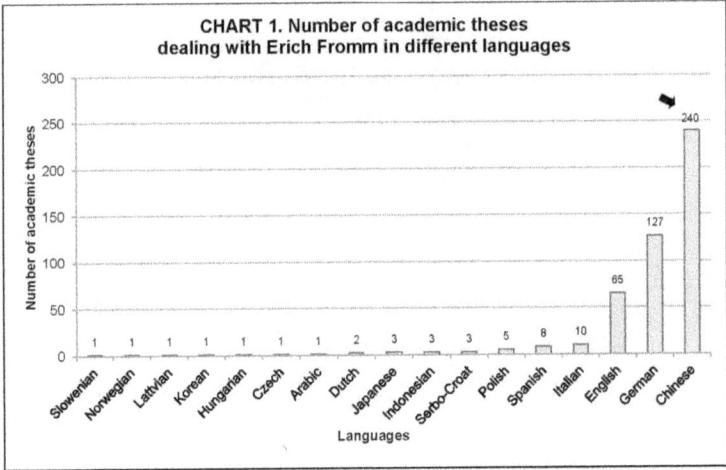

CHART 1. Number of academic theses dealing with Erich Fromm in different languages

According to data from Erich Fromm *online*, OPUS4: http://opus4.kobv.de/opus4-Fromm/home (September 17, 2014) and CNKI [China Knowledge Resource Integrated Database KNS], http://oversea.cnki.net/kns55/default.aspx (September 17, 2014).

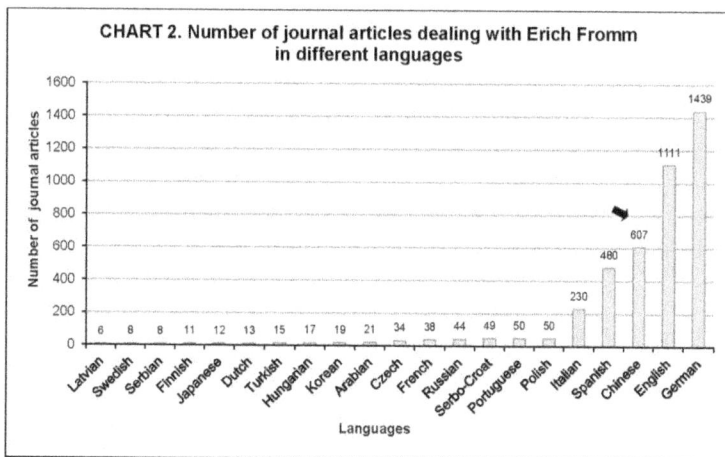

CHART 2. Number of journal articles dealing with Erich Fromm in different languages

Number of articles > 5.

According to data from Erich Fromm *online*, OPUS4: http://opus4.kobv.de/opus4-Fromm/home (September 17, 2014) and CNKI: http://oversea.cnki.net/kns55/default.aspx (September 17, 2014).

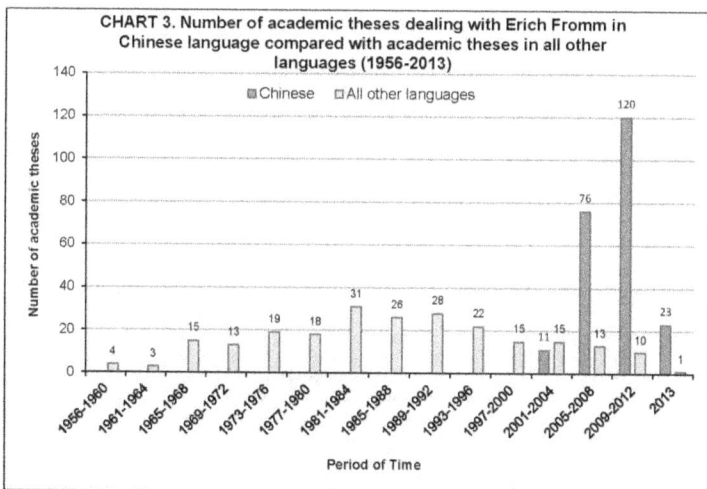

CHART 3. Number of academic theses dealing with Erich Fromm in Chinese language compared with academic theses in all other languages (1956-2013)

According to data from Erich Fromm *online*, OPUS4: http://opus4.kobv.de/opus4-Fromm/home (June 12, 2014) and CNKI: http://oversea.cnki.net/kns55/default.aspx (June 12, 2014).

CHART 4. Categorization of contributions dealing with Erich Fromm

	Journal articles	Academic theses
I. CONTRIBUTIONS ON FROMM	**520**	**154**
1 Erich Fromm and his basic theories	*125*	*23*
– Family and social background of Fromm	10	-
– Psychoanalysis and Marxism / Analytic social psychology	35	3
– Dynamic character and social character	61	2
– The nature of man	19	18
2 Man and society	*194*	*66*
– The social unconsciousness	16	3
– Escape from freedom	76	19
– Alienation / Alienation of the consumer behaviour	60	21
– Capitalism critics and "sane" society / Humanization of the technologic society	42	23
3 Theory and praxis of humanism	*170*	*37*
– Marxism as humanism	25	3
– Humanistic psychoanalysis	13	2
– Humanistic ethics	58	10
– Religion	7	1
– Education	15	6
– The art of loving	52	15
4 Other subjects, not categorized contributions	*31*	*28*
II. APPLICATION OF FROMM'S THEORIES TO LITERATURE AND ART STUDIES	87	86
III. CONTRIBUTIONS MENTIONING ERICH FROMM	ca. 19.000	

Zimmer (2014b), page 3 (PDF version), supplemented by more recent data.

CHART 5. Contributions on Fromm: Ranking of thematic groups according to the number of contributions

Escape from freedom (95)

Alienation / Alienation of consumer behaviour (81)

Humanistic ethics (68)

The art of loving (67)

Dynamic character and social character (63)

Capitalism critics and "sane" society / Humanization of the technologic society (65)

Psychoanalysis and Marxism / Analytic social psychology (38)

The nature of man (37)

Marxism as humanism (28)

Education (21)

The social unconsciousness (19)

Humanistic psychoanalysis (15)

Fromm's family and social background (10)

Religion (8)

Zimmer (2014a), page 4 (PDF version), supplemented by more recent data.

CHART 6. Authors and number of publications dealing with Fromm (selection)

Name (Period of time, Number)	Department, University	Academic thesis on Fromm (Year)	Theme on Fromm
KONG Wenqing (2008-2000, 10)	Department of Philosophy, East China Normal University, Shanghai, 200062	Frommian Autonomic Morality and Its Revelation on Moral Construction in the Chinese Social Transformation (2007)	Humanistic ethics, religion, freedom, nature of man, Fromm's Jewish roots
DENG Zhiwei (2011-2005, 9)	The Center for Studies in Moral Culture, Hunan Normal University, Changsha, Hunan 410081	E. Fromm's Neo-humanistic Ethics (2008)	Consumption ethics, peace ethics, religious ethics, Frankfurt School
ZHANG Heping (2006-2001, 8)	Editorial Department of Northwest Normal University, Lanzhou, Gansu 730070	[Not on Fromm]	Historical Materialism, alienation, nature of man, peace, ethics
FANG Xingfu (2012-2007, 7)	College of Foreign Languages, Central China Normal University, Wuhan, Hubei 430079	On Erich Fromm's Theory of Hominology (2008)	Human existence, modern relationships, production and consumption, Marx / Freud, character, alienation
YAN Yurong (2010-2008, 5)	Department of Social Sciences Teaching, Shandong Institute of Business and Technology, Yantai, Shandong 264005	[Not on Fromm]	Humanistic ethics, moral, humanistic religion, education

Zimmer (2014b), page 8 (PDF version), supplemented by more recent data of CNKI (June 12, 2014).

CHART 7. Universities and number of academic theses dealing with Fromm and the application of Fromm's theories to literature and art (selection)

University	Number of theses (period of time)	Number of theses about the application of Fromm's theories to literature and art studies (Period of time)
Jilin University, Changchun, Jilin	**15** (2013 [2], 2012 [4], 2011, 2009, 2008 [3], 2007 [3], 2006)	3 (2012, 2009, 2007)
Heilongjiang University, Harbin, Heilongjiang	**10** (2011 [5], 2010, 2009, 2008 [2], 2007)	1 (2007)
Hunan Normal University, Changsha, Hunan	**7** (2011, 2008 [3], 2006, 2005, 2004)	3 (2012, 2010, 2007)
Huazhong University of Science and Technology, Wuhan, Hubei	**6** (2011 [2], 2009 [2], 2008, 2004)	-
Central China Normal University, Wuhan, Hubei	**4** (2012 [2], 2008, 2006)	3 (2012, 2011[2])
Shandong Normal University, Jinan, Shandong	**4** (2007 [2], 2004, 2001)	3 (2011, 2009, 2008)
Henan University, Kaifeng, Henan	**4** (2012 [2], 2011, 2010)	3 (2012, 2011, 2006)
Central South University, Changsha	**2** (2010, 2000)	1 (2012)

Zimmer (2014b), page 9 (PDF version), supplemented by more recent data of CNKI (June 12, 2014).

**CHART 8. An example for the structure of a doctoral dissertation
on Erich Fromm (2008)***

**Title: Another Marx: One Humanism Annotation. On Fromm's Humanistic Interpretation
of Marxist Philosophy**

Author: CHAI Tingting
Supervisor: LIU Fusen
Discipline: Marxist Philosophy
University: Jilin University, Changshun
Year, Degree: 2008, Doctoral thesis

Executive summary (4-9)

Introduction (9-15)

1. The paper's origin (9-10)
2. The main idea of the paper and the attempt to solve the problem (10-12)
3. The study's perspective (12-15)

CHAPTER 1: MARXISM: FROMM'S IDEOLOGICAL PREMISE (15-38)

I.   The Frommian revival (15-20)
     (A) Marx: Marxism and vulgar materialism (15-18)
     (B) The "Manuscripts": basis for Fromm 's humanistic theory (18-20)

II. The Marxist Historical Materialism, humanistic modification (20-30)
     (A) Critique of vulgar materialism (20-25)
     (B) Only a humanism of Marx (25-30)

III. Humanism is not Marxist (30-38)
     (A) Idealism: the inevitable end of the humanism (30-32)
     (B) "New" materialism: Marx's idealistic philosophy liquidation (32-38)

CHAPTER 2: IDEOLOGIC BEGINNING OF HUMAN NATURE: FROMM (38-65)

I.   A socio-biological theory of human nature (38-50)
     (A) The logical starting point: people's existence-antinomies (38-42)
     (B) Potential: human nature of self-initiative (42-46)
     (C) Human nature: the production of non-alienated man (46-50)

II. Fromm's humanistic view of human nature fate (50-65)
     (A) Dynamic of human nature and the ideal of human nature (50-54)
     (B) Not able to unlock the mystery of the "history" (54-65)

CHAPTER 3: ALIENATION: FROMM 'S HUMANISTIC THEORY CORE (65-105)

I.   Fromm's theory of alienation (65-81)
     (A) The development context of alienation (65-71)
     (B) Fromm's interpretation of Marx's early theory of alienation (71-74)
     (C) Alienation: a subjective experience (74-78)
     (D) 'Not look like he should be'' (78-81)

II. Fromm's theory of alienation inherent reflection (81-85)
     (A) Fromm's theory compared with Marx's theory of alienation (81-83)
     (B) Fromm's theory of alienation inherent contradictions (83-85)

CHART 8. An example for the structure of a doctoral dissertation
on Erich Fromm (*continued*).

III. Fromm's theory of alienation predicament (85-95)
    (A) Marxist ideological transformation: Fromm's theory of alienation empty field (85-90)
    (B) The central concept of the "Manuscripts" is not equal to the central concept of the Marxist
    philosophy (90-95)

IV. The historical existence: the core of the theory and principles of interpretation
    of Marxist philosophy (95-105)
    (A) Survival: the core concepts of the Marxist philosophy (95-98)
    (B) Historical Materialism historical (98-105)

CHAPTER 4: HUMANISM: FROMM'S HUMANISTIC THEORY (105-146)

I. The traditional humanism (105-114)
    (A) Humanism and its historical evolution (105-109)
    (B) A mindset: Marxism is humanism (109-114)

II. Marxism: thorough humanism (114-124)
    (A) Humane socialism (114-120)
    (B) Natural: people's practice activities derived (120-124)

III. The Frommian humanism theory of regret (124-133)
    (A) The body of the abstract thinking and people's existence (124-129)
    (B) The pursuit of "the other side of the world", "idealistic" (129-133)

IV. Marx's critique of traditional humanism and beyond (133-146)
    (A) Survival: a new evaluation scale of the humanitarian (133-136)
    (B) The history of humanism (136-139)
    (C) A new humanistic ethics: institutional ethics (139-146)

Summary (146-151)
References(151-163)
Doctoral studies during the academic (163-164)

Abstract (Chinese) (164-168)
Abstract (English) (168-172)

Cited English language literature

Buber, Martin (1966).The Origin and Meaning of Hasidism, translated by Maurice Friedman.
Evans, Richard I. (1963) Dialogue with Erich Fromm.
Fromm, Erich (1950) Psychoanalysis and Religion.
Fromm, Erich (1965) Socialist Humanism: An International Symposium.
Fromm, Erich (1960) Let Man Prevail - A Socialist Manifesto and Program.
Fromm, Erich (1963) The Dogma of Christ and Other Essays on Religion, Psychology and Culture.
Fromm, Erich (1963) The Heart of Man: Its Genius for Good and Evil. Religious Perspectives.
Fromm, Erich (1966) You Shall Be as Gods: A Radical Interpret. of the Old Testaments and Its Tradition.
Funk, Rainer (1996): Erich Fromm's Approach to Psychoanalysis. A Seminar on "Social Character".

*Automatic translation from Chinese to English, slightly corrected by M. Z.

According to data from Dissertation topic (*structure*): http://www.dissertationtopic.net/doc/1652769 and CNKI (*bibli-ography*): http://www.cnki.net/KCMS/detail/detail.aspx?QueryID=0&CurRec=3&recid=&filename=
2008128962.nh&dbname=CDFD2008&dbcode=CDFD&pr=&urlid=&yx= [shortened: http://tinyurl.com/cjzntfb] (both
April 13, 2013), in: Zimmer (2014b), page 10-11.

CHART 9. Master theses to the thematic group "Escape from freedom" (selection, 2008-2013)

Title	Discipline	University	Author	Year
The Criticism of Escaping from Freedom to the Sane Society [从逃避自由到健全的社会]	Marxist philosophy	Shandong University, Jinan	Du Pei	2013
The Theory of Psychic Mechanism - Critique on Fromm's "Escape from Freedom" and Contemporary Enlightenment [弗洛姆逃避自由的心理机制批判理论及当代启示]	Foreign philosophy	Southwest University, Chongqing	Tao Xiangfeng	2013
An analysis of the Psychological Mechanism of Fromm's Escape from Freedom and Its Contemporary Value [弗洛姆"逃避自由"心理机制的解析及当代价值]	Foreign Marxism	Harbin Poly-technic Uni. Harbin	Liu Yanan	2012
Research on Fromm's Freedom Thoughts [弗洛姆自由思想研究]	Basic principles of Marxism	Heilongjiang Academy of Social Sci., Harbin	Ning Xin	2012
An Analysis of the Thought of Fromm's "Escape from Freedom" [解析弗洛姆的>逃避自由<思想]	Foreign philosophy	Jilin University, Chang-chun	Dun Haiwei	2012
Fromm's Theory of "Escape from Freedom" [弗洛姆"逃避自由"理论述评]	Foreign Marxism research	Heilongjiang University, Harbin	Cai Lingling	2011
An Inquiry into Fromm's Ethical Thought of "Escape-from-Freedom" [弗洛姆的>逃避自由<伦理思想研究]	Ethics	Hunan Normal University, Chang-sha	Tan Zhaojun	2011
An Analysis of Fromm's Freedom Plight Theory [对弗洛姆的自由困境理论探析]	Foreign Marxism	Harbin Normal University, Harbin	Zhang Jun	2011
A Comparative Study of Fromm and Marx's Theory on Human Liberation [弗洛姆与马克思关于人的解放学说比较研究]	Marxist philosophy	Huazhong University of Science & Technology, Wuhan	Jiang Ziyu	2009
Escape from Freedom to Pursue Freedom [从逃避自由到追寻自由]	Marxist philosophy	Ideological and Political College, Chengdu	Qiao Yajun	2009
A Research on Fromm's Freedom [埃利希弗洛姆的自由思想研究]	Marxist philosophy	East China Normal University, Shanghai	Ding Nais-hun	2009
Fromm's "Escape from Freedom" Theory and Its Impli-cations [弗洛姆的逃避自由理论及其启示]	Marxist philosophy	Heilongjiang University, Harbin	Zhang Yingli	2008
Investigation into Fromm's "Escape from Freedom" Thought and Its Meaning for the Present [弗罗姆"逃避自由"思想及其当代意义]	Marxist theory and ideological and political education	Xiamen University, Xiamen	Ceng Cairu	2008

New compilation according to data from CNKI: http://oversea.cnki.net/kns55/default.aspx (June 12, 2014).

CHART 10. Master theses with the application of Fromm's theories to literature and art sciences studies (selection, 2011-2014)

Author	Writer's work; other subject of evaluation	Fromm's theories (from point of view of the authors)	Student	Year
Carver, Raymond Clevie (1938-1988)	Short fictions (1983-1988)	Alienation (also the alienation theory of Marx)	ZHOU Yingqi	2014
Amis, Martin (born 1949)	Novel London Fields (1989)	Different types of alienation	KONG Fang	2013
Fitzgerald, Francis, F. Scott (1896-1940)	Novel Tender is the Night (1934)	Alienation	XIONG Houmei	2013
Garcia Márquez, Gabriel (1927-2014)	Novel Hundred Years of Solitude (1967)	Loneliness	LAI Chen	2013
McCullers, Carson (1917-1967)	Novel The Heart is a Lonely Hunter (1940)	Loneliness	LI Min	2013
Müller, Herta (born 1953)	Novel Reisende auf einem Bein (1989), Engl.: Traveling on One Leg	"Negative"-, and "positive" freedom theory	ZHANG Ji	2013
Auster, Paul (born 1947)	Novels The New York Trilogy (1987)	Alienation between man and society, consumer alienation	REN Huan	2012
Banks, Tyra & US-Television Station	Television "Reality" Show: America's Next Top Model (since 2003)	Consumer alienation (also: concepts of H. Marcuse, Ben Agger)	MA LIHUI	2012
Didion, Joan (born 1934)	Novel Play It As It Lays (1970)	Escape mechanisms, negative and positive freedom, spontaneous activity	CHEN CHAOYAN	2012
Morrison, Toni (born 1931)	Novel The Bluest Eye (1970)	Alienation (also the theories of Marx, Freud)	JIANG QIAN	2012
Murdoch, Iris (1919-1999)	Novel The Sea, the Sea (1978)	Escape from freedom	WANG HUANA	2012
Steinbeck, John (1902-1968)	Novel The Winter of Our Discontent (1961)	Alienation	LIU Xiaofeng	2012
-	"Abuse" in psychological aesthetics	Escape from freedom, theory of love	Hu Yingjing	2012
Bellow, Saul (1915-2005)	Novel Mr. Sammler's Planet (1970)	Alienation (also: Marx)	Yu Xianghong	2011
Bulgakov, Mikhail (1891-1940)	The White Guard (1926); The Master and Margarita (1966)	The interpretation of dreams (also Freud, Jung)	Lu Ye	2011
DeLillo, Don (born 1936)	Novel White Noise (1985)	Alienation of consumer behavior and by technology (also: Marx, Lukács, H. Marcuse)	Liu Pengfei	2011
Drabble, Margaret (born 1939)	Novel The Millstone (1965)	Humanistic psychoanalysis, nature of man	ZHU YANYAN	2011
Poe, Edgar Allan (1809-1848)	Author's Life and Work, psychological origins of his horror tales	Psychoanalysis (also Karen Horney: neurotic fear)	MA DI	2011

Zimmer (2014b), pages 28-31, new compilation, supplemented by newer data (2013 and 2014) from CNKI: http://oversea.cnki.net/kns55/default.aspx.

Chart 11. Chinese research fund for Fromm's psychology and philosophy (selection)

Name and description of the fund	Publications supported by the fund: Title, author, year of publication, author's institution
Jiangxi Province, College of Humanities and Social Sciences Research Project "Humanitarian Protest against Anonymous Authority - Interpretation of Erich Fromm's Philosophy" (ID: XYSK10YB11) [江西省高校人文社科研究项目"对匿名权威的人道主义抗议——弗洛姆'不从'理念之解读"(编号:XYSK10YB11)]	Humanitarian Protest against Anonymous Authority - An Interpretation on Fromm's Disobedience Ideology [弗洛姆的"不从"理念对匿名权威的抗议] YUAN Luoya (2012) Ideological and Political Teaching Department, Jiangxi University of Technology, Nanchang 330098
Jiangxi Province, College of Humanities and Social Science Research Project (MKS1236) [江西省高校人文社会科学研究项目"对匿名权威的人道主义抗议——弗洛姆'不从'理念之解读"(MKS1236)]	An Interpretation on Fromm's Social-Psychoanalysis Thought [弗洛姆"社会心理分析"思想的理论来源述评] YUAN Luoya (2013) Ideological and Political Teaching Department, Jiangxi University of Technology, Nanchang 330098
Psychological Science Planning Project in Heilongjiang Province, "Fromm's Social Psychology and Its Contemporary Value" (item number: 20110003) Initial Results [黑龙江省心理科学规划项目"弗洛姆社会心理学思想及其当代价值研究"(项目编号:20110003)的阶段性成果]	Review on Fromm's Thoughts of Social Psychology in Recent Years [近几年弗洛姆社会心理学思想研究述评] WANG Heyan, ZHANG Zhishun & SUN Chenguang (2012) School of Marxism Studies, Northeast Petroleum University, Daqing 163318
Psychological Science Planning Project in Heilongjiang Province, "Fromm's Social Psychology and Its Contemporary Value" (item number: 20110003) Initial Results [黑龙江省心理科学规划项目"弗洛姆社会心理学思想及其当代价值研究"(20110003)阶段性成果]	Logical Progress of Freedom in the Development of Western Traditional Philosophy [自由在西方传统哲学发展中的逻辑进程] Xu Xiaoyu (2012) School of Philosophy and Society, Jilin University, Changchun 130012; School of Marxism Studies, Northeast Petroleum University, Daqing 163318
Zhejiang Provincial Education Department Issues "Modern Research on Fromm's Consumer Alienation Critique" (item number: 20070611) [浙江省教育厅课题"弗洛姆对消费异化的后现代性批判之研究"(20070611)]	Fromm's Criticism and Reconstruction of Consumption Alienation [弗洛姆对消费异化的批判与重建] Xu Huifen (2012) Department of Ideological & Political Studies, Jiaxing University, Jiaxing, Zhejiang 314001
Social Fund Project in Hunan, "Fromm's Humanitarian Ethics" Research (item number: 04YB019) [湖南省社科基金课题"弗洛姆人道主义伦理学研究"(项目号04YB019)]	Erich Fromm's Ethical Thoughts of Peace [弗洛姆人道主义和平伦理思想] DENG Zhiwei (2007) College of Public Management, Hunan Normal University, Changsha, Hunan 410081
Social Fund Project in Hunan, "Fromm's Humanitarian Ethics" (item number: 04YB019) Initial Results [湖南省社科基金课题"弗洛姆人道主义伦理学研究"(04YB019)阶段性成果]	Analysis on Erich Fromm's Three Ethic Propositions [浅析弗洛姆的三个伦理命题] DENG Zhiwei (2007) College of Public Management, Hunan Normal University, Changsha, Hunan 410081

New compilation according to data from CNKI: http://oversea.cnki.net/kns55/default.aspx (September 26, 2014).

CHART 12. Discussion - Theses

Contributions on Fromm

(1) Social and cultural changes taking place in China are critically and carefully monitored and evaluated by Chinese scholars. Fromm's social psychological theories that inspire critical thinking are highly valued in here.

(2) The reception of Fromm focuses on the controversies about his theories as a representative of "Western Marxism" and as a humanist thinker.

(3) Authors primarily come from the following academic fields: "Marxist Philosophy", followed by "Ethics" and a large number of different mostly socio-scientific subject areas. "Psychology" is found only rarely among the disciplines, and "Psychoanalysis" not at all.

(4) The authors discuss certain "classic" theories of Fromm in terms of their significance to theory and practice. The framework for the theory is mainly determined by different varieties of Marxism, but also by ethics as a philosophical discipline. As far as practice is concerned, usually aspects of current social relations are discussed. The focus is on the question of the possible implementations of Frommian theories.

(5) The authors handle Fromm's theories in quite pragmatic ways: they select the pieces which fit into the framework of their theory or their practice ideas and leave the other theoretical aspects aside.

*Contributions with the application of Fromm's theories
to literature and art studies*

(1) The background of the authors is predominantly "English Language and Literature". Central figures in the literary interpretation are Fromm's theories of alienation, of love and his concept of "escape from freedom".

(2) Fromm's social psychological concepts occupy a certain place in literature and art sciences of China. The use of Frommian theories is justified by the fact that they are more up to date and useful than previous patterns of interpretation, for example, following Freud.

According to Zimmer (2014a), page 14f. (PDF version).

CHART 13. Suggestions for future projects

(1) Translation of the websites *Erich Fromm online* [http://www.erich-fromm.de] and *International Erich Fromm Society* [http://www.fromm-gesellschaft.eu] into Chinese.

(2) Publication of the journal of the International Erich Fromm Society *Fromm Forum* in Chinese language.

(3) Translation of the *Erich Fromm Complete Edition* into Chinese (including the subject and name index and the editor's notes).

(4) Translation of exemplary contributions (theses, journal articles)* from Chinese into English.

(5) Initiation and support of doctoral- or master theses on the reception of Fromm in China by German speaking Chinese authors or by Chinese speaking German authors.

(6) Conference at a university in China about the Fromm reception in China.

(7) Conference at a university in Germany about the possibilities of Fromm's humanistic thinking concepts in China.

* See examples in Zimmer (2014b), pages 34-39 (PDF version). – According to Zimmer (2014a), page 15f. (PDF version).

Cited Literature

The page references in the text above refer to the English language PDF versions on the Website "Erich Fromm online" http://www.erich-fromm.de.

Zimmer, Manfred (2014a) Erich Fromm in China. Überblick über die Rezeption seines Denkens (1961-2013), *Fromm Forum*, No. 18/2014, pages 159-169; Internet: Erich Fromm *online*: http://www.erich-fromm.de/ [Reception of Erich Fromm, A Survey Paper on Erich Fromm in China], PDF version, 16 pages [in German].

Zimmer, Manfred (2014b) Erich Fromm in China. Überblick über die Rezeption seines Denkens (1961-2013), Anlage zum Artikel im *Fromm-Forum*, No. 18/2014, pages 159-169; Internet: Erich Fromm *online*: http://www.Erich -fromm.de/ [Reception of Erich Fromm, A Survey Paper on Erich Fromm in China], Appendix to the Article in *Fromm-Forum*, No. 18/2014, PDF version, 48 pages [in German].

Acknowledgements

I thank *Rainer Funk* for the encouraging support of the "Erich Fromm in China" project, *Alexei Sesterheim* and *Herman Adèr* for critical review and help with the translation of this article. Many thanks to Mrs. *Yap Teng-Teng* for careful examination of the bibliography and for her help in all questions regarding Chinese writing and language.

Reflections on the Conference

Anna Müller-Hermann and Adrian Kind

Report of the observer Anna Müller-Hermann

First of all, I would like to thank the International Psychoanalytic University of Berlin and the Erich Fromm Foundation for organizing this conference and to express my gratitude to Dr. Rainer Funk for inviting me as student observer and to all the speakers and participants, who made this a truly remarkable event.

The lectures, which covered a variety of topics, were very interesting and inspired me for conducting further research on Erich Fromm's work. I was particularly interested in the social appliance of his theory in the work of Michael Maccoby "Los pequeños hermanos" and Sonia Gojman de Millán's projects in Mexico, which show what a tremendous impact a loving and supporting environment can have on the life of human beings and indicate the value of Fromm's concept of the social character and how it can be used fruitfully today.

Another positive outcome of this conference was that I learned more about Erich Fromm as a person. This helped me understand the interconnectedness between his life and his work. He was a social thinker and an activist with humanistic ideals, a man who lived his life according to his beliefs and who had the courage to speak about them. In times of growing indifference and passivity, Fromm can be recognized as a role model for the productive human being. The integrity of his life and work, his authenticity, directedness, his productive art of being and loving, his need for constant self-improvement, his courage and love of life, are all necessary characteristics for the development of the human being.

Moreover, Fromm believed that opinions, science, society etc. have their foundations in values and that the relevant question to consider is whether they are conscious or not, and whether they are life enhancing (good) or life denying (bad). So two questions I take with me from this conference are: What are my values? What is my purpose in this life and do I live according to that?

But of course, Erich Fromm did not only apply these things to his personal life. He was concerned with the future of this world. He was a political man with a vision of hope for humanity. Despite the terror of WWII, the Cold War, and the threat posed by the development of nuclear weapons, he did not lose his faith in the immense potential of humankind.

His books, although written some fifty years ago, are today more accurate than ever.

I believe this is due to a universal truth he speaks, which resonates strongly with his readers. We cannot continue to be on the path we are today. We need a new humanistic paradigm, based on love and reason, realizing our interconnectedness and our responsibilities towards this planet earth and the future generations.

Lastly, I would like to congratulate my university for enabling us to have a seminar on Erich Fromm taught by his closest assistant Dr. Rainer Funk. It is a great honor for us to be able to learn from such a connoisseur of Fromm and classes taught by Dr. Funk have been inspiring and thought provoking. It surely is time for a rediscovery of Fromm.

Thank you for listening.

Report of the observer Adrian Kind

First of all I want to thank you for the opportunity to contribute this conference and reflect on what we have heard.

I, as a person who is personally invested in Freudian psychoanalysis and Critical Theory, had a special interest in this congress. As someone, who is mainly familiar with the works of Fromm before his separation from the Institute of Social Research, I am happy to hear about his later work and, what Frommian analysis means today, but also to have a look at a different line of theory that once arisen from the same lap, the ideas of Freud and Marx.

Among the plenty of interesting and important lectures, I can just pick up a few topics that seem important, at least to me and my work.

The first important discussion I would like to point out, was on the topic of the problematization of the growing importance of neo-positive thinking on the one hand and post-structural thinking on the other hand in social science. This matter is interesting for those of us who want psychoanalysis to be considered a science. A science that can, in its Freudian or Frommian way, explain the suffering of individuals *in* society, based on a theory of subject, group, and society. We do not need more psychology of numbers, statistics and experiments, or postmodern speculation as an alternative and I hope that the meaning of the question "What can I know?", as one of Kant's fundamental questions of philosophy, will be recognized as deserving more of our attention, in our reflection on psychoanalysis as science. I do not mean the discussion about qualitative and quantitative methods which is prevalent in today's scientific discourse, but I mean, expanding the discussion to talk about the premises of *any* method and epistemology. This could show us that the understanding of what a scientific finding is, in its state of the art in social science, is partially wrong. This is a problem that becomes more and more evident in the philosophy of the last decades, for example in the works of authors associated with Critical Realism or Materialistic-Dialectical philosophy.

Another topic that I was very interested in was covered in the lectures on the social character and the theoretical or practical work done in relation to it. For me the idea of social character, proposed by Erich Fromm and by critical theory, is one of the most important concepts in psychoanalytic social psychology, with the theoretical potential to provide a strong counter balance to situationism theory in academic personality psychology, which is not able to tell us anything about the inner structures of an individual and the reasons they have to resist or adapt to changing social circumstances. For me, as one of two tutors of a Student Seminar for psychoanalytic authoritarianism research, here at the International Psychoanalytic University in Berlin, it is an exciting idea to link the works of Fromm and the works of Critical Theory in order to see the connections and differences. I would be very much interested in expanding this dialogue further, here at the IPU.

It was also interesting for me to see that the reading of Freud's drive concept, his concept of narcissism and his idea of abstinence, here was quite different from other readings in contemporary Freudian psychoanalyst that I am familiar with. For many psychoanalytic theorists Freud's was understood right from the beginning as an inter-subjective theory. As I feel invited to re-read Fromm, I would like to invite you to a second reading of Freud, or if you like, of the works of Freudian authors like Alfred Lorenzer, André Green, Heinz Müller-Pozzi and our dear Professors Lilli Gast and Christiane Kirchhoff, all covering discussed topics. It would be interesting to see what the discussion would look like, after such re-reading on both sides.

Last but not least I will mention Marxism. I do not know how relevant the reading of Marx is for many of you. I heard his name during the conference in a few contexts, and, of course, in the impressive lecture of Prof. Anderson and the audience discussion. If we want to do justice to Fromm and the other Freudo-Marxists, we have to take seriously the Marxist element in their theories. Also we must not forget about the importance of a fundamental critique of power relations and its connections to political economy. This critique leads to the need to overcome capitalism, and introduce an alternative organization of society that allows humans to avoid all unnecessary suffering. To work towards this project Freudo-Marxists should develop their theoretical psychoanalysis and integrate the advanced Marxian theories that developed in the years after the collapse of the Soviet Union. The value of a critical engagement with Marx, promoted by Moishe Postone and Ingo Elbe just to name two outstanding authors, could be very productive in the future work. In the end, the only political and social goal of theory and practice of psychoanalysis can be, to follow all three categorical imperatives of Kant, Marx and Adorno, in use of their knowledge about the unconscious mind.

Thank you very much for your visit at the International Psychoanalytic University and your attention to my remarks.

About the Authors

Anderson, Kevin B., PhD, is a Professor of Sociology, Political Science, and Feminist Studies at University of California, Santa Barbara. He has worked in social and political theory, focusing on Marx, Hegel, Marxist humanism, the Frankfurt School, Foucault, and the Orientalism debate. Among his recent books are the *Rosa Luxemburg Reader* (2004, coedited with Peter Hudis) *Foucault and the Iranian Revolution* (with Janet Afary, 2005), *Marx at the Margins* (2010), and *The Dunayevskaya-Marcuse-Fromm Correspondence, 1954–78* (2012, coedited with Russell Rockwell). In 2000, he and Richard Quinney received the International Erich Fromm Prize for their edited volume, *Erich Fromm and Critical Criminology: Beyond the Punitive Society.* He has also published several articles on Fromm and Marxism.

Bierhoff, Prof. Dr. Burkhard, is a sociologist of education teaching at Brandenburg University Cottbus–Senftenberg, Department of Social Work. He is a founding member of the International Erich Fromm Society. Habilitation thesis (in German): *Erich Fromm. Analytische Sozialpsychologie und visionäre Gesellschaftskritik* (Opladen 1993). He published extensively on social psychology and social theory. Research areas of interest include: educational theory, theory of the subject, lifestyles, consumption and sustainability.

Braune, Joan, PhD, is an Assistant Professor of Philosophy at Mount Mary University in Milwaukee, Wisconsin, USA. Her book *Erich Fromm's Revolutionary Hope: Prophetic Messianism as a Critical Theory of the Future* was published in Fall 2014 through Sense Publishers's Series "Imagination and Praxis: Creativity and Criticality in Educational Research." Braune has published contributions on Erich Fromm in two other edited volumes through the same Imagination and Praxis series (*Reclaiming the Sane Society: Essays on Erich Fromm's Thought* and *We Saved the Best for You*), and she has been published in *Radical Philosophy Review*, *Fromm Forum*, *Marx & Philosophy Review of Books*, and the *American Catholic Philosophical Quarterly*. She has presented on Fromm or Critical Theory at close to twenty academic conferences.

Buechler, Sandra, PhD, is a Training and Supervising Analyst and graduate of the William Alanson White Institute. Her Training Analyst and most of her supervisors worked with Fromm, and were clearly inspired by him. Her first book *Clinical Values. Emotions that Guide Psychoanalytic Treatment* (Analytic Press, 2004) pays tribute to the work of Sullivan and Fromm. Her other books: *Making a Difference in Patients' Lives. Emotional Experience in the Therapeutic Setting* (Routledge, 2008), *Still Practicing. The Heartaches and Joys of a Clinical Career* (Routledge, 2012), and *Understanding and Treating Patients in Clinical Psychoanalysis: Lessons from Literature* (Routledge, 2015) clearly owe a tremendous debt to Fromm's influence.

Cortina, Mauricio MD, living in Silver Spring MD, is a psychoanalyst and Director of the Attachment and Human Development Center at Washington School of Psychiatry, Washington D.C., belongs to the Faculty of the Institute of Contemporary Psychotherapy and Psychoanalysis, Washington D.C. He is a Member of Sociedad Méxicana de Sociopsicoanálisis, A.C. (SEMSOAC), Mexico D.F., and a Fellow of the American Academy of Dynamic Psychotherapy and Psychoanalysis.

Deguchi, Takeshi, PhD, is an Associate Professor, Department of Sociology, Graduate School of Humanities and Sociology, The University of Tokyo. From 2005 to 2006, he worked as a visiting scholar at the Institute for Social Research at the University of Frankfurt (IfS). His recent work in English is *Critical Theory and its development in post-war Japanese sociology: Pursuing true democracy in rapid capitalist modernization* (2013) in A. Elliott, M. Katagiri, and A. Sawai (Eds.), *Contemporary Japanese Social Theory* (Routledge).

Dietrich, Dr. Jan, is an Associate Professor for Old Testament at Aarhus University, Denmark, and currently Director of PhD-studies for Theology, Philosophy, and History of Ideas at Aarhus University's Graduate School, Arts. His research interests include: the History of Law and Ritual as well as the Anthropologies, Mentalities, and Modes of Thinking in ancient Israel and its surrounding ancient Near Eastern cultures. Since 1998, he is one of the editors of *Fromm Forum*, the International Erich Fromm Society's journal.

Funk, Dr. Rainer, psychoanalyst and Erich Fromm's Literary Executor, lives in Tübingen (Germany). He belongs to the Board of the International Erich Fromm Society and the Erich Fromm Foundation. Along with organizing the Erich Fromm Institute at Tübingen and editing Fromm's writings, his own publications generelly address social psychological topics. In the last years he analyzed a new social character, an orientation that is enthusiastic about constructing reality anew while suffering from an unconscious unbounded self.

Gojman de Millán, Sonia, PhD, Psychologist and Psychoanalyst UNAM; Secretary General of the International Federation of Psychoanalytic Societies (IFPS) from 2000 to 2008. She is training and a supervising analyst at the Seminario de Sociopsicoanálisis A.C. (SEMSOAC) and a certified Trainer from the University of California, Berkeley, on the Adult Attachment Interview AAI, in English and Spanish.

Hardeck, Prof. Dr. Jürgen, studied Science of Religion, Philosophie and Sinologie. He wrote a dissertation on *Religion in the Works of Erich Fromm*. He works in the Ministry of Culture of Rhineland-Palatinate (Germany) and is one of the advisory directors to the executive board of the International Erich-Fromm-Society. 2005 he published *Erich Fromm. Leben und Werk*.

Jimenez, Luis MD, MA., Dip. Psy, PhD, is a psychoanalyst, medical doctor and sociologist, graduated from IMPAC. Clinical and Research Director (School of Psychology – Counselling and Psychotherapy, University of East London). He has contributed to Fromm's related events and conferences over the years including the IFPS 50th anniversary conference. Has also published on various aspects of gendered identities, neoliberal subjectivities and work change as well as intergenerational transmission of trauma within a psychosocial and Frommian perspective in *Fromm Forum* and *International Forum of Psychoanalysis.*

Johach, Dr. Helmut, born in 1941, studied philosophy, sociology and pedagogy and was trained in methods of Humanistic Psychology. Until 2006, he worked in the areas of: adult education, teacher's training and therapy of young alcoholics and drug addicts. He is a member of the Extended Board of the *International Erich Fromm Society* and one of the editors of *Fromm Forum.* Publication: *Von Freud zur Humanistischen Psychologie.* Bielefeld (Transript) 2009.

Kind, Adrian, student at the International Psychoanalytic University in Berlin.

Maccoby, Michael, PhD, is a psychoanalyst and anthropologist who is a globally recognized expert on leadership. After receiving a doctorate from Harvard in 1960, he and his wife travelled to Mexico where he worked with Erich Fromm for eight years. With Fromm, he co-authored *Social Character in a Mexican Village* (1970). Graduated from the Mexican Institute of Psychoanalysis, he became a training analyst. Back in the United States, he began a series of studies of leadership and projects to improve the quality of working life in the US, UK and Sweden. For his work in Sweden, he was made Commander of the Royal Order of the Polar Star. Dr. Maccoby has taught at Harvard, the University of Chicago, the University of California at Santa Cruz, the Washington School of Psychiatry, Sciences Po, and the Saïd Business School, Oxford. He is the author or co-author of fourteen books. The most recent one is titled *Transforming Health Care Leadership* and *Strategic Intelligence.*

McLaughlin, Neil, teaches sociological theory at McMaster University in Canada. He has written extensively on the reception and reputation of Erich Fromm in North American academic and intellectual life. He also writes about the sociology of the public intellectual more broadly, with case studies on David Riesman, George Orwell, Noam Chomsky, George Soros and woman public intellectuals in Canada. His most writing on Fromm is an extended book review essay called "Erich Fromm's Critical Theory: Prophetic, Scholarly or Revolutionary?" in the *Canadian Journal of Sociology* 40(2), 2015 (https://ejournals.library.ualberta.ca/index.php/CJS/).

Mieth, Prof. Dr. Dietmar, hold the Chair of Theological Ethics/Social Ethics at the Universities in Fribourg, Switzerland (1974–1981) and in Tübingen,Germany (1981–2008). Studies in Theology, Philosophy and Literature. He was Editing Director at the International Theological Journal CONCILIUM (1978–2001); Founder and Chairman of the Center for Ethics in the Sciences at the University of Tübingen (1985–2001), Founder of the European Society of Catholic Theology (1989), Counsellor in the Group on Ethics in the Sciences and New Technologies at the EU-Commission in Brussels (1994–2001) also at the European Council and the German Parliament. He was awarded a Federal Cross of Merit of Germany 2007. President of the "Meister Eckhart Gesellschaft" (since 2008). He is a Fellow of the Max Weber Center for Advanced Studies at the University of Erfurt, Germany (2009 until present). He published thirty books as author (and other thirty others as an editor) on Social Ethics and Ethics in the Sciences, on Meister Eckhart, on Narrative Ethics. Recently he is a co-editor of the Cambridge Handbook on Human Dignity and author of Meister Eckhart (Collection Denker), Edition Beck, Muenchen 2014.

Millán, Salvador, MD, Psychiatrist and Psychoanalyst UNAM. He is a training and supervising analyst of the Seminario de Sociopsicoanálisis A.C (SEMSOAC) directing the weekly clinical case presentations; co-editor of "Espacio Psicoanalítico", the online journal for romance languages of the International Federation of Psychoanalytic Societies (IFPS).

Müller-Hermann, Anna, student at the International Psychoanalytic University in Berlin.

Omelchenko, Nikolai is a Professor of the Philosophy Department at Volgograd State University (Russia). He graduated from Lomonosov Moscow State University (1978), then he obtained his second PhD at St. Petersburg State University (1997). He was a Fulbright Scholar-in-Residence at Mansfield University (PA, USA) in 2001/2002 academic year. His main research interest is in philosophical anthropology. He has more than 135 publications including *An Essay on Philosophical Anthropology* (Volgograd State University Press, 2005). He edited *The Human Being in Contemporary Philosophical Conceptions* (Newcastle upon Tyne (Cambridge Scholars Publishing), 2009). From 1993, he is a member of International Erich Fromm Society. He is interested in Fromm's profound ideas of humanity, its progress, trajectory and its goals.

Otte, Dr. Rainer, MA, studied philosophy, comparative religion and the history of art at the universities in Marburg and Tübingen. He specialized in anthropology and psychoanalytic theory. Since 1987, Dr. Otte worked as a journalist in the fields of medicine, economy, psychology and philosophy, writing for renowned newspapers. As an author and director, he realized television programs and films; two of them were devoted to Erich Fromm. He is the author of books discussing the paradigms of modern medicine (*Thure von Uexküll*, 2001; *Wenn Ethik der Fall ist*, 2003) and philosophical ideas in modern societies (*Wenn weniger mehr ist*, 2012; *Windpassagen*, 2014).

Panfilova, Tatiana, PhD, Professor in the Department of Philosophy, Moscow State University, Institute of International Relations, Russia; member of the International Erich Fromm Society; member of the Philosophical Society of Russia. She has translated some of Erich Fromm's writings from English into Russian: *Beyond the Chains of Illusion*, *The Revolution of Hope*, and the Appendix to *The Anatomy of Human Destructiveness*.

Zimmer, Manfred, Dr. rer. nat., ecological chemist & environmental verifier; member of the International Erich Fromm Society since 1985, editor of some IEFG-proceedings; for several years he has been occupied with the reception of Fromm's thought in countries of Southeast Asia, especially China.